The Letters of Robert Giroux and Thomas Merton

THE LETTERS
of
ROBERT GIROUX
and
THOMAS MERTON

Edited and Annotated by

PATRICK SAMWAY, S.J.

Foreword by

JONATHAN MONTALDO

University of Notre Dame Press

Notre Dame, Indiana

Manufactured in the United States of America

Library of Congress Cataloging-in-Publication Data

Giroux, Robert.

The letters of Robert Giroux and Thomas Merton /

edited and annotated by Patrick Samway, S.J.

pages   cm

Includes bibliographical references and index.

ISBN 978-0-268-01786-6 (pbk. : alk. paper) —

ISBN 0-268-01786-7 (pbk. : alk. paper)

1. Giroux, Robert—Correspondence.   2. Editors—United States—Correspondence.
3. Book editors—United States—Correspondence.   4. Merton, Thomas, 1915–1968—
Correspondence.   5. Trappists—United States—Correspondence.   6. Authors,
American—20th century—Correspondence.   7. Authorship—Correspondence.
8. Authors and publishers—United States—Correspondence.   9. Publishers and
publishing—United States—Correspondence.   I. Merton, Thomas 1915–1968.
II. Samway, Patrick H., editor.   III. Montaldo, Jonathan, writer of foreword.   IV. Title.

PN149.9.G57A4   2015

070.5'1092—dc23

2015017675

Contents

Foreword

JONATHAN MONTALDO

Although I had begun reading Thomas Merton's autobiography in 1958, ten years after its publication when I was thirteen, and then proceeded to read Merton methodically until I caught up with his latest book, I never entertained a notion to visit him at the Abbey of Our Lady of Gethsemani. A friend, also in his early twenties and an avid Merton reader, did indeed maneuver a fifteen-minute conversation with Merton in Kentucky. I never envied his opportunity. Merton's literary "voice" and transparent spiritual journey attracted me. I never thought of writing him a fan letter or encountering his celebrity in the flesh.

On the other hand, I was enthusiastic when in the 1980s I had the chance to meet Robert Giroux, the editor of *The Seven Storey Mountain* and twenty-five other Merton books. I realized his handshake placed me one degree of separation from T. S. Eliot, Robert Lowell, Virginia Woolf, Flannery O'Connor, and a host of other literary luminaries whose books Giroux had edited. After maneuvering myself into knowing him better, I also learned the hand I shook had greeted famous friends, such as Maria Callas, Jackie Kennedy Onassis, and Igor Stravinsky. A few years before his death on September 5, 2008, at age ninety-four, Giroux allowed me to record extended interviews with him on camera, sixteen hours of interviews in all! I prompted him off camera, which was a good thing: my being on film, often open-mouthed and wide-eyed, would have been distracting as Giroux reminisced with gusto about his long history as an editor, recounting his favorite stories about writers and friends he had known. I marveled as he detailed his exceedingly rich experiences as a major American literary editor and publisher, first at Harcourt, Brace and then at the New York house that eventually bore his name, Farrar, Straus & Giroux.

I have long anticipated this edition of the correspondence between Thomas Merton and Robert Giroux ably edited and annotated by Patrick Samway, S.J., one of Giroux's closest friends and confidants, and a university professor of American literature. Father Samway has more than rewarded my patience. These letters, produced in the trenches of hard labor, bring to light a reluctant but creatively facile monastic writer and his hands-on-the-business-tiller editor, yet always the writer's true advocate. They reveal the necessary shaping of a text that would hopefully excite its readers to ponder God and garner profit for all concerned. The reader is present at the creation of a book from pages of often undisciplined but highly evocative writing. Talk of deadlines and of royalties are continuing subjects here, but what fascinates is realizing how much Giroux contributed to honing the monk's prose and developing Merton's brand, as he often gave Merton's writing its form and more than twice crowned his books with great titles: *The Sign of Jonas* and *No Man Is an Island.* Giroux's letter to Merton dated February 13, 1951, offers particularly good evidence of his deft editorial hand as he critiques the development of *The Ascent to Truth.* This behind-the-typewriter view of their collaboration also reveals how little glamour attends the making of what will become a classic text, which Giroux once defined as a book that remains in print. He and Merton collaborated to produce many of these.

Beyond the business of publishing, these letters are studded with personal revelations. Merton often expresses to his editor that he should write "slower and more prayerfully" (September 9, 1949). Rather than become famous, Merton wanted to become "the simplest of all priests" (May 12, 1949). He longed to work in the fields and "be a monk for a while" (February 15, 1951). Giroux was always sympathetic. He knew firsthand the cost of Merton's writing career to his genuine, monastic vocation, yet he remained confident that Merton would work out the paradoxes of being a Trappist monk and famous writer. He defended Merton's writing against critical readers who wrote personally to him against a supposedly silent monk publishing so prolifically. In response, Giroux would send them a preprinted card (thus, this critique must have been a frequent occurrence): "Writing is a form of contemplation."

This collection admirably joins other volumes of Merton's correspondence that have been gathered in books, a genre of his that should continue to proliferate since Merton was an inveterate letter writer to persons both famous and unknown. While his journals are naturally important for intimate background, his letters offer epiphanies of his broad and hospitable humanity that are hard to come by in any other format. I commend this well-edited dialogue with enthusiasm as another perspective into the man whom Giroux described simply as "a great and important American thinker and writer."

Notes on the Text

The letters are arranged chronologically, as far as it is possible to determine dates with accuracy. Where dates are incomplete or missing, I have relied mostly on the evidence within the letters to assist me in determining the dates as accurately as possible. I have tried to preserve the physiognomy of the letters in order to allow the reader to appreciate the stylistic habits and preferences of the writers. Minor typographical infelicities have been silently corrected, but I have made every effort to retain creative spelling and usage wherever the meaning can be gleaned from the context. Handwritten marks are presumed to be made by the sender unless otherwise noted. Editorial interpolations—missing words and corrections of obvious errors affecting sense—are enclosed in [square brackets], as are any contextual annotations other than footnotes. I have made uniform the format of the dates of the letters and have occasionally stylized some of the letters, mostly by correcting spelling mistakes and regularizing punctuation. These letters, either originals or duplicates, were found in the following locations: the private archives of Robert Giroux; the archives of Harcourt, Brace; the Thomas Merton Center at Bellarmine University in Louisville; and the Manuscripts and Archives Division of the New York Public Library.

In preparing these letters for publication, I am most grateful for the assistance of the following persons: Robert Giroux; Charles F. X. Reilly; Dom Damien Thompson, O.C.S.O.; Patrick Hart, O.C.S.O.; Hugh James and Dorothee McKenna; Thomasine O'Callaghan; the Merton Legacy Trust (Anne McCormick, Mary R. Somerville, Peggy Fox); Paul M. Pearson and the Thomas Merton Center at Bellarmine University in Louisville, Kentucky; my student assistants at Saint Joseph's University (Cara Donaldson, Christine Skalka, and Mary Sarajean Black); Dominic Roberti; Professors JoAlyson Parker and Peter Norberg; the Saint Joseph's University English Department; the Jesuit Community at Saint Joseph's University; Tina Smith and the staff of the Archives of Harcourt, Brace; the staff of the Manuscripts and Archives Division of the New York Public Library; and especially my thoughtful literary agent Albert LaFarge. The Estate of

Robert Giroux gave permission to publish his letters, and the Thomas Merton Legacy Trust gave permission to publish Merton's letters.

Sigla:
Naomi Burton: NB
New Directions: ND
Farrar, Straus & Cudahy: FSC
Farrar, Straus & Giroux: FSG
Robert Giroux: RG
Harcourt, Brace: HB
James Laughlin: JL
Thomas Merton: TM
Patrick Samway, S.J.: PS

Introduction

When twenty-year-old Thomas Merton entered Columbia College on New York's Morningside Heights in January 1935, he brought with him a remarkable background few of his American fellow students—certainly not Robert Giroux—could easily have fathomed. Born on January 31, 1915, in Prades, France, Tom, as his mother preferred to call him, did not spend his childhood enjoying life in the picturesque foothills of the Pyrenees. Rather, his seemingly mismatched parents—his father Owen, an artist, native New Zealander, and member of the Church of England, and his mother Ruth, likewise an artist, native Ohioan, and confirmed pacificist in the Quaker tradition—attempted to eke out an existence in a country they little knew. Though the French Catalans of this region tended to identify themselves with their non-Francophone neighbors, they nevertheless felt at this time the impact of the German invasion on their native French soil in the Northeast. The advance of war impelled the Mertons to move on July 16, 1916, to Flushing, New York, not far from Douglaston, where infant Tom's maternal grandparents lived. The Mertons followed the war news on the radio intensely as the German military commanders vowed to "bleed France white" at Verdun, an apparently vulnerable target northwest of Strasbourg on the way to Paris. Though able to halt the German advances here during the heavy snows of February 1916, French and British troops nevertheless suffered over five hundred thousand casualties at the Battle of the Somme. From Flushing, the Mertons could only have felt relieved by President Woodrow Wilson's declaration of war on Germany on April 6, 1917, followed by the arrival of General John J. ("Black Jack") Pershing's American Expeditionary Force in June.

Amid the traumatic events of the war, the physical and emotional dislocation of young Tom soon increased, made more intense by the death of his mother on October 3, 1921, just as his brother John Paul was about to celebrate his third birthday. Owen sometimes took his older son on his painting excursions up and down the Long Island Sound and Cape Cod, and then, in October 1922, to Bermuda, where Tom's father had an amorous affair with the novelist Evelyn Scott, whose name Merton does not mention in *The Seven Storey Mountain*. Without a family, a school, or a church, young Merton lacked comforting, customary routines, a situation further aggravated when his father took him, at age ten, back to southern France in July 1925 and enrolled him in the Lycée Ingres, a boarding school in Montauban, near St. Antonin, where his father took up residence. Though the adult Thomas Merton had a tendency to see France as an ideal place, in *The Seven Storey Mountain* he sometimes revealed his childhood scars: "And I would plead with Father to let me out of that miserable school, but it was in vain. After about two months I got used to it and ceased to be so unhappy. The wound was no longer so raw: but I was never happy or at peace in the violent and unpleasant atmosphere of those brick cloisters."[1] The isolation from his grandparents and brother—and, to some extent, his father, especially when his father moved to Murat in the province of Auvergne in the winter of 1926—must have taken an additional toll on his young psyche. Most likely because his father sought a better environment to sell his paintings, Merton was taken in 1928 to Ealing, England, to live with his great-aunt Maud Pearce, a sprightly and charming woman, and her husband Benjamin. He later reflected that his father's death in a London hospital on January 18, 1931, brought him to a low point in his life: "I became a true citizen of my own disgusting century: the century of poison gas and atomic bombs."[2] In the summer after his father's death, he returned to Douglaston briefly and then sailed back to England for his final schooling at Oakham in the East Midlands beginning in 1929.

Once finished with his secondary education at age eighteen, and having enjoyed a vacation by himself in Italy, he obtained, in 1933, a prized scholarship to Clare College, University of Cambridge. Yet, his academic year there proved to be disastrously bitter—exacerbated by the emptiness he felt; no doubt the bitterness was related to fathering a child out of wedlock, a situation that has never been fully explained. Merton's biographer cryptically states, "Whether the matter was a threatened breach-of-promise case or an affiliation order (paternity case), it seems clear that some legal settlement was made."[3] And his close friend, Edward Rice, believed that the mother and child were killed in the Blitz. Yet, according to Paul Pearson, director of the Thomas Merton Center at Bellarmine University in Louisville, Rice, when interviewed by Michael Mott, would only admit that a woman Merton knew had a child.[4] (Giroux never knew about this situation while Merton was alive.) Merton's self-evaluation at Cambridge, especially after he had lost his scholarship for poor grades, clearly indicates that he was ready for a change of heart and behavior: "I . . . had turned out to be," he says in his autobiography, "an extremely unpleasant sort of person—vain, self-centered, dissolute, weak, irresolute, undisciplined, sensual, obscene, and proud. I was a mess. Even the sight of my own face in a mirror was enough to disgust me."[5] This time, his return to Douglaston reflected an intense desire to find some type of liberation. One thing became eminently clear to him: he had broken all physical ties with England and would never return there again. Enrolling as a sophomore at Columbia College in upper Manhattan might offer him, in spite of the Great Depression, an elite education, new friends, and an opportunity to pursue his talents—and maybe even an opportunity to develop a latent spirituality.

Little did Merton know that when he entered the *Columbia Review* office on the fourth floor of Columbia's John Jay Hall most likely during his first year on campus, he would meet someone who would have a great impact on his life: Robert Giroux, then a college junior and the *Review*'s coeditor. The first thing Giroux noted, as related in an unpublished talk on Merton, was Merton's overall demeanor: "Blond and blue-eyed, his height was average, he had a stocky and solid build, and even . . . was beginning to bald. He was good-natured, extremely articulate, and laughed a lot." Since Merton and Giroux were taking one of Mark Van Doren's courses, the two students soon felt comfortable discussing with one another Van Doren's approach to literature and Renaissance drama. Giroux undoubtedly read Merton's story, "Katabolism of an Englishman," in the September 1935 issue of the *Jester*, the college's humor magazine, and perhaps wondered whether the desire of the story's narrator to transfer from Cambridge to Columbia had any autobiographical basis. When Merton handed Giroux another story, entitled "In the Street," Giroux never forgot, as he says in his talk, the significance of the moment:

> It was a description of an auto accident he had seen on Broadway with a dead man's body lying in the street, his pack of cigarettes in a pool of blood. It was vividly written, the language was alive, and I said I would print it if he shortened it by one-third. He said, "Fine, but *you* do the cutting," and we shook hands. Without knowing it, I had become his editor.

Though Giroux had seen similar stories about street life and city vignettes, he knew instinctively then and there that Merton was going to be a serious writer.

Except for their interest in literature and publishing, Merton and Giroux seemingly had little in common. Born on April 8, 1914, Giroux grew up in a decidedly blue-collar Jersey City, New Jersey, where his father, Arthur Joseph, suddenly stopped working as the foreman of a local silk factory, thus causing great financial and emotional strain on the family. His mother, Katherine Regina Lyons Giroux, provided for the family's needs by doing fine sewing to support her five children, as her husband spent many of his idle days handicapping the horses. Young Robert excelled in grade school and was selected to attend the all-scholarship,

Jesuit-run Regis High School on East Eighty-Fourth Street just off Park Avenue in New York. He eventually received a partial scholarship to Columbia in 1932. In fact, he felt so confident in his ability to succeed academically that he left high school during his last semester to work as a copy boy on the *Jersey Journal*, giving him valuable work experience he cherished throughout his life.

On and off for a year and a half, Giroux worked at the *Jersey Journal*. His mentor there, editor Lillian Brown, early on recognized and appreciated his incipient talents, and took him and his friends to concerts, various museums, and sites of historical interest—and even, as he recalled, to cocktail parties! She was the one who had encouraged him to apply to Columbia; his mother, perhaps because she was thinking of the cost connected with sending her other children off to college, had serious reservations about his continuing his education (none of Giroux's four siblings went on to college). Giroux, in the year between high school and college, assisted Brown in collecting and editing engaging and informative articles in the "Club Section," a part of the paper oriented to both young adults and older readers that discussed the social and literary gatherings, on topics ranging from chess to cartooning, from editorial writing to drama (see the issues of April 30, 1932, and May 7, 1932, for examples). In retrospect, he saw his work at the newspaper as the perfect type of apprenticeship for entering the world of publishing, and he cherished throughout his life this valuable newspaper experience, focusing as it did on daily communication and the value of the written word. If anything, this was a marvelous formative time for him, particularly as it instilled in him a sense of his own worth. Though the larger world was quickly opening up in front of him, he knew he would still have to live at home as a college student. In fact, he lived almost his entire life in Jersey City, except for short stints in New York City and when he served as an administrative officer from 1942 to 1945 for Carrier Air Group Nine aboard the USS *Essex*.

Giroux recalled that during his senior year, he saw Merton occasionally; they became friends, but did not have the close friendship Merton had with fellow classmates Robert Lax (a semester ahead of Merton, with whom he carried on a lifelong zany correspondence, collected in *A Catch of Anti-Letters* [1979] and *When Prophecy Still Had a Voice: The Letters of Thomas Merton & Robert Lax* [2001]), Adolph ("Ad") Reinhardt, Robert Gerdy, Seymour ("Sy") Freedgood, and Edward Rice. Merton's recollection of Giroux in *The Seven Storey Mountain* is understated, to say the least, given the fact that Giroux edited the very words that Merton wrote: "Giroux was a Catholic and a person strangely placid for the Fourth Floor. He had no part in its feuds and, as a matter of fact, you did not see him around there very much."[6] Yet Giroux had a good reading of his friend. In Giroux's eyes,

Columbia for Merton resembled what it was to most American college students then: the hot jazz records of Duke Ellington and Louis Armstrong, fraternity beer parties, athletics, student publications, dating, smoky barroom seminars in the early hours of morning, Alice Faye, W.C. Fields, Charlie Chaplin, Don Ameche, and the Marx brothers movies at the local movie house, called the Thalia, and, in between, classes. He saw Merton preoccupied with jazz, French literature, running track, the fiction of James Joyce, and especially the new poetry of W.H. Auden, Louis Mac-Neice, and Stephen Spender. He sensed, too, that Merton was ripe for the rejection of established authorities, a mind-set that prompted him to flirt with communism. "But he was an intelligent person as well as a restless one," Giroux observed in his talk, "so that when it began to bore him and he took an objective view of the situation, he was able to see the lack of logic in its methods and objectives. His Communist activity soon ceased."

In his book on Merton, Ed Rice described his friend from a slightly different perspective, as someone "dressed like a businessman, in a neat suit and a double-breasted chesterfield topcoat, carrying a leather briefcase full of papers, articles, books and drawings."[7] In all, Merton's classmates seem to agree that he was articulate, energetic, and decisive when he had to be, and full of himself. Despite Merton's affability and great sense of humor, Giroux, however, sensed that, underneath it all, he was lonely and rather sad.

In addition to Mark Van Doren's humanistic influence on Merton and especially Giroux, who later wrote *The Book Known as Q: A Consideration of Shakespeare's Sonnets* (1982), Daniel Walsh (1907–75), a visiting faculty member in philosophy, introduced Merton to the writings of Saint Thomas Aquinas and two contemporary Thomists: Étienne Gilson, whose recently published *The Spirit of Mediaeval Philosophy* Merton read in the winter of 1937, and Jacques Maritain, whose *Art and Scholasticism* (1930) proved essential while Merton pursued his graduate studies. Walsh had done his BA and MA at the University of Toronto, as well as a PhD at Toronto's Pontifical Institute of Mediaeval Studies; while there, he had come to know Gilson, one of his professors. Gradually, Merton began to readjust his values and read and wonder about the Catholic Church. Gilson caused a radical shift in Merton's way of looking at life, as he records in his autobiography:

The result was that I at once acquired an immense respect for Catholic Philosophy and the Catholic faith. . . . When I put this book down, and had ceased to think explicitly about its arguments, its effect began to show itself in my life. I began to have a desire to go to church—and a desire more sincere and mature and more deep-seated than I had ever had before. After all, I had never before had so great a need.[8]

From Maritain, he learned, as Giroux said in his talk, "the real concept of virtue without which there can be no happiness because virtues are precisely the powers by which we can come to acquire happiness that in the end constitutes everlasting peace. And soon he accepted all the full range and possibilities of religious experience right up to the highest degree of glory." Curiously, during their college years, the subject of religion never came up between Giroux and Merton; the former never had any idea during this time that the latter would ever have considered becoming a Catholic. And when Giroux graduated in May 1936, he never expected to see his friend again.

When Merton entered his senior year at Columbia, he became editor of the yearbook, which noted that an in-house poll had cited him as the college's "best writer." His work on the *Jester* as the art editor helped pay for his college tuition. Because of the recent deaths of his maternal grandparents Samuel Jenkins and his wife Martha, Merton had vacated his grandparents' house on Long Island in early summer of 1937 to take an apartment on West 114th Street near the Columbia campus. Because he had a few more courses to take to complete his degree, he did not graduate until early 1938, after which he decided to stay on at Columbia to pursue an MA in English, fascinated, as he had been since his youth, by the poetry of William Blake, the subject of a thesis he started writing in September 1938.

Writing, reading intensely, taking summer school classes, and having a chance to reflect on his past and future, Merton decided one day in August 1938 to go to Mass, as he said in his autobiography, for the "first time in his life," at Corpus Christi Church adjacent to Columbia.[9] When asked what there was in Catholicism that drew Merton to it, Robert Lax stated succinctly, "I think the feeling of God's concern for the world, God's mercy toward sinners, actually made a strong appeal."[10] That November, in the same church, Merton was baptized and received his first Communion. Ed Rice acted as his godfather. More and more, Merton was finding a part of his life that had, up to this point, evaded him. After he received his MA in February 1939, he moved to 35 Perry Street in the West Village and decided to pursue a doctorate, with a projected dissertation on the poetry of Gerard Manley Hopkins, S.J. While the strictly academic life had its appeal, Merton was not totally convinced it was for him. In April, he took a trip to Bermuda, where he had lived with his father in the winter of 1922–23. It was at this time in his life that he confided in Dan Walsh that he felt he had a vocation, perhaps to the Jesuits—even attempting to follow Saint Ignatius's Spiritual Exercises on his own. Merton rejected the Jesuits, as he wrote in his autobiography, because they were "geared to a pitch of active ministry and military routine."[11]

With a good bit of time on his hands, he joined Bob Lax and Ed Rice for a short vacation that summer in Olean, New York, the site of the

Franciscan-run Saint Bonaventure College. While there, Merton plotted out and wrote three variants of the same novel, all romans à clef: *The Straits of Dover, The Night before the Battle,* and *The Labyrinth,* as well as *The Journal of My Escape from the Nazis,* published in 1969 as *My Argument with the Gestapo: My Macaronic Journal.* Talking to a number of Franciscans and seeing their manner of life, he applied for admission to the order, hoping to enter their novitiate the following fall, but once his interviewers learned what had happened at Cambridge, he was turned down by them in July 1940. (It should be pointed out, too, that Merton had not, from a canonical point of view, been a Catholic long enough to be accepted into a religious order.) He taught English composition for a semester at Columbia for the fall 1939 semester and then taught as an assistant professor of English at Saint Bonaventure from the fall of 1940 to December 1941, earning forty-five dollars a month plus room and board.

When Robert Giroux started working at Harcourt, Brace & Company in January 1940, he learned that the typescript of *The Straits of Dover* by Thomas James Merton had arrived. As one of the readers, Giroux was one-third of the way through it before he realized it was written by his friend. "It was the story of a young man floundering around in Greenwich Village," he recalled in his unpublished talk. He believed it was well written but that, in the end, it failed to add up. "There was little drama in it and it lacked a resolution. During the next six months Naomi [Burton, Merton's agent at Curtis Brown, Ltd.] submitted two other novels, neither of which worked. They were actually rewritings of the first novel and at the end the hero was still floundering around."

Giroux was not alone in his evaluation. On February 7, 1940, an anonymous in-house reader at Harcourt, Brace gave his opinion of *The Straits of Dover:*

> One of those strange novels which seem to concern lots of people, and have no particular plot. The most constant figure in this is a boy who was in school in England, went to Cambridge for a bit, and ended up at Columbia. Also involved are a stupid millionaire, his wife, a show girl who was after him, a left-wing intellectual, a Hindu mystic, etc., etc., etc. I think Mr. Merton's got something, but not quite enough to do anything about. No.

Stanley P. Young, a senior editor at Harcourt, Brace, added his typed personal comments seventeen days later: "Some interesting writing here, but it wobbles around as a story and never hits a strong narrative line. No."

At Perry Street, Merton must have been upset by Young's brief letter of the same date, which noted that while the editors had read *Straits of Dover* and enjoyed much of the writing the firm had decided not to publish it. Young had added, however, that he would like to consider any work that

Merton might send him in the future. Young's handwritten notes about *The Labyrinth*, dated March 26, 1940, are equally direct: "This is a revised version of 'The Straits of Dover' which came in and was rejected (with interest!) several weeks ago. It will still need to be rejected (with interest!). Merton is a talented young man but his story moves with a mazy motion even though there are many isolated passages of insight and strength." The same day, Giroux wrote a short note to Young: "I will write Merton, independently, in about a week, after you've had a chance to reject—encouragingly, I hope." On March 29, Young wrote a second letter to Merton, care of his Douglaston address:

> As I told you over the telephone, my vote on your manuscript was no, but as this was a revision, I checked it against others here and all of us feel about the same way: that our interest in you is sufficiently galvanized by your manuscript to make us want to see anything you may do. Whether or not you enter the Franciscans, I think you will go on writing novels. From what I can gather from this manuscript, the bug is working under the skin. I am really sorry that we don't feel that this is the one to launch you with, but let me hear from you.

In all, the editors of Harcourt, Brace (*including* Robert Giroux) turned down Merton's earliest sustained creative efforts, including the version of the novel entitled *The Man in the Sycamore Tree* that Burton sent Giroux in April 1941, as Giroux mentions in an interview with Paul Wilkes.[12] Merton, likewise, received rejections for his early fiction from Farrar & Rinehart, Macmillan, Viking, and Knopf.

One summer day in 1941, as Giroux was browsing in the Scribner's Book Store on Fifth Avenue, someone touched his arm. It was Tom Merton, whom he had not seen since he had left Columbia. Merton explained that he had just been to the offices of the *New Yorker*, where their Columbia classmate, Robert Gerdy, was on the staff, to submit some of his poems, though Gerdy encouraged him to write instead about Gethsemani. Giroux squinted a bit in wonderment. "Oh, it's a Trappist monastery in Kentucky, where I recently made a retreat at Eastertime," his friend explained. "Well, I hope you'll write about Gethsemani," Giroux said with a slight note of encouragement. "It sounds fascinating." Merton indicated that he had no intention of writing such an essay. As they shook hands in parting, Giroux said, "Tom, I hope you'll go on writing." Giroux was most surprised to receive a phone call in early December from Van Doren saying that Merton had left his job at Saint Bonaventure College and had entered, at age twenty-six, Our Lady of Gethsemani Abbey, taking the religious name of "Maria Louis." None of Merton's friends thought they would ever hear from him again, especially as they incorrectly believed that Merton had taken a vow of silence. Since Merton had left the manuscripts of his poems with Van Doren with the intention of sending them to James ("Jay") Laughlin at the publishing firm called New Directions, his voice, albeit a poetic one, would be heard and read in *Thirty Poems* (1944).

The years passed, as Merton adjusted to his life as a Trappist monk in rural Kentucky and as Giroux, returning from his career in the Navy in early 1946 and soon becoming editor-in-chief at Harcourt, Brace, started editing the works of Hannah Arendt, W. E. B. DuBois, T. S. Eliot, William Gaddis, Randall Jarrell, Jack Kerouac, Bernard Malamud, Flannery O'Connor, William Saroyan, Jean Stafford, Robert Penn Warren, Eudora Welty, Edmund Wilson, and Virginia Woolf, among others. Unknown to the outside world, Merton with the encouragement of Dom Frederic Dunne, O.C.S.O., the abbot, wrote his autobiography. The impression that Merton gave Giroux was that he really did not want to write this work, but was obliged to do so. Yet, according to Michael Mott, the original impetus for the autobiography seems to have come from Merton, not the abbot.[13] He was not alone in his willingness to write about his early life as a religious. Little did he know that his contemporary, Avery Dulles, the son of the U.S. secretary of state John Foster Dulles—a position previously held by Avery's great-grandfather, John W. Foster, and his great-uncle, Robert Lansing—had converted to Catholicism in 1940, while a student at Harvard College. He had entered Harvard in the fall of 1936, about the same time that Merton had encountered Giroux in his *Review* office. After a year and a half at Harvard Law School, Dulles served in the Navy, doing liaison work with the French Navy, for which he was awarded the *croix de guerre*. In 1946, he entered the Society of Jesus, and as a novice wrote his *A Testimonial to Grace*, which recounts the story of his conversion and spiritual growth. Though Dulles approaches the story of his conversion less from a strictly biographical point of view, he and Merton intersect in their narratives at key points:

> On apprehending the dignity of reason and its true relation to reality I all at once felt at home in the universe. It is impossible for me to exaggerate the sense of joy and freedom which came from this discovery. I soon found myself reading avidly the modern Aristotelians— Catholic authors such as Jacques Maritain and Étienne Gilson—and adhering to the logic of their doctrine with a fervor which I could hardly capture today.[14]

And, like Merton, Dulles went on to be a renowned figure in Roman Catholicism, mainly through his books and articles on systematic theology, for which he was made a cardinal in February 2001 by Pope John Paul II.

Both Burton and Merton thought it good to submit his 694-page manuscript (reduced from 800 pages by the Trappist censors) to Giroux, which

Burton did in December 1946. In great peace and solitude, Merton had a chance to review the events that led up to his arrival at Gethsemani and find a perspective that would later resonate with thousands of others, especially those who had been radically shaken by World War II. Giroux wondered whether he had gone out on a limb when he asked Donald Brace to read the manuscript. "Do you think it will lose money?" the senior editor asked. "Oh no," Giroux replied, "I'm sure it will find an audience. I don't think we'd lose any money, but whether we make any is problematic. Merton writes well, and I wish you'd take a look at it, Don." "No, Bob," Brace said, "I'll read it in print. If you like it, let's do it." In his talk on Merton, Giroux gives a larger context to this particular text:

> When the abbot suggested that he write his life story, Merton resisted. One reason he had become a monk was in order to reject his past life, of which he was anything but proud. But once he began to write, it poured out. He wrote freely, with no thought of the Trappist censors. "I don't know what audience I might have been thinking of," he admitted. "I suppose I just put down what was in me, under the eyes of God who knows what is in me." He was soon trying to tone down the original draft for the censors of the Order, who had criticized it severely, especially the account of his year at Clare College, Cambridge, during which he became the father of an illegitimate son.

Giroux did not cut much of the first edition, though he did spot one section that needed reworking.

After receiving Brace's approval, Giroux phoned Burton and then telegraphed Merton at the end of December 1946: "MANUSCRIPT ACCEPTED. HAPPY NEW YEAR." Merton then wrote to Burton on January 2, 1947, informing her that he gave Giroux a free hand with the editing. For Giroux, as he mentions in the introduction to the book's fiftieth-anniversary edition, the main flaw was the essay, or sermon, with which the book opened—an example of misplaced "fine" writing:

> When a man is conceived, when a human nature comes into being as an individual, concrete, subsisting thing, a life, a person, then God's image is minted into the world. A free, vital, self-moving entity, a spirit informing flesh, a complex of energies ready to be set into fruitful motion begins to flame with potential light and understanding and virtue, and love, without which no spirit can exist. It is ready to realize no one knows what grandeurs. The vital center of this new creation is a free and spiritual principle called a soul. The soul is the life of this being, and the life of the soul is the love that unites it to the principle of all life—God. The body that here has been made will not live forever. When the soul, the life, leaves it, it will be dead.[15]

Giroux wisely said that Merton should explain right off who he was, where he came from, and how he got there. Merton's revised opening began: "On the last day of January 1915, under the sign of the Water Bearer, in a year of a great war, and down in the shadow of some French mountains on the borders of Spain, I came into the world." For Giroux, it was personal, concrete, vivid, and got the reader involved in the story immediately. Giroux went on to suggest editorial problems with the conclusion of the book, to which Merton positively and enthusiastically responded, including the addition of five and a half pages of material that had recently appeared in the Catholic journal *Commonweal*. In addition, after Merton received the proofs on January 26, 1948, he cut at least eight thousand words.[16] The celebrated author Evelyn Waugh, who edited the British edition under the title *Elected Silence*, wrote to Giroux on July 20, 1948: "I regard this as a book which may well prove to be of permanent interest in the history of religious experience. No one can afford to neglect this clear account of a complex religious process." In light of this and other superb comments, Harcourt, Brace increased the first printing from 5,000 copies to 12,500, knowing that they might still need more copies. In fact, its pre-publication sale was 20,847 copies, with the original cloth edition exceeding 600,000 copies!

Behind the scenes, however, a crisis was developing. Merton told Burton that a final Trappist censor had refused to give his permission for the book to be published, unaware that a contract had already been signed. The censor objected to Merton's "colloquial prose style," and advised him to put the book aside. Giroux gave immediate and helpful advice: present the matter to the abbot general. According to Merton, the head of the order in France had told him to go ahead and write as he pleased and to use all the slang he wanted, but he would not countermand the judgment of any censor. Finally, the censor did an about-face, leaving Merton to his own devices concerning matters of style. After finished books were distributed in August 1948, Merton tried hard not to change his monastic routine, with more or less success. In Giroux's long and distinguished career, he never had a book as popular as this one.

When Abbot Dom James Fox, O.C.S.O. (1896–1987), invited Giroux and other Merton friends, including Jay Laughlin, Sy Freedgood, Dan Walsh, Bob Lax, and Ed Rice, to the monastery for Merton's ordination on May 26, 1949, Giroux brought along copy number 200,000 of the autobiography in a special leather binding. In his comments about editing this book, Giroux reflected on its worldwide appeal:

> Why did the success of *The Seven Storey Mountain* go so far beyond my expectations as an editor and publisher? Why, despite its being banned from the [*Times* "best seller"] list, did it outsell all other nonfiction books in the same months? Though few readers believe it, publishers

cannot create bestsellers. There is always an element of mystery when it happens: why *this* book at *this* moment? The most essential element of success is right timing, which cannot usually be foreseen. *The Seven Storey* appeared at a time of disillusion, following the Second World War, when another war—the cold war—had started and the public was ready for a change from disillusion and cynicism. Second, the story Merton told was unusual: an articulate young man with an interesting background leaves the world and withdraws into a monastery. Third, it was a tale well told, with liveliness and eloquence. No doubt there were other reasons, but the combination of the right subject at the right time presented in the right way accounts for a good part of the book's success.[17]

Giroux often talked to me about the success of this book, how it was lively and eloquently written, and of his friendship with Merton, particularly during the two pilgrimages I made with him from Jersey City to Gethsemani, where we were the guests of the abbot, Dom Damien Thompson, O.C.S.O., and Merton's former secretary, Brother Patrick Hart, O.C.S.O. Giroux believed that Merton's journey through life was one of exploration, keeping his eye on God, on the eternal verities, and on the world God created—thus seeing all the relationships and resulting congruities and incongruities. As Merton's books became known throughout the world, Merton, too, enlarged his imaginary mindscape. "Some people would say that Merton found a home in the monastery," Giroux explained in his interview with Paul Wilkes. "It may be true, but that doesn't take one iota away from his achievement. Many people have found homes in monasteries, but few have developed as remarkably as he did. The ambience never really explains the art itself."[18] In short, Merton was very much a man of his own times, who had a deeply felt spirituality rooted in Cistercian forms of prayer and in the traditions and sacramental life of the Catholic Church. He flourished in the seclusion of the monastery, due in large part to his searching imagination and his desire to communicate through the printed word. To those who believed that a Trappist monk should keep silent both in and out of the cloister, Giroux would send them a succinct six-word card he had printed: "Writing is a form of contemplation."

During the early months of 1955, Giroux, increasingly dissatisfied with the interpersonal dynamics at Harcourt, Brace, decided that he needed to move elsewhere, especially given the desire of the firm's new president, William Jovanovich, to focus more on textbooks and less on literature. Giroux wrote to his friend, Paul Horgan, on March 27, 1955, that he was terribly upset by the anti-Catholic statements directed at him by some in the office. Once Giroux had made up his mind, he delayed leaving until early spring so that he would be in a position to collect his pension. Naomi Burton learned of Giroux's situation and, in turn, she introduced him to Sheila Cudahy, who set up a dinner meeting, where Giroux was formally invited by Roger W. Straus Jr., John Farrar, and Cudahy in February 1955 to join Farrar, Straus & Company (soon to become Farrar, Straus & Cudahy). The conditions were not complicated; Giroux would start in April and have an initial contract for five years. According to the new arrangement, Straus was president and owner and Giroux would hold the position of vice president, become a member of the board of directors, shareholder, and editor-in-chief. Cudahy, having previously owned a publishing firm in Italy with her husband Georgio Pellegrini, would retain her post as vice president. She would continue to focus on children's books, as well as books that might appeal to Catholics.

When Giroux arrived at his new first-floor office at 101 Fifth Avenue, he found the firm poorly managed, and thus spent considerable time establishing a decent house library and archives so that copyrights could be properly filed. Approximately seventeen authors followed Giroux to his new firm, including John Berryman, T.S. Eliot, Paul Horgan, Randall Jarrell, Jack Kerouac, John LaFarge, S.J., Robert Lowell, Thomas Merton, Jean Stafford, Peter Taylor, and eventually Bernard Malamud and Flannery O'Connor. Just before Giroux left Harcourt, Brace, he was proud to have edited *The Recognitions*, by William Gaddis, an author whom he admired and who eventually received two National Book Awards, but who decided not to follow him. When Eliot cabled his desire to remain with Giroux as his American editor, Giroux saw this as a "rare act of generosity and friendship." Donald Brace simply handed Giroux the telegram that Eliot had sent and left his office without saying a word. Straus later said that Giroux's arrival in 1955 was "the single most important thing to happen to this company."[19] Giroux already knew that Roger Straus, who came from a privileged background, could count on family financial resources; his mother was a Guggenheim and his father's family owned Macy's department store. His paternal grandfather, Oscar Straus, was secretary of commerce during the presidency of Theodore Roosevelt. While still serving in the U.S. Navy, Straus had begun planning to start his own publishing firm, and he enlisted James Van Alen to help get the firm started in 1945, but because of pressure from his own family, Van Alen never formally became involved and preferred to put his energies into playing professional tennis. In addition, Straus contacted another friend of his, John Farrar, a Yale graduate who had worked for the *New York World* and then became well known in publishing circles as editor of the *Bookman*. He was the founder of the Breadloaf Writers' Conference at Middlebury College in Vermont in 1926. Later as editor-in-chief of George Doran Company and then a founding member of Farrar & Rinehart, he had the publishing background Straus needed, and after finishing his assignment in the Office of War Information, he joined the new firm.

Straus and Giroux had met in New York during World War II when the latter was stationed on the aircraft carrier USS *Essex*, one of whose pilots,

Lieutenant George M. Blair, had been shot down at Truk, a Japanese base on the Caroline Islands, on February 18, 1944. After the successful U.S. attack on the Japanese base there, a large task force maneuvered to participate in the pilot's rescue. Later, Blair found it difficult to be interviewed about the situation, but with Giroux's assistance, he was able to tell his story. Giroux took his written account, "Rescue at Truk," to Lieutenant Straus, who was serving as a censor for the Navy. Straus approved the article and it was eventually published in *Collier's* (May 13, 1944), for which Giroux received a check for $3,000, half of which he sent to Blair. Thus the Giroux-Straus friendship was formed, though not without serious ups and downs, as Giroux explained to me in some detail during the years I knew him. But in the beginning, both were eager to get started and make the firm successful, which they did with great éclat.

On Maundy Thursday, in early April 1955, Giroux wrote on Farrar, Straus & Cudahy stationery to Merton at Gethsemani:

> I deeply regret the misunderstanding which occurred during my last weeks at Harcourt, Brace and which resulted, despite my promise to you, in the final corrections not being made in the first printing of NO MAN IS AN ISLAND (save for twelve specially made copies). I think now that the firm probably acted in good faith, though they still question mine. . . . I am grateful to Harcourt, Brace for having released you from their contract, and I know that their doing so is due mainly to Naomi's skill and tact in an extremely difficult situation.[20]
>
> P.S. Cable from T.S. Eliot confirming his leaving Harcourt, Brace and coming here [FSC] too!

Revealing a new energy and ready to start afresh, he also wrote an unpublished "private and personal" letter on April 21, 1955, to John Berryman in South Minneapolis, Minnesota:

> As you may have heard, I have left Harcourt, Brace after fifteen years to join this firm. I had thought my troubles were over when [Eugene] Reynal resigned last December, but this was a miscalculation; his leaving only confirmed the ascendency of the textbook people. William Jovanovich (or Don Giovanovich as I like to think of him) and John McCallum are The New Men. Denver Lindley, an old one whom I have always liked, will last as long as they can use him.
>
> In any event, here I am loaded with honors (vice president, member of the board of directors, stockholder) and as excited as Alfred Harcourt and Donald Brace must have been when they left [Henry] Holt in 1919. I've known Roger Straus since we were in the Navy together; John Farrar and Sheila Cudahy are old friends. We're a young

firm, and at the same time the oldest survivor (perhaps the only, now that [William] Sloane [Associates] has fragmentized) of the postwar publishers. We publish [François] Mauriac, Edmund Wilson, [Alberto] Moravia, Colette, [Marguerite] Yourcenar, Alec Waugh, and [Giovanni] Guareschi among others.

I want to build up the American list in general (I think our European list has great distinction), and the poetry list in particular. I would like to start with *Homage to Mistress Anne Bradstreet.* I can now sign contracts myself, and there will be none of the Harcourt, Brace ambivalence—editor proposing and management disposing. May I publish your poem . . . ? We are going to do Eliot's new play (he staggered me by cabling "I will come along with you"), and Cal Lowell has agreed to publish the prose book he is working on (a memoir) with us; his poetry, alas, is tied up (I tied it up, of course).

So come on, and join your friends. Will you wire me collect and tell me we can submit a contract for the Anne Bradstreet; I'll offer you good terms.

I plan to come out your way [Minneapolis] in early May for a brief visit; I have to get back by May 11th when Uncle Tom [Eliot] arrives from London to stay at my apartment. It will be good to see you, and to talk over lots of things, but meanwhile let me know about the poem, by telegram preferably.

With so many talented authors aboard, Giroux wasted no time getting back to editing, including that spring some notable works: *The Vagabond* by Colette; *The Selected Letters of Anton Chekhov,* edited by Lillian Hellman; *Flesh and Blood* by François Mauriac; *A Ghost at Noon* by Alberto Moravia; *Keats* by John Middleton Murry; and *Island in the Sun* by Alec Waugh.

Giroux, however, was not the only one adjusting to change. As anyone who has lived for a long time in a religious community knows, life within the cloistered walls is far from easy. In addition to the books and essays he wrote, Merton not only dealt for ten years (1955–65) on a very personal level with the Trappist novices in his charge—listening to them and discerning how they could become the Trappists they were called to be—but also carried on an extensive correspondence. Paul Pearson estimates that Merton wrote to approximately twenty-one hundred correspondents between the years 1963 and 1968, though, admittedly, not all of their letters are of major import. At the same time, it should be mentioned that for many years Merton's letters were read for the most part by his abbot, who often had to pass judgment on what Merton was trying to accomplish. From a spiritual point of view, the abbot, as the superior of all the monks in the abbey, knew where Merton wanted to go, but given the complexities of the situation, he had no road map to guide him, as a fair number of letters in this present volume make clear. At times, Merton and Fox clearly locked horns. John Eudes Bamberger, O.S.C.O., M.D., whom Merton mentored when he was master of scholastics (1951–55), once told Paul Wilkes,

> I think the relationship between Merton and Dom James Fox not only began well, I think it ended well, but there were many rough periods in between. We can't forget that for many, many years Merton saw his abbot every week, discussing his work and so on. He also acted as the abbot's spiritual director for a long period, and they were very open with one another. That just doesn't happen unless there is something positive going on year after year.[21]

In turn, Dom James Fox had to deal with *his* superiors, the various abbots general, who had to pass final judgment on Merton's writings after they had consulted with other Trappists, some of whom were not sympathetic to Merton's manner of discussing the Trappist manner of life. As an editor, Giroux faced these clerics and their views head on, whether by writing to or meeting with Abbot Fox at Gethsemani or in New York, or by asking prominent Catholic scholars, such as Jacques Maritain, to show their approval of Merton's writings. Clearly, Giroux never wavered in his support of his friend.

Thus, Giroux always remained steady in his professional and private friendship with Merton, encouraging him to continue writing, explaining in great detail what his books would look like, and giving publishing details that authors enjoy knowing, even when Merton could not keep track of all his writings—let alone foreign rights to his books, which caused him enormous difficulty. As Merton dealt with his programmed spiritual life, the monastic prayer schedule—as outlined in *The Waters of Siloe* (1949), a history of the Cistercian Order and an examination of the characteristics of Cistercian life—included the Canonical Hours of Matins and Lauds at 3 a.m., Prime at 5:30 a.m., Tierce at 7:45 a.m., None at 11:07 a.m., Vespers at 4:30 p.m., and Compline at 6:10 p.m., in addition to the community Mass, meals, and work in the monastery. Furthermore, he met with more and more visitors over the years, as his ecumenical circle of friends expanded to include non-Christians and those interested in the civil rights of all human beings on this globe. Merton kept an extraordinary daily schedule.

Given Giroux's reluctance to say anything to impede Merton's productive international influence and despite Naomi Burton's objections, Merton never severed his relationship with his other publishing firm, New Directions. Over the years, he was often overwhelmed by the details involved in planning one book after another. When, on his own initiative, he signed a contract on October 19, 1962, with Macmillan to publish a book entitled *Prayer as Worship and Experience,* he did not realize the import of his action, particularly as he was still under contract to Farrar, Straus & Cudahy. Roger Straus and Warren Sullivan, both presidents of their respective firms, almost took the case to court. When Merton apologized in a letter to Sullivan on July 3, 1963, he took responsibility for the apparent impasse: "The whole thing is my fault. Though I acted in ignorance and good faith, I am nevertheless objectively guilty of an injustice." He asked that their contract be terminated; in addition, he would willingly withdraw the book from publication. A month later, Sullivan wrote to Abbot Fox agreeing with him that the book should not be published and that the manuscript would be sent back to Merton. The advance of $5,000 was returned to Macmillan. Had Merton received Giroux's important letter of March 28, 1962, which for some unexplained reason never arrived in his mailbox, he would never have continued his relationship with Macmillan. No one, it seems, emerged from this unpleasant situation without feeling hurt. Throughout this difficult period, Giroux sought to maintain a personal and professional equilibrium in discerning how he could best help Merton continue as a productive writer.

As Giroux and Merton reached the end of their mutually agreed-upon contractual relationship in July 1965, Burton, who had become an editor at Doubleday, continued to write to Merton, finally persuading him to publish at least one book with her firm. In a letter to Burton, dated August 17, 1965, Merton says that he must withdraw more and more into solitude and live the life of a semihermit. "I know, if one can ever be said to know, that this comes from God and that I must obey him." Burton, for her part, reflected on her declining relationship with Merton:

> I was so struck in reading over several of Tom's letters by his real kindness, by his good advice to me, but most of all by his saying that he needed my advice on his work from a business point of view. And so I deserted him. Since I have left the literary agency where I worked for so many years I have written Tom seldom. The old exchange of thoughts and ideas is lost.[22]

In the mid-1960s, Merton's life was changing as he moved into his hermitage and lessened his ties with the other monks still residing in the abbey, as he became involved in the spring and summer of 1966 with a nurse who worked at a hospital in Louisville (see his journal entries in *Learning to Love: Exploring Solitude and Freedom*), and as he increased his contact with men and women of other faiths, either through letters or visits they made to him. He would have been the first to admit that the trajectory of his life, at that point, was not what he would have imagined on the day of his entrance to Gethsemani in 1941.[23] In a letter dated August 15, 1967, to former Trappist Colman McCarthy, he asked a probing question:

What am I doing personally? Without going into details, I can say I am to a great extent living on the margin of life at Gethsemani and concentrating on my own personal task, my own development and my contacts with people in my own fields, such as (a) poets and other writers and artists; (b) with Buddhists, Hindus, Sufis and people interested in the mystical dimension of religion, whether Christian or other.[24]

Astonishingly, with all the traffic in the abbey's mailroom, Merton made only three trips while Dom James was abbot: to search for a new site for a foundation in Ohio in the mid-1950s; to a workshop in 1956 on psychology at St. John's Abbey, Collegeville, Minnesota; and in 1964 to New York for a meeting with the Dr. Daisetz T. Suzuki. But no one, either in or out of Gethsemani, could have foreseen the manner of Merton's death.

Beginning in September 1968, Merton traveled to California, Alaska, and Asia, ultimately to attend a conference of Eastern and Western monks in Bangkok, during which he died of an accidental electrocution, "at the height of his powers," according to Giroux.[25] Rembert G. Weakland, O.S.B., Benedictine abbot primate and later archbishop of Milwaukee, and one of the conference's organizers, described to Paul Wilkes how Merton's body was found on the floor of his room, during one of the rest periods, with a tall electric floor fan fallen across his body. The fan's velocity-control box lay right against his flesh (he had just taken a shower) and on his skin "the area around the box was burned pretty badly and that burn extended down on the whole of the right side of Merton's body."[26] For Giroux, this image of the dead Merton brings to mind the last words of *The Seven Storey Mountain*, the conclusion of "the conversation with Our Lord" which he had written in 1947: "*That you* [meaning himself] *may become the brother of God and learn to know the Christ of the burnt men.*" When Giroux reflected with me on Merton's life, not long before his own death, he stressed Merton's energy, an intellectual energy fully supported by physical energy. His Trappist friend wrote every day of his life, by hand, by typewriter, in his journals, on trains, on airplanes, wherever he was. Merton's letters by hand were wonderful to look at, he said. The words just raced across the page. Giroux was once reminded of an original hand-written Mozart score he had seen, especially in realizing how quickly both men composed their works. For Giroux, this was evident from the very first time he edited Merton's story as a college student at Columbia. Merton, twenty-seven years a Trappist, died on December 10, 1968, the anniversary of his entrance into the Trappists, which also happened to have been the birthday of Dom James Fox, who had stepped down as abbot during the first week of September 1967 to pursue the life of a hermit as Merton had done. He died at age ninety-one on Good Friday 1987 and was buried next to Merton.

NOTES

1. TM, *The Seven Storey Mountain* (New York: Harcourt, Brace, 1948), 49.
2. Ibid., 85.
3. Michael Mott, *The Seven Mountains of Thomas Merton* (Boston: Houghton Mifflin Company, 1984), 84.
4. See Edward Rice, *The Man in the Sycamore Tree: The Good Times and Hard Life of Thomas Merton* (Garden City, NY: Doubleday, 1970), 19. Interview with Paul Pearson by PS (July 7, 2010).
5. TM, *Seven Storey Mountain*, 132.
6. Ibid., 155.
7. Rice, *Man in the Sycamore Tree*, 25.
8. TM, *Seven Storey Mountain*, 175.
9. Ibid., 206.
10. Robert Lax, interview by Paul Wilkes, in *Merton by Those Who Knew Him Best*, ed. Paul Wilkes (New York: Harper & Row, 1984), 68.
11. TM, *Seven Storey Mountain*, 260.
12. Wilkes, *Merton by Those Who Knew Him Best*, 17.
13. See Mott, *Seven Mountains of Thomas Merton*, 226–28.
14. Avery Dulles, S.J., *A Testimonial to Grace* (New York: Sheed & Ward, 1946), 25.
15. TM, *The Seven Storey Mountain*, Fiftieth Anniversary Edition with an introduction by RG (New York: Harcourt, Brace & Company, 1998), xiv. See also RG, "Editing *The Seven Storey Mountain*," *America*, October 22, 1988, 273–76.
16. See TM, *Entering the Silence: Becoming a Monk and Writer*, ed. Jonathan Montaldo (San Francisco: HarperSanFrancisco, 1995), 160.
17. RG, "Editing *The Seven Storey Mountain*," 276.
18. Wilkes, *Merton by Those Who Knew Him Best*, 25.
19. Quoted in Ian Parker's "Showboat," *New Yorker*, April 8, 2002, 60.
20. In a letter dated March 29, 1955, NB informed John McCallum at Harcourt, Brace that TM wanted to be released from his contract with this firm because he would like to continue having RG as his editor. The release was signed on April 4, 1955.
21. Wilkes, *Merton by Those Who Knew Him Best*, 118.
22. Naomi Burton, *More Than Sentinels* (Garden City, NY: Doubleday, 1964), 72.
23. TM, *Learning to Love: Exploring Solitude and Freedom*, ed. Christine M. Bochen (San Francisco: HarperSanFrancisco, 1997), 37–126.
24. See *Thomas Merton: A Life in Letters*, ed. William H. Shannon and Christine M. Bochen (New York: HarperOne, 2008), 53.
25. RG, "Lecture on Thomas Merton," Saint Peter's College, Jersey City, NJ, October 7, 1999.
26. Wilkes, *Merton by Those Who Knew Him Best*, 162.

The Letters of Robert Giroux and Thomas Merton

Harcourt, Brace & Company, Inc.
383 Madison Avenue
New York 17, N.Y.

Frater M[aria] Louis, O.C.S.O.[1]
Abbey of Our Lady of Gethsemani
Trappist, Kentucky

Dear Tom:

Please forgive my delay in replying sooner but the seasonal rush has been upon me. First of all, the proofs arrived in very good order and I was delighted with your cuts, all of which are very much to the good. Second, I have been in consultation with Mr. [Francis X.] Connolly, of Fordham and the Catholic Book Club, who has had some excellent suggestions which will be evident in the revised proofs which will be ready in several weeks. Third, we have received the imprimatur of the Archbishop of New York.[2]

I hope all of this is good news. Also, the reference to [former classmate, Stephen] Aylward has been caught and deleted. And a review copy of FIGURES FOR AN APOCALYPSE arrived from New Directions. It is a handsome book, worthy of the contents. I find the title poem particularly impressive, one of your best, and for personal reasons I am especially fond of part III of the poem. I think it an excellent idea to have included the essay on "Poetry and the Contemplative Life" [*Commonweal*, July 4, 1947]

Incidentally, it was one of Connolly's points that many readers will find the ending of THE SEVEN STOREY MOUNTAIN beyond comprehension. He liked the essay on "Active and Contemplative Orders" in Commonweal [December 5, 1947] tremendously and thinks that, because it represents a less extreme position than the present ending,* it should be used as the conclusion of the book. In any event, I am having it set up and you can judge the alternatives in proof.

Ever yours,
Bob /s/

*My own feeling is: let the reader catch up with you, or himself, in due course. But I admit justness to the point from the viewpoint of the audience. Let us decide on proofs.

P.S. FOUR QUARTETS and MURDER IN THE CATHEDRAL have gone to you by separate cover, and will be charged to your account.[3]

1. TM was a monk of the Abbey of Our Lady of Gethsemani in Kentucky. His religious title was *Frater*, Latin for "brother" (sometimes abbreviated as "fr."); Maria, in honor of Our Lady (see the letter dated July 22, 1951); and Louis, after Saint Louis of France. The initials after TM's name refer to his religious order: Order of the Cistercians of the Strict Observance. Since this order was influenced by the Cistercians of a monastery in France called La Trappe, the monks of this order are known as Trappists. Even when ordained a priest, and commonly referred to as "Father" or "Fr.," a Trappist might refer to himself, as a sign of humility, as *frater*.

2. After TM wrote a book, it had to receive the *nihil obstat* (a Latin phrase declaring that the publication is not offensive to faith or morals) of two censors of the Trappist Order as well as the *imprimi potest* (indicating that the book can be published) of the abbot. Then it was sent to a diocese or archdiocese for a *nihil obstat* from a *censor librorum* (an official with the authority to censor a book) of the Catholic Church before receiving the *imprimatur* (likewise indicating that a book can be published) from a designated highly placed church official. After Vatican Council II, this procedure was simplified.

3. *Four Quartets* (1943) is a book containing four poems written by T.S. Eliot: "Burnt Norton," "East Coker," "The Dry Salvages," and "Little Gidding." Eliot's play *Murder in the Cathedral* concerns the death of Saint Thomas Becket, archbishop of Canterbury, England.

DECEMBER 15, 1948

Abbey of Gethsemani
Centenary 1848–1948
Trappist, Kentucky

Dear Bob:

I am dazzled by the huge ad, the sales figures, the fan mail. I note that in the middle of that picture on the ad is our late Reverend Father Abbot walking wisely into the distance and I have not much difficulty figuring out who has been praying this book into the money—and, what is more akin to his spirit, into the apostolate.[1]

The fan letters were very comforting. However I got one snorter from a New York priest who ended up by saying he believed I would eventually apostatize from the Church for being such a smart-aleck. A kind of counterweight to the Archbishop [Cardinal Francis Spellman], and it will help me to behave.

One thing I want to ask. Please will you tell Sister Maris Stella to have the writer of that beautiful poem send it to [James] Laughlin [of New Directions] and tell him that I suggest it for inclusion in a Catholic Anthology he is slowly getting up?[2]

In great haste I close. Pray for me next Tuesday, I am supposed to be ordained subdeacon. It is also our hundredth anniversary. Thanks for the great check—thank Naomi [Burton].[3] To both of you a very holy Christmas. God bless you.

In Christo Rege [In Christ the King],
fr. Louis /s/

---

1. Dom Frederic Dunne, O.C.S.O. (1874–1948), was the abbot of the Monastery of Our Lady of Gethsemani from 1935 until his death on August 4, 1948. He was succeeded by Dom James Fox, O.C.S.O., who, when he resigned his office in September 1967, was, in turn, succeeded by Dom Flavian Burns, O.C.S.O., who preached at TM's funeral.

2. James ("Jay" or "J") Laughlin (1914–97) graduated from Harvard in 1939. His family had amassed a huge fortune in the steel business, allowing him to start the publishing firm of New Directions in 1936, which published some of the works of Ezra Pound, William Carlos Williams, Dylan Thomas, Marianne Moore, and Wallace Stevens, among others. *Thomas Merton and James Laughlin: Selected Letters*, ed. David D. Cooper (New York: Norton, 1997), details the friendship of TM and JL that began with the publication of TM's collection of poems, *Thirty Poems* (1944). For information about this Catholic anthology, never published, see *Thomas Merton and James Laughlin: Selected Letters*, 7–8.

3. Naomi Burton (Mrs. Melville E. Stone) (1911–2004), TM's friend and literary agent at Curtis Brown Agency, came to the United States in 1939 from her native England. Her lengthy correspondence with TM was most important in the development of his career as a writer. With Patrick Hart, O.C.S.O., she coedited *Love and Living*, and she also wrote about her friendship with TM in her autobiography, *More Than Sentinels*.

FEBRUARY 14, 1949

Our Lady of Gethsemani
Trappist-Cistercian Abbey
Trappist, Kentucky

Dear Bob:

By way of a Valentine, I got some nine thousand bucks from Naomi and I am sending you six pages of Author's Note which I think are very necessary to soothe future priest-readers of WATERS [OF SILOE]. They will be touchy about my treatment of, say, Fr. Vincent de P[aul] Merle.[1]

I gather that you are keeping the book for next fall. Quite O.K. But I would deeply appreciate it if you could find some way of getting it in galleys quick, so that I can send them immediately to the Abbot General in Rome and get him to approve them, give us a letter of specific approbation, and bring the whole works back when he comes to Gethsemani early this summer.[2] We need to work fast because he'll need leeway, being very busy, though very willing to do this.

Thanks for Dorothy Sayers, Wm. [William] Empson and Eliot.[3] Especially Empson. In a couple of days I hope you'll be getting the new job N[ew] Directions did for us, SEEDS OF CONTEMPLATION.[4]

I am glad the [SEVEN STOREY] MOUNTAIN is doing so well. Did I tell you I got a beautiful letter from Jacques Maritain?[5] It came to me via Harcourt [Brace & Company], maybe you saw it. I wrote him and we have been writing back and forth. He is certainly a wonderful and most benevolent person. My favorite fans are some little children on Long Island, who go to Communion for me and one of them, a boy of eleven, wants to become a Trappist.

Well, there goes the whistle. God bless you.

fr. M. Louis /s/

1. See TM, *The Waters of Siloe*, 83–100. Rev. Vincent de Paul Merle (1768–1853) founded the monastery of Petit Clairvaux in Nova Scotia, Canada.

2. Dom Dominique Nogues, O.C.S.O., served as the abbot general of the Order of Cistercians of the Strict Observance from 1946 to 1951.

3. Dorothy Sayers, an English-born author, was the author of *The Unpleasantness of Bellona Club* (1928), *Gaudy Night* (1935), and *The Mind of the Maker* (1941), a book that relates the creative process in art to the Holy Trinity. Her literary creation, Lord Peter Wimsey, appears in eleven novels and twenty-one of her short stories. William Empson, an English-born literary critic, is renowned for his book *Seven Types of Ambiguity* (1930). T.S. Eliot won the Nobel Prize for Literature in 1948.

4. TM, *Seeds of Contemplation* (New York: New Directions, 1949).

5. Jacques Maritain (1882–1973), a French Catholic layman, was a noted Thomistic philosopher. In the early 1930s, he lectured at the Pontifical Institute of Mediaeval Studies at the University of Toronto. Subsequently he taught at Columbia University, the University of Chicago, the University of Notre Dame, and Princeton University. Two of his influential books were *Art and Scholasticism* (1930) and *Creative Intuition in Art and Poetry* (1953). Daniel Walsh introduced TM to Maritain at a talk Maritain gave on social action in 1939. On February 10, 1949, TM wrote a long, almost chatty, letter in English to Maritain, thanking him for his kind remarks on TM's booklet *What Is Contemplation?* (Holy Cross, IN: Saint Mary's College, 1948). TM says that he is trying to block out time to write a book on theology, but is finding the going a bit difficult, though he does realize that for him "sanctity is quite probably connected with books and with writing and with intellectual drudgery. . . . To be a theologian demands a severe interior asceticism, and when I find myself sighing for a life of simplicity and solitude and obscurity I wonder if, after all, I am not just seeking luxury."

MARCH 18, 1949

Frater M. Louis, O.C.S.O.
Abbey of Our Lady of Gethsemani
Trappist, Kentucky

Dear Tom:

I enclose herewith sample pages of WATERS OF SILOE. As you will see, we have got away from the ubiquitous Electra. The body type is Janson and the display type is Cochin. I find it extremely attractive and I hope you do.

The printers are just now completing composition and the first batch of galley proofs will go out to you Monday morning. We have scheduled the book for publication in October.

I can send you a duplicate set for the Abbot General in Rome, but perhaps it would expedite matters for you to write him separately and for us to airmail them right from the office. Please let me know your wishes in this matter.

I can understand the necessity for the author's note in the WATERS OF SILOE, but I hope you will have no objection to our placing this at the end of the introduction to the book rather than at the beginning.

THE SEVEN STOREY MOUNTAIN is still selling beyond my wildest expectations and there is no sign of it letting up. Total sales to date are 154,245, and there are 171,000 copies in print.[1] The whole publishing world knows that it is the number 1 non-fiction best seller although it has just reached the number 2 spot on the so-called "bestseller lists."

I spent the other evening with the Mark Van Dorens who spoke of you most affectionately.[2] If I am not mistaken Dorothy [Van Doren] is taking her first steps along the road to faith. I have also been seeing Bob Lax,[3] who is the same as ever. He did not think you would mind his showing me some of your drawings. I know that they are sketches which you did not intend for publication, but if you do anything which might lend itself to such use, may I see them? There is tremendous interest in anything that you may do—too much interest no doubt from your point of view. But your book and your writing have already done an incalculable amount of good and the interest springs from a great hunger.

New Directions is to be congratulated on having made such a beautiful book out of SEEDS OF CONTEMPLATION. I read through avidly and with the greatest satisfaction. It is admirable in every way and I only regret that we did not have the honor of publishing it.

Ever yours,

[Robert Giroux]

1. By the end of the first year in print (October 3, 1949), *The Seven Storey Mountain* had sold 275,054 copies.

2. Mark Van Doren (1894–1972), Pulitzer Prize–winning poet and critic, taught English literature at Columbia University from 1920 to 1959, and had a great influence on both RG and TM, as evidenced in TM's premonastic journal *Run to the Mountain: The Story of a Vocation* (1995). Inspired by Van Doren's work on Shakespeare, RG wrote *The Book Known as Q: A Consideration of Shakespeare's Sonnets* (1982). In his *Autobiography* (1958) and in his *Selected Letters* (1987), Van Doren includes a number letters that indicate his deep friendship with TM.

3. Robert Lax (1915–2000), who figures prominently in TM's *The Seven Storey Mountain*, was a fellow student at Columbia College with TM and RG. He converted to Catholicism from Judaism. In 1962, he moved to the Greek isles, eventually settling on Patmos, before returning in 2000 to his hometown, Olean, NY.

MARCH 21, 1949

Frater M. Louis, O.C.S.O.
Abbey of Our Lady of Gethsemani
Trappist, Kentucky

Dear Tom:

Enclosed herewith are the first 39 galleys of WATERS OF SILOE. I also enclose the original manuscript as well as a duplicate set of galleys for your files. Please return the manuscript with the marked set of proofs. If you want to wait until the entire book is in your hands before returning proofs, that is OK. It would be an advantage however to have it returned in sections just as soon as possible. I will await your instructions regarding our forwarding a set of proofs to your Abbot General.

I have indicated on galley 6 the spot where I think your new copy, "Note on the Function of a Contemplative Order," should be inserted. I would change the first page of the new copy as indicated on the enclosed sheet; this all right with you?

With all good wishes.

Yours,
[Robert Giroux]

[NO DATE]

Dear Bob:

I am working on the proofs now. The book certainly looks fine and I am crazy about that Cochin [font]. Here are a few changes I'd like made in the MOUNTAIN.

In haste, I throw this in the mail. Only one thing I'd like to say at once: I want you to come down, if you can, for my ordination. We are hoping it will be on Ascension Day, May 26th, but it is not yet certain. That will be a very good time because the Abbot General will be here; you can meet him. For him, could you let me have an extra set of page proofs, to give him as soon as he arrives, probably middle of May or earlier. Then perhaps he could let you have the letter when you come down. I have written to Bob Lax and Jay Laughlin about coming and mean to write to Mark [Van Doren]: but it is a bad time for teachers.

All the best in Christo,
fr. M. Louis
Tom /s/

Changes to be made in the SEVEN STOREY MOUNTAIN.

p. 215 line 12 delete "with his ancient, ailing mother"

p. 12 line 8 from bottom. "Episcopal" instead of "Episcopalian"

p. 26 line 7 "It is what many Protestant children hear . . ." instead of "It is what all etc. . . ."

p. 243 top line. Delete "It is one reason for the number of drunken Irishmen in the world on Saturday nights for as we know, and it is quite true . . ."

p. 141 line 8 delete "sort of a"

p. 277 line 2 delete "irish"

MARCH 29, 1949

Frater M. Louis, O.C.S.O.
Abbey of Our Lady of Gethsemani
Trappist, Kentucky

Dear Tom:

The first 39 galleys arrived today. Thanks for returning them so promptly. We've now sent all the galleys except for the front matter and Author's Note; I hope they have arrived safely.

I very much want to come down for your ordination and will plan for May 26th unless I hear from you otherwise. When Mark [Van Doren] phoned today he said he would try to make it if he possibly could. Meanwhile, I'll send you that extra set of proofs for the Abbot General at the end of the week.

Yours,
[Robert Giroux]

MARCH 31, 1949

Frater M. Louis, O.C.S.O.
Abbey of Our Lady of Gethsemani
Trappist, Kentucky

Dear Tom:

I enclose herewith a specially bound set of proofs for the Abbot General. Please let me know what the wording should be for the "Nihil Obstat." Should I delay submitting the proofs to the Archdiocese of New York for Cardinal [Francis] Spellman's imprimatur until after it has been cleared by the Abbot General? I shall hold this up until I hear from you.

With best wishes.

Sincerely yours,
[Robert Giroux]

APRIL 2, 1949

Abbey of Gethsemani
[Letterhead]

Dear Bob:

Here is the front matter. One thing I would like to add: a dedication to Evelyn Waugh.[1] What do you think? He did me a big favor editing the MOUNTAIN in London and he was very friendly down here.

What about a few notes on monastic terms in the back. It might help, but I don't want to take up too much space. Another thing I thought of was a time table of the monk's day.

Many thanks for the elegant proofs for the General. I am making careful corrections because I don't want to say unjust or untrue things about people who were very holy.

> In Xto [In Christ],
> fr. M.L. /s/

1. Evelyn Waugh, a noted satirical English author of such novels as *Decline and Fall, Vile Bodies, Scoop, A Handful of Dust,* and *The Loved One,* edited the British edition of TM's autobiography, entitled *Elected Silence* (1949), and TM's *Waters of Siloe* as *Waters of Silence* (1950).

APRIL 7, 1949

> Abbey of Gethsemani
> [Letterhead]

Dear Bob:

Here are all the galleys back. I went over the end of the Prologue again and want to put in an insert, pertinent quotes from the [papal] Bull Umbratilem, about three hundred words in selected type.[1]

Will you send the N.Y. censor the page proofs containing the corrections that have been made in this round? I'll give the General the proofs you sent when he arrives.

Robert Speaight was here and we had a talk.[2] He glanced over the galleys and liked the book and asked for proofs to be sent to [the English publishing firm of] Hollis & Carter, saying they would be interested.

How are you coming with your consideration of the photographs? I hope the desire to win over a book club doesn't lead you to sacrifice the pictures. I'll take a cut in the royalties if necessary to get as many as possible in. Really, they will add tremendously to the book.

Speaight spoke about replacing a couple of American chapters by chapters on England and Ireland, in the event of an English edition.

When [Thomas] Sloane [of the Devin-Adair Company] does the index, please ask him to be sure and get in items like "Penance," "Mary," "Contemplation," "Liturgy," etc. These will be useful for monastic readers.

Did you think over the idea of a glossary?

Have a good Holy Week and Easter. Do you know that marvelous book, "Le Mystère Pascal" by Louis Bouyer?[3] It is something that would help one to get a tremendous amount out of this season. It is hard for even monks to realize how much Easter means: but everything is there.

May God bless you and give you every grace.

> In Corde Christi [In the Heart of Christ],
> fr. M. Louis /s/

1. The *Apostolic Constitution* of Pope Pius XI, entitled *Umbratilem*, approved the statutes of the Carthusian Order in 1924.
2. Robert W. Speaight, a British actor and writer who came to prominence as Becket in the first production of T. S. Eliot's *Murder in the Cathedral*, edited and wrote a foreword to the British edition of TM's *Selected Poems* (1950).
3. Rev. Louis Bouyer, a French Lutheran minister who converted to Catholicism in 1939, cofounded the international ecumenical review *Communio* and was the author of a number of books about the history of spirituality, including *The Spirituality of the Middle Ages* (1968).

[NO DATE]

Abbey of Gethsemani
[Letterhead]

Dear Bob:

Here is an insert that goes in near the end of the Prologue. I marked the place in the galleys: it is a quote, and should be, I suppose, solid, in smaller type, indented, etc.

The dedication should simply read:

To
Evelyn Waugh

Okay?

I'll get busy right away on the glossary and the other thing, and keep it short in order to get it in quicker.

Could you slip into the Bibliography:

Gethsemani Magnificat, Trappist Ky, 1949.

Happy Easter.

In Xto Rege,
fr. M. Louis /s/

APRIL 13, 1949

Frater M. Louis, O.C.S.O.
Abbey of Our Lady of Gethsemani
Trappist, Kentucky

Dear Tom:

Thanks for getting the galleys back so promptly. As I write you, the quoted material from Umbratilem for the Prologue has arrived, so we can proceed with paging. We'll submit pages to the censor of the Archdiocese of New York.

We are now working on the photographs. There's a rich selection to choose from; they are really an excellent group of pictures and we want to use as many as possible. We've chosen as frontispiece the archway of the [Abbey of] Fontenay cloister and will work this design into the title page.

Have the photos all been cleared for use in the book? And how about credits? We'll check these on the illustration proofs.

Naomi should send finished proofs or perhaps books to Robert Speaight for their consideration on English publication. You'll probably want to do a rather different version for them, as suggested.

Please rush copy of the glossary and time-table. We'll be all set then except for index. I hope Sloane will be free to do this but he's working for another publisher right now.

I enclose a full page ad which ran on the back page of this Monday's New York Times. Also an article in Time magazine (their third on MOUNTAIN—something of a record). Sales as of yesterday total 169,507, with 186,000 copies in print.

> Ever yours,
> [Robert Giroux]

HOLY THURSDAY [APRIL 14, 1949]

> Abbey of Gethsemani
> [Letterhead]

Dear Bob:
  Here is the time-table.
  Does that wind up everything?

> In Xto,
> fr. M. Louis /s/

P. S. Your letter just came in, with the TIME story. About the pictures, those marked on the back as coming from one [photographer Yvonne] Sauvageot, in Paris, will, some of them, need to be paid for at twelve dollars a throw, and a credit line will be given. Also credit line to those marked Jahan, and the Georgia barn shots, etc., will be credited [John] Manning. I'll catch all that in proof. Look forward to seeing them. Happy Easter. I'll keep you specially in mind at Communion, and today (oops, it is now Holy Saturday) I sing the exultet [Easter chant] and bless the Paschal candle, or light it, anyway, after the Abbot has blessed it.

APRIL 18, 1949

Frater M. Louis, O.C.S.O.
Abbey of Our Lady of Gethsemani
Trappist, Kentucky

Dear Tom:
  Happy Easter!

Many thanks for the time-table and for indicating the credits required for photos. I don't know at this moment how many [Yvonne] Sauvageots we want to use, but we shall not be deterred by the fee.

Yours,
Robert Giroux

MAY 12, 1949

Abbey of Gethsemani
[Letterhead]

Dear Bob:

This is to confirm the ordination date: two weeks from today, on the 26th, Ascension Thursday.[1] It seems incredible. I look forward to seeing you and I hope you will be able to stay over the Saturday when I sing my first solemn Mass. After that Mass, I hope we can arrange a dinner, all of us together, with the Abbot General and Father Abbot and it seems that Clare Boothe Luce is coming down also.[2] So be sure to stay all three days if you possibly can. I'll say a low Mass, Deo volente [God willing], on the Friday morning, and give Communion to those who wish to receive it.

The cover design, I mean the jacket design of <u>Waters</u> is simply swell. That angel might have walked that way right off one of those twelfth century manuscripts!

With best regards—and pray for me to become the simplest of all priests!

In Corde Christi,
fr. M. Louis /s/

1. The Feast of the Ascension, a celebration of Jesus' ascension into heaven after his resurrection, occurs forty days after Easter.

2. Clare Boothe Luce, a noted American author, socialite, and a major benefactor to the Abbey of Our Lady of Gethsemani, read page proofs of *The Seven Storey Mountain* during the summer of 1948. She served as the U.S. ambassador to Italy (1953–56) during the presidency of Dwight D. Eisenhower. She is buried in Mepkin Abbey in South Carolina.

[NO DATE, MOST LIKELY MAY 19, 1949]

Abbey of Gethsemani
[Letterhead]

Dear Bob:

In haste, just before going on retreat I send all I have finished of Waters—meaning everything except bibliography and glossary.

Everything looks fine.

However, our Abt [Abbot] General has not arrived yet and when he does he will be too busy. I think we had better skip the idea of his letter after all. Just go ahead with the book as it is. But I'll give him the proofs you sent and he will like them. Maybe he could give us a statement we could use as a blurb—but I don't know if that would be proper. We shall see.

God bless you. Pray for me in this momentous week. Hope to see you next Thursday. Stay three days if you can!

All the best.

In Christ,

fr. M. Louis /s/

MAY 19, 1949

Frater M. Louis, O.C.S.O.
Abbey of Our Lady of Gethsemani
Trappist, Kentucky

Dear Tom:

Jay Laughlin and I have made airplane reservations for Wednesday, 25th, and will arrive in Louisville around 5:37 E.S.T. I understand from Jay that we shall be able to get to the monastery about 7 o'clock. It was wonderful news to have confirmation of your ordination date and I very much look forward to the great event.

As Mark Van Doren has doubtless written you, he will, alas, be unable to attend. He is expecting an old student of his for a doctor's examination on that date, and the man is flying here from England. Jay and I shall, Deo volente, be ringing the bell at the Gatehouse some time around 7:00 on Wednesday.

Ever yours,

[Robert Giroux]

JUNE 7, 1949

Rev. M. Louis, O.C.S.O.
Abbey of Our Lady of Gethsemani
Trappist, Kentucky

Dear Tom:

Many thanks for the Utah monastery [Our Lady of the Holy Trinity in Huntsville] photographs which have just arrived. They are going to use the one with the mountain as backdrop. It's a magnificent shot.

I enclose herewith a duplicate set of proofs of the index to WATERS—not for proofreading (we are doing that here)—but to catch any errors of omission on the part of the indexer.

It was a most wonderful visit we all had, more wonderful than I can say. I am most grateful to Reverend Father Abbot for his courtesy in allowing me to come, and for the great consideration shown to all of us while there.

Ever yours,
Robert Giroux

JUNE 11, 1949

Abbey of Gethsemani
[Letterhead]

Dear Bob:

I am returning the index with a few perfunctory notes only. Further changes can be made in a later edition. I'd like to get more detail on points like "contemplation," etc., by citing passages that deal with it without perhaps using that very word. I'll catch all that when I go through the book.

We all certainly look forward to seeing the book and I think it will have a profound effect in the Order—although I may get a few brickbats for some of my ideas about De Rancé, etc.[1] We have all been busy here with the regular visitation and I have seen a fair amount of the Abbot General but mostly on business. It is a good thing we dropped the notion of the letter from him because he is very busy and not very well, and it is a good thought to spare him—but he is very happy about the success of the MOUNTAIN. He even made an oblique reference to that and SEEDS [OF CONTEMPLATION] in the official report of the visitation, but that, perhaps is a family secret so don't be telling it around, it would sound as if I we're promulgating the contents of the report!

Needless to say, Bob, it was wonderful to have you all here and you must come again when it will be less official and when you can rest and think and read and pray.

God bless you.

In Corde Xti,
fr. M. Louis /s/

---

1. Rev. Armand-Jean le Bouthillier de Rancé (1626–1700) was an abbot of the Monastery of Notre Dame de la Trappe in France. He dedicated himself to reforming monks of the Cistercian Order.

JUNE 21, 1949

Rev. M. Louis, O.C.S.O.
Abbey of Our Lady of Gethsemani
Trappist, Kentucky

Dear Tom:

The index changes you requested have all been made and I enclose a duplicate set of page proofs herewith for your files. Don't bother to return them unless you find some howlers which need correction.

I also enclose the first proof of the photographs. I am delighted with the texture and tone of this spread, and I am told that the finished product will be even a little better. You may keep these proofs if you wish.

I had lunch with Dan Walsh [on] Friday.[1] What a wonderful person he is! I intend to see more of him. We had a good talk about your new book, THE FIRE AND THE CLOUD.[2] We are both of the opinion that it may be your best prose work to date.

Ed Rice was good enough to show us proofs of some of the photographs he took at Gethsemani.[3] They came out very well, indeed.

With all good wishes.

Sincerely yours,
Robert Giroux

P.S. By separate cover I am sending you a set of page proofs for reference. The book is beyond the correction stage; it is now in foundry and in fact corrections were made on the pages. I will send a set of sheets early in July, and if in your reading of this you find any errors, we will pick them up in the next printing.

1. Daniel Walsh (1907–75), a visiting professor of philosophy from 1936 to 1955 at Columbia College, taught courses such as the philosophy of Saint Thomas Aquinas. TM was one of his students. Walsh was a professor at Manhattanville College of the Sacred Heart in Purchase, NY, from 1934 to 1960. On May 14, 1967, he was ordained a priest at age sixty for the Archdiocese of Louisville. He is buried at Gethsemani.
2. An early version of what would eventually become *The Ascent to Truth*.
3. Edward Rice (1918–2001), publisher and photojournalist, attended Columbia College with TM and RG. He was the editor of the *Jester*, Columbia's humor magazine, in his senior year. In addition, he founded and edited the Catholic magazine *Jubilee*. In 1970, he chronicled his friendship with TM in *Man in the Sycamore Tree*.

JULY 1, 1949

Abbey of Gethsemani
[Letterhead]

Dear Bob:

Thanks for the set of page proofs and for the proofs of the pictures which certainly look nice. The Month [a journal published by the English

Jesuits] wants to print excerpts from the book, and does not want to depend on Hollis & Carter for access to copy. Would you consider sending them a set of proofs, or a completed copy of the book if it will be forthcoming within a month or six weeks—or sheets or something. I think they can wait for a finished book, anyway. Apparently Elected Silence is not out yet.[1]

The French editor wants to cut a little. He is coming over here this fall, he says.

I gave Archbishop Yu Pin, of Nanking, oral permission to go ahead and present a small, edited, Chinese digest of the book for non-profit distribution among Chinese Christians and non-Christians. He seemed to think it would do a lot of good. He is a very impressive person by the way.

The man to contact at The Month is Fr. H. D[eryck] Hanshell, S.J.; they are at 114 Mount St., London, W.1.

I think that is about everything at the moment. It is the season of sweat in Kentucky. I am glad we had such nice weather when you were all down here. I keep you daily in the Mass, which does not cease to be the only thing that really absorbs me. In fact it gets to me more and more so every day.

> Sincerely in Christ,
> Tom
> fr. M. Louis /s/

P.S. I see I have been ambiguous about "the book." In paragraph one I mean Waters. In two, Elected Silence. In three, Seven Storey Mountain.

---

1. *Elected Silence*, the British edition of *The Seven Storey Mountain*, was published in 1949 by Hollis & Carter. By July 13, 1949, the American edition had sold 251,000 copies.

JULY 15, 1949

> Abbey of Gethsemani
> [Letterhead]

Dear Bob:

I am enclosing some pictures that I obtained from a French photographer—one who did some of the stuff we are using in Waters. These pictures are of some fascinating old monasteries down in the south of France where I was born, on the road to St. James of Compostella. One of the monasteries is Cuxa, the cloisters of which are uptown New York now. I'd like very much to make these pictures and perhaps others into a book. Let the pictures do most of the work, and I'd write a preface and some captions. I think it would make a very effective job. So I am submitting the pictures to you first, and if you can't see your way to doing it I'll send them to Jay—or perhaps you could pass them on to him.

Also, in the line of picture books, if you think it would be interesting, I think I could easily get the photographers who did the <u>Gethsemani Magnificat: [Centenary of Gethsemani Abbey]</u> to work around all the Trappist monasteries in this country and make an interesting book on them, although perhaps this would be pretty well out of your line. Anyway, here is the material on the French cloisters. I'd be glad to know what you think about the cloister idea. The other can wait.

I thought I had something else on my mind that I wanted to ask you about but it has slipped out for the moment. I am glad you and Dan liked the <u>Cloud and the Fire</u>. That is a job I must take slowly however. I'll get it done in time. There is no hurry there, either. It needs thought, and above all prayer.

All the best. God bless you.

In Corde Christi,
Tom
fr. M. Louis /s/

JULY 26, 1949

Rev. M. Louis, O.C.S.O.
Abbey of Our Lady of Gethsemani
Trappist, Kentucky

Dear Tom:

THE WATERS OF SILOE has just come to my desk in sheets, which I enclose herewith. I am very much pleased with its appearance and I hope you will be.

The Imprimatur of Cardinal Spellman arrived from Msgr. [Monsignor] John M. Fearns. In an accompanying letter, he pointed out a few typographical errors, all of which you caught (they had to read uncorrected proofs) except for the following:

xxi (footnote): Change "Q. 182, a.1, ad 2." to "q. 182, a.2, ad 3."
xxxv: insert hyphen between "Garrigou" and "Lagrange."
p. 102, third line from bottom, they suggest "teaching" would sound better than "education."
p. 127, second paragraph from bottom, they ask "Is 'Apostolic Delegate' the correct term? An Apostolic Delegate was in the U.S. only from about 1890."[1]
p. 269, line 4: should "virtutem" be "virtutum"?
p. 287 (footnote): should "unas" be "unus"?

Let me know if you want any of these corrected in the next printing.

Our advance sale of WATERS is terrific—already over 20,000 copies in advance of publication, which is now set for September 15th. The photos are really beautiful; we had to include two additional pages at the last minute, of which I'm sure you will not disapprove. With our special binding and jacket and the illustrations, this 380-page book is five dollars worth and we are pricing it at $3.50. I hope to send you finished copies shortly.

We are consulting about the monastery photo book right now. If it is to be done, I think we should do it. The prints you sent are not, however, good enough to reproduce from, our designer tells me. Can you get larger prints, or better yet negatives? And would the French photographers take an outright payment for book rights? We'd prefer this to royalties. Send me whatever additional material you have at hand. Better still, if you could start on a dummy, we could then proceed to get estimates and know just what the manufacturing problem is.

I am speaking at Columbia (Earl Hall) on THE SEVEN STOREY MOUNTAIN on August 2 and at Fordham on August 8.

With all good wishes to yourself and to Father Abbot.

Sincerely,
Robert Giroux

1. In an undated letter to RG, TM suggests that maybe the term "Nuncio" could be substituted for "Apostolic Delegate." He also says that Madame Yvonne Sauvageot has a variety of pictures, should RG want to look at them.

JULY 30, 1949

Abbey of Gethsemani
[Letterhead]

Dear Bob:

I have the sheets of WATERS now and they look fine. I have gone over the Prologue and Note and am sending you some corrections which ought to go through, if convenient, before too many more thousand are printed. I'd like to have the book with these corrections made fall into the hands of the more technical reviewers. For the average layman, okay as it stands.

As early as possible I'd very much appreciate having a dozen finished books to sign and send to important people . . . Maritain and some men in Rome, our Abbot General, etc. Could these count as publicity copies?

Could you take care, in due course, of sending a copy each to Bob Lax, Dan Walsh, Mark [Van Doren], Sy Freedgood, Jay Laughlin, and take these from the ones coming to me as author's copies?[1] The rest of the authors copies send here eventually. How garbled is this message?

In the illegible scrawl I sent the other day, I meant to ask you to put through all the corrections suggested by the censor. And as to the picture book, we can get full-size prints by writing to the address on the back of the samples. The name is Mme. Y. Sauvageot.

Have not yet seen the pictures that go with WATERS. But could you please send me back the pictures we did not use? I have to return some to a man in France.

God bless you. The book is swell.

Tom

fr. M. Louis /s/

1. Seymour ("Sy") Freedgood (1915–68), a close friend of TM, was one of his classmates at Columbia College. Later, he was an editor at *Fortune* magazine. It was through Freedgood that TM met the Hindu monk Brahmachari, who greatly influenced TM's religious sensibilities.

AUGUST 4, 1949

Rev. M. Louis, O.C.S.O.
Abbey of Our Lady of Gethsemani
Trappist, Kentucky

Dear Tom:

It's a great pleasure to send you herewith two copies of THE WATERS OF SILOE. Eight additional author's copies are due you and I shall be glad to send those out to any addresses you may indicate, or shall we ship them all to you at Gethsemani? I should tell you that I have already sent copies to your aunts at Douglaston [Freida ("Nanny") Hauck and Elsie Jenkins]. Everyone here is delighted with the appearance of the book, particularly the illustrations, endpapers, and binding. We have used an excellent stock of paper for the first edition of 25,000 copies. We are shortly going to press with a second printing (which includes those corrections). We are not sure that we will have the same good luck with the paper and I would therefore advise you to get in a supply of first edition copies for your library as soon as possible, and I will see that some are put aside for your use.

Copies of the English edition of ELECTED SILENCE have just reached my desk. Have you seen it? Evelyn Waugh's preface is particularly good and I think they have done a nice job of production. But I was rather surprised to note that the abridged edition of the text actually makes a bigger book than THE SEVEN STOREY MOUNTAIN. I shall be glad to send you an extra copy of the English edition which was sent here if you would care to have it.

With best wishes.

Sincerely yours,

Robert Giroux

AUGUST 5, 1949

Rev. M. Louis, O.C.S.O.
Abbey of Our Lady of Gethsemani
Trappist, Kentucky

Dear Tom:
Your letter of July 30th answers mine of August 4th which crossed it. I'm sending a dozen publicity copies by separate cover. Author's copies have gone to Mark Van Doren, Dan Walsh, Robert Lax, Ed Rice, Seymour Freedgood and James Laughlin. These, with the two copies to your aunts, make eight and the two already sent finish the ten. If you need any additional, do not hesitate to let me know; they can be considered publicity copies.

The new corrections have gone to the printer. The two new insertions on the best religious Order and on Trappists as business men will necessitate resetting several pages, but it ought to be done.

I'm returning the photographs not used in THE WATERS OF SILOE by separate cover.

With best wishes.

Yours,
[Robert Giroux]

P.S. I'm sending down two extra copies of WATERS, one, if you'll be good enough to autograph it, for myself; the other for an inscription for Gerry Gross, who designed the book (it is all too evident) as a labor of love.

AUGUST 6, 1949

Abbey of Gethsemani
[Letterhead]

Dear Bob:
The books just came and they are simply fine. All who have seen them here are enthusiastic. Father Abbot is away but I know he will like it. I just signed a copy for Clare Luce whose feast day is this week. Please send all the other author's copies here and ten others besides for me to send around to various people, as I said in the last letter. Thanks for sending copies to Douglaston. Will you send one to Bob Lax, one to Dan Walsh, one to Mark, one to Sy Freedgood, one to Ed Rice?

I haven't seen hide nor hair of the first edition of ELECTED SILENCE. I am sure they will be sending me one, but if you have no use for that extra copy . . .

Thanks for putting the corrections in the second printing. I'd like to have sheets of that printing bound up for the Holy Father as we did with the MOUNTAIN. Will you attend to that, Bob? Jay knows the place, they did a good job. I'd be very grateful. Then charge whatever is to be charged to the royalty account. I haven't heard from Rome yet about the others.

By the way, in Waters: credit line <u>Manning</u> should go on "Monks Dinner USA," "New World Script Building Temp. Monastery" and "Acolyte." This last title is not quite correct. He is really making his thanksgiving after Mass. Why not just say: "After Communion." On the big Gethsemani pictures would you give a credit line <u>Terrell Dickey</u>?

Thanks again Bob, the book is splendid.

God bless you,

[Thomas Merton]

AUGUST 8, 1949

Rev. M. Louis, O.C.S.O.
Abbey of Our Lady of Gethsemani
Trappist, Kentucky

Dear Tom:

Many thanks for your note of the sixth. I'm awfully glad to know that you like the looks of WATERS. Gerry Gross really did a marvelous designing job, I believe. Copies have gone out to Bob Lax (in the Virgin Islands) and to the others. I'll check with Jay as to the binder and get sheets of the second edition to him.

I'm glad to have the extra credits for the photos. They are too late even for the second printing, since we ran off 50,000 copies of the illustrations at the beginning. We had to do this as a precaution, since the special gravure press is not always available, and also it was more economical to do so. (On small runs the cost of WATERS is such that its price would be nearer to $5.00 than to the present $3.50; in short, readers are getting a bargain.) However, in future runs the changes will be made. I assume that these corrections are not important for the specially bound copy.

The mistake on the "Acolyte" photo is my fault. Is he not kneeling at the <u>side</u> of the altar? This led me to assume that he was serving at Mass, rather than performing it. We'll change it to "After Communion."

Thanks for the information on Mme. Sauvageot, to whom I shall be writing. What about the American foundations? Are you thinking of this as a purely European photo book?

The copy of ELECTED SILENCE goes to you by separate cover. With best wishes.

Yours,

Robert Giroux

AUGUST 10, 1949

Rev. M. Louis, O.C.S.O.
Abbey of Our Lady of Gethsemani
Trappist, Kentucky

Dear Tom:

The director of the School of Journalism at Fordham University, Father Alfred Barrett, S.J.—the man who asked me to speak about THE SEVEN STOREY MOUNTAIN—is a poet who very much wanted you to see his book of verse. He inscribed the enclosed copy for you. He was part of the group of Catholic poets who were active about a decade ago—Sister Madaleva, Leonard Feeney, and so on—the generation just preceding yours and mine.[1] I suppose he is concerned lest this group be not included in your anthology. At any rate, here is his book. I rather like his sonnet on Thérèse of Lisieux.[2]

Yours,
Robert Giroux

1. Leonard Feeney, S.J., defended the strict interpretation of the Roman Catholic doctrine, *extra Ecclesiam nulla salus* (outside the Catholic Church there is no salvation), arguing that no non-Catholic will be saved. In 1953, he was excommunicated from the Catholic Church and dismissed from the Society of Jesus. Sister M. Madaleva Wolff, C.S.C., poet and author, served as president of Saint Mary's College, Notre Dame, IN, from 1934 to 1961.

2. Saint Thérèse of Lisieux, a French Carmelite nun often called "The Little Flower of Jesus," was canonized a saint in 1925.

AUGUST 13, 1949

Our Lady of Gethsemani
[Letterhead]

Dear Bob:

The big box with fourteen copies of WATERS arrived. Does this include the two you want signed? I'll send them along at any rate. Also ELECTED SILENCE. Thanks very much. I really like the appearance of the English edition too. But really. WATERS is beautiful. Photos came back too.

Thanks also for the proofs on the Note, for the second edition.

My idea for the photo book was to make one exclusively devoted to those southern French cloisters. They are not monasteries of our Order. What I thought of doing was having short bits of poetic prose to go with groups of pictures. For instance where there are one or two groups of capitals, showing Biblical scenes, I could do some prose on the things represented. The pictures would always have the pages to themselves, perhaps different stock, and text to face. Perhaps the book would run like that all through: Picture—text—picture, etc. However, I'd have to read up on the monasteries before I started and I have no material.

When I mentioned a Trappist picture book, that was a separate enterprise, but it could be more or less along the same lines. However, it would be more living and topical. I'd like it to cover monasteries everywhere. In fact, what I would like most of all would be a picture book of the contemplative life everywhere—but it would be an awful job to get the stuff together. Still, perhaps I could go to Europe to do it: but it would be an awful headache.

I am going to get busy and sign those copies of WATERS and send them all around. Did I tell you Jacques Maritain promised to write a preface to the French translation of MOUNTAIN?

Well, I am busy as usual. I am trying to crowd all letter writing into Saturday afternoons so as to have the rest of the week free for real writing. Still, I am trying to write slower and pray more while I write so that everything I do is contemplation. It is fine when it really goes that way.

God bless you.

Tom
fr. M. Louis /s/

P.S. The monk kneeling at the side of the altar is there <u>after</u> Mass because it was in the hayloft and that was probably the best corner he could find.

AUGUST 17, 1949

Abbey of Gethsemani
[Letterhead]

Dear Bob:

Father Abbot wants to order twenty copies of WATERS OF SILOE [in] the first edition, for the monastery.

Will you please bill the Abbey and address the books to Father Abbot? Thanks.

In Corde Christi,
Tom
fr. M. Louis /s/

P.S. I am sending a signed copy to E. Waugh, of course. How many more do you think should go to him? I don't know the procedure when one dedicates a book to someone. Anyway, will you send him 3 on the royalty account, if you think that is enough?

AUGUST 18, 1949

Rev. M. Louis, O.C.S.O.
Abbey of Our Lady of Gethsemani
Trappist, Kentucky

Dear Tom:

We are shipping 20 copies of WATERS OF SILOE, first edition, to Father Abbot and are charging them to your account.

The three extra copies for Evelyn Waugh, as Dedicatee, seem right and proper to me, and we are forwarding them to him today.

The English reviews of ELECTED SILENCE are fascinating. A full page in the Times Literary Supplement was very good. I believe Naomi is sending you a copy of this. You will be amused to see how they mis-read your account of Seymour Freedgood pointing to the cat as [the Hindu] Bramachari. I enclose an ad from the English trade magazine which indicates that they are really in their third printing. Congratulations.

With best wishes.

Yours,
Robert Giroux

AUGUST 23, 1949

Abbey of Gethsemani
[Letterhead]

Dear Bob:

I have just received fifty or so more contact prints (small) of that southern French business, cloisters, villages, etc., this time more landscape and more life, people, etc., which convince me that the whole business will make a thrilling picture book, with bits of poetic prose interspersed. Are you interested enough in it for me to go ahead and tell Mme. Sauvageot to blow me up enlargements of all these small prints so that we can really go to work? I think I shall do so anyway, because if you do not want it Jay will. Anyway, please let me know quick so that I can write to her early next week or if possible this Saturday.

Have you contacted her? Have you paid her for the stuff we used in WATERS? Perhaps you could send her a copy of WATERS and this would show her that we are not fooling. It will certainly impress her, it is so beautiful.

Incidentally, about WATERS, Clare Luce wrote to me and remarked that she thought it was a mistake to put it forward as a kind of sequel to MOUNTAIN since it is really such a different book. People will be expecting a continuation of the autobiography and therefore they will be inclined to kick at passages which they would not otherwise regard as slow. I mean, the utterly different tempo of this book will be apt to irk them if they buy it on the grounds that it will move on like the MOUNTAIN. Really I too think it is not the right angle to work on. Let them know, perhaps, more bluntly what the book is. However, you can tell much better than I.

Still busy, as usual. At the moment I am cleaning up SEEDS [OF CONTEMPLATION] for a second edition.

I close in haste. God bless you. All the best. Everybody likes WATERS immensely. Sending the signed copies.

In Corde Christi,
Tom
fr. M. Louis /s/

AUGUST 30, 1949

Rev. M. Louis, O.C.S.O.
Abbey of Our Lady of Gethsemani
Trappist, Kentucky

Dear Tom:

Invitations to talk about THE SEVEN STOREY MOUNTAIN and your work keep coming in. I have just agreed to speak to the Saint Thomas More Crusaders at New Haven early in October.

Clare Luce is mistaken in thinking that we are presenting WATERS as a "a kind of sequel to THE SEVEN STOREY MOUNTAIN." Our jacket, it is true, refers to WATERS as a "companion volume" but that is quite a different thing. It is a companion volume, and it will have all the more meaning for readers because they have already read THE SEVEN STOREY MOUNTAIN. It will be evident to anyone who has the book in his hands for two minutes that it is quite different from your autobiography. The booksellers have all seen advanced copies, they know its nature, and their orders continue to come in. The advance sale has now reached 42,738 copies with 50,000 copies in print before publication. There is no denying that the success of THE SEVEN STOREY MOUNTAIN has had a great deal to do with this. If the order of publication had been reversed there would probably be quite a different story. THE SEVEN STOREY MOUNTAIN has stimulated a tremendous interest in Trappists and in the monastic and contemplative ways of life. Only yesterday the Herald Tribune printed a story about Trappists. I don't think they would have sent their reporter out on this story if it were not for the MOUNTAIN. In our advertising and promotion of WATERS we are making it quite clear that the book concerns the monastic life in general. Our big bookstore poster is centered around the figure of the gardener at Aiguebelle [in southeastern France] which is included among the illustrations in the book. It might interest you to have a copy of the poster. Perhaps it could be displayed in the bookstore at Gethsemani. In any event, I am shipping one to you by separate cover. I am also enclosing a copy of an ad which appeared in this morning's <u>Times</u>, announcing the sale of copy number 250,000 of THE SEVEN STOREY MOUNTAIN.

Have you any idea when we might expect delivery of the manuscript of THE CLOUD AND THE FIRE? If it were finished by the end of October, for example, we could definitely plan on spring publication. If, however, you will not have finished with it before the end of the year, we should like to plan for next fall. Please let me know about this as soon as you can.

As to the picture book, we are of course very much interested. The quality of Madame Sauvageot's work is simply terrific, and it will be a very beautiful book. I am sending her a copy of WATERS. I think you are safe in telling her to make blow-ups of the pictures. Ask her to send the charges for this preliminary work so that if for any reason the book is not brought to a successful conclusion we can reimburse her. We are not exactly sure whether all the French pictures in WATERS are her work. Did she cite any charges in sending them to you? I should certainly like to straighten this out, and I don't want her to think that we tried to use the material without reimbursing her.

I am delighted to learn that Jacques Maritain is writing the Preface to the French translation. Will there be any other foreign editions besides the French? I should very much like to have news of all the foreign languages into which THE SEVEN STOREY MOUNTAIN is going to be translated.

Yours,
Robert Giroux

AUGUST 31, 1949

Abbey of Gethsemani
[Letterhead]

Dear Bob:

The WATERS are being read in the refectory and one or two changes came to mind. I am enclosing sheets to show what they are. On the whole the book is well liked here.

I am sorry I have delayed so long in signing those copies. I am doing so right now and getting them in the mail at once.

Can those bills please be taken care of on the royalty account?

All the best,
God bless you.

In Domino Christo [In Christ, Our Lord],
Tom
fr. M. Louis /s/

P.S. Is Gerry Gross right for the name of the designer?

SEPTEMBER 6, 1949

Rev. M. Louis, O.C.S.O.
Abbey of Our Lady of Gethsemani
Trappist, Kentucky

Dear Tom:
Thanks for the further changes in the text. I will send proofs of these and see that they are incorporated in the next printing.
I have just heard that Hollis & Carter are taking WATERS. What good news! They want to borrow the illustrations. Should I tell them that Mme. Sauvageot may have to be paid?
Do let me know about THE CLOUD AND THE FIRE when you can.

Ever yours,
Robert Giroux

P.S. The bills will of course be charged to the royalty account. The designer's name is Gerry Gross.

SEPTEMBER 7, 1949

Abbey of Gethsemani
[Letterhead]

Dear Bob:
Thanks for your letter. I quite understand about the publicity of WA-TERS. I see your point all right.
Here is a correction—urgent because it is a silly mistake that will arouse a lot of people in Kentucky—

p. 130, line 7 "St. Joseph's Cathedral, Bardstown," should be substituted for "St. Peter's Cathedral . . ."

As soon as the printing with the corrections in the "Note," etc., is ready, will you please send me a dozen copies? When that edition is ready, review copies should be sent to "The Thomist," 487 Michigan Ave., N.E., Washington, D.C.; La Vie Spirituelle, 29 Boulevard de la Tour Maubourg, Paris, 7e.

Much curiosity about Trappists has been aroused in South Carolina where we are soon to make a foundation. Ads in the Charleston and Columbia papers might be a good idea.

If I had something else to say I'll remember it at mental prayer this evening.

God bless you.

> In Corde Mariae [In the Heart of Mary],
> Tom
> fr. M. Louis /s/

SEPTEMBER 9, 1949

> Abbey of Gethsemani
> [Letterhead]

Dear Bob:

I forgot all about THE CLOUD AND THE FIRE. That must wait. I cannot get down to it until I am more in the clear. I intend to rewrite everything I sent you, and need time to study and pray before I can get into the book. Let us put it off until, say, spring 1952. I want to take it slowly and carefully.

I think the photographic job should come next. My idea now is for a sort of prose-poetry text, very brief of course, to accompany the pictures. I'd need more time and more pictures, and also some reading, before I could turn out any of it. I think the book would do for fall of next year.

Meanwhile I have been working on one of our 12th-century writers, Aelred of Rievaulx.[1] A study of him has been needed for some time. The book would comprise biography, study of his doctrine and selected texts from his writings, all in Latin and some not printed even in Latin. This could make an attractive book, and I may be able to let you have it in January or February, but let's not rush. We can keep it for spring 1951, at least. I have finished the biographical part. A nun is helping with the translations of his texts but the doctrinal section requires study and reflection, Bob, and it will be better if I do not hurl myself into it wildly. I want above all, now, to slow down on production and turn out more careful and more meditative work.

Let me know what you think of these projects. Then there is always that book on the Mass. I badly want to do it. That could wait until after the CLOUD [AND THE FIRE]—or do you think it should come first?

Really, I want to be able to work slower and more prayerfully now that we have a good start and there is a fair amount of stuff in print, to keep us going for a while.

All the best. God bless you.

> In Corde Christi,
> Tom
> fr. M. Louis /s/

P.S. The only pictures in the W[aters] of S[iloe] for which we need to pay Mme. Sauvageot are the three accredited in her name. Did you send W. of S. to the editors of the <u>Month</u> who want to print some parts of it.

---

1. Saint Ailred of Rievaulx (1110–67), a Cistercian monk, wrote *The Mirror of Charity* and *On Spiritual Friendship*. His name has been regularized in all cases as Aelred.

SEPTEMBER 12, 1949

Rev. M. Louis, O.C.S.O.
Abbey of Our Lady of Gethsemani
Trappist, Kentucky

Dear Tom:
I should have caught the error regarding St. Joseph's Cathedral, Bardstown [Kentucky]. I passed it often enough with Jay during our visit and was amazed at its size and beauty.

We'll send review copies to <u>The Thomist</u> and <u>La Vie Spirituelle</u>. I assume you mean the second edition, but of course you made further corrections which we'll get into a third printing. Is it the latter printing you want us to send them by any chance? Incidentally, we are advertising THE WATERS OF SILOE in South Carolina.

Ever yours,
Robert Giroux

P.S. A Jesuit teacher who read an advance copy writes us: "One little passage troubles me—on the top of page 231: 'These (stone jars) are now distributed around the various altars in the church, and the servers of Mass empty the basins into them at the <u>lavabo</u>.' I cannot make anything of that sentence at all."

P.P.S. As I sign, your letter of the 9th arrives. OK, let's plan on THE CLOUD AND THE FIRE for the spring of 1952. It's more important than anything else, save perhaps the book on the Mass, which I'd like to see come first—fall of 1950, maybe? The photo book will be fun, but it's worth considering at this point whether the enormous amount of work and detail it will involve are proportional to the product. If you feel ready and eager for it, so be it; we certainly want to do it, and fall of 1950 sounds right. Aelred of Rievaulx is new to me and sounds fascinating. I'd like to see the biographical part, if I may; I'll return it, of course.

Best of all is your determination to slow down on production. That is important at this point—I feel this strongly. Are there any other unfinished books committed for Jay or elsewhere?

SEPTEMBER 16, 1949

Abbey of Gethsemani
[Letterhead]

Dear Bob:

Here is a little something I have been keeping in reserve for you. I wanted to read it all, but have not had time to get through it completely. I think it is an amazing book, although it will need a lot of editing and perhaps rewriting here and there. Don't be scared by the absurd title.

It is the narrative of a Trappist laybrother in one of our French Abbeys. He is British born, and was imprisoned by the Nazis during the war. He escaped and made his way through France, Spain, and Portugal, and finally got back to England. This is his story. It is well told and very exciting, full of wit, very original and I think if it were handled properly it would make a tremendously good book. The only trouble is that the language is not so wonderful and much of the writing is far too crude and sloppy, but don't you think someone could clean that up easily enough?

The Abbot General told me about this ms. and I got in contact with the Brother (Brother Martin, at Thymadeuc, in Brittany) who sent it along. I told him to write fifty pages about his life in the monastery to begin with. For my own part, I can write an introduction giving his past career which is colorful (Lt. Colonel in British Secret Service, etc. World War I, novice in Spain, etc.) He is writing that now, and inventing names for the people in the book, to replace initials. I think it is swell. Tell me how it looks to you.

All the best,

In Christo,
Tom
fr. M. Louis /s/

P.S. As a tentative title I am thinking of "Chastised but not Killed." His name is Bro. M. Martin Caillard, O.C.R.

SEPTEMBER 29, 1949

Rev. M. Louis, O.C.S.O.
Abbey of Our Lady of Gethsemani
Trappist, Kentucky

Dear Tom:

I have just had a most unpleasant conversation with Mr. Manning, who took the Georgia photographs used in WATERS OF SILOE. He claims that we had no right to use the photographs without his permission and that the Georgia monastery had no right to release them to you. You will doubtless be hearing from him directly, and he will doubtless enclose a large bill.

Don't worry your head about this. I am simply preparing you for the event, and when his letter and the bill arrive just forward them to me at once.

Our lawyer will have to handle this and it would be helpful to know from the Georgia foundation if <u>they</u> commissioned the photographs; that is, can you find out if they asked him to do the job or whether it was the other way around—did he ask them and get their permission to roam around the place taking his pictures? He claims that the photographs are his property, and that they are copyrighted. I pointed out to him that the copies which you forwarded to me contained no copyright notice, as they should. His reply was that he had sent a "courtesy set" unmarked to the monastery for their files. He also claims that with this set he sent a covering letter asking the monastery not to release them for publication. It is most important to know whether this latter claim of his is true. Could you check this?

I hate to bother you with the matter, but it appears that Mr. Manning requires firm handling.

Ever yours,
Robert Giroux

OCTOBER 6, 1949

Rev. M. Louis, O.C.S.O.
Abbey of Our Lady of Gethsemani
Trappist, Kentucky

Dear Tom:

Brother Martin's story of his escape from the Nazis is an extremely interesting job, but I am afraid it is not for our list. As you say, it needs editing, cutting, and proper handling, for it is an unusual and bizarre story, with the stamp of an individual on it. I particularly enjoyed Part III, the escape section. The lack of restraint, the language, and even in the incidents, will amaze many readers. To some degree, the narrator acts like a clown and is taken for a clown by others, but of course he's nobody's clown. One of my favorite sentences in the book occurs near the end: "A dear old Air Force Officer was aboard with a bottle of Johnny Walker. He rendered first aid. It was a merry voyage." The book is quite English in manner and in attitudes towards other nationalities; that is part of its charm—and its limitation too, from our point of view. Naomi should certainly see it and I am sure she will handle it successfully for the Order and place it. Shall I pass it on to her? I won't tell her about it, until I hear from you. Meanwhile I'll hold the manuscript here. I couldn't be more grateful for your thoughtfulness in sending it to me and I'm disappointed, if only for that reason, that we've decided against taking it on.

St. Aelred is wonderful and I shall write you at length about it shortly. Has the thought occurred to you of combining two short books under one title (the other being the book on St. Bernard, which we very much want to do also)—a title like TWO SAINTS. This is not however meant to be the letter about your writing program and I'll go into this more fully in my next. But offhand what do you think of the combination idea? (I think incidentally that the St. Aelred story should start in England on page 29).

The WATERS OF SILOE is having a wonderful reception. I have a file of letters from religious and teachers all over the country and shall be sending these, along with reviews. We now have 75,000 copies in print: I'm sure we have just begun. This week was the first anniversary of publication of THE SEVEN STOREY MOUNTAIN. Remember copy no. 200,000 which I brought down in May? Well, we have already reached no. 300,000 and, with the present upswing in sales (perhaps related to the publication of WATERS), there's a chance we may reach no. 350,000 by Christmas.

With all the best.

Yours,
Robert Giroux

P. S. I enclose our anniversary day ad. Also the New Yorker ad which just came in today!

OCTOBER 10, 1949

Abbey of Gethsemani
[Letterhead]

Dear Bob:

Sorry to have delayed about the Manning business. You will see from the enclosed letter that I had to wait for our Father Abbot to come back from France so that I could find out from him, as he was the one in charge in Georgia at the time. He says, as I wired, that Manning presented himself, in fact made a big nuisance of himself, as the representative of Click, took pictures for Click and gave the monks prints of the pictures as the only compensation for their courtesy. There were no strings attached and he did not send any letter about not releasing the pictures. No such letter is preserved in Georgia and no one remembers one and it is the custom in our monasteries here to assume that when we give someone the right to come in and take pictures of us, we in turn receive the right to print the pictures if we need them in any of our publications. It is only a fair exchange. Of course Waters of Siloe is a different thing, but we had no reason to expect that he would object to the publication of the pictures. I suppose you would be as willing as we would be to pay a reasonable fee for the use of the pictures, but I assume he is now suing for damages or lese majeste [slighting behavior toward a person to whom deference is due] or something terrific.

Go ahead, Bob, and give the Bro. Martin ms. to Naomi. He has written that a new beginning is on the way over—some thirty pages of monastic material to start out with. I'll shoot that straight to her. Let's assume that the title of the ms. for the time being is <u>Chastised but not Killed</u>. If she can't get anyone else to use it, I think people like Kenedy or Declan-McMullen (if they exist) or Devin Adair would be very glad to get it, or even Sheed & Ward [all publishing houses].

About St. Aelred: rather than combine just Aelred and Bernard, it would be better to do Bernard and his school including Aelred and several others, but that would make the material I have so far written on Aelred too long and it would knock out all the translations and selections which, remember, the sister is doing and which were the original excuse for the volume. I'd much rather go on from where we are and make a full-length study of Aelred with this anthology of selections, a good definitive sort of book about him, and then do the same for St. Bernard. What do you think about selections from Bernard? I mean along with the biography and the doctrinal study? It has been very well done in French and I think it is needed.

I am so glad <u>Waters</u> is going well. I feel good about it, on the whole and a lot of people, especially monks and priests, are saying it is the best one I have done so far. I am surprised that it is so well liked.

The reason why I want to go into Aelred in some detail is that he is quite a man on the theology of Love and I think something very convincing can be made out of his message.

Sometime I want to make a few more minor corrections on <u>Waters</u>, but too busy now. Meanwhile, is a copy being bound for the Holy Father? And can you send review copies of both <u>Waters</u> and <u>Mountain</u> to the magazines <u>Dieu Vivant</u>, 27 Rue Jacob, Paris 6e and <u>Vie Spirituelle</u>, 29 Boulevard de la Tour Maubourg, Paris 7e, and <u>Cross and Crown</u>, Rosary Coll[ege], River Forest, Illinois (only <u>Waters</u>). Did you send one to the <u>Thomist</u>?

I guess that's all for the moment.

God bless you.

In Corde Christi,
Tom
fr. M. Louis /s/

NOVEMBER 7, 1949

Rev. M. Louis, O.C.S.O.
Abbey of Our Lady of Gethsemani
Trappist, Kentucky

Dear Tom:

We have had a request from the editor of the Chicago <u>Tribune</u> Book Section, Mr. Frederick Babcock, that you contribute a Christmas message to their readers. They specify between 300 and 600 words, and it can of course take any form you please, poetry, prayer, essay, or story. They have a tremendous audience in the mid-West and cover a much larger area than simply the state of Illinois. As a matter of fact, they fan way out both West and South in an area in which there has been marked response to all your writing. I sincerely hope that you will be able to contribute something; it's really worth your while from every point of view. This is something of a rush, alas, as all deadlines are. They need it November 19, but I am sure it could be stretched a couple of days if you assure delivery. In any event, please let me know whether this is possible, and I shall get in touch with Mr. Babcock.

With all good wishes.

Sincerely yours,
Robert Giroux

P.S. I have had several requests from bookstore people, both here and in Chicago, who are Catholics, for medals from Our Lady of Gethsemani. Do you think you could send me about five of them?

NOVEMBER 9, 1949

Rev. M. Louis, O.C.S.O.
Abbey of Our Lady of Gethsemani
Trappist, Kentucky

Dear Tom:

Naomi has written me about the book which you wrote, under obedience, some time ago about the stigmatic Cistercian saint in the 13th century, for which I understand Bruce is the publisher.[1] Naomi tells me that you wondered if they could be prevented from advertising it in a big way. One very effective way of preventing their advertising it improperly would be Father Abbot's requesting them not to use the by-line Thomas Merton in any way, shape, or form, but restricting it solely to the use of the name Father Louis. Of course their contract with you or with the monastery may have specified Thomas Merton, in which case the suggestion is useless. But if it doesn't, and if Father Abbot concurs in the wisdom of such a course of action, and if as a result the Bruce Publishing Company cancels publication, I herewith guarantee its publication under our imprint.

I think it's extremely important, not only to the monastery but for the effectiveness with which your work will reach the general public, that you limit the number of books which appear under the name of Thomas Merton very severely. The name will carry more weight, and the works will go farther, the fewer you publish each year. This is really a matter of serious concern, and I know that you feel it to be so by the fact that you bring up the question of this book. If the above suggestion seems right and proper

to Father Abbot, I hope he will put it into effect, and I assure you that we will cooperate on our part to the fullest extent.
    With all good wishes.

Sincerely yours,
Robert Giroux

1. TM, *What Are These Wounds? The Life of a Cistercian Mystic, Saint Lutgarde of Aywières* (Milwaukee: Bruce, 1950).

[NO DATE]

Abbey of Gethsemani
[Letterhead]

Dear Bob:
    In haste I am sending the Chicago Tribune thing hoping that you will forward it to the correct address if the thing seems to be what is wanted. About the medals—what kind do you want? St. Benedict? I'll get the bookstore to send some.

In Corde Christi,
Tom /s/

NOVEMBER 14, 1949

Rev. M. Louis, O.C.S.O.
Abbey of Our Lady of Gethsemani
Trappist, Kentucky

Dear Tom:
    This is to acknowledge receipt of the essay on "Reading as a Path to Contemplation" for the Chicago Tribune. I think you've done an excellent job and they are lucky to get it. I was delighted to find [Franz] Kafka and [Karl] Barth and [Johannes] Tauler and [Evelyn] Underhill along with [Léon] Bloy and [Leo] Tolstoy and [Fyodor] Dostoevsky.
    The requests for medals were not specific—I assume medals of Our Lady. However, does the bookstore have a catalogue or order sheet? If so, send that and then I can check back with the bookstore people who inquired.

Ever yours,
Robert Giroux

DECEMBER 1, 1949

Dear Tom:
    It's a pleasure to send to you, by the hand of Naomi Burton, a copy of THE LAW OF HOLY MASS by Father Joseph Francis. Your library doubt-

less contains many reference books covering the general rubrics of the missal, but this little work is so compact and so well put together that I think you might find it useful. I have, of course, an ulterior motive in sending it—that is, your book on THE MASS. I would very much like to see you do it as your next book, say the fall of 1950. As you know, I thoroughly agree with Naomi and Mr. T. F. Burns [of Burns & Oates Publishers] that your books should be limited to one a year, or perhaps to three books every two years, and I do think you should concentrate on the major works like THE LIFE OF ST. BERNARD and THE CLOUD AND THE FIRE, and I take it from your own thoughts on the matter that you agree.

I want to re-affirm by this post our offer to publish the book which you wrote under obedience about which I wrote you in my last letter. I understand that you have already written to Bruce [Publishing Company] and have had no reply. I should advise your putting it in Naomi's hands and having her arrange for the recapture of the book rights from Bruce and drawing up an agreement with Harcourt, Brace.

I also want to confirm by this mail our offer to publish your book on St. Aelred. I shall want to work out the details of this with Naomi after I have seen the complete manuscript. Perhaps she will be able to bring it back with her. We could perhaps go ahead with whatever preliminary editorial work may be needed on this, and hold up the scheduling of publication until such time as we have a clearer picture of your subsequent books.

This is purely personal but I have heard that a young man whom I knew in Jersey City—an ex-Navy man—has joined the Cistercian Order because of THE SEVEN STOREY MOUNTAIN. His name is James Carlin and he is a very fine person indeed. Perhaps you know him already at Gethsemani.

With all good wishes.

Sincerely yours,
Robert Giroux

JANUARY 11, 1950

Rev. M. Louis, O.C.S.O.
Abbey of Our Lady of Gethsemani
Trappist, Kentucky

Dear Tom:

On January 30th, the Catholic Writers' Guild of America is going to make their Golden Book Award for non-fiction to THE SEVEN STOREY MOUNTAIN.[1] They write us as follows:

The Catholic Writers' Guild gives annual awards to the outstanding fiction, non-fiction and religious book written by a Catholic. The award consists of an inscribed Golden Book to the author, and a golden scroll to the publisher of the book. These awards are based on recommendations received from Catholic colleges all over the country, but the final selections are made by our special Award Panel, consisting of Rev. Robert I. Gannon [S.J.], former president, of Fordham University, Very Rev. Msgr. John S. Middleton, Sec'y [Secretary] to His Eminence for Education, Hon. James A. Farley, and Miss Gretta Palmer, well-known Catholic author. The Guild will hold its annual Award dinner, Monday, January 30th, at eight o'clock, in the Perroquet Suite of the Waldorf Astoria.

I shall be on hand, and so will Naomi, on January 30th. Perhaps you may wish to send them a message of acceptance on this occasion and, if so, I shall be glad to pass it on for you.[2]

I am leaving for Italy on February 16th. I shall stay about a week in Rome and, since I have heard that His Holiness [Pope Pius XII] is particularly interested in writers and editors, I shall not be surprised if I am granted the privilege of an audience. If this occurs, do you think it would be in order to bring along presentation copies of your books? I know that Jay arranged to have specially bound copies forwarded previously, but I have never heard whether these have been acknowledged. In any event, I see no reason for not presenting additional copies, do you? Are there any errands I could perform or any people that you would like me to see while I am in Rome? Please let me know. It would be a pleasure if I could be of help in any way. This is my first trip to Europe and I am looking forward to the whole journey with eagerness. I shall be spending most of my time in Italy, but I am coming back by way of Paris and London (where I shall drop in on Hollis & Carter).

I hope we may expect the St. Aelred manuscript soon. I very much want to get it in the works before my departure. It ought to be in proof before Easter, even though we are not publishing until early fall. We want to have as good-looking a book as possible, in the manner of THE WATERS OF SILOE. Would there be any illustrative material available for the Saint Aelred?

You may remember last May our discussing an illustrated edition of THE SEVEN STOREY MOUNTAIN. I have since written to your aunts and they have very courteously said they would put all the material on hand at my disposal if I should want to examine it. The feeling here is that if we are to do an illustrated edition, we should re-set the text and re-design the book from start to finish. If we re-set, this will give us the opportunity to include the portions originally omitted. I have been in correspondence with Sister Marie Thérèse [Lentfoehr, S.D.S.], who recently printed one of the sections in the <u>Catholic World</u>.[3] What do you think of the idea of a new enlarged edition with all the original material reinserted? You could also make changes in any other part of the text you see fit. I should first like to have your reactions to the proposal and then, if you approve, I should like to know whether you would be free to send us your corrections for the text in the near future or whether you would wish to keep it as it is. Whether you make any changes in the text or not, I think it would be appropriate to include a short prefatory note to the new edition.

I was delighted that Naomi made the trip to Gethsemani. We have had many talks about it and I think it has had a very great effect on her. She is a really fine person.

With best wishes.

Sincerely yours,
Robert Giroux

1. From June 1 to December 31, 1949, *The Seven Storey Mountain* earned $47,000 in royalties.

2. On December 21, 1949, NB wrote to TM that she had gone ahead with a definite contract with HB for TM's next four books, with an option of the French cloister book. She expressed dismay that JL and ND would like to publish TM's *Journal* and counseled him to decide on a publisher once he had actually completed the book. She then shared with TM portions of three letters she received from JL that focused on the question of who would publish TM's books in the future. Her opinion was that ND did not have the organizational skills to handle this particular book, though this firm might, in the future, continue publishing TM's poetry. In this correspondence, JL did not hide his ambitious side. NB's letter to RG, dated February 2, 1950, mentioned that JL had even suggested that HB and ND jointly publish TM's work. TM deep down felt an obligation in this particular case to ND. RG's long and well-reasoned letter to NB, dated February 6, 1950, recalled that HB so far had sold a total of 404,409 copies of TM's first two books and that the present dilemma was really a moral one: "Should New Directions hold Tom to what Tom considers is perhaps a moral obligation, and then act against Tom's interest? Could you allow it? Tom would not care; he has said so. But surely you must care." RG felt that the decision as to who should publish the *Journal* should not be left to TM, but to someone such as the abbot. He continued to feel upset about TM's continued involvement with ND. In a letter dated October 16, 1950, RG wrote to NB: "I respect Tom's scruples about promises to Jay, but not any more than his promises to us." RG was even willing to bring up the matter with the abbot.

3. Sister Thérèse Lentfoehr, S.D.S. (1902–81), had a long friendship with TM, beginning in 1939, when she first wrote him praising one of his poems. She became an avid collector of Mertoniana, and her collection now resides at Columbia University. She is the author of *Words and Silence: On the Poetry of Thomas Merton* (1979).

JANUARY 14, 1950

Trappist-Cistercian Abbey
Our Lady of Gethsemani
Trappist, Kentucky

Dear Bob:

This morning I signed the contract and am sending it off to Naomi. It was certainly a great pleasure to do so. It is rather a comfort to have things on a very stable basis like this. I plan, as you know, to take my time and work along slowly and peacefully—and thoroughly.

Meanwhile about fifty really remarkable photographs have come in from France, completing the collection on those Southern French cloisters and covering a lot of other aspects of that same countryside. It will make a delightful book, and one in which I will not write very extensively. I would now like to get enlargements of the small prints I sent to you. What would you like me to do: send you the photographs I have, and let you judge on them (they are big enough to give an idea of how they would be laid out) or do you want to wait until there is some copy written? This will take time, as I will have to read up on it. If you want to wait, then please send me all the small contact prints I sent you so that I may procure enlargements.

I can also send you a Spanish book of picture and text that might suggest possibilities for layout and design on this job.

Here is a letter that came in from England. Can you think of anything worth doing about it?

With all best wishes, as usual. Have I yet wished you a Holy New Year? If not, here it is. I know God will bless you. I continue to keep you in my Mass each day. Your friend [James] Carlin seems to be doing very well. He looks healthy and proves it by kneeling at the door of the refectory doing penance and displaying sledge hammers he has broken while at work. His name is Frater Gregory.

In Corde Christ,
Tom
fr. M. Louis /s/

P.S. Many thanks also for the little Christmas book which is very nicely done.

JANUARY 16, 1950

Trappist-Cistercian Abbey
[Letterhead]

Dear Bob:

Your letter was given to me just after my other one went out the other day.

I am enclosing a proper (?) reply for the golden book outfit.[1]

It is swell that you are going to Italy. By all means, take a copy of WATERS to his Holiness. We sent the MOUNTAIN last time, specially bound, and I got a letter back from Montini, of which I will enclose a photostat if I can find one around. Sr. [Sister] Thérèse [Lentfoehr, S.D.S.] had some made.[2] But the letter was from Msgr. [Giovanni] Montini and I have no guarantee that the Holy Father read the book at all. I can ask Father Abbot some pointers about how to get a private interview with His Holiness. Meanwhile, you ought to drop in on our Abbot General, at Piazza Santa Prisca, n.12, on the Aventine [Hill]. He is Dom Dominique Nogues, as you remember from the imprimatur [formal approval] and he would be glad to chat with you I am sure. If you like I can give you a note of introduction. You might also call on Father Paul Philippe, O.P., at the Angelico [Pontifical University of Saint Thomas]. He is professor of mystical theology there and has been writing some nice letters back and forth. He is a friend of Jacques Maritain. Then there is Mgr [Giuseppe] De Luca who has shown great interest in our stuff and has written about it in the Osservatore Romano [Vatican newspaper]. He would be very interested, I think. His address is: Via delle Sette Sale, 19, Rome.

About the Aelred manuscript: there are two reasons why we must wait on that one, Bob. First I haven't been able to do any work on it since I have been teaching. Did you know that? I have a very heavy schedule teaching mystical theology and an orientation course for novices, not that I have many classes, but I have to build up the courses from the foundations, on no previous material as this is our first experiment in them. I will get back to the book in due time. But meanwhile it is also important that I wait for the appearance of an unpublished tract of St. Aelred on psychology, his De Anima. This is expected soon—maybe this year. I'll find out. I can't very well go on without preparing to include it somewhere and it will naturally affect many of my statements about other parts of his work.

The enlarged edition of the Mountain still appeals to me. I would like to see the extra bits put in but I would also like to go over the book again and perhaps cut here and there. It would definitely be a new edition, and a prefatory note would be in order.

If you are going to Europe, would you be able to take in the little corner of France (down by the Catalan border, above Barcelona) where the cloister pictures, etc., come from? You might be able to pick up some ideas and information that would help a lot with the book. I would give a lot to be able to get down there myself. Still it would not justify your going out of your way without another cause.

May your trip to Europe be a happy and fruitful one. If you run across any good new books about the Mass, I will be able to use them eventually on the job I am to do for you. I am reading up on that as I go along. Most of these jobs just require a lot of study and thought—and above all prayer.

Again, with all best wishes.

In Christo Domino,
Tom
fr. M. Louis /s/

1. See the letter dated January 11, 1950.
2. Monsignor Giovanni Montini, later Pope Paul VI, served in the Vatican's State Department from 1922 to 1954.

FEBRUARY 13, 1950

Rev. M. Louis, O.C.S.O.
Abbey of Our Lady of Gethsemani
Trappist, Kentucky

Dear Tom:

The Golden Book Award Dinner was an impressive affair. Your message of acceptance was quite moving, and I hope I did it justice in delivering it. The main event was a talk by Father [Edmund] Walsh [S.J.] of Georgetown; he's a marvelous speaker besides having that aura of goodness which gives added meaning to everything he says. His remarks on THE SEVEN STOREY MOUNTAIN were particularly apt. I enclose a copy of the program, which Naomi and I have autographed. She put quotes around Editor, and expected me to put them around Agent but, as you will see, I surprised her. Dan Walsh was also a guest at the Harcourt, Brace table and it was good seeing him. I hope the Golden Book arrived safely at the monastery. I carried it uptown and down on the evening of the dinner and felt quite proud of myself when I walked into the office with it safely next morning. I've heard that Hollywood "Oscars" are used as doorstops; I'm eager to know to what ingenious use the Golden Book will be put at the Abbey.

I've wired you for letters of introduction to Dom [Dominique] Nogues and the others you thought I might see in Rome. I'm taking over special copies of THE WATERS OF SILOE, just in case there is a special audience with His Holiness because of Cardinal Spellman. I look forward to Italy and Europe more eagerly than I can tell you. It's my first trip abroad, you know, except for the South Pacific on an aircraft carrier [during World War II]. But getting to Rome at this particular time is wonderful and I'm fortunate indeed to have this opportunity.

You are quite right to postpone the Saint Aelred manuscript until De Anima is published. It would not make sense even if you had full time to work on it, to complete the book with the impending appearance of his tract on psychology. Your Aelred book will come in good time, and there is no rush about it.

I am concerned to learn from Naomi that the Journal may be coming along next. She tells me that you expect it to be a bigger book than it originally appeared, and that it may in fact be a Harcourt, Brace book. Jay apparently thinks so too, for he has been good enough to suggest joint publication.[1] I remember from way back how very much you were interested in the Journal form. That day we met at the Harcourt, Brace office (in 1941?) after you had returned from retreat at Gethsemani, we spoke about this. You mentioned Georges Bernanos and I of course thought of your JOURNAL OF MY ESCAPE FROM THE NAZIS. At any rate, next to autobiography it is surely the most personal form in literature. It sounds to me as if it might well be your most important book and I honestly doubt that New Directions will be able to handle it. Jay's proposal of joint publication makes sense only if he does a limited signed edition and we do the regular trade edition. What he is actually proposing is that we do the <u>same</u> edition. This is impossible. It will confuse booksellers who won't know who to order from; it will cause confusion in the trade and bad feeling among booksellers, and do harm to your name and your work. I know Jay's intention is good, but Naomi agrees that this kind of joint publication is an impossibility. Well, we shall work this out with good will when the manuscript is ready. We should want to make restitution to Jay in any way he suggests. Perhaps one of the other books under contract would be more suitable for New Directions; or even more than one. We shall be willing and ready to make any adjustment that Jay considers equitable. I know that Jay wants the good work of your books to reach the widest audience possible. That is what we want, and is what with our resources we can do for a particular kind of book better than New Directions. THE WHALE AND THE IVY sounds like that kind of book to me. I understand there may be drawings; I'm most eager see the Journal, I assure you.

I'm sending you two copies of THE SEVEN STOREY MOUNTAIN <u>sans</u> binding. These are for corrections and emendations for the revised edition. Should I get the omitted portions of the manuscript from Sister Thérèse, or can you provide manuscript and indicate where you want inserts in the book? I'm consulting on illustrations and we'll send you blueprints of suggested layouts on my return from Europe (March 28th).

I wish I were able to get to southern France, by the Catalan border. What you have written of it, and the cloister pictures appeal to me greatly. But my five-and-a-half weeks are all too few as it is; I'm returning by way of London, you know, and the four days there will probably be ridiculously few as it is. I think, on the photographic books, that we ought to have some copy first, and at least a tentative layout along your own lines. Why not get enlargements of the small prints you sent me? I'll return these by separate cover today. Keep a record of all the expenses you incur for enlargements and otherwise, so we can figure them as part of the originals: have the photographers indicated what their usual charge is? (Mr. Manning's were so exorbitant that we want to avoid that kind of pitfall in the future.)

I'll write from Rome and various spots in Italy. Until my return at the end of March.

Yours,
Robert Giroux

1. JL wrote to RG, in a letter dated August 2, 1950, saying that he had received several letters from TM and NB indicating that the projected *Journal* was being written for him and would be published by ND.

MARCH 28, 1950

Dear Bob:

If my calculations are right, you must be back. Thanks for the card from Lucerne. I hope you had a fine journey and am eager to hear all about it.

Will you please pay Mme. Sauvageot for the pictures credited to her in Waters. She will accept whatever you think is the proper rate. She says magazines pay $50.00 a picture but expects to get less for book work. Her address is 59 Rue Scheffer, Paris, XVI.

She has done a very fine guide book, illustrated, of the route from Paris to Nice and is anxious to publish it over here. It is well worth seeing and I am giving her your name. She is the one who is doing the cloister stuff. Incidentally, when I ask you to pay her, I mean of course that you do so for me and charge it up to our royalty account if you will be so kind.

She said something about a Bach festival being held in the middle of the country that the cloister book is about, and that many Americans will be going there, which would add to the appeal of the book, but I am afraid the time is too short to finish it for the festival.

We have all been down with the flu here, and most of us are still pretty groggy. I am writing back and forth to England to try and get my hands on that Aelred De Anima which is apparently close to publication.

More later. God bless you.

In Corde Xti,
Tom /s/

APRIL 20, 1950

Harcourt, Brace & Company, Inc.
[Letterhead]

Rev. M. Louis, O.C.S.O.
Abbey of Our Lady of Gethsemani
Trappist, Kentucky

Dear Tom:

My body is back in the States, but my soul is still in Europe. What a wonderful trip it was—too much, in one way, seeing so much in so short a space of time: Italy, Switzerland, France, England, Ireland—but a bird's-eye view can be just as revealing as a magnified closeup; and it was all so novel and fresh to my eye that I find I've forgotten nothing. Rome was, of course, the high spot. And our audience with His Holiness the climax of the pilgrimage. He said Mass in the Vatican apartments, to which we were shown by Swiss guards at 7:30 in the morning. It was a medium-sized room, beautifully painted, with an altar set up on a platform. He appeared in a doorway to the left quite suddenly, dressed all in white, the nobility of his face and demeanor quite overwhelming. He changed into vestments quite slowly and Mass began. I could hardly believe I was there; after Mass was finished, he had them bring a chair and sat down before the altar. We filed up one by one; I had a copy of THE WATERS OF SILOE under my arm. I kissed his ring. He spoke excellent English, in a melodious voice, thanked me for the book, told me that editing was "a noble profession," and gave me a little blue packet stamped with the Papal arms. Inside there was a medal with his head engraved in profile on one side and a picture of the Holy Door of St. Peter's and "Anno Santo 1950" on the other.

I believe I told you of meeting Dom Nogues at the monastery of Tre Fontane. I took some movie films and they came out beautifully. Perhaps I could bring them down this spring. I'm sure I could rent a projector in Louisville. Would a showing of such films be allowed? There's also one taken inside St. Peter's at the beatification ceremony [March 5, 1950, Blessed Dominic Savio]. It's rather dark, but the Pope's entry on the <u>sedia gestatoria</u> [papal chair] is quite good. Also some excellent shots of St. Mark's in Venice in color.

I have two medals for you and Father Abbot, for which the chains have to be fixed. They are medals of Our Lady of Fatima, blessed at the shrine, and also blessed by the Pope. The chains I found at Our Lady of Tre Fontane; they also are blessed by the Pope. I hope they will be ready by Monday and will send them along.

In London, of all places, I picked up a copy of <u>The Month</u> and read the section of your journal entitled "September, 1949." I think it's magnificent! It's very much related to THE SEVEN STOREY MOUNTAIN and we surely must publish it. Today Naomi spoke to Jay and told him she feels that Harcourt, Brace should publish the <u>Journal</u>. I'm very happy about her decision because I think it's the right one. She has not shown the manuscript to either of us, naturally, but I know from the excerpt in <u>The Month</u> that we want to do it. It may be your most important book. I'd like us to do it in the fall, if possible. It would be desirable, for one thing, because Bruce's handling of the St. Lutgarde book [*What Are These Wounds? The Life of a Cistercian Mystic, Saint Lutgarde of Aywières*] has been appalling, and ought to be counteracted. Incidentally, I have told Naomi that we will be glad to transfer another book to Jay for the <u>Journal</u>.

I hope we can publish the Journal this fall, and that we can get the text into proofs in the next few weeks. I'd love to bring the proofs down to you in May or June, and bring the films too, if I may. It would be good to see you again.

Ever yours,
Bob /s/

P.S. I've taken care of Mme. Sauvageot.

APRIL 24, 1950

Rev. M. Louis, O.C.S.O.
Abbey of Our Lady of Gethsemani
Trappist, Kentucky

Dear Tom:

I enclose the medal and chain from Fatima and Tre Fontane respectively.[1] I probably made them sound much more elaborate than they are but, as you might expect, coming from those places they are quite simple and inexpensive. The medal, actually, is the most beautiful I saw in all my travels (and you can imagine how the Italian hawkers turned up at our busses every morning with something "new" or "special"; they even caught on to having a "liquidation sale" at "bankrupt prices"!). By this same mail, I am sending a similar medal and chain to Abbot Fox.

You may not have seen the enclosed review from La Vie Spirituelle. Incidentally, this reminds me: do you regularly get copies of The Month and Commonweal (in which I recently enjoyed your essay on "Self Denial and the Christian")? If not, please let me know and I'll see that they get to you—or any other magazines or books you might want. Don't ever hesitate to ask me to track down anything of this sort; I'll enjoy doing it.

Tomorrow, April 25th, is royalty day at Harcourt, Brace and we are sending [the literary agency of] Curtis Brown our check for some $47,000 for sales of THE SEVEN STOREY MOUNTAIN and THE WATERS OF SILOE from June through December 31, 1949. I think that's a magnificent record and I feel very happy about it. You will be hearing from Naomi shortly when it has cleared through their accounting department. Sales of the two books have slowed up since the middle of March, and that's another reason for our planning the Journal for this fall.[2]

Ever yours,
Robert Giroux

1. Fatima, located in Portugal, is the site where the Virgin Mary appeared to three children. Tre Fontane, located in Rome, is a Cistercian abbey.
2. NB wrote to TM, in a letter dated April 26, 1950, reiterating that she was extremely worried about JL's "total lack of business sense." She feared that it would be confusing if ND and HB both advertised publication of the same book, even though the first would do a limited edition and the second a regular trade edition.

MAY 1, 1950

Trappist-Cistercian Abbey
[Letterhead]

Dear Bob:

Many thanks for your letters and their enclosures, especially for the delightful Fatima medal which I am wearing now. I am happy that Our Lady showed me this kind attention, through your instrumentality. It will bring me many graces.

The best news of all was that you intended to come down soon. We are all looking forward to your visit. Father Abbot will be away until the thirteenth of the month, however. It will be swell to see you and this time we will have more leisure to talk a little and work things out—it won't be a "state occasion" like last May.

The Journal problem however has reached an unexpected settlement. It will perhaps be a disappointment, but on the whole I think it is the best yet. Father Abbot has simply decided that it would be imprudent, for many reasons, to publish such a book at such a time. It is so unheard of a project that many would be completely unable to understand it. They would interpret the appearance of such a book in a light very unfavorable to the monastery, to the Superiors and to the author. These would be in a minority, but they would nevertheless be a minority that might cause an awful lot of trouble for Father Abbot and for the house. I see nothing for it but to let the whole thing go until I am tucked away six feet underground—if people are still interested when that time comes.

However that makes it easy for Naomi and you and Jay all right. I shall go on writing the thing sporadically, I suppose. It is hard for me to get much on paper these days; I have to spend all my time and energy preparing stuff for classes. But that will all go into the making of the four books on our contract.[1] I don't feel like hurrying too much over the new edition of the <u>Mountain</u> but whatever you say will be okay.

We can talk about everything when you get down here. Oh—the movies can't be shown here, Bob. One of the General Chapters passed a statute against that. I bet they would be a lot of fun though. I look forward to hearing all about Rome. Did you manage to find Fr. Paul Philippe [O.P.] and Msgr. [Giuseppe] De Luca?

With all best wishes.

> Sincerely in Christ,
> Tom
> fr. M. Louis /s/

1. TM had signed a contract with RG to write four books: *The Ascent to Truth* (1951); a life of Saint Aelred (not completed as such); a book on Saint Bernard (*The Last of the Fathers* [1954]); and a book on the Holy Mass (unwritten), plus an option for two additional works (letter of RG to NB, dated February 6, 1950).

JUNE 6, 1950

> Our Lady of Gethsemani
> [Letterhead]

Dear Bob:

The other day I heard from Naomi of the death of your father, and I am writing to say that we are sorry to hear of it and are praying for the repose of his soul. I am remembering him in my Masses and I am sure Father Abbot will be doing the same. May Our Lord bring him quickly to the vision of the blessed in heaven.

Naomi also said that you had written telling us when you were coming down, but neither Father Abbot or I have got the letter. In any case, perhaps your plans have been changed somewhat. We will be expecting you, nevertheless. I look forward to seeing you again and to having a chance to talk more fully with you—and at leisure. I have been working again on the Cloud and the Fire, on a new plan, trying to make it all transparently clear to everybody. It will not be a long book, but I think it will be full enough to be much more than slight. I described it to Naomi in terms that made it seem like little more than a pamphlet and she seems to feel that such a book as that should not be my next. The thing will shape up into something worth while, I believe. But I am taking my time as the pressure of work and what not is turning out to be a little too much for me physically and I have to take things easily, so they say.

The more I think about it, the happier I am that the Journal is not to be published.

With best wishes, as ever.

> In Spiritu Sancto [In the Holy Spirit],
> Tom
> fr. M. Louis /s/

JUNE 16, 1950

> Harcourt, Brace & Company, Inc.
> [Letterhead]

Rev. M. Louis, O.C.S.O.
Abbey of Our Lady of Gethsemani
Trappist, Kentucky

Dear Tom:

The solution to the JOURNAL problem was unexpected, but I am sure that it is absolutely right, and one of the reasons I am sure is your own reaction to the decision. There is great wisdom behind the decision and, ultimately, I am sure the greatest good will be accomplished by this course of action. I hope that Father Abbot will agree to entrust the manuscript of the JOURNAL to our safekeeping, as it grows, and that its eventual publication in the far distant future will also be entrusted to Harcourt, Brace.

I have written to Father James [Fox] asking permission to come down over the Fourth of July weekend. I would have come sooner if the death of my father had not intervened. I am very grateful for your consoling words and your promise to remember him in your prayers.

The news about THE CLOUD AND THE FIRE and THE PSALM OF CONTEMPLATION is very exciting.[1] Is there any chance of our being able to bring out the PSALM around Christmas time? In any event I do want to discuss these and other matters and have the kind of leisurely visit that was not possible on the previous "state occasion."

Ever yours,
Bob /s/

1. The second title is evidently an early title for TM's book on the psalms: *Bread in the Wilderness* (New York: New Directions, 1953).

JULY 5, 1950

Rev. M. Louis, O.C.S.O.
Abbey of Our Lady of Gethsemani
Trappist, Kentucky

Dear Tom:

Just a note to tell you how very much I enjoyed my visit to Gethsemani, and to enclose (a) the Cambridge University Press catalogue announcing the Joan Evans book on page 10, and (b) the announcement of Anne Lindbergh's article on Dom Alexis [*Life*, July 3, 1950].[1]

I spoke to Gerry Gross, our designer, this morning about your doing the illustrations for THE PSALMS AND CONTEMPLATION, and he was highly enthusiastic. After we discussed the text, he said that he didn't suppose there would be "illustrations," strictly speaking, but decorations, but I shall await your sketches before I concur in this distinction. In any event, the sooner you can send us something—and the sketches can be as rough as you wish—the easier it will be to work out the design. Gerry is eager to do this job and I think we shall have a book which will make a very attractive Christmas gift.

I realize that I am speaking somewhat prematurely after only a telephone conversation with Naomi, but she seemed to think, offhand, that it was agreed that Harcourt, Brace would do the next book. In any event, even if we have to work it out that Jay does THE PSALMS AND CONTEMPLATION rather than us, we shall be glad to make available to him the designs and artwork which we may have completed.

Typewriter ribbons, carbon paper and stationery should be reaching you shortly by separate cover. The least that Harcourt, Brace can do is to make such staples available. Please let me know if you are in need of any other stationery materials.

Ever yours,
[Robert Giroux]

1. See the letter dated August 2, 1950.

JULY 14, 1950

Our Lady of Gethsemani
[Letterhead]

Dear Bob:

Thanks for the Dom Alexis article. I have not yet had time to go through it. Fr. Jean Daniélou, a very eminent French theologian, from the Institut Catholique, was here and gave a talk and I was busy with him until Mass today.

Here are the best we can do in the way of Mass cards. Sorry I have been so long about it.

Oh, incidentally, about Daniélou: I'd like to dedicate the Psalm book [*Bread in the Wilderness* (1953)] to him as that is precisely his field. Just make it "To Jean Daniélou, S.J." or to Father Jean Daniélou, S.J. I sent the ms. off to Naomi the other day, more than doubled. Tripled in fact. It is around eighty pages. If you want bibliography, index, let me know. I think I can let you have some drawings to look at within three weeks. Let me know if there are any special requirements.

After it was all finished I began to wonder how Naomi would like the idea of a book by Christmas. I had forgotten that she seemed opposed to the immediate publication of anything.

Jean Daniélou is one of the editors of Dieu Vivant, which you saw here.[1] He wants perhaps part of the book for that in French and an article by me and they plan to publish a translation of a poem. That's all for the moment. God bless you. It was wonderful to have you down here and certainly much was accomplished that could never have been swung in a letter.

As ever.

In Corde Christi,
Tom
fr. M. Louis /s/

1. *Dieu Vivant: Perspectives Religieuses et Philosophiques* was a journal published in Paris.

JULY 20, 1950

Rev. M. Louis, O.C.S.O.
Abbey of Our Lady of Gethsemani
Trappist, Kentucky

Dear Tom:

Naomi is still brooding about the Psalm book and of course I hope the decision will be favorable. I shall see that the Dedication is made to Father Daniélou; I would have given much to hear his talk. We are looking forward very much to doing the drawings and I shall of course pass them on to Naomi after we have seen them.

I do hope that all the typing materials have finally reached you. Many thanks for the Mass cards.

Ever yours,
Robert Giroux

JULY 27, 1950

Our Lady of Gethsemani
[Letterhead]

Dear Bob:

Have I thanked you yet for the paper, carbon and typewriter ribbons? If not, I am very sorry. They were welcome indeed. Thanks too for the [Carl] Jung book which I have begun and find very interesting.

You probably have received a few rough sketches I did. They are not precisely what I want, but they give the general idea. I'll try to produce more in time. Meanwhile Naomi has written that she does not feel sure that the Psalm book ought to be the next one. But by now perhaps that has all been discussed between you. I will be happy to learn the outcome. Will you please send me the copy you took from here? I mean on the Psalms? I need it to fit in with the carbons of the new stuff to have a complete copy of my own.

Perhaps you should let Naomi look over the ms. of the Cloud and the Fire—the new one—to see if that ought to be the next book.

I promised Daniélou proofs of the Psalm book so that he could take excerpts of it for <u>Dieu Vivant</u>, but I assume the book will not be anywhere near the setting up stage for a long time. However, if you do set it up let me have an extra set of proofs please, for this purpose. Meanwhile, I have found the chewed up remains of that Dutch cover for the 7 S.M. [*The Seven Storey Mountain*], which is enclosed. I keep praying for you and all your intentions. Pray for me too. At the moment I think I had better do a little reading to prepare the way for the first part of the Cloud.

As usual, all the best wishes.

In Corde Christi,
Tom
fr. M. Louis /s/

JULY 28, 1950

Rev. M. Louis, O.C.S.O.
Abbey of Our Lady of Gethsemani
Trappist, Kentucky

Dear Tom:

I have read BREAD IN THE WILDERNESS, think it marvelous, and have told Naomi that we want to publish it. Since Father Abbot approved publication in December, and even suggested illustrations, Naomi seemed reassured. In any event, I have no doubts. There remains the problem of New Directions and Naomi has agreed to clear it with Jay and offer him the picture book in substitution. I gave Naomi the photos and although this book is already under contract we will be glad to make the rearrangement. We must act fast, as you have certainly done, and I am asking our designer to get up sample pages at once.

BREAD IN THE WILDERNESS is a wonderful improvement over the original manuscript of PSALMS AND CONTEMPLATION. We like the Preface in particular. It states exactly what the general reader may expect, yet invites him further rather than repels him. I don't think an Index is called for; as for bibliography, the footnotes are thorough. I've marked up the script for the printer and we are ready to shoot—as indeed we must if December publication is to be realized.

The sketches and illustrations arrived, and they are beyond our expectations. I particularly like the head of Christ, the one called "Christ unveils the meaning of the Old Testament," and the sketch of the monkish figure (in the finished drawing the habit is better drawn but the nebulous and anonymous face is better in the sketch, we feel).[1] Anyway Gerry Gross will prove [*sic*] up one drawing to show you what processes we can use and how various media will work out. We want to do the illustrations on different stock from the text—and give a full page to each illustration. We ought to have eight at least, plus a frontispiece to make nine. The three kings and Balaam and such Old Testament subjects illustrate the text wonderfully, but there ought to be variety also—and your sketches indicate that you agree.

As to the text, you will next see galley proofs if all goes well. Should we not have a Nihil Obstat and so on? I take it the censors have already passed on it—or that proofs will be all right. It will be a perfect December book; I'm delighted about it.

Ever yours,
Robert Giroux

P.S. For jacket can you do a spot drawing—loaf of bread, or bread and basket, or broken bread?

1. No drawings by TM were included in *Bread in the Wilderness.*

AUGUST 2, 1950

Rev. M. Louis, O.C.S.O.
Abbey of Our Lady of Gethsemani
Trappist, Kentucky

Dear Tom:

The big book on CLUNIAC ART OF THE ROMANESQUE PERIOD by Joan Evans has just arrived, and I'm forwarding it this afternoon by separate cover. It's a beautiful book.

Your letter of the 27th apparently crossed mine of recent date. I expect that Naomi has now written further about BREAD IN THE WILDERNESS; after all, Father Abbot, you and I all feel that it should be done. Naomi's objection seemed to rest on the point that the book is too "technical"; that is a good reason for making it the next one: a book on prayer at Christmastime could hardly be considered exploitation (and that, after all, was the cause for concern). In any event, I don't find it as special as she does, and your preface takes care of that point beautifully.

I do hope you go on with the drawings and get them out of the way. You will soon be hearing from Gerry Gross on this; he is awaiting some proofs based on the sketches you sent in.

BREAD IN THE WILDERNESS seems the perfect precursor to THE CLOUD AND THE FIRE. I've reread Part Two of the latter and I think it's excellent—much better organized than the original manuscript I saw, and the subheads help enormously. Is Part Three anywhere in sight?

The part of "The Psalms and Contemplation" which I took away is now with Naomi, and I will ask her to return it to you to fill out your duplicate copy of the new stuff. Why not wait for proofs for Fr. Daniélou? I do hope we can go ahead and set it up. My understanding is that Naomi is now going to clear it all with Jay, and offer him the picture book (this Cluniac art book undoubtedly has some items that ought to be included).[1]

I'm glad to know that the paper, carbon, and typewriter ribbon have reached you. If you need anything further, please let me know.

Charlie Reilly ran off the films the other day and they came out amazingly well.[2] Color films bring out values that aren't visible to the unassisted eye; the shots in the woods which I didn't expect to come out are particularly good.

Ever yours,
Robert Giroux

1. JL wrote to NB, in a letter dated August 2, 1950, saying that he would be glad to publish the book on the cloisters if HB would relinquish it, though he did not consider it a fair exchange for the book on the Psalms, which he believed she and TM had promised him. He did not believe that RG had any right to usurp publishing rights in this case, in view of what he thought was TM's very definite commitment: "From everything I know about him, Bob is certainly not the kind of person who would want to take something that belonged to someone else." JL sent RG a copy of this letter. The next day NB replied to JL that there was no question of RG "crowding" her, as she put it. Caught in a dilemma, NB wrote RG, in a letter dated August 7, 1950, that even if JL received the right to publish the *Journal*, it could not be published just then.

2. Charles F. X. Reilly was a good friend of RG.

AUGUST 19, 1950

Our Lady of Gethsemani
[Letterhead]

Dear Bob:

Naomi tells me she has been trying to contact you without success and hopes you are not sick. I have visions of your stomach trouble down here having turned into an ulcer or something. I hope and pray you are all right.

You got Jay's letter and you know that he insists on my keeping my promise to him, about <u>Bread</u>. I think you understood, Bob, that I was only turning the ms. over to you on condition that you would cede it to Jay in the event he insisted on having it. I could not do otherwise as I had several times formally promised it to him. It is a great pity the book cannot come out this Christmas over the Harcourt, Brace imprint, all the more so as Gerry Gross's proofs have just arrived and they are beautiful. Would you object to Jay using the ideas as to color, etc.? Well, now I suppose the book will be delayed.

Naomi seems against quick publication of this book. How do you now feel about its appearance? My impression when you were here was that you decidedly wanted to see it in print so that there would be something around to take away the taste of the Lutgarde book [*What Are These Wounds? The Life of a Cistercian Mystic, Saint Lutgarde of Aywières*]. This effect will be produced even if Jay prints it—although I well understand you wanted it over Harcourt's imprint. Then there is the other thing—the <u>Cloud</u> is progressing well. I hope to deliver it to Naomi, for you, in December. If you like I will send you part one as soon as I have finished it. Then I will revise part two and go on to part three. Let me know if you want part one right away (i.e., September or October). Then, I have had the good fortune to receive enough material to finish the Aelred book too. This from the man in England who was working on him and who has very kindly given me photostats and some of his own mss. Since I am now hot on the trail with the <u>Cloud</u> I'd like to finish that first, because this material on Aelred needs to be studied. That can be done in conjunction with theology class work at the very same time while I am finishing the Cloud, then I can move right in on Aelred. But all this points to a crowding of books in 1951 or 1952 unless <u>Bread</u> comes out now, when it is in the clear. I have written Naomi to this effect, but the understanding is of course that the <u>date</u> of the appearance of <u>Bread</u> is subject to the okay of Harcourt, Brace, owing to the "next book" problem. I do feel that this question of spacing makes sense. Let me know how you feel about it.

Meanwhile you have the cloisters [book]. I can do that whenever you please. I'd like to do a fairly decent little text for it, not leave it exclusively a picture book. Say fifty pages of writing? Plus captions of course.

And now that brings me to the Cluniac art book. It is simply tremendous. Really, that is a major book. I do not tire of looking at it. It gives me endless ideas and I know the text will be very valuable when I get around to studying it, in due time. Thanks very very much for it. It is a terrifically expensive present: to whom am I indebted? To you personally or to Harcourt, Brace? If it is to you, I feel abashed that you have gone to such expense. The Jung will come in handy for part one of the <u>Cloud.</u>

Well, Bob, it is too bad about <u>Bread</u>: but I know you understand. You'll soon have the other stuff anyway. I'll be sending you some more of the Journal to file as more is typed. Naomi writes in a strain that indicates she refuses to look upon that book as posthumous. . . . However there is not much she can do about it.

I repeat that I hope you are all right. Thanks again for everything. With best wishes and prayers, as ever, God bless you.

In Corde Christi,
Tom
fr. M. Louis /s/

SEPTEMBER 18, 1950

Rev. M. Louis, O.C.S.O.
Abbey of Our Lady of Gethsemani
Trappist, Kentucky

Dear Tom:

I have been laid up with a bad cold, and I am just beginning to feel myself again. Forgive me for not having written sooner. I have been greatly distressed by what seems to me an unnecessary series of misunderstandings.

Of course there was never any question about the Psalms book being promised to Jay! I knew this. Also you made it clear that only if Naomi and Jay agreed with you, Father Abbot, and myself that BREAD IN THE WILDERNESS should be published in December could Harcourt, Brace go ahead.

But since it was further understood (and you expressly stated this) that Harcourt, Brace was to publish your next book, whatever it turned out to be, it seemed clear to me what your wishes were.

I should have (a) asked you to write Naomi saying that BREAD IN THE WILDERNESS was to be your next published book and (b) asked you to write Jay saying that this would mean that Harcourt, Brace would publish it and that another substitution, or some kind of compensation, would be made. I also understood that BREAD IN THE WILDERNESS had been promised to Jay in place of the Journal; since the Journal is now in the way of becoming an historical fact rather than a contentious problem, the basis for the promise seems to have been blurred considerably.

Because neither of these points was cleared up, I ran into two difficulties: first, Naomi's very sincere feeling that BREAD IN THE WILDERNESS ought not to be your next book. I disagree. She thinks it a "technical" book, but aside from the biography of St. Bernard and St. Aelred (and even there in good part) all your writing from now on is bound to be "technical." THE CLOUD AND THE FIRE is surely going to be so—and, say I, so much the better. In short, I don't agree that because BREAD IN

THE WILDERNESS is "difficult" or "technical" it ought not to be your next book. I also thought that, with Father Abbot's agreeing it would be all right to go ahead in December, this would answer Naomi's objection.

Secondly, Jay, on the other hand, felt that I was "crowding" you and Naomi. I was simply going on the assumption that BREAD was to be your next book, and that, since we were to publish your next book, this was it. The chief obstacle is, of course, Jay's assertion that the book on the Cloisters is not a fair exchange for BREAD IN THE WILDERNESS. This strikes me as unjust and I can only wonder, why isn't it fair?

I worked very hard to get the text of BREAD IN THE WILDERNESS ready for the printer. I copy edited the script page by page myself. I got Gerry Gross to rush rough proofs of the drawings, to guide you in doing the final sketches, etc., etc. (I think, incidentally, that these have come out beautifully, with the green background especially—or do you prefer the olive?). The manuscript is all ready to go into proof at this moment.

I cannot help wondering why we cannot go ahead. It required only two steps: (1) a decision on the part of Father Abbot that this should be your next book and (2) the reaffirmation of the principle that Harcourt, Brace should publish your next book. When I visited with you over the Fourth, it seemed to me that these two points were established. We spent every effort in determining Point No. 1, and came to what seemed to me a happy decision in Father Abbot's office. Point No. 2 was never questioned. Why therefore can we not proceed with the plans agreed upon?

It must be agonizing for you to have this kind of tug-of-war going on and it is not restful to the publisher's nerves either. Why do we not draw up a program of all your commitments (no matter how small or trivial you may think them to be), and then agree mutually on an order of publication and on the timing, in so far as it can be foreseen?

If you want BREAD not to be the next book, I will concur, of course, and wait for the manuscript of the CLOUD AND THE FIRE in December. I had occasion to read what you gave me again and again while convalescing and I like it enormously. It will be a wonderful book to do, with illustrations too, I hope.

With best wishes to you and Father Abbot.

Ever yours,
Robert Giroux

SEPTEMBER 21, 1950

Our Lady of Gethsemani
[Letterhead]

Dear Bob:

Your wire and your letter reached me at the same time. I just answered the wire and now for the letter.

About BREAD IN THE W.—there is no room for further action, Bob. It was promised to Jay. Jay wants the book. He therefore has to have it. I gather from your letter that it can only be the next book if Harcourt has it. In that event, it will have to wait until after I have sent you the completed ms. of the CLOUD AND THE FIRE—and on that I am compelled to take my time as I want it to be carefully done. I think I can let you have it next spring early or late, and I also think it ought to be a good solid book. I am trying to make it that. Without being commercial, I have a kind of feeling that it is going to sell all right; the first part is shaping up that way. It is a little different from what you have seen so far. What I had lined up for the third part I am going to drop as unnecessary, and wind the book up with a very thorough treatment of the Gifts of the Holy Ghost following John of St. Thomas. This will make it complete and you will like it. I might do just one illustration—a sort of frontispiece. See later.

I am sorry you were laid up, and of course I am most grateful for all the trouble you have taken over BREAD. I especially liked Gerry Gross's proofs, in green above all. I am very sorry that my vagueness precipitated all this trouble and caused everyone a lot of extra work and worry. But Bob, you can see there is nothing more I can do about it now. A promise is a promise. Jay will wait until we get the signal to go. That will also please Naomi—until she sees how technical the CLOUD is. Still, it is less technical than BREAD.

They sent me to the hospital for a check-up. I have a mild case of colitis which they are clearing up with a new diet. I am supposed to rest somewhat and get out in the air more, but I can swing things so that this will not necessarily slow down any really productive work. I hope so anyway.

From now on I'll try to make sure that all future books come out on a schedule approved by Naomi and agreeable to everyone. For the moment, it's CLOUD next, then BREAD. Do you want the Cloisters after that?

God bless you.

As ever,
Tom
fr. M. Louis /s/

SEPTEMBER 25, 1950

Rev. M. Louis, O.C.S.O.
Abbey of Our Lady of Gethsemani
Trappist, Kentucky

Dear Tom:

I am relieved to learn that you went to the hospital merely for a check-up. It sounded more serious when I first heard about it from Jay. I am glad that you are at home again, and on a new diet. Fresh air and rest are the best medicines of all. My cold did not really clear up until I got outdoors one sunny afternoon (and spent it, oddly enough, out at the Cloisters near Fort Tryon Park, mostly in the herb garden and the reconstructed cloister of Cuxa).

I am delighted to learn that you think you can have the completed manuscript of THE CLOUD AND THE FIRE ready in early spring. The earlier the better. As you describe it, it is shaping up beautifully, and I know that I will like it. A frontispiece illustration, and perhaps a vignette or design for the jacket, would be marvelous and would give it a really personal and individual touch.

Don't hesitate to send parts of the manuscript along as you finish them. We should be happy to do the retyping here.

As ever,

[Robert Giroux]

OCTOBER 27, 1950

Rev. M. Louis, O.C.S.O.
Abbey of Our Lady of Gethsemani
Trappist, Kentucky

Dear Tom:

I believe I've already told you about the autobiography of Dr. Karl Stern, the Montreal psychiatrist. It's called THE PILLAR OF FIRE. Proofs have just come in, and I am sending you a set of galleys herewith. I am most anxious to know what you think of it, and so is the author. It's an extraordinary story, as you will see, and it is bound to have a tremendous impact. It would mean much to us, and to Dr. Stern, to have a quote from you, to use on the jacket. I hope that you will find time to read his story, and I know that when you do you will want to say something on its behalf. I will be eager to hear from you.

Incidentally, I am sending you by separate cover the new edition of T.S. Eliot's SELECTED ESSAYS. The book ends (in the essay entitled "Modern Education and the Classics") with these sentences:

> The only hope I can see for the study of Latin and Greek, in their proper place and for the right reasons, lies in the revival and expansion of monastic teaching orders. There are other reasons, and of the greatest weight, for desiring to see a revival of the monastic life in its variety, but the maintenance of Christian education is not the least. The first educational task of the communities should be the preservation of education within the cloister, uncontaminated by the deluge of barbarism outside; their second, the provision of education for the laity, which should be something more than education for a place in the Civil Service, or for technical efficiency, or for social or public suc-

cess. It would not be that tawdry adornment, "education for leisure." As the world at large becomes more completely secularized, the need becomes more urgent that professedly Christian people should have a Christian education, which should be an education both for this world and for the life of prayer in this world.

Ever yours,
Robert Giroux

NOVEMBER 22, 1950

Our Lady of Gethsemani
[Letterhead]

Dear Bob:
They have been keeping me here in the hospital for some time, mainly to make me rest. They are checking up on various things too. My chest is a little shaky but that does not mean I have anything like TB. Father Abbot dropped in on the day of my (minor) operation bringing the galleys of Stern's book and Eliot's Essays and your letter. Many thanks for everything.

First, about PILLAR OF FIRE. I liked it very much. It is a fascinating book to me. It is another one of those conversions which is symptomatic— a kind of type-reaction to the Holy Ghost, one that will probably be the pattern for many more to come. If you want to quote me on the subject, you can say something like this—of course I mean what I say:

Karl Stern's conversion to Catholicism would be the death of the nineteenth-century myth that science and religion are incompatible, if that myth had not already died long ago. He not only shows that a scientific attitude of mind is no obstacle to Catholic faith, but that a scientist who is fully aware of the implications of his science, is bound to accept the Catholic faith. At the same time, however, he does not make the mistake of trying to give a purely "scientific" explanation of his conversion. I am especially interested in the eschatological character of his conversion. The thinly disguised Old Testament Messianism in Marx has hitherto offered Communists a promise of a religious satisfaction which Communism itself will necessarily refuse them. I think someday many people are going to follow the road that Stern has travelled.

I am going back to the monastery at the end of the week. This delay will not hold up the Cloud and the Fire too much, if at all. I can still get it to you by March, if my mind will stick to one simple plan and not get off into a more involved treatment of the subject than the book requires. That I think is the crux of this problem.

The doctors have told me that I must not overwork. This is simply another indication that I must approach my writing in a somewhat different way—it must grow out of more reading and thought, and prayer. All this means is longer intervals between books. My stuff needs to grow out of the ground without being pushed and forced. There is no sense in rushing anyway.

Well, it is time to say the office, so I will get this in the mail.

God bless you. I'll be praying for you on Thanksgiving day—and every day. Give my best to Naomi; I haven't yet had a chance to write to her. But I guess I haven't really anything urgent to write about anyway.

As ever.

In Corde Christi,
Tom
fr. M. Louis /s/

DECEMBER 21, 1950

Our Lady of Gethsemani
[Letterhead]

Dear Bob:

I suppose this will reach you too late to bring you my best Christmas wishes. In any case you will know that I prayed for you in my Masses, asking Our Lord to bring you all the blessings of this season.

Father Abbot told me the good news about the reprint rights for the MOUNTAIN and WATERS. I was thinking of going over the whole of the MOUNTAIN before letting it out as a reprint. But I have not had time. I would like, though, to have the following sentences cut—same old ones. Just wipe them out this time.

> p. 26—l. 7 "It is what many . . . religious training."
> p. 26—l. 13, 14, 15. "And since this fitted . . . crooked and immoral."
> p. 65, lines 11, 12, 13, 14 from bottom: "It is a class religion . . . coherence up to now."
> p. 174—change bottom line to read as follows: "idea of ours, let alone any sensible image could delimit the being of God."
> p. 220, cut from line 18 to line 35: "In other words he was able . . . a single system."

I also would like them to drop that <u>Commonweal</u> article, pp. 414: "America is discovering . . ." to p. 419 "all other works put together." There has been a lot of criticism of the theology involved here and I have restated the whole position more clearly in an article which would be for that collection of articles, if ever . . .

Would you please ask someone to send these same changes to Miss Weiner at Curtis Brown so they can be made in subsequent foreign editions?

Work on the CLOUD goes steadily, with medical interruptions when I have to go to Louisville on routine check-ups. But they are a nuisance.

Well, God bless you. Hope all is going well.

> Sincerely in Christ,
> Tom
> fr. M. Louis /s/

DECEMBER 30, 1950

> Our Lady of Gethsemani
> [Letterhead]

Dear Bob:

Many thanks for the Christmas card—what an angel!—and the book which is marvelous. And now for business.

This appears to me to be a good idea. Work on the Cloud is going along well in spite of interruptions. I am well on the way to having the part I am doing now finished in the next month or two. But now, look. This part is so much of a unit, and so much more technical and the divisions are all so much longer than the other that it really forms a completely separate book. You have not seen it. You will agree as soon as I send it to you, but I would rather finish it first.

Here is my suggestion. The part you have now is also an almost complete unit. Just needs ten pages or so at the end and a new beginning and some touching up here and there. Don't you think it would make a nice small book by itself? As I see things now that is what it ought to be. Let's go ahead with that and it will be a great boon to me in the following ways:

1—It will produce two books instead of one. It will give us plenty of time to work on this second book which is deep and difficult and requires immense care. I expect to have to do a lot of careful going over which would hold up the whole job. In conscience I must do this. But the part you have is simple and straightforward, even in a certain sense popular. It would be quite easily touched up.

2—It will solve that "next book" question which, though more or less abstract, is producing an unwelcome pressure that gets in the way of my work. I would like to lift that silly burden. It would give me more freedom and I could move. The only thing I ask is that I be allowed to finish the section of this one I am working on (not the whole 2nd book, just two weeks work or so) before touching up your book there. Would you meanwhile glance over the ms. you have and see if you do not think it would make a good book, and what would be required in your opinion to round it off.

The second book demands the title we had been thinking of—or rather a better one (?) Fire Cloud and Darkness for the explanation of these symbols is all in this one. Meanwhile I will think up a title for the other.

I am really convinced that the section you have there needs to go out as a small book by itself and that this other should be solid and concentrated on one technical point, which it is. Also, it is unified by being consistently concerned with the doctrine of St. John of the Cross.

I get this off in haste. Sending a copy to Naomi. Best regards to you both. God bless you. I hope this idea will work out because it will help me and I think it will satisfy your desire to get something quickly in print.

As ever.

Tom
fr. M. Louis /s/

JANUARY 20, 1951

Trappist-Cistercian Abbey
[Letterhead]

Dear Bob:

Here is another piece of that FIRE CLOUD AND DARKNESS ms., which I think Naomi gave you. This is the second book, the one which is not any longer anything to do with the ms. I gave you last summer. Let us call that other one at least for the time being THE SCHOOL OF THE SPIRIT. I haven't heard from you on it. I can finish it fairly quickly, I hope. You can still have it more or less by March if you let me know you want it then. I am trying to finish a section of F[ire] C[loud] and D[arkness] of which I have all the ideas lined up. The thing has been going well and I am beginning to think there will be something to it. I do not want to hurry over it too much.

Incidentally, a chapter in FIRE called the "Problem of Unbelief" might well be taken out and go into a volume of essays we were speaking of. As also might another section, about Jung, which Naomi has.

I am also sending a drawing I meant to send for Christmas although I did not get around to it then.

With best wishes, as ever.

In Corde Christi,
[Thomas Merton]

FEBRUARY 4, 1951

Our Lady of Gethsemani
[Letterhead]

Dear Bob:

Father Abbot was happy with the big check. Naomi will give you the dope on the project about exclusivity. I know you have every right and reason to suggest and even sort of demand it—if you should want to. We haven't made a definite decision. One reason is—dropping Jay flat means, in effect, shutting the door of the monastery on him, because he would never come back. And he needs to come here. You can see our point. He need not get more than poems or little scraps of things that you wouldn't touch.

Here is another piece of Fire Cloud and Darkness. Ten pages more and I will have finished the section I have on my mind so much and will then polish off (God willing) the School of the Spirit for some time in March. At least that is the plan. If I should get an exceptionally hot idea on F[ire] C[loud and] D[arkness] I would have to pursue it. Did I mention that material is shaping up for that book of articles? We have a lot to think about with these mss. Plenty to work on and, if things go as they ought, we can really produce something with them. I do not want to rush with anything except the School, which should come out as a popular introduction to the mystical life or something like that. The others should be mature and solid especially FCD. Hope to hear your reactions.

God bless you—as ever.

Tom
fr. M. Louis /s/

FEBRUARY 11, 1951

Trappist-Cistercian Abbey
[Letterhead]

Dear Bob:

Good news. I am sending you the last two chapters of Fire Cloud and Darkness in two separate envelopes. This on account of a strike I hear of. Apparently they will not take heavy items.

This brings the first draft of the book to an end, with the exception of a prologue which it needs in order to state the theme quite definitely. No need of many words for that. The book will need cutting and revision. I got enough ideas to finish it all off in the last few days. By the grace of God I have written a lot in the last month. The book needs nothing new except perhaps some things might suggest themselves.

Thus I am able to fulfill my promise of delivering a completed book by March. At the same time, there is a question about this being the next book. I would personally like to think about it for a while.

At the moment, what do you say about carrying on with the project presented in the last two or three letters I have written: let me try to finish the School of the Spirit soon—can do it easy by the end of Lent—and bring it out as a simple and short book for next Christmas. Then we can have the summer to think over Fire and make the necessary revisions, besides I want some theologians to go over it. It is of course a more substantial piece of work than anything I have attempted so far and I really want it to be good.

Incidentally, the ms. of Fire begins with a chapter called Vision and Illusion, the page being numbered 70. It needs a new start, along with the Prologue I spoke of but otherwise it is a complete unit, except perhaps that we might take out the chapter Problem of Unbelief (p. 168) and use it in the volume of essays.

I am eager to hear what you have to say about these jobs, and would like to have a definite idea of what our plans are going to be. My health is okay. That is one reason why the work went ahead fast. That and the grace of God and a relic of St. John of the Cross which the Carmelites gave me— and then another bigger relic of St. John of the Cross which Sr. Thérèse gave me, and which finished off the book.

God bless you, happy Lent.

In Corde Christi,
Tom
fr. M. Louis /s/

FEBRUARY 13, 1951

Harcourt, Brace & Company, Inc.
[Letterhead]

Rev. M. Louis, O.C.S.O.
Abbey of Our Lady of Gethsemani
Trappist, Kentucky

Dear Tom:

There is so much to write about that I shall have to divide it all up into two or three letters. This letter is about the new book. I'll write separately about Jay and our proposal of exclusivity, which I'm sure we can solve charitably and justly at the same time, and I shall also write Father Abbot about this and other matters.

I think the new book is terrific. It is mature, and solid, and unified by being consistently concerned with the doctrine of Saint John of the Cross. Just because it has all these virtues, my advice is that we publish it as your next book, at the end of summer or in early fall. The shorter book, THE SCHOOL OF THE SPIRIT, can follow later—similarly with the book of essays.

At first reading, I must confess, the new book was tough going. The opening pages on "Vision and Illusion" were particularly confusing, with its consideration of the philosophies of the East. I tried it out on other readers, sympathetic ones, and they found it even more difficult than I did. We couldn't see where you were going, or what you were getting at; of course, the reader needs some sense of your aims almost before he starts reading. So I read through the entire manuscript, down through the "Loving Knowledge of God," which came last week. Then I started in again on "Vision and Illusion," with a pretty good grasp of the whole book. With a keener eye, I now saw that all the elements in the opening chapter, which you develop so skillfully later on, need only slight rearrangement to help the reader "get into" the book, and that the obstacles to his doing so were quite expendable, editorially speaking. For one thing, the reader has to see at once that what you are writing about really concerns him, as an individual, that it is not "abstract" at all, but really vital. Pascal's example of the gambler, at the end of the chapter, really hits home. That is contemporary life; it gets to the core of the problem you are discussing, and it has the virtue of being a vivid extract from a writer relatively modern. It also immediately enables you to cite Saint Gregory of Nyssa, and his commentary on Ecclesiastes, and so on. The only way I can show you my editorial suggestions on this most important opening chapter is to enclose a transcript of the whole thing.

I also found that when I reached page 168, "The Problem of Unbelief," it was like coming to an oasis in the desert. It's witty and pungent and fascinating. But I also realized that it doesn't belong there, and actually interrupts the development of your text at this late stage; so I wasn't surprised by your suggestion that it might be taken out and made part of the book of essays. But I think it can be put to better use, as chapter two of this book. It also made the paragraphs in "Vision and Illusion" on faith and reason more meaningful for me, and I therefore suggest that you put these at the end of the opening chapter, to lead right into "The Problem of Unbelief," as indicated on the enclosure. Chapter 3, "On a Dark Night," has a most felicitous opening reference to Pascal's gambler; the continuity is therefore perfect. The reader is now well into the book, and having been led this far, I think he will go on.

Another thing that will lead the reader on is a different title. I've tried FIRE, CLOUD AND DARKNESS out on everyone—Naomi, friends*, visitors like Karl Stern—and, as the bebop set would say, it doesn't exactly send them. Even when I explain the Moses symbol, they like THE CLOUD AND FIRE better. Yet, thanks to your book, I now realize that "darkness" is the most important of the three words. However, there is a phrase in your opening chapter (page 83 of your typescript) which struck me forcibly, and everyone here thinks it would be a wonderful title: THE ASCENT TO TRUTH. I like it for many reasons. It implies a gradual development of thought, perhaps ascending in difficulty. It implies some kind of journey, and the journey image occurs regularly in the book (see page 187, etc.). Finally, it echoes THE ASCENT OF MOUNT CARMEL, and is wholly fitting for a book about the doctrine of Saint John of the Cross.

This title will be immediately attractive to readers. People are searching for Truth these days, and want to get above the morass of everyday life. THE ASCENT TO TRUTH will say something to them, at once, which FIRE, CLOUD AND DARKNESS will not. I recommend the new title wholeheartedly, as editor, publisher, and reader. Naomi tells me she likes it very much. Please give it full consideration. It's your phrase, and I hope you make it the title.

Query: you mention "ten pages more"; will that mark the end of this book? I shall look forward to their receipt, in any event. Do you think a preface or introduction is necessary? I'm inclined to think not, at this point, but it depends on what you think needs saying. As to the whole manuscript, if you agree about the new opening, I'm inclined to think that the latter part will need only a minimum of polishing. I'm all for getting it into proofs during March. Once it's in type, you will doubtless find places that require some revision, but that's safe enough to do on galleys.

Illustrations: Having seen what you can do in this line, I'm eager to know whether there's a possibility of your doing at least a frontispiece drawing, or maybe three part titles—burning bush, pillar of cloud, darkness. Or perhaps a portrait of Saint John of the Cross, or a drawing of that diagram you mention, the two false roads and the true road. How about trying your hand at some sketches? We'd like to use the same two-color process we proposed for BREAD IN THE WILDERNESS.

Of course, I'd like to see us put out the first illustrated book by you. I think color and drawings will in no way detract from the new book; they should, in fact, be an attraction.

So much for the moment. Read over the enclosed revision** of the opening of the book, and either send it back with your corrections, or let me know if it's all right to go ahead. And let me know what you think about the other points.

Ever yours,

Bob /s/

P.S. I went over to Morningside [Heights] to hear Father [Martin] D'Arcy [S.J.] (of Campion Hall and [Evelyn] Waugh fame) at Corpus Christi [Church] on Sunday—a wonderful sermon on the gospel for the first Lenten Sunday.

P.P.S. We have been sent a translation of THE WHITE PARADISE, [Petrus] van der Meer de Walcheren's book on [the monastery of] La

Valsainte [in Switzerland]. Incidentally, I hear that a Carthusian community has been started in Vermont under Father Vernon Moore.

*"Sounds like Winston Churchill," said a Boston friend.

**Still being typed. I've decided to mail this off and ms. will follow.

FEBRUARY 15, 1951

Our Lady of Gethsemani
[Letterhead]

Dear Bob:

I got your letter last night and I am glad you like the new book. Although I would have liked more time to mull over it, I am willing to push ahead and get it out for this fall. The new title, ASCENT TO TRUTH is okay—except the ear does not distinguish between "ascent" and "assent" in such a phrase.

I realized the first chapter would have to be remodeled. Please send me your transcript right away so that I can get busy. I still think the book needs a short prologue, which I will write. Let's not set up the False Mysticism Chapter as it is; I want to rewrite it. There is also some rewriting to be done in the Blindness of the Wise. If you have done any editorial work on your copy, please let me have it back. I will work over the top copy which I have here and send it in for the printer. It is going to be a penance for the typesetters.

Okay. Problem of Unbelief as the second chapter, if you think so.

You have by now, the last two chapters which I sent in two separate envelopes on account of a strike or something.

As for illustrations—I will think about them. I would really like to do some, but at the moment I do not see quite what I can do. I am not too good on burning bushes and pillars of fire and the Mountain diagram requires a lot of lettering, which I am bad at. No reason why someone else shouldn't do it. But that might spoil the effect you are aiming at.

Meanwhile, I have to get out a pamphlet to go with those records of our chant which is supposed to come out at Easter, and I am in the same old rush as ever. When we get this Ascent under way, I really want to drop things and do some field work and be a monk for a while, especially as there is likely to be a great log-jam of books again if I finish up THE SCHOOL OF THE SPIRIT quickly, on top of this and the one Jay has.

This is all for the moment.

Best wishes, as ever. I will get the copy to you as soon as I can, but please do not set up the one you have there.

God bless you.

In Corde Christi,
Tom
fr. M. Louis /s/

Our Lady of Gethsemani
[Letterhead]

Dear Bob:

It seems to me that the most practical thing to do is to send you this manuscript piece by piece as I go over it. I do not know if you are sending me the copy you had there. If it comes I'll send back the part corresponding to this. I have cut the chapter called Blindness of the Wise as it only holds up the movement. I am writing some more on False Mysticism as this is important. I do not know how you will take to the new first chapter, but I think it is needed.

Above all, I hope you will like the title. The quotation from Job explains it and it avoids the ambiguity I spoke of last time. I'll send more in a couple of days. You'll have the whole thing ready for the printer first week in March. You can send this right away to the press if you like. Glad to be moving with this job. God bless you.

In Corde Christi,
Tom
fr. M. Louis /s/

P.S. I like your editing of Vision + Illusion fine.

Trappist-Cistercian Abbey
[Letterhead]

Dear Bob:

I am enclosing another piece of THE ASCENT TO LIGHT. As far as I am concerned it is ready to print. I meant to say in my last letter that you had better hold your copy (I mean the carbon) there in case you did any editorial work on it, as I am sending this stuff in fast. If the copy comes here I'll send it right back.

Another thing: there might be a lot of perplexity in the minds of readers arising from the fact that I talk about St. John of the Cross, St. Thomas, and John of St. Thomas. What about a short biographical note on these and maybe also on Pascal, Gregory of Nyssa and one or two others? Let me know. God bless you.

In Jesus,
Tom
fr. M. Louis /s/

FEBRUARY 28, 1951

Our Lady of Gethsemani
[Letterhead]

Dear Bob:

Here is the last corrected part of THE ASCENT TO LIGHT. I am surprised that I did not find much to change. It seemed to me that there was a lot of work to be done. Maybe I will see more changes in the galleys.* I hope it reads all right. Have you all the sections now? Hope to see galleys soon. Meanwhile I'll be thinking about drawings or some kind of illustrations. Maybe I could get a good picture of St. John of the Cross from somewhere.

God bless you. As ever.

In Corde Christi,
Tom
fr. M. Louis /s/

*Please send two extra sets of galleys—one for our censor + one for a theologian to go over.

FEBRUARY 28, 1951

Rev. M. Louis, O.C.S.O.
Abbey of Our Lady of Gethsemani
Trappist, Kentucky

Dear Tom:

I'm delighted to know that you're revising the book, and hope you'll continue sending it in piecemeal. The first 139 pages arrived yesterday, and I'm pleased to know that the editing of "Vision and Illusion" was OK. I'll hold the other copy of the whole book for the time being, unless you need it.

That's a beautiful quotation from Job, but I don't think the new title is right. The word "Light" is too abstract; the title doesn't say to the reader what THE ASCENT TO TRUTH says. The toughest critic I've confronted is Tom Burns, manager of Burns & Oates and Hollis & Carter (who incidentally sends you and Father Abbot his very best regards and regrets very much that business in New York prevented his getting to Kentucky—he says he'll make it next trip over). He thinks THE ASCENT TO TRUTH is tops, and it was his firm and family who published [John Henry] Newman's THE GRAMMAR OF ASSENT! I pointed out your concern over the homonyms, but Burns thought that the specialists who were reminded of Newman would, after all, be literate enough not to confuse "Ascent" with "Assent." And the point is that every one likes the first title; I've never experienced such unanimity of response and I've never been more sure of the title. The word "Truth" is a touchstone of our times; it's been abused so, and yet underneath people really are seeking the truth. I've got no affirmative reactions to THE ASCENT TO LIGHT, and I leaned over backwards to get honest responses. Anne Ford thought it might be taken for a scientific work, a book on physics or such! Please, let's stick to THE ASCENT TO TRUTH.

I think your preface is excellent, and there's no doubt in my mind that we'll have finished books for the fall. Incidentally, Naomi and Burns both asked me to have the manuscript retyped, so that Hollis & Carter won't have to wait for American proofs. So I'm having the job done here. We won't send it to the printer until we have the entire manuscript, but we can get sample pages, binding, etc. Do you have any special preferences in this direction? Would you like the WATERS OF SILOE typeface and page design, for example, or something different from any we've had before? Please let me have your thoughts on these points.

Ever yours,
Robert Giroux

P. S. The other two sections have just arrived—through Part II; many thanks! I think biographical notes on the people you cite is an excellent idea. Let's do it.

MARCH 2, 1951

Rev. M. Louis, O.C.S.O.
Abbey of Our Lady of Gethsemani
Trappist, Kentucky

Dear Tom:
Just a note to acknowledge receipt of a final section of the manuscript which arrived late Friday afternoon.

I've made a note about two extra sets of galleys for the censor and theologian.

Let's not give up the idea of an illustration or two altogether. A frontispiece may be the right solution.

Yours,
Robert Giroux

MARCH 3, 1951

Our Lady of Gethsemani
[Letterhead]

Dear Bob:
Just got your letter. Glad you are typing the book there. I will get busy on the biographical notes. I would like to hang on to the quote from Job anyway, although I give in on the title. I still think it is ambiguous but it

doesn't make much difference because very few people will read the book out loud. (You see I have been eating 9 yrs [years] in a monastic refectory!) About the type. I would like something quite new in type and page design. I like Elzevir No. 3 as a body type—or Estienne or Granjon but have kind of a good feeling about Elzevir for this one—and maybe a different format. It is going to be a harder book to read; we should have more spaces. About headings—please, please, never again Weiss italic although it was nice in the Mtn [*The Seven Storey Mountain*]. What I like most of all is the Caslon (?) you used on the Collected Poems of William Empson. Would that go nicely with one of the above types I mentioned? I think the title page of Empson would suggest something nice. By the way, we have discovered a brilliant artist among our laybrother novices.[1] He suddenly broke out one day and designed a marvelous vestment. I was the first one to wear it, too. He likes the sort of 12th-century business that suggested the angel on the jacket of Waters. I have already given him the Cluny book to devour. Can you dig up anything else of the type?

Glad you will have the book ready for fall. At this distance, can I indulge my Carmelite devotions some more? There are a lot of Carmelite feast days, any one of which would make a nice publication date. Oct. 3rd, St. Thérèse, Oct. 15th St. Teresa, Nov. 24, St. John of the X [Cross].

How about coming down again this summer? Or before the summer? As ever, all the best. God bless you.

> In Corde Christi,
> Tom
> fr. M. Louis /s/

P.S. Look, I know this gets everybody mad, but I have been reading that Journal of My Escape from the Nazis and there are some pages of funny writing that could be trimmed out and printed just for the fun of it. The idea makes Naomi wild, but I still cherish it. I could easily drop the double talk, or just leave one section of concentrated double talk which might be funny to someone on this earth besides myself . . . Oh, well. Thanks a lot for typing the book. I'll pray hard for whoever has the penance of doing it.

1. Probably Lavrans Nielson.

MARCH 9, 1951

Rev. M. Louis, O.C.S.O.
Abbey of Our Lady of Gethsemani
Trappist, Kentucky

Dear Tom:
The jacket sketch of THE ASCENT TO TRUTH has just reached my desk and I send it along herewith at once. The artist is Arno Scheule, who

did THE WATERS OF SILOE, and I think he has done a most imaginative and successful job of design, particularly in his handling of the burning bush. If you have any suggestions, now is the time to make them. I should add that this represents the third stage of design, and I know you will see at once the amount of thought which has gone into it. My personal suggestion, if I had any at all, would be to make the background at the top of the cloud really pitch black—that is, perhaps a completely black border right across the top to represent the ascent to darkness. I am enclosing a return envelope since we will have need of the sketch just as soon as you are through with it.

With best wishes.

Sincerely yours,
Robert Giroux

MARCH 15, 1951

Our Lady of Gethsemani
[Letterhead]

Dear Bob:

The jacket design is really splendid. I suppose the dark left side of the design is to represent the "darkness." It seems to me to suffice. My only idea would be a more spiral effect in the flames, to suggest the spiral ascent of the thoughts in the book. Or is this being too subtle? In any case, I do not attach great importance to it.

At present the biographical notes occupy me, and I think I will make them more than just notes, but a separate essay that could go in as an appendix, but which will treat all those concerned in the light of the main theme of the book, and show how it was their function to assert these crucial doctrines in moments of spiritual crisis that confronted the whole Church.

That's all for the moment. Get this off in a hurry. It is really a fine design. But it also reminds me that I have been having so much fun, out at work in the fields, that I nearly set fire to the whole forest the other day, while burning some brush out towards the lake.

God bless you, and may you have a very happy Easter.

In Corde Christi,
Tom
fr. M. Louis /s/

MARCH 19, 1951

Our Lady of Gethsemani
[Letterhead]

Dear Bob:

Here are the biographical notes.

One question remains open: do you think they would be better at the beginning or at the end?

Happy Easter. Eager to see proofs.

As ever.

God bless you,
Tom
fr. M. Louis /s/

[marginal notes: apophasis—denial; apophatic: in quotes on page two but not on p. one; Webster: "negative"]

MARCH 29, 1951

Our Lady of Gethsemani
[Letterhead]

Dear Bob:

Here are the final pages of the book—the insert that was to complete the chapter on "False Mysticism." I think you now have everything and we can go to press!

Incidentally, Jacques Maritain is eager to go over the proofs, which will be an immense help. His address is 26 Linden Lane, Princeton, N.J. Will you also send proofs to Dan Walsh?

By the way, Father Abbot informs me that Dan wrote and said he was in favor of my original title—Fire Cloud and Darkness. Father Abbot likes that too. In fact, he told me to write and tell you so. So you see that it is not absolutely unanimous for your side. However, I am not particularly excited about it. My only feeling is that Fire, etc., has more to do with the theme of the book and also, incidentally, it fits the cover much better. However . . .

Incidentally, too, the more I think of that splendid cover the less I am inclined to put one of my own silly drawings in the book. But there is still time. If you want one, you must pray the Holy Ghost to give me a very special inspiration.

I keep repeating that you should come down again this summer.[1] By the way, when you were in Rome or elsewhere did you hear anything of the canonization of one Father Charbel, a hermit?[2] I am very interested in anything that can be found out about him. He is either being canonized around now, or already elevated to the altar.

As ever, all the best.

God bless you,
Tom
fr. M. Louis /s/

1. RG visited TM at the abbey on April 12, 1951.
2. On December 5, 1965, Pope Paul VI officiated at the ceremony of the beatification of Rev. Charbel Makhlouf, during the closing of the Second Vatican Council. In 1976, the pope signed the decree of canonization of Blessed Charbel, which took place on October 9, 1977.

MAY 21, 1951

Harcourt, Brace & Company, Inc.
[Letterhead]

Rev. M. Louis, O.C.S.O.
Abbey of Our Lady of Gethsemani
Trappist, Kentucky

Dear Tom:

Naomi has told me the news of your wedding-present to her, and I can only say how wonderful I think it is. I am delighted that Father Abbot has reconsidered his decision about the Journal, and is allowing publication of special sections of it. It will do an enormous amount of good, and one very salutary effect will be to scotch erroneous impressions about life in a monastery. I shall be eager to see the manuscript when Naomi is ready to pass it along, and I shall be writing you about it shortly thereafter.

Meanwhile, I am glad to tell you that we have finally settled on the Estienne type for THE ASCENT TO TRUTH. I enclose the sample pages, and I hope you consider them as attractive as I do. The Estienne is wonderfully open and readable, and it has real distinction as well. We have decided to put all the source footnotes in the back of the book, so as not to discourage the general reader right off. Don't you agree this is sound?

One important thing: we want to do very attractive endpapers—as effective as those for THE WATERS OF SILOE. Have you any ideas? Best of all would be some kind of drawing or design by you—even a little design which could be duplicated over and over to form an endpaper pattern. It should not clash with the jacket, whose design you know, but rather contrast with it. Second best would be a photograph endpaper, something almost abstract—an arch, or doorway, or spire. Do you have access to anything of this sort in those French monastery photos?

I have been buried in work, and feel that I owe you a good many letters. Maybe I'll come down again this summer instead. Anyway, THE ASCENT is on the linotype machines, and galley proofs will soon be coming through. So more later.

Ever yours,
Bob /s/

CORRECTIONS: THE ASCENT TO TRUTH

p. 16 lines 16–17: omit "as He is in Himself"
p. 38 line 11—delete "True, since the existence . . . accessible to reason."
Reset next sentence as follows "Any denial of God's existence involves us at least materially in a sin against faith."
p. 68 line 8. after "achieved" add "in the order of faith,"
line 10—reset to read "anything that is supernaturally seen or heard . . ."
line 12 reset to read "medium of any clear species."
p. 70 line 6—reset to read "images or clear representations in the soul"

p. 82 line 11—reset to read "with God above the level of any distinct image or idea"

p. 192 lines 6–7 reset to read "values that are appreciated in a mode as yet beyond the reach of the intelligence."

p. 193 line 17—"true God beyond the level of clear concepts" (add word "clear")

p. 194 last line reset—"the will enjoys an experiential contact with God by love"

p. 202 line 18 delete "for the mind and will . . . medium of concepts"

p. 219 line 26—reset to read "It does not grasp Him in a distinct concept."

p. 252 line 6—reset to read "According to St. Thomas, two great saints . . ."
line 10—delete "Elias"
line 16—delete whole sentence "That however . . . which it was granted."

p. 253 line 7—delete "Elias."

p. 258 line 18—delete "supraconceptual"

p. 259 line 12 from bottom—"key is a body of truths about God."
Delete next sentence "These . . . believe"

p. 260 delete lines 13–17: "So perfect . . . itself and God."
Reset line 17—"This union of Love with God does not [incomplete word]
Line 4 from bottom, delete "in fact," reset "identified by grace with Christ"
delete last words of page and top of page "in such a way . . . Divine Persons."

p. 262 line 7—reset to read "certain can be clear to the intelligence that apprehends its certitude."
line 11—delete "cannot" substitute "do not."

p. 263 line 11 from bottom—change "without any concepts" to "beyond distinct concepts." In the remaining section of the page delete three times the word "Faculty" and substitute in each case "aptitude."

p. 268 line 7—change to read "conceptual complex containing the truth to which we assent."
line 5 from bottom reset to read "terms of the credible proposition."

p. 272 line 8 from bottom—delete sentence "The only substance . . . Himself."

p. 274 line 6—add word clear "transcends clear concepts"

p. 278 line 12—delete "as He is in Himself" substitute "intimately experienced"

p. 280 line 4—delete "This love . . . Himself"
line 14—delete "as He is in Himself"

p. 294 line 6—reset to read "mystically identified."

p. 296 line 2—delete "in such a way that . . . glory of God."

p. 299 line 6 from bottom—delete "sees" and substitute "experiences"
next line—delete last lines "with a clarity so great . . . comparative obscurity."

p. 315 lines 8 and 9—"raised the intelligence above distinct concepts and took it beyond . . ."

MAY 25, 1951

Rev. M. Louis, O.C.S.O.
Abbey of Our Lady of Gethsemani
Trappist, Kentucky

Dear Tom:

Have you read the edition of Walter Daniel's LIFE OF AELRED whose jacket I enclose? If not, I'll send the book along to you when I finish dipping into it. Let me know.

Yours,
Robert Giroux

MAY 29, 1951

Rev. M. Louis, O.C.S.O.
Abbey of Our Lady of Gethsemani
Trappist, Kentucky

Dear Tom:

Galley proofs will be here on June 8th, a Friday and I will get them to you by Monday the 11th. Our manufacturing department asks if you can get them back to us with corrections by Friday, the 15th? It will be an enormous advantage if you can, because we shall then be able to have page proofs before our printer's holiday shut-down at the end of July. Do you think you can follow this schedule?

Incidentally, shall we wait for page proofs for your censors and for the imprimatur—so that all your corrections are contained therein—or will galley proofs do? Please let me know right away, since I may have to order extra galleys.

Ever yours,
Robert Giroux

MAY 31, 1951

Our Lady of Gethsemani
[Letterhead]

Dear Bob:

I doubt if I can handle the proofs on such short notice. To begin with, things usually lie around the place for a couple of days before they even get into my hands. Besides I have a heavy new job, spiritual director of the students, and don't know if I could put them off for a week. However I shall definitely do my best.

Page proofs ought to be good enough for the censors—in fact, better for them. By the way could you send galleys to Jacques Maritain?

Yes, I have the Aelred book here and plan on using it when I get back on that job.

Did you find a good photograph for those end sheets? I like the Estienne very much. I am working slowly on the revision of What is Contemplation in conjunction with another pamphlet and some additions. It ought to make a book about 75 to 100 pages long and I thought of calling it A GRAMMAR OF INTERIOR PRAYER.

As for the Journal I am eager to hear your reactions. The title is inadequate. Do you think DEAD MAN'S DIARY would be too sensational—what I mean to explain is that the person in that Journal is, I have suddenly discovered, just as much a thing of the past as the central figure in the Seven Storey Mountain.

Finally, those Columbia record people have put out a record of our [Gregorian] chant with some notes by me, but they have ballyhooed the notes in such a way as to make it appear that I am the one giving a spoken commentary on the chant. This is very bad for several reasons, one of which is that I have refused several times to make any recordings of my voice, reading poetry, etc. Now everybody thinks I am talking on the record, when in fact it is one of the novices. What do you suppose we can do about this?

In haste—God bless you.

In Corde Christi,
fr. M. Louis /s/

P.S. Many thanks for Daniel's new book. I expect to enjoy it.

JUNE 17, 1951

Our Lady of Gethsemani
[Letterhead]

Dear Bob:

I am returning the galleys of the ASCENT corrected. You will notice that I made a big cut on the last galley—I felt it to be absolutely necessary as the material in question just got in the way and very badly, although it might be all right in itself. If you want to put it in somewhere else, all right. But certainly it must not be allowed to mess up the ending—it makes everything go dead just when the book is hitting its climax.

Presumably the footnotes are coming later and you do not want me to correct them this trip. I will have the other set of galleys to work with in case they suddenly arrive after this has gone off. I like the type immensely and the book seems to have turned out pretty well. But I will wait and see what various theologians have to say. Did you send galleys to Jacques Maritain?

What chances are there of October publication? How are you making out with the Journal?
    God bless you, as ever.

In Corde Christi,
Tom
fr. M. Louis /s/

JUNE 19, 1951

WESTERN UNION
ROBERT GIROUX
HARCOURT BRACE CO
383 MADISON AVE NYK

PROOFS MAILED MONDAY.

FATHER LOUIS

JUNE 20, 1951

WESTERN UNION
FATHER M. LOUIS
ABBEY OF GETHSEMANI
TRAPPIST, KENTUCKY

GALLEYS HAVE ARRIVED[.] MANY THANKS[.] NEED MANUSCRIPT URGENTLY[.] CAN YOU RUSH AIRMAIL[?] ALL YOUR CORRECTIONS SEEM EXCELLENT AND YOU WERE RIGHT TO MAKE FINAL CUT[.] LETTER FOLLOWS[.] BEST REGARDS[.]

BOB

JULY 9, 1951

Rev. M. Louis, O.C.S.O.
Abbey of Our Lady of Gethsemani
Trappist, Kentucky

Dear Tom:
    This is urgent; please use enclosed airmail envelope for return.
    In the 25¢ edition of THE SEVEN STOREY MOUNTAIN, which Signet is doing, all the changes, including the deletion of the five pages 414–19, have been incorporated. However, the Federal Trade Commission laws are so stringent, that Signet is afraid that they will be prosecuted for presenting an "abridgment" instead of the whole text! To get around this absurd difficulty, we have proposed an Author's Note, explaining that these are

indeed "corrections"—not an abridgement. Their lawyer asks for the enclosed wording.

Is this OK with you? I'm sure that any minor re-phrasing is agreeable to them so long as the same points are covered. Also they want you to sign, either "Thomas Merton" or with initials, as indicated. I'll be most grateful if you can return this at once.

The page proofs of THE ASCENT TO TRUTH are now being prepared, and I hope to have them soon after July 15th. Your corrections were really impressive; Evelyn Waugh ought to see them. If we're to keep to September publication, however, we shall have to OK the pages with no changes except of downright errors. The footnotes (all in the back) will be the next biggest job. They must be made uniform, and putting them all together will show up the discrepancies.

We have a stunning double-spread title page. And as end-papers are using the enclosed photo by Mme. Sauvageot. I've already written her about this and sent our check. We shall use the same lithograph process as for THE WATERS. What is the significance of the XII at the bottom of the cross, do you have any idea?

Yours,
Robert Giroux

JULY 10, 1951

Our Lady of Gethsemani
[Letterhead]

Dear Bob:

The Author's note for the Signet edition is quite all right with me. I'd prefer the signature T. M. I have made two minor changes in the wording. I really am glad the book is coming out in a 25 c[ent] edition.

The photograph for the endsheets is swell. The reason why there is a XII cut in the base of the cross is that it is the twelfth station in an outdoor way of the cross leading up the mountain behind St. Martin du Canigou. I look forward to seeing the title page. The book really seems to be shaping up well.

About page proofs—I shall try my best to get them in with only the most essential corrections but remember the censors. I have not yet had a chance to send our galleys to the theologian I was thinking of. Has Maritain seen them, and has he suggested any changes? The galleys are still with the censor of the Order. Remember the New York censors too. I don't think we'll be able to make September publication at this rate. Let's settle for October 15th, the feast of St. Teresa [of Avila]. By the way, what are you doing about the Author's note? I didn't see it in the galleys, and I know Dan and Jacques Maritain wanted some changes made. And how about the biographical notes?

When do you want to go to work on the HB [Harcourt, Brace] second edition of the Mountain? What about the Journal? I have not been able to do a thing on the revisions of What is Contemplation lately but much was done a month ago. God bless you.

As ever.

Tom
fr. M. Louis /s/

JULY 13, 1951

Our Lady of Gethsemani
[Letterhead]

Dear Bob:

Here is a letter from Dr. [Lawrence Sidney] Thompson, the head librarian at the University of Kentucky and I think if you can send him the things he wants it would be worth while [for a display of Merton's *The Ascent to Truth*]. I have practically nothing left here except two or three sheets of notes which I am letting him have for keeps. Of course I suppose he means to return the ms.

Will you please send me an extra set of page proofs? I think Fr. Paul Philippe, the Dominican from Rome who plans to be here in August, will be my best bet as a censor.

Will you also send a set of proofs to Sister Thérèse who wants to get out a review in time for the fall number of Renascence? Her address is:

Sister M. Thérèse, SDS
3516 West Center Street
Milwaukee 10, Wis.

Am trying to clear the way so as to be free to work on the proofs next week.

A wonderful long poem in honor of N.D. [Notre Dame] de la Garde (Patroness of Marseilles) just came in from Lax.

God bless you—as ever.

Tom
fr. M. Louis /s/

JULY 18, 1951

Rev. M. Louis, O.C.S.O.
Abbey of Our Lady of Gethsemani
Trappist, Kentucky

Dear Tom:

Here are the galley proofs of the footnotes, in advance of the page proofs which are due here on Friday. As you can see, there are a great many queries about inconsistencies and missing notes. We are running them in two columns, and I think readers will find them convenient and easy to follow.

I send them at once so that you will have a head start, though of course you lack the proper key without the page proofs. I was going to return the manuscript from which they were set but I realize that your cuts in the galleys may have eliminated some footnotes and thus affected the numbering. It's not an easy proof-reading job and only you can do it. Please airmail them back as soon as you can. I'm enclosing two duplicates in case things get complicated—one set on light paper. Don't forget that the set to return is the one marked in green ink!

Didn't Dan Walsh tell you that Maritain read galley proofs? He told me that Maritain likes the book very much. I'm writing Dan today to follow this up; I want him to read page proofs.

I'm reading a fascinating and scholarly study by Father [Josef] Jungmann, S.J. which has a good deal of the early history of the rite of the Mass. I'll forward it to you soon, unless of course you already have it.

Many thanks for returning the "Author's Note" so promptly. They may want all your corrections for their edition. I suppose it's foolish to suggest that you go through THE SEVEN STOREY MOUNTAIN in your "spare time" and make all the corrections you want made and send the book as soon as you can. Do you need extra copies for this purpose? If so, let me know.

Page proofs will follow. We must keep to September—and we can if you return them and footnotes and the rest at once.

Our artist has designed a beautiful double-page spread for the title page, in two colors. I think it's marvelous. This is only a rough proof enclosed, but it gives you a good idea. I hope you like it.

Yours,
Robert Giroux

JULY 18, 1951

Rev. M. Louis, O.C.S.O.
Abbey of Our Lady of Gethsemani
Trappist, Kentucky

Dear Tom:

I enclose front-matter proofs. No need to return these, except if you have corrections. We do need a title for Part One, as soon as you can provide one.

It was at Dan Walsh's suggestion that I omitted the reference to Father [Jean] Daniélou, S.J. He seemed to think it would unnecessarily mislead many theologians. Perhaps you will disagree. As for myself, deeply moved as I was by your mention of me in the preface, I would find it embarrassing to ask for an exception to our house policy in this regard. It is a rule here that editors are not to be mentioned in dedications and acknowledgments, but should remain anonymous. There are many good reasons for the rule, and my concurring in it in no way detracts from my deep gratitude to you for your kindness.

Yours,
Robert Giroux

JULY 20, 1951

Our Lady of Gethsemani
[Letterhead]

Dear Bob:

Here is the front matter with new title for Part One and corrections in the author's notes. For the title to Part One, I have scribbled Cloud and Fire. If you prefer The Cloud and the Fire, or Fire Cloud and Darkness— take your choice. And if you still don't like any of them try the Burning Bush. In any case, some one of these will throw light on the marvelous jacket and title page. Since we first planned this I watched a lot of fires, when we were out burning brush in the woods, and the jacket sure has the spirit of those fires.

I can't figure out about Maritain—he wrote me that he had not seen the Ascent to Truth. Maybe the explanation is that he thought it was still the Cloud and the Fire. In any case, did he make any corrections? That is what I am most eager to know. And please ask Dan to make every slightest correction that seems to him to need to be made. I absolutely must have this book correct in every detail. Please be sure to send me a duplicate set of page proofs for Fr. Paul Philippe, O.P., from Rome who is to arrive here in a couple of weeks. He can spot any serious error and we can rush it in. Meanwhile, he can let me know what ought to be changed for later editions. The other galleys are with our Order's censors. And don't forget the N.Y. censor. Too bad you are out of the author's notes but not out of his gratitude anyway!

The Footnotes can be gone over for corrections and I'll get the page references, etc., later. I can't do anything about page reference for footnote 16 on galley 61 because I don't have the duplicate set of proofs, but you can catch it when the footnotes come back. Yes? Or else write me quick what part and what Chapter it comes in.

I just can't do anything about the new edition of the MOUNTAIN until after August. Let Signet go ahead with what they have, and let HB [Harcourt, Brace] bring out the new mountain which will have significant changes—namely some of that stuff Sister Thérèse dug out of the ms. I think this would be much better for you and for all. And what about illustrations? I have done little or nothing about them but we might run a picture of the monastery and of a few places and of Lax and all the fellows with beards maybe . . .

Father Abbot says he is coming to town; maybe you can talk about the Journal. I'll get this off fast now. God bless you always. Hope page proofs come soon. If it has to be September, make it the day on which St. Thérèse died, which is I think the 30th. How about sending a copy to every Carmelite convent—or am I going Cecil B. DeMille on you??? God bless you always—

Tom

fr. M. Louis /s/

JULY 20, 1951

Rev. M. Louis, O.C.S.O.
Abbey of Our Lady of Gethsemani
Trappist, Kentucky

Dear Tom:

Here are the page proofs. They are, as you will note, extraordinarily clean. I hope you will not find it necessary to make further changes. And in order to expedite matters, I suggest the following procedure: After you have gone through them, would you wire me collect to the effect that page proofs are OK and you are returning the galleys?

I have not sent you the master pages, so there is no need of returning the pages enclosed. We shall, however, have urgent need of the galley proofs which you made with your corrections, and the sooner you can mail these back to us, the happier we shall be.

By wiring "OK" I shall assume that you want us to proceed with the very few corrections which the printer has noted—such as capital letters for the "Gift of Understanding." If you do find that other changes are required, please return just those pages in which the changes occur.

I hope you have been able to proceed with the footnotes. We can't, of course, release the pages to the printer until these also have been returned to us.

I have already sent off a set of proofs to the Censor Librorum for the New York Archdiocese, and I am confident that there will be no difficulty in obtaining an Imprimatur.

With best wishes.

Sincerely yours,
Robert Giroux

JULY 22, 1951

Our Lady of Gethsemani
[Letterhead]

Dear Bob:

Do you mind adding the names of the various saints to be included in the Biographical Notes? At this stage, I think the additions to front matter involve no difficulty.

What do you think about a note somewhere telling what the picture on the end sheets represents—namely the view from the Abbey of Saint Martin du Canigou, in Southern France. Maybe this has no importance to anyone however.

At the end of the Author's Note, you can just put "Fr. M. Louis Merton." I guess a lot of people couldn't figure out the Maria [Latin, for Mary]. Keep O.C.S.O. Maybe it would be just as well to delete about the 9th anniversary, etc., and just put Abbey of Gethsemani, Lent 1951. Okay?

I can do an index quick if you send me the page proofs quick. What about the man at the University of Kentucky?

Don't forget to leave room for the imprimatur. In case I forget to tell you, the two censors Ex Parte Ordinis [on behalf of the Cistercian Order] will be Fr. M. Maurice Malloy, O.C.S.O., and Fr. M. Paul Bourne, O.C.S.O., with of course the General as in previous books. I am still waiting for their nihil obstats.

In the biographical notes, if you can still fit in 3 to 500 words on St. Bernard, please let me know very quick because I think many in the Order would be offended if he were left out.

As ever—God bless you.

> Tom
> fr. M. Louis /s/

JULY 23 [1951]

WESTERN UNION
REVEREND M LOUIS
ABBEY OF OUR LADY OF GETHSEMANI
TRAPPIST, KENTUCKY

OK 500 WORDS [ON] SAINT BERNARD[.] PLEASE RUSH COPY[.] WE DECIDED AGAINST INDEX[.] PROOFS HAVE ARRIVED[.] REGARDS[.]

> BOB

JULY 24, 1951

> Trappist-Cistercian Abbey
> [Letterhead]

Dear Bob:

The page proofs have come and I am working on them. Here is the stuff on St. Bernard. I hope it is not too long. You really must let me do an index for a later edition, for the book requires it. There will also I am sure have to be corrections in a later edition. We are going into this one terribly fast. Material like this needs to be seen in perspective.

However, if I can get the opinion of people who can give an authoritative judgment I shall feel safe even about the first edition. That is why I particularly want to know in some detail the reaction of Dan Walsh and Jacques Maritain.

However there is one obstacle that will still slow us down. Only one of the censors of the Order has the galleys. The other has seen nothing. Father Abbot is going to write to them both and tell them to get busy. But it is simply not licit for us to send the material to press without their nihil obstat, and I hope you will wait. Meanwhile, to speed things up, perhaps you could send a set of proofs at once to:

> Rev. M. Maurice Malloy, OCSO
> Censor Deputatus
> Our Lady of Guadalupe
> Pecos, New Mexico

You can mark it official business, rush and everything else and explain the affair to him in a note. By that time he should have Fr. Abbot's letter. But we can't proceed without him.

I am enclosing a few pages on which I made changes.

The book really seems to be shaping up well, from the material point of view. Thanks for all you have done.

God bless you.

> Tom
> fr. M. Louis /s/

JULY 26, 1951

WESTERN UNION
ROBERT GIROUX
HARCOURT BRACE CO
383 MADISON AVE

[PAGE] PROOFS RECEIVED[.] WILL FINISH FRIDAY[.] MUST AWAIT
CENSORS OF [TRAPPIST] ORDER[.]

> FATHER LOUIS
> TRAPPIST, KY

AUGUST 7, 1951

Rev. M. Louis, O.C.S.O.
Abbey of Our Lady of Gethsemani
Trappist, Kentucky

Dear Tom:

The enclosed note of acknowledgment has just come in from Father Malloy [M. Maurice Malloy]. I am very pleased with his notation that he is "profoundly impressed by a first reading." I also had a note from

Monsignor Fearns, and I am sure that the Imprimatur will soon be in our hands. I have just had a note from Father Abbot, who is in New York, and I expect to be seeing him shortly.

Because of the addition of the biographical note on Saint Bernard, I had to cut two pages. This was quite a job, but I took a lot of time and (if I say it myself) I don't think they are any the worse for the cutting. But they had to end on page 335, and I agree with you that you couldn't omit the note on Saint Bernard. When the revised proofs came back, I found that there were a few lines to spare, so I reinserted two sentences in the note on John of Saint Thomas. I have typed these in the margin of the proof. We also decided, for the sake of design, to limit the Author's Note to two pages. It has, therefore, been set down in slightly smaller type, but nothing has been deleted.

In short, the first edition is now ready, pending the release of the censors. I think this is going to be one of our handsomest books and I look forward to the finished copies. The binding will be a black cloth stamped in gold; it will match the jacket perfectly.

With best wishes.

Sincerely yours,
Robert Giroux

AUGUST 10, 1951

Rev. M. Louis, O.C.S.O.
Abbey of Our Lady of Gethsemani
Trappist, Kentucky

Dear Tom:

I had a splendid visit with Father Abbot yesterday. While he was here we put in a call to Father Paul at Conyers [the Trappist monastery in Georgia], since we were uncertain as to whether he had received the proofs. He told Father James [Fox] that not only had he received them, but that he was within 20 pages of the end of the book. Since we know that Father Maurice and Monsignor Fearns are also well along with their reading, I expect that we shall have the release before very long.

Dan Walsh wrote a very fine letter about your book. I have had the pertinent passages copied, and I enclose them. I also enclose the final proof of the contents. I hope you agree that it has come out very well.

With Naomi's permission, Thought magazine, the Fordham University Quarterly, is running chapters 15 and 16 in their Autumn number. This will come out around the time the book is published. Father [William] Lynch [S.J.], the editor, has asked if she would return the proofs by Monday, August 20th. I enclose a return envelope addressed to him.

With all good wishes.

Sincerely yours,
Robert Giroux

AUGUST 11, 1951

Our Lady of Gethsemani
[Letterhead]

Dear Bob:

Thanks for the new page proofs of the biographical notes and front matter. Two small last minute corrections: in the imprimatur Dom Dominique [Nogues] ought to be O.C.S.O. like the censors of the Order. (The last General Chapter made us all uniformly use the initials O.C.S.O.—formerly there had been a choice [O.C.R., Order of Reformed Cistercians].)

And then in the Author's Note, towards the end, if you don't mind, strike out "dear" from my dear friends Dan Walsh, etc. Nothing against Dan, but I got a qualm of conscience about being too effusive with nuns. Just leave it as "my friends . . . etc."

By the way, could you start right away to make arrangements for a specially bound copy for the Holy Father. Another idea—I recently saw a catalog of Danish book bindings and was much taken with them. I thought it might be a nice idea to have a small number of copies of all our books done in some of these nice bindings for presentation purposes, etc. Henrik Park is the binder I am thinking of mostly. If you don't know anything about him, I think someone at the Museum of Modern Art might be able to tell you. Do you like the notion? This would only involve a few dozen books.

With best wishes, as ever: God bless you.

Sincerely in Christ,
Tom
fr. M. Louis /s/

AUGUST 16, 1951

Our Lady of Gethsemani
[Letterhead]

Dear Bob:

The release has come through from our Georgia censor. It depends on one correction, in galley 62. I think this one can be made without too much trouble.

He suggested some other changes and as far as I am concerned the ones enclosed can go through at your convenience. We can at least keep them for a second edition if we don't throw them into this one.

Dan Walsh was down here and left yesterday—after getting up at one o'clock and going through the night office of the Assumption [of Our Lady], etc., with us! It was good to see him. He likes the book all right but is not sure whether Maritain saw the whole thing or not.

Does this make it impossible to have a publication date in September? October 15, the feast of St. Teresa [of Avila], is a good day. So too is Oct. 4th, feast of the Little Flower [St. Thérèse of Lisieux]. Could you send me a set of unbound pages, on which I could start making corrections for the second printing?

With best wishes, as ever—God bless you.

> In Corde Christi,
> Tom
> fr. M. Louis /s/

P.S. Fr. Paul Philippe from Rome, (teaches at the Angelicum) has been here for 3 weeks. Did not have time to go over the ms. He has some interesting material on the interior life—you might like to see some of it. Let me know.

AUGUST 20, 1951

Rev. M. Louis, O.C.S.O.
Abbey of Our Lady of Gethsemani
Trappist, Kentucky

Dear Tom:

The corrections have just arrived, and we are bending every effort to make them in foundry [*sic*], particularly the one on galley 62 (or page 196–97). You may have forgotten that you had already changed the phrases about "biological functions," etc.; your page proofs will indicate the first change. In any event, those lines are being changed again as you indicate.

On page 197, in order to fill out the line, after deleting "and even if they were, we would fail," I had to make the new paragraph begin: "Nevertheless, all the reality that exists, and all the goodness of everything that exists and is good can be," etc. The first "that exists" is new; I hope it's okay—I knew no other way of expanding without changing your meaning.

Likewise, on galley 4, after changing "the truth" to "truth" I had to emend "so far" to "so very far."

We are still trying to keep to September 20 and we will if we can. I'll let you know if it changes.

I am off to England on September 14, to see the London publishers. Hollis & Carter are aiming at publication by Christmas. I'm relaying all your corrections as I get them, but if you prefer them to have a later edition, I suggest that you write Mr. T. F. Burns, their director, to this effect and have Naomi do so. Actually their edition will be in conformity with our final first edition. Anyway I'll be at the Savoy Hotel after September 19, if

I can go to bat in any way. Tom Burns is an excellent man, I think (he's the Burns of Burns, Oates & Washburn too).
    With best wishes.

Ever yours,
Robert Giroux

P.S. I'm glad you saw Dan Walsh; I hope to before I sail.

AUGUST 23, 1951

Rev. M. Louis, O.C.S.O.
Abbey of Our Lady of Gethsemani
Trappist, Kentucky

Dear Tom:
    Some time ago you asked me to inquire about Father Charbel. Perhaps you have the answer by now regarding this French hermit, but if not I was given the name of Rev. T. Lincoln Bouscaren, S.J., at Borgo Santo Spiritu, 5, Rome.[1] He is in charge of the causes for beatification and canonization of Jesuits. Father Charbel doesn't sound like a Jesuit, but this was the only lead I could get, and it might be worth following.

Ever yours,
Robert Giroux

1. See the letter dated March 29, 1951.

AUGUST 30, 1951

Our Lady of Gethsemani
[Letterhead]

Dear Bob:
    Here is Fr. Maurice's nihil obstat. I gather he has already communicated it to you. One correction which I have marked in the letter has to be made in the first edition. It means the deletion of the word "saints" in the passage concerned. Will you please make this correction and return the letter to me? I would like to follow his other suggestions in a later edition.
    I shall write and tell him this and I hope you will mention it in your letter if you have not already written. This now gives us the go signal on the book. Will you please communicate these essential corrections (this one and the one from Fr. Paul in Georgia) to Tom Burns before September 7th?
    I close in haste wishing you a good trip to Europe. I think the book is going to turn out very well but I hope that people will not think it is

supposed to be a best-seller because perhaps the best-seller audience might be disappointed in it—a bit thick for them. Too technical. However, I hope the main errors have been corrected and of course please let me hear any theological reactions. I sent a chapter to be translated in La Vie Spirituelle and another for Dieu Vivant.

God bless you always.

In Corde Christi,
Tom
fr. M. Louis /s/

AUGUST 30, 1951

Rev. M. Louis, O.C.S.O.
Abbey of Our Lady of Gethsemani
Trappist, Kentucky

Dear Tom:

An advance copy of the book has just come from the printer, and I have sent it along under separate cover.

This is a set of sheets for Hollis & Carter. Naomi tells me that she has written you, and them, setting a deadline of September 15 for England. These sheets contain all the corrections I have had from you and from Father M. Maurice Malloy which are going into our second printing. If you add any others you have, and get them off by air mail, they should reach Hollis & Carter in plenty of time. I suggest that you address the package to Mr. T. F. Burns, and mark it "Urgent—Proofs."

When I wrote on August 20 there seemed to a fighting chance to get the last changes into foundry, but I then learned that the sheets were off press. The plates have since been changed, and I'll send you confirmation proofs shortly. If you have further changes you wish to make, let me have them at once.

To whom do you wish to send complimentary advance copies? If you would send us a list of names, we shall mail out the books. Or if you wish to inscribe them personally, let me know how many copies you want. I'm having two copies specially bound, and have written the binder you recommend. I hope you like the looks of the book; it seems to me the most handsome job of book-making I've seen in a long time. And my re-readings of the text convince me more and more that it's your best writing.

Ever yours,
Robert Giroux

P.S. I enclose some comments of Father M. Maurice with the sheets.

Our Lady of Gethsemani
[Letterhead]

Dear Bob:

Thanks for your letter and the sheets which I sent off immediately to London. I did not see the one correction Fr. Maurice thought important and so I presume you have relayed it to Tom Burns from the letter. Please return the letter, when you have finished with it.

Thanks for getting in touch with the Danish binder. About special copies, can you let me have some cards to sign and then I will send them back with a list of addresses. However please also let me have a dozen or so copies as soon as possible to sign and send from here also.

It is a great pity that several thousand copies will be in circulation without the corrections desired by our two censors. This will certainly get me in trouble with them, although the corrections were slight. I am bound, as a matter of obedience, to wait for their corrections to be inserted before anything gets out. I can see that this was a great nuisance to you and that the book had to go on schedule and that you did your best to make the adjustment. Nevertheless, because of my obligation, I simply have to wait on the censors and next time there will be no alternative but to do so. It is just one of the professional hazards of being a monastic writer—because I am only a writer <u>per accidens</u>. The accent is on the word monastic. I am obliged to be a monk, but am in no way obliged to write anything. In order to placate them we ought to insert as many as possible of their corrections in the second edition. You have them all there, I suppose. How about these from Fr. Maurice? I presume they will absolve us from making changes that would throw out the paging. Hope you have a fine trip—may God bless it and all you undertake.

Ever yours in Him.

Tom
fr. M. Louis /s/

Harcourt, Brace & Company, Inc.
[Letterhead]

Rev. M. Louis, O.C.S.O.
Abbey of Our Lady of Gethsemani
Trappist, Kentucky

Dear Tom:

I have rushed through the deletion of "saints" on page 146, and changed it to read "It is possible that there are some contemplatives etc." The first printing got through without this correction, but oddly enough Father Maurice did not mention it in the set of proofs he sent me. I'm sorry if I have caused any difficulty, but doesn't your later phrasing cover the point anyway: "They cannot be saints unless they belong at least invisibly to the Church"?

I return Father Maurice's very interesting letter herewith. I seriously disagree about translating foreign phrasing and "difficult" words in the next edition. If only Father Maurice knew how common the word "ambivalence" is nowadays; too glibly common, I'm afraid. And "ersatz happiness," "oriental notion of Karma," and "Zen Buddhism or Patanjali's Yoga" present no difficulties whatever. Readers who want to explore the latter two are free to, if so inclined, but you have no obligation to explain them in this text. As for "apophatic," you explain it sufficiently on page 17. "Ontologically" and "ascesis" you have used in other writings; there are always dictionaries for intelligent readers. As for the Latin, unless you assume a certain amount of culture in your reader, how can you ever write? Most of the phrases are self-explanatory and sometimes you paraphrase in the next sentence. In the long run, readers will catch up to you. Presenting them with a few verbal problems is actually good. T.S. Eliot has done this throughout his career; the words become his property, like "objective correlative." Isn't this all to the good? As editor and publisher, I strongly advise that you leave them.

I enclose page proofs of the corrections so far made. You may keep these! I'll send page 146 along when ready, and any others that we correct meanwhile for the next printing.

I don't sail until midnight of a week from Thursday, so if you have any last minute instructions, please send them along. I'll be seeing Tom Burns, of course.

I almost forgot. We do have a fine statement (the first to come) from the editor of Thought [William Lynch, S.J.]: Here it is:

> The Ascent to Truth is a very good and very solid book. One thing Thomas Merton has helped us to realize afresh is how much the reaching of the very apex of human liberty and divine contemplation depends on fidelity to reason and concepts, to the human Christ and the Church of men. He helps to dispel any pantheistic or liberal concept of mysticism.

Ever yours,
Bob /s/

SEPTEMBER 10, 1951

Trappist-Cistercian Abbey
[Letterhead]

Dear Bob:

Perhaps there is still time to reach you before Thursday, to wish you a pleasant and profitable trip. But above all I want to say how pleased I am with the ASCENT TO TRUTH which arrived the other day—also with your corrections in the new printing. The new cover, with the blue effect, was a pleasant surprise. The whole job was even better than I was expecting it to be. It is outstandingly well done. Please thank all who contributed to it, from me. I am glad you think it is a solid book—and glad the Jesuits think so. I hope they will all agree with Father Lynch. If that happens it will be a real triumph. Especially if the Dominicans also agree. But I think there will still be many minor points to polish up. Among other things there are three picayune corrections in the jacket blurb. But I feel I ought to suggest them since in fact the blurb has more influence usually than the book itself. First I think we ought to say "the summit of truth is reached in contemplation" instead of "the way to truth is through contemplation" since some truth can be reached without contemplation. Second, it is more correct to say "Mystical contemplation is symbolized by the dark night etc." than "the contemplative way of life is symbolized . . ." because the contemplative way of life covers a lot of ground that the dark night does not cover. Every Trappist leads a contemplative life but not every Trappist has mystical contemplation. Finally there was a correction made in the book, in a sentence quoted in the blurb. It should read "God is never fully known unless He is loved . . ." Can you put these through? Since the reviewers will be so mystified that their revues will simply be copies of the blurb, I think this is really important.

Thanks again, Bob, for all the work you have done on this book. I thoroughly agree with your attitude toward Fr. Maurice's suggestion—translating all Latin tags, explaining all difficult words, etc. However, I did not want to come out on the point flat footed all by myself, but with you behind me I will. It is after all a purely editorial question and you are the one who knows. May God bless your trip.

As ever.

In Corde Christi,
Tom
fr. M. Louis /s/

SEPTEMBER 14, 1951

Rev. M. Louis, O.C.S.O.
Abbey of Our Lady of Gethsemani
Trappist, Kentucky

Dear Tom:

Thanks for your good letter of the 10th. We shall certainly change the jacket, and in fact I have already sent the revisions through. I enclose the changed plates for all the other corrections.

Monsignor Fearns phoned me on Tuesday, to say that he had some suggestions and notes from the reader's report to send on to you "for your consideration." I asked if these were things that "had to be changed." He said no, they were "suggestions which were entirely up to you," and that he was sure that you would want to consider them. I told him that you had already made many changes on the basis of suggestions from the censors in your Order, and on your own initiative. I reminded him that his office had phoned us early in August to say that the book was OK, and he acknowledges this.

What happened, I am inclined to believe, is that the first reader or readers were not fully equipped for the subject. Finally, after their first call, it got into the hands of an expert, or at any rate of someone with pronounced familiarity with mystical theology. When I asked Monsignor Fearns if the suggestions of "omissions" were to be followed, he said again no, they were really "suggestions" and you might not agree. In short, this is an advisory letter. Why they could not have got it to us in August (they were sent to proofs on July 19th), I don't know except that it probably got in this reader's hands much later—after they phoned us originally about going ahead.

I've had a copy made of the reader's report, to help you in case others are consulted. One difficulty: they did not return their set of proofs (censors amaze me with their lackadaisical approach to practical details, and their casual sense of time). Also, these proofs were paged differently from the galleys and from the final pages, so that the numbers in the reader's report are not helpful. But I am sure that you know the text well enough to find the places referred to. Meanwhile, I'm searching for an old proof copy with this paging, and will send it as soon as possible.

Considering all the difficulties in our way, I am amazed that the book has turned out so well. The first reactions are all terrific. Dan Walsh called to say that the book is marvelous.

But I have learned a lesson. Next time we shall get duplicate manuscripts to all the censors; we shall get guarantees that their first reactions are also their last ones; if they want to have second thoughts or "further suggestions" to give us fair warning and we'll hold everything; and so on. Then, only after the manuscript has been OK'd will we set up in type. In the case of the ASCENT TO TRUTH I think it was the seeing of it in type which gave you some of your best thoughts about it for revisions. And surely there are few subjects more subtle than this one. I am certainly amazed at the intensity of the first reactions. The Catholic Book club, headed by Father [Harold] Gardiner, S.J., expects it to be one of their most widely read choices.[1]

Yours,

Robert Giroux

1. By September 25, 1951, 38,000 copies had been sold.

JANUARY 3, 1951 [1952]

Rev. M. Louis, O.C.S.O.
Abbey of Our Lady of Gethsemani
Trappist, Kentucky

Dear Tom:
    I enclose plate proofs of all the pages on which you had corrections. We
are also sending a set to Monsignor Fearns to show him that the changes
have been made for the second edition. And isn't that good news—a second edition, I mean—after a first edition of 45,000 copies? Yes, the new
printing is 10,000 copies and of course I hope that it's only the beginning
of many more.
    Further good news: THE ASCENT TO TRUTH has just been awarded
the Golden Book Award by the Catholic Writers Guild of America. I enclose a copy of the letter from their President, which I hope you will show
to Father Abbot. Needless to say, I shall be on hand for the presentation,
together with Anne Ford and others from Harcourt, Brace. Doubtless
they will hope to have a message from you, as they did on the previous occasion. The other books getting awards are TOTAL EMPIRE by Edmund
Walsh, S.J. and the short stories of Richard Sullivan of [the University of]
Notre Dame.
    This surge of interest in THE ASCENT TO TRUTH, and the recent
number of re-orders, make us feel that the release of BREAD IN THE
WILDERNESS ought to be considered most carefully. We are convinced
that one of the reasons for the success of THE ASCENT despite the
difficulties of its text is that it has the Catholic market almost to itself at
the moment; competition is non-existent. It would be a mistake surely to
have a new Thomas Merton book compete with this one while it is still
going strong.[1] Don't you and Father Abbot agree? Please let us have your
thoughts on this, because we do wish to do what is right, for this book and
for all your work.

                                                    Ever yours,
                                                    Robert Giroux

    1. In a letter dated January 17, 1951, RG proposed to NB that HB henceforth act as the
exclusive American publisher of TM. RG wanted to prevent any confusion if and when TM
made contractual arrangements on his own. A day later, NB emphasized the fact that *Seeds
of Contemplation* succeeded to the extent it did because of the reputation of *The Seven Storey
Mountain*. She urged TM to publish all his works with HB in the future. Ten days later, TM
wrote a long letter to NB, vacillating between ND and HB, thus leaving the dilemma unresolved. Abbot Fox wrote to NB, in a letter dated February 1, 1951, saying that TM would
still like to give ND his future "minor works." He agreed that Garden City Publishing Company and New American Library could still be considered for books that would be reprinted. Discussion of this matter continued for a good while. On June 29, 1951, TM wrote
to NB: "Neither I nor Jay nor Bob nor you want to fight about it and the details of the question are so involved and so picayune that we would not get anywhere by fighting anyway."

RG feared that parts of the *Journal* would be excised by TM and then given to ND to be printed as pamphlets or small books. RG and JL subsequently agreed that HB would publish *The Sign of Jonas* and that ND would publish *Bread in the Wilderness*.

JANUARY 7, 1951 [1952]
Harcourt, Brace & Company, Inc.
[Letterhead]
Rev. M. Louis, O.C.S.O.
Abbey of Our Lady of Gethsemani
Trappist, Kentucky

Dear Tom:
I'm glad that you liked Illustration. It struck me as an unusually good issue, too, and I thought the color photos of the Vence chapel breathtaking. Shall we ever see its like in this country? I believe we shall.

This note is in part to send you some of the reviews of THE ASCENT [TO TRUTH]. Even The New Yorker came through nobly, to my astonishment. I like [John] Wu in Commonweal best. I was annoyed by the Rev. James Pike in the Sunday Times who says that "Pascal fares badly" at your hands; I'd say the opposite. (Incidentally, why they gave it to the Protestant chaplain of Columbia instead of Father [John] Daly or Father [George] Ford, I can only surmise. I wonder if they'd go out of their way to give a book of Protestant doctrine to a Papist?) The other reviews are truly miscellaneous, including the amazing Mr. and Mrs. Field who like everything—Truman Capote, [William] Faulkner and what have you. I hope one of the good quarterlies, like Cross Currents (do you see it? If not I'd like to get you a subscription) or Thought, will do a long serious review. I'll keep you posted.

With regard to your query about the pamphlet, of course we would have no objection to your using the last chapter of THE WATERS OF SILOE in it, as long as credit and copyright notice were included.

The correction on page 88 of ASCENT, suggested by Dan Walsh, leaves us one line short. You gave us the wording: "It arrives at a valid and sure knowledge of God's supreme Being mirrored in His Creation." Can you expand, or add another short sentence? Six or seven words ought to do it.

I'm proceeding with editorial work on the Journal and I promise you that there will be plenty of time in this case. I would like to see the contents and whatever manuscript is available on the other spiritual book project, including "What Is Contemplation?" In fact, I'd also like to see the Saint Aelred manuscript if it can be spared. Has that necessary work yet been published that we were waiting for—the Aelred text, I mean?

Ever yours,
Bob /s/

MARCH 29, 1952

Our Lady of Gethsemani
[Letterhead]

Dear Bob:

Thanks for your card from Cuba which came in this morning. I am happy about the Journal. I do not think you had the whole thing. At any rate, here is an important section that was written since I sent you all that you have. Would you like to go over it and have it typed also, then we can work on the ms.

Here are the things we are going to need:

1) An extra typescript for the censors of the Order. They may want to send it to Rome also; they are getting more fussy. But Father Abbot also wants to go over this carefully. Anyway, if we could have two copies it would be a big help. You keep one. Did you have that many made? If not, one will have to do. I can send both back of course.

2) For the illumination of all concerned at this end—will you please state clearly in a letter I can pass on to them just what your editorial aims are, the thoughts and themes you most desire to see brought out? They are certain to want to cut some of the matter that you like. For my own part there are one or two sections that I would like to keep—I have marked those in this last part.

3) It is possible that we might get a few sketches that I have done and put them in the book. The good ones have been sent all over the place, but we could gather them in. Jay is not using the stuff I did for <u>Bread in the Wilderness</u>.

4) Title: I think at last we should change it to "THE SIGN OF THE PROPHET JONAS" because of one of the last entries, as you will see. I can also write a prologue and an epilogue. I think the book needs a word of explanation perhaps.

5) Along with sketches, maybe a few photographs of Gethsemani? Only God forbid that we should do anything that would attract any more postulants.

6) Do you formally wish me to continue writing this Journal? If so I will try. It is getting to be almost the only thing I can decently write with my other work. However, I'll send you class notes of stuff that may conceivably get written up in the St. Bernard book.

7) How is the <u>Ascent</u> going? I am still waiting for proofs of <u>Bread</u> from Jay so that is shaping up very slowly. It would be well to let him get it out in time to leave a decent interval before the Journal comes out. What date do you have in mind?

It is good to get working on this. In the summer I ought to have more time for it. Right now I am quite pressed, so I stop and try to get this into the mail. God bless you always, hope to hear from you soon. Coming down this summer?

In Christ,
Tom
fr. M. Louis /s/

APRIL 7, 1952

Rev. M. Louis, O.C.S.O.
Abbey of Our Lady of Gethsemani
Trappist, Kentucky

Dear Tom:

I am delighted to have the JOURNAL up to as recently as Saint Patrick's Day. I think the new material, which I read quickly this morning, is excellent, particularly the next to last entry (February 26) on "different levels of depth." I almost think that this should go in as a kind of prologue, similar to the repeated paragraph in THE WATERS OF SILOE.

Altogether I find the JOURNAL magnificent from every point of view— your own good, the good of the Order, the good of the Church, and a good influence on readers—and I think you should continue writing it.

As to the title: I'll admit that I like THE WHALE AND THE IVY, despite objections from two very sympathetic readers that the word "ivy" does not occur in the Bible. It's called "a gourd," and "a caster-oil plant," and in another version "a tree," none of which is as nice as ivy. One of the readers pointed out that an ivy plant could not grow by itself; I retorted that the whole story is hardly naturalistic, but I see what he means. How about THE SIGN OF JONAS? If readers don't know he is a prophet, they'll find out soon enough.

Editorially speaking, there should, I think, be a somewhat different organization of the JOURNAL. It is now divided into years; I would rather see it divided into other categories, such as "Diaconate," "Priesthood," etc.—periods of your life, that is, or some such division. There would not have to be more than three parts. We could use the years decoratively, of course, as running-heads or sub-heads, so that the reader would be fairly certain of the date no matter where he opened the book. Three terrific photographs, one for each of these parts, would be wonderful. I don't mean that they should involve you personally, or indeed the image of any monk, but they could, for example, be photographs of the altar or the Chapter room or the fields or any such image.[1] I think they could be full-page reproductions and reproduced in gravure. Pen-and-ink sketches would be a natural corollary to entries in the JOURNAL, and I should like to see as many of these as you can manage.

Many thanks for the class notes on Cistercian theology. I am fascinated by the outline and I wish I were attending some of your lectures. I think I may be down to visit you in May.

Meanwhile I have sent off to you two copies of the manuscript. Would you consider the original copy as the master copy intended for the printer and make your corrections thereon? The other can be sent off at once to the Censors of the Order. I will of course send on, after it is copied, the new material which arrived this morning. This does, however, remind me that there is one large section that seems to be missing, but perhaps that is intentional. There is nothing whatever for the first part of 1948. That is, page 89 of the new typescript is the last entry for 1947 (December 28), and page 91, the next entry, is for October 15, 1948. Do you want it that way or is it simply that I failed to get a part of the manuscript?

The trip to Cuba was part of my vacation and I had a most wonderful time. It is, as you found it to be long ago, a wonderfully religious country in the very best sense. I hope it did me some good.

With all good wishes.

Yours ever,
Robert Giroux

1. Monks usually met in a Chapter room that was used daily for the second part of Prime and a subsequent talk by the abbot. It was also used to discuss issues concerning the well-being of the monastery.

APRIL 11, 1952

Our Lady of Gethsemani
[Letterhead]

Dear Bob:

Am just mailing to you under separate cover the missing material for 1948. That completes the whole book. There will still be a lot of editorial work at this end. Be sure and send a letter to edify censors with the exact kind of matter you think needs to be given a break in editing [*sic*]. They will want to cut everything that shows life in the monastery as it really is. You can help save a few pieces by stressing the fact that nothing is to be lost + everything gained by this material (written 7 St. Mtn. [*The Seven Storey Mountain*]) and that at least the essence of best descriptive passages should be kept—just softening up language maybe.

Let me know if ms. is delayed in reaching you. Look forward to receiving the ms. from you + getting to work right after Easter.

My best wishes for Easter—I'll have you in my Easter Mass.

In the Risen Christ,
Tom
fr. M. Louis /s/

MAY 16, 1952

Rev. M. Louis, O.C.S.O.
Abbey of Our Lady of Gethsemani
Trappist, Kentucky

Dear Tom:

I am enclosing* with this note a general editorial letter on the JOUR-
NAL, in duplicate copies, so that you can send one of them on to the censor of the manuscript.

I also enclose the very unusual jacket sketch which our Art Director has
designed. As you can see, it's composed around the Jonas title and, the
more I think about it, perhaps that is the right one. The all-seeing eye
above and the suggestion of an ocean wave below make a really striking
pattern. I hope you like it as much as we do. The only criticism I had was
that the proportions should be reversed slightly: the lettering of the title
larger, the symbols smaller.

What do you think of the colors? They strike me as unusual and altogether appropriate. The copy in the blue box at the bottom was written in
by the designer and is by no means final. Nevertheless I rather like it, although the word "experiences" is perhaps not the right one. I am enclosing
a return envelope with this jacket design since we have need of it for our
forthcoming conference. Can you send it back at once? I am also enclosing
a photostat, together with some color swatches, which you can keep.

Have you had any thoughts about a frontispiece illustration? We want
something as good as those in THE WATERS OF SILOE and THE AS-
CENT TO TRUTH.

With all good wishes.

Ever yours,
Robert Giroux

*Sending later.

MAY 20, 1952

Our Lady of Gethsemani
[Letterhead]

Dear Bob:

The cover design is very striking. I like the Old Testament character of
the thing. The ms. is still here; I have gone over it carefully. I am waiting
to write a prologue and epilogue. I have redivided it into more pertinent
sections. At the beginning of each section I plan to write about a page, giving an outline of what happened during that period [when] I was talking
to the Abbot General about the book.[1] He said it must be true—not too

idealistic a picture of the Order, but at the same time nothing that could be twisted around against us. I am hoping to preserve the general trend of the "story."

Meanwhile we have some photographs. The best is the "Old Garden House." We can send you negatives of some of these so that you can get better prints made than we can make here. Here are some I have at hand. Have you any thoughts about the other material I sent in? I still want to get together "What is Meditation," "Balanced life of Prayer" and "What is Contemplation" into a little simple book.[2] Plenty of time. When do you think the Sign of Jonas would be coming out?

Don't forget you are coming down here this summer! God bless you. As ever.

> In Corde Christi,
> Tom
> fr. M. Louis /s/

1. Dom Gabriel Sortais, O.C.S.O., served as abbot general of the Trappist Order from November 13, 1951, until his death on November 13, 1963.
2. This material was never collected into a book. An article called "What Is Medition?" was eventually published in *Sponsa Regis* 31 (February 1960): 80–87. *A Balanced Life of Prayer* was published as a twenty-two-page pamphlet by the abbey in 1951 and reprinted in *The Merton Annual* 8 (1995): 4–21. *What Is Contemplation?* had already been published.

MAY 22, 1952

> Harcourt, Brace & Company, Inc.
> [Letterhead]

Rev. M. Louis, O.C.S.O.
Abbey of Our Lady of Gethsemani
Trappist, Kentucky

Dear Tom:

I am happy to know that you like the cover design for THE SIGN OF JONAS. Some of the photographs you sent are really first-rate, and there are five for which we should very much like to borrow the negatives: the cows going over the hill (I hope that streak down the middle is not in the negative); Old Garden House (by which I assume you mean the lovely wintery shot); the pick and shovel line ([photographer Sergei] Eisenstein might have taken it); and the shot of the monk standing in the woods (is it you?) looking out over the hill.* Unfortunately the photographs of the steeple are too fuzzy, as is the one of the figure seated almost in camouflage by the brookside. But perhaps we can do something with the other five, and to expedite your mailing of the negatives I enclose a stamped return envelope.

I enclose some sample pages. As you can see, we have gone back to the Janson type of "Siloe," and I think it will make a handsome page. We have decided to shift the dateline for each entry from the left-hand margin to the right, so that the reader can begin the copy more or less unimpeded by a caption. As you can see, the artist drew in the big letters for "1947" on the half title page. Now that you are re-dividing the manuscript into more pertinent sections than dates, we shall of course use another design.

I like the idea of a page of outline at the beginning of each section enormously. It amounts to an inspiration, and it might very well provide the one structural device needed to fuse the book more completely into an integrated whole. Have you any duplicate typescripts of these new pages? I am eager to read them just as soon as possible.

My impression about the other material you sent in is that it will make a very effective little book. "What is Meditation?," "The Balanced Life of Prayer," and "What is Contemplation?" are perfectly related and I would like to speak to you about our doing the three of them together in one volume.

I say "speak" since it looks pretty definitely as if I may be able to pay you a visit either the first week in June or right after our sales conference is ended—that is, the week of June 16th. It's probably more realistic to count on the latter date since I expect to be terribly busy up 'til that time. But just as soon as it is definite, I will get in touch with you in the hope that there may be no obstacle at your end to my coming down.

Ever yours,
Bob /s/

*Also the one at the statue of Our Lady.

JUNE 4, 1952

Our Lady of Gethsemani
[Letterhead]

Dear Bob:

Thanks much for your last letter. Here are the negatives, or rather a few of them. Some are different views from those you have seen. Under separate cover I am sending some kodachromes and a whole roll of stuff on the woods, none of which is very good.

I have not yet had a chance to write those little in-between sections for the beginning of each part of the book, nor the prologue. Maybe I can get them done before you come down. Glad you are coming. I will try to get things organized so that we can put all in final shape and line up something for the little book on prayer. I want to do a lot of rewriting on those three pamphlets, but there is no hurry. When you are here I hope to show you some drawings that might go in JONAS. I have some old ones, but would like to do some more.

The Janson type looks just right, and I am appending the new section titles, so that the art man can go ahead designing the various half-title pages.

Looking forward to your visit—with best wishes and prayers. As ever.

In Christ,
Tom
fr. M. Louis /s/

JUNE 6, 1952

Rev. M. Louis, O.C.S.O.
Abbey of Our Lady of Gethsemani
Trappist, Kentucky

Dear Tom:

Many thanks for your letter of June 4th. I am delighted to have the negatives, but I can't find among them the shot which we particularly prefer—that is, the scene in the woods in which a single monk is framed in the left margin of the picture. Presumably it will appear on the roll, but the fact that you say "none of which is very good" makes me doubt this since the still I have in mind is quite good indeed. So if it is not included in the roll, can you possibly get hold of the negative and send it on separately?

The section titles are magnificent, completely appropriate, exactly what I had hoped would turn up, and it pleases me immensely to see that "The Whale and the Ivy" gets in anyway.

I hope that you can get the in-between sections, for the beginning of each part of the book, written before I come down. If you can possibly send me here some of the drawings which might possibly go in JONAS, I could bring down various layouts and proofs of various types of reproduction. If these are done, and if you are free to send them, I wish you would do so now. I am glad you like the Janson type. I think it's right, and I think we shall have a very handsome book.

Dan Walsh is now reading one copy of the manuscript and his early reaction is very favorable indeed. I'll bring down all his comments. My visit begins to look like late June now. Perhaps it might even have to go over until after the Fourth of July. In any event, I'll get there just as soon as I can extricate myself from New York.

Yours,
Robert Giroux

JUNE 10, 1952

Our Lady of Gethsemani
[Letterhead]

Dear Bob:
All the decent drawings I had have been given away—to Clare Luce or to Sister Thérèse. Do you have the latter's address? I also gave away a lot of them to a Brazilian called Alceu Amoroso Lima, who is in Washington somewhere.[1] Here are a few I had lying around—a head of Our Lord and a lot of unidentified spots. Some of these are rather dizzy, and I suppose you want to keep them all more or less on the same level. Anyway, I can give them names if you want me to.

I have signed a few.

Must get this off. I will try to do some others if I get time. With best wishes.

In Christ,
Tom
fr. M. Louis /s/

1. Alceu Amoroso Lima, a Brazilian writer and activist, served as the director of Catholic Action in Brazil.

JUNE 17, 1952

Our Lady of Gethsemani
[Letterhead]

Dear Bob:
I have rewritten the outline for the beginning of Section I, and I have written a prologue for the whole book. If you think they are okay, could you type them? Meanwhile I will go on with the other in-between outlines.

Looking forward to your visit—with best wishes and in haste.

Yours in Christ,
Tom
fr. M. Louis /s/

JUNE 19 [1952]

WESTERN UNION
FATHER LOUIS
ABBEY OF OUR LADY OF GETHSEMANI
TRAPPIST, KENTUCKY

PLAN TO FLY DOWN WEDNESDAY THE TWENTY-FIFTH[,] ARRIVING AROUND TWO O'CLOCK[.] PLEASE WIRE COLLECT IF AGREE-

ABLE TO FATHER ABBOT AND YOU[.] PLAN TO RETURN FRIDAY
AT FOUR[.]

BEST WISHES[,]
BOB GIROUX
HARCOURT[,] BRACE

JUNE 21, 1952

WESTERN UNION
ROBERT GIROUX
HARCOURT BRACE AND CO
383 MADISON AVE NYK

WEDNESDAY FINE EXCEPT FATHER ABBOT AWAY UNTIL JULY
6TH[.] COME ANY WAY UNLESS [YOU] SPECIALLY WISH TO SEE
HIM[.]

MERTON

JUNE 23 [1952]

WESTERN UNION
FATHER LOUIS
ABBEY OF OUR LADY OF GETHSEMANI
TRAPPIST, KENTUCKY

THANKS [FOR YOUR] TELEGRAM[.] WILL COME WEDNESDAY[,]
JULY NINTH INSTEAD IF AGREEABLE DUE [TO] COMPLICATIONS
HERE AND THEN [I] CAN ALSO SEE FATHER ABBOT[.] EPILOG AR-
RIVED TODAY[.] EXCELLENT[.]

GIROUX

JULY 7, 1952

WESTERN UNION
FRATER M LOUIS
ABBEY OF OUR LADY OF GETHSEMANI
TRAPPIST, KENTUCKY

ARRIVING WEDNESDAY AROUND ONE[.] PLEASE WIRE COLLECT
WHETHER OK [FOR] YOU AND FATHER ABBOT[.][1]

BOB GIROUX

1. On July 11, 1952, Abbot Fox sent RG the finished manuscript of *The Sign of Jonas*, which he believed would prepare the way for the reception of *Bread in the Wilderness*, to be published by ND. He also noted that other unfinished manuscripts might be suitable for HB: *St. Aelred; An Introduction to the Bible; Escape From the Nazis; Meditations; St. Bernard of Clairvaux*; and *Cloisters in the Pyrenees*.

JULY 14, 1952

Harcourt, Brace & Company, Inc.
[Letterhead]

Rev. M. Louis, O.C.S.O.
Abbey of Our Lady of Gethsemani
Trappist, Kentucky

Dear Tom:

I had a wild trip back to Louisville with the two secular priests.[1] Since my plane didn't leave until 4:30, they decided to be tourists and stopped first at Lincoln's log cabin, and then Fort Knox, by which time a pile-up on the main road to Louisville sent us on a detour over to the West via Brandenburg and a dinky ferryboat across the Ohio river (which broke down on the trip just prior to ours and was stranded on the other side for forty-five minutes!). In other words, by the time I got to the airport, I felt as if I had already driven to New York and back.

It was a most wonderful visit with you, and I thank you for it. I have a vivid and pleasant recollection of our walk in the woods to the lone house. The upset stomach seems quite unreal now, though it was certainly concrete enough at the time. It was so good to get away from New York and the office and my desk and the telephone and publishing schedules to the Kentucky hills and the quiet of the guest house and the 5:30 risings (which I enjoyed) and seeing you and Father Abbot.

I have just sent off to Dom Gabriel Sortais the duplicate copy of THE SIGN OF JONAS. The Epilogue has been re-typed and on re-reading I am more certain than ever that it is the right ending to the book.

I spoke to Naomi on the telephone this morning. She is still not back at the Curtis Brown office, but I am to have lunch with her this week. There's a rumor in the book trade that New Directions is being sold, but I'm sure that it's false and that it derives from Jay's taking a job with the Ford Foundation.

About the Christmas cards: Tom Humason, our salesman, would like to send out a mailing piece to the 350 Catholic bookstores on our list. He thinks he can get orders for the Christmas cards from all over the country, not only New York, although he pointed out that it's a little late for such orders (apparently most accounts order Christmas cards in February). Father Hilary this morning sent me about fifty "flyers." Will you thank him for his letter and ask him if such a mailing to Catholic bookstores is OK with him—that is, is he sure it will not duplicate any other mailings that might have been sent from the monastery. If it is OK, would he send me 300 additional flyers. Tom Humason tells me that these mailings have always been extremely effective, so warn Father Hilary that he might be inundated by Christmas card orders.

Since I know Dan Walsh would be most interested to see the "firewatch" addition, I am taking the liberty of sending him a copy.[2] Please give my very best regards to Father Abbot and tell him I am sorry not to have said *au revoir* to him in person. And I mean *au revoir*, since I hope to be able to get down again at the earliest opportunity.

Yours ever,
Bob /s/

P.S. I forgot to ask you last week: Can the Archbishop of Louisville give the Imprimatur to THE SIGN OF JONAS? If so, would you like him to, rather than [the Archbishop of] New York? Technically, the book is printed in New Jersey, although published in New York. I raise the point because the Censor Librorum here is very slow, and I am thinking of every means of cutting corners.

P.P.S. Many thanks for those extra pages of the manuscript. I missed them today, and wondered where they had strayed.

I hope the "landscapes" + decorative pieces for Jonas flow from your pen! (I'm ordering an India Ink fountain-pen!) Can we make opening line of Epilogue, "Watchman, what of the night?" [See Isaiah 21:11]. Dan [Walsh?] thinks all Latin should be translated—[it] frightens readers.

---

1. While at Gethsemani, RG assisted TM in putting the finishing touches on his journal, *The Sign of Jonas*. In an undated letter written from the abbey's "Scholasticate," TM mentioned to RG that he was not sure whether, when they last met, he had given RG material about his ordination and the flu epidemic of 1950. TM said that if RG did not have this material, TM would be glad to send it to him.
2. See the letter dated July 21, 1952.

JULY 17, 1952

Our Lady of Gethsemani
[Letterhead]

Dear Bob:

Here is another section preface—for part four. Maybe I can finish the other two tomorrow.

Perhaps we could use as title for the Prologue: "Journey to Nineveh" after all. Unless you want to call it "The Sea-Beast."

In guise of a dedication, could you put somewhere on a page in the front the following:

Gloria tibi Domine
Qui natus es de Virgine.

Let me know what happens when you contact Jay. I have not yet written to the General.

With best wishes, as ever.

In Corde Christi,
Tom
fr. M. Louis /s/

JULY 18, 1952

Our Lady of Gethsemani
[Letterhead]

Dear Bob:

Here are the remaining introductions to the last two parts. I have only written one page for part six. I hope that will do. I am looking forward to proofs. Can you please send me a "reader's set" of galleys for Father Abbot—and for my confessor? I mean just one, for both of them. Now that I have finished these sections, I will get the whole thing off to the censors.

With best wishes and blessings.

In Christ,
Tom
fr. M. Louis /s/

MONDAY [AFTER JULY 18, 1952]

Our Lady of Gethsemani
[Letterhead]

Dear Bob:

Here is the introduction to Part Three. The rest follows in a few days. We are all upside-down with the blessing of new bells. Again, it was fine to have you here and I think the book will be fine. Dan may come down next weekend for Rod Mudge's profession [as a Trappist monk].

Best wishes—and prayers.

Sincerely in Christ,
Tom
fr. M. Louis /s/

JULY 21, 1952

Rev. M. Louis, O.C.S.O.
Abbey of Our Lady of Gethsemani
Trappist, Kentucky

Dear Tom:

The last three introductions to the six parts of Jonas arrived this morning. I think some of your best writing is in these pieces; I couldn't be more delighted with the job you have done, and the success with which they fit into the design of the book. I was deeply moved by the introduction to part five, which is indeed "The Whale and the Ivy." The brevity and economy of the final piece is just right, and the single sentence about citizenship at the end perfectly foreshadows the Fourth of July "firewatch" epilogue to the book. Well done, and many thanks.

The part four piece is, I think, too long and ought to be reduced from six pages. I'd like to see it start on page three with this sentence, "That which is most perfect and most individual in each man's life," etc. right on to the end. The earlier part is wonderful and true, but it's a question of where to cut. Anyway, I am enclosing clean copies of all the new material. If anything seems to need further changing, either let me know now, or fix it on the galleys (which you will be getting very soon).

The manuscript has gone off to the Abbot General without any explanation from us. I hope some mail censor doesn't immediately send it back to the United States for censoring here!

I see Naomi again tomorrow. I think all will be well.

Tell Father Hilary to let me know about the Christmas card mailing. The salesmen may become impatient. It's simply a matter of telling us to go ahead, or not to. If yes, we shall need 300 stuffers. I hope it's yes (and we shall be glad to do it all at our expense); but of course it should not be yes, if Father Hilary has already done a direct mailing to Catholic bookstores around the country. (On second thought, I can't even see very much danger in duplication. If they've seen the stuffer already, they have only to ignore the repetition.) But do let me know.

> Yours ever,
> Robert Giroux

JULY 23, 1952

> Our Lady of Gethsemani
> [Letterhead]

Dear Bob:

Many thanks for your letter.

I was sorry to hear of your hair-raising tour of Kentucky. I sent the ms. off to the censor [in the Trappist monastery] in Georgia, but the epilogue is incomplete. Could I have a carbon of your typescript for him, please?

Still haven't written to Dom Gabriel [Sortais]. Will do so right now, as I have important business on all sides. It might be embarrassing for him to write a letter of introduction. What would you say to a letter by some bigshot American bishop, e.g. Card[inal] Spellman? Or is this just wacky? I think perhaps it is. Don't ask anybody until I get a reaction from Rome.

Yes, I think the firewatch is the right ending. Change the Latin if you wish. One of the censors will almost certainly suggest translating all the Latin into English, or throwing it out altogether. I'd like to keep Latin in the text and put the translation in footnotes.

About the diocesan censor: anything but Louisville, please! They keep books from six to eighteen months. Why not sound out Newark? That is the diocese where Rahway is, isn't it? We have three choices, you know: the printer gives us one. The most cooperative censor I have hit is Milwaukee—where Bruce [Publishing Company] has his impenetrable den and his toe-hold on the hierarchy.

With zeal for religious poverty I write on the other side of this same page. I hope you find it. Fr. Hilary was very pleased at your message and thanks you. I don't know if he wrote and gave you the green light, or if he intends me to do so. In any case the light is green, and many thanks. I am getting up energy for the landscape sketches as soon as the pen arrives. I have thought of many ideas, and would have started already with a pencil if I had not been so busy. Yesterday the district forester was here, praising our planting of seedlings and the progress of the same.

Well, I'll write to the General now.

As ever, with very best wishes.

Yours in Christ,
Tom
fr. M. Louis /s/

P.S. Clare Luce wants galleys of the new book and offered to write a blurb. Maybe that is a good idea, backed by a few other opinions. I can't think of any suggestions except that T. S. Eliot is the one man who is so objective and honest and clear that I would be grateful for anything that came from him, because even if he thought the book was bad, he would say so in a way that would help me—personally I mean.

JULY 29, 1952

Rev. M. Louis, O.C.S.O.
Abbey of Our Lady of Gethsemani
Trappist, Kentucky

Dear Tom:

I am sending, separately, the galley proofs of THE SIGN OF JONAS. There are three sets—one on air mail paper for forwarding to Rome if you decide to do so. The only omission is the prefatory matter to Part I and this will be following shortly.

I think our printer has done an extraordinary job, almost a record-breaking one. I hope you like the looks of the typography as much as I do.

I am sending you another letter about more personal matters. I simply want to thank you for your very moving and wonderful letter.

Yours ever,
Robert Giroux

AUGUST 7, 1952

Gethsemani

Dear Bob:

Here are a few sketches. I haven't had time to really get down to work on them yet and so they are not much good. I only really like one of them. But they will give an idea for layouts. Let me know what to go ahead with. I also enclose a sort of abstract spot. I might be able to do a few of these. Let me know.

As ever.

God bless you,
Tom
fr. M. Louis /s/

AUGUST 11, 1952

Our Lady of Gethsemani
[Letterhead]

Dear Bob:

This is just a note to tell you that the proofs all arrived safely and I have sent them out and around, and have also gone through the main set myself once and am going through it again.

The Abbot General wrote that he received the manuscript and passed it on to a monk who knows English well and is broad-minded and competent to judge. The General has also himself kindly promised the prefatory letter we asked. His intention however is to hand the ms. with his *imprimi potest* and the censor's suggestions to Dom James at the General Chapter in the middle of September. We will therefore have to wait that long before we can advance much further. Perhaps it would be safe to get the book in page proofs as soon as I make the changes undoubtedly to be suggested by the American censors. I am very glad Dom Gabriel will write a prefatory letter.

What is your desire with regard to Latin in the text? I have been unsystematically translating some but not all of it into English footnotes.

Censors may have something to say too—one had an editorial opinion of his own on the point, in the Ascent to Truth.
    With best wishes—as ever.

In Jesus.
Tom
fr. M. Louis /s/

AUGUST 15, 1952

Rev. M. Louis, O.C.S.O.
Abbey of Our Lady of Gethsemani
Trappist, Kentucky

Dear Tom:
    I had a wonderful lunch with Jay Laughlin today, and all is well. He is agreeable to THE SIGN OF JONAS coming out first, and in fact sees the wisdom of it and indeed the advantage thereby for BREAD IN THE WILDERNESS. I gave him a copy of Father Abbot's letter (the one of July 11th you gave me, listing all the future books), to avoid misunderstanding. I met him at his sumptuous air-conditioned, thickly-carpeted office at the Ford Foundation; he has the sleekest, most expensive dictaphone ($750) I have ever seen, and he was rightly sheepish about all the decor. What a far cry from New Directions! He's flying to India for the Foundation, to do an anthology of Indian writers. It occurred to me that the anthology could be done without his leaving New York, but it seemed mean to say so. Anyway I am delighted that he took the publishing program in good spirit since, as you know, I was very much concerned about his attitude.
    I have just spoken to Naomi and to Dan about my lunch with Jay, and they are both happy that he concurs.
    Many thanks for your letter of August 11th about the galleys. Now that the road is clear with Jay, we want to proceed as fast as possible and publish in early October. Since the book is being printed at Country Life Press in Garden City, the censor librorum of the Brooklyn diocese will read it and the imprimatur of Bishop [Thomas E.] Molloy will be used. I've already spoken to the diocesan censor, Father [Thomas W.] Smiddy, S. T. D., and he was very pleasant and helpful and, I feel certain, will expedite matters.
    How wonderful of Dom Gabriel to write a prefatory letter! I'm for this one thousand percent and I sincerely hope it comes through.
    Proof schedule. Can you get the corrected galleys back to me before August 29th? I'd very much like to return them to the printer for paging before I go off to Canada (Carmen [RG's fiancée] and I will be at Murray Bay until September 15th). Don't you think it would be safe now to go into pages?

I'm delighted that the Abbot General has already passed the proofs on to a monk who knows English well. Now that it's being read in Rome, and by the Censors here, there ought to be few snags left. As a lay reader, it strikes me as a wonderful tribute to the Cistercian way of life, a book that will do good for the Order, and for its readers. I am more convinced than ever that Dan is right in saying that this is your best book. I'm more pleased than I can tell you about the Fourth of July ending; it's absolutely right.

About Latin, I don't see why we have to be exhaustive in translating all of it. The more difficult, yes, but one of the readers here was astonished at her ability to figure out the Latin, and I think it's somewhat condescending to render every phrase into English. Dan disagrees, however, and thinks all the Latin should be rendered in footnotes. Some readers, he feels, will think that something is being withheld from them. It will be all right with me if you follow your present plan, or decide to translate every word.

My present state of happiness about my forthcoming marriage, and Reverend Father's solemnization of it, is beyond the power of words. Carmen and I are sending you an invitation as a symbol of our oneness with you. You will be there in spirit on August 30th, in our thoughts and in our prayers.

Ever yours,
Robert Giroux

AUGUST 27, 1952

Rev. M. Louis, O.C.S.O.
Abbey of Our Lady of Gethsemani
Trappist, Kentucky

Dear Tom:
This has been the most productive day for THE SIGN OF JONAS. Your proofs arrived this morning, and while I haven't yet gone through all of them I expect to have done so before leaving the office. Second, I have just had a telephone call from Monsignor [John J.] Heneghan, Censor Librorum for the Brooklyn diocese. He has told me that everything is in order and that there are only five or so major points that he wishes to take up with you, and that he is doing so by letter today. I tried to find out what the probable corrections would be so that I could get them into the galley proofs, but I had no luck, and of course propriety requires him to communicate with you first. But if you would rush them here at once, Miss [Lavania] Jones will see that they are incorporated in the galley proofs during my absence.[1]

Incidentally, I sent the Brooklyn censor a set of specially bound proofs which has different pagination from our galleys. Could you possibly correlate the corrections with a duplicate set of galleys so that Miss Jones will know where to make the corrections?

As for the drawings, we have not quite worked out the problem, and at the moment it looks as if we will not include any at all. I think you are right about the crucifixions, which don't really develop the text. The sketches of the steeple and the water tower do; they are part of the landscape, but the trouble is that being very much alike we can't use more than one or two, and I don't think that would be enough. So unless you can find time to do more "landscape" sketches, I think we shall have to forget about illustrations. The endpapers in the jacket will be decoration enough. In any event I think your two drawings in the Clare Luce book have come out beautifully—the John of the Cross and Thérèse of Lisieux.[2]

Half of Cuba arrived yesterday for the wedding. There are enough Consuelos and Juanitas and José Marias and Conchitas to people a Spanish novel. I can hardly wait for Friday afternoon to greet Father Abbot at the Westchester airport. I have met Mrs. [Ann] Skakel, a wonderful person whose style is definitely operatic and who even resembles [opera singer] Helen Traubel.[3] She has a beautifully bound collection of your works and the marvelous library of Catholic books.

I can't tell you how grateful Carmen and I are for your wedding present of your Mass this Saturday.

Ever yours,

[Robert Giroux]

1. In a set of four letters dated August 30th to September 12th, 1952, Miss Jones and TM discussed revisions contributed by an unnamed theologian and one of the censors of the order. TM had hoped to send the revisions in time for the page proofs though he was too late for the new galleys. Monsignor Heneghan sent Miss Jones the required imprimatur. TM also requested that the kodachromes he supplied to RG be sent back.

2. *Saints for Now*, ed. Clare Boothe Luce (New York: Sheed & Ward, 1952).

3. Ann Skakel was the mother of Ethel Skakel Kennedy, wife of Robert F. Kennedy. Skakel, who corresponded with TM, died in a plane crash in 1955 along with her husband. Daniel Walsh was godfather to Kathleen Kennedy. The Skakel family were longtime benefactors to Gethsemani.

[LATE AUGUST 1952]

WESTERN UNION
REVEREND M LOUIS
ABBEY OF OUR LADY OF GETHSEMANI
TRAPPIST, KENTUCKY

[I] MUST HAVE [THE] MANUSCRIPT [OF THE SIGN OF] JONAS IN ADDITION TO PROOFS RECEIVED[.] MY LETTER MAILED YESTERDAY[.] REMEMBER ME SATURDAY[.][1]

BOB GIROUX

1. Abbot Fox presided on August 30, 1952, at the marriage of RG and Carmen Natica de Arango, the daughter of Cuban aristocrat Don Francisco de Arango, third Marquis de la Gratitud, and his wife, the former Doña Petronila del Valle. After the death of her sister, Doña Mercedes, the fourth Marquise, Doña Carmen became the fifth Marquise de la Gratitud. RG at times spoke to me about his marriage and the canonical dissolution of this marriage in October 1968 and his divorce a year later.

SEPTEMBER 18 [1952]

WESTERN UNION
FATHER LOUIS
ABBEY OF OUR LADY OF GETHSEMANI
TRAPPIST, KENTUCKY

MOST URGENT[.] WE RECEIVED ADDITIONAL CORRECTIONS OF FATHER MAURICE [MALLOY] FOR SIGN OF JONAS[.][1] JUST HAD LETTER FROM FATHER JAMES [FOX] INDICATING [THAT THE] ABBOT GENERAL'S APPROVAL [IS] COMING SOON[.] DELIGHTED IMPRIMATUR GRANTED BY BISHOP OF BROOKLYN[.] CAN YOU WIRE COLLECT WHEN FATHER MAURICE'S CHANGES WILL BE SENT[?] PAGES COMPLETED AND [WE ARE] HOLDING PRICES[.] MEANWHILE [WE ARE WAITING] FOR [THE] FINAL PLATE CHANGES[.]

LOVE[,]
BOB GIROUX

1. Father Malloy's one page of comments, dated September 5, 1952, contains no substantive negative criticisms; in fact, Father Malloy notes that he "found great beauty and edification in the journal as a whole."

SEPTEMBER 19, 1952

WESTERN UNION
ROBERT GIROUX
CARE HARCOURT BRACE INC.
383 MADISON AVE

CENSOR DENIED NIHIL OBSTAT[.] DEMANDING CHANGES BUT SENT A REPORT TO ABBOT IN FRANCE[.] CONSEQUENTLY DON'T KNOW WHAT CHANGES [ARE] ESSENTIAL [OR] WHAT [ARE] OPTIONAL[.] CENSOR [IS] IN HOSPITAL[.] HAVE GALLEYS HERE[.] WILL SEND SOME CHANGES QUICK[.] MUST WAIT [TO] CONSULT CENSOR[.] FOR OTHER DELAY[,] ABOUT 10 DAYS[.] SORRY[.]

MERTON

SEPTEMBER 19, 1952

Our Lady of Gethsemani
[Letterhead]

Dear Bob:

Today's wire contained all the essentials about Fr. Maurice, who is in the hospital, while his letter has gone to Dom James in France. I'm enclosing the galleys containing the changes which I am accepting without having to ask him what he means. At the same time, I am returning to him a number of galleys, some of which contain vague marks referring to his notes which I do not have. The chief thing about his censorship is that he has taken upon himself the task of completely re-editing some of the most important parts of the book. For instance, he practically demands the deletion of Galleys 77, 78, 97 and 100, as well as the story about the hunters on the enclosure wall and the jeep and the junk wagon dream. His remarks on galleys 77, 78, etc. amount to the fact that he finds them "incomprehensible" and that they will not appeal to "my readers." His judgments do not bear at all on faith or morals and are purely literary. I have returned these galleys to him, asking precisely what he objects to and what I am to do to obtain a nihil obstat. Incidentally, another galley he has marked, apparently for the flames, is my first meeting with J. [Laughlin]. Also he demands punctuation of a quote from Eliot's "Four Quartets." I send you one galley I have deleted for him. That can go, it is not important, and I have assured him that 107 and 108 are just about all gone. You can make these changes then, and wait and pray. I have told him he can wire you the nihil obstat collect—if he has no more changes to make than these I send you. Otherwise he is to send his changes back to me and I will pass them on to you. Thanks for your card from Canada. Everything sounds swell. Dan sent me the clipping from the Times with Carmen's picture and I congratulate you again! God bless you both. I keep you in my Mass.

As ever.

In Christ,
Tom
fr. M. Louis /s/

SEPTEMBER 25, 1952

Rev. M. Louis, O.C.S.O.
Abbey of Our Lady of Gethsemani
Trappist, Kentucky

Dear Tom:

Father Maurice sent in his Nihil Obstat this morning by telegram.[1] Needless to say, I was very much relieved to hear from him. We have started to make the corrections he suggests, but for the life of me I can't understand why he wants most of them made. I am therefore consulting with Father James on his return next Tuesday, and I will let you know what develops.

Meanwhile, as the enclosed cable indicates, and as you have doubtless heard from the Father Abbot himself, a real bombshell has been dropped on us. The Superior of an English monastery, who has read the manuscript for the Abbot General, apparently takes the position that the diary form is not appropriate. If this position is upheld, there can of course be no book called THE SIGN OF JONAS.[2] My private opinion is that the position is extremely untenable, and I can only hope that the Abbot General reconsiders the whole matter. Anyway, I at once consulted Dan Walsh and Naomi Burton, both of whom were stunned by the news, as indeed all of us here at Harcourt, Brace have been. Considering the wonderful reaction on the part of the book clubs, the granting of the Imprimatur by the Archbishop of the Brooklyn Diocese, and the extraordinary response we have already received from bookstores across the country, I really think a less unilateral consideration might be given to the problem.

Meanwhile we shall hope and pray. In any event, Dan and I hope to be seeing Father Abbot on his arrival here and I shall be in touch with you soon thereafter.

Devotedly yours,
Robert Giroux

1. After spending twelve days in the hospital for cancer surgery, Father Malloy wrote to TM, saying that he noted a levity in TM and a preoccupation with worldly affairs, such as dealing with literary people, that ill befit a Trappist monk. He counseled TM to give a "genuine picture of Cistercian life as it is lived today." He asked TM's forgiveness for delaying the publication of his book (see also letter dated September 26, 1952).

2. In a letter dated September 21, 1952, Abbot Fox informed RG that the abbot general had several abbots read the typescript and they all concurred that the book should not be published. In a letter to TM dated October 6, 1952, NB noted that Monsignor Fearns raised a number of points about *Bread in the Wilderness* that he wanted answered.

SEPTEMBER 26, 1952

Our Lady of Gethsemani
[Letterhead]

Dear Bob:

I am afraid there is very bad news from the censor's end of things—in the Order. It is my fault for having let you go ahead and set the book up, but it looks as if the <u>whole thing</u> is condemned! I never in the world expected that bad a reaction. This is the combined effect of the censor in New Mexico—I send you a copy of his report which finally reached me!—but above all of the censor chosen by the General, who is Prior of a monastery over there. The latter holds that the book would ruin me. Another Abbot was called in to read the ms. and agreed that it should not be published as now stands. So much I gather from a practically illegible note of Father Abbot. All I can gather of hope is the suggestion of one of these European readers. Quote: "He spoke so highly of some of the spiritual passages. He suggested to save the beautiful passages and recast the book in some form other than diary form." From this I think we could point out that the book has been heavily advertised as a Journal and keep the diary form and—then cut. I am expecting letters of the European Censor and the General. After that, I will let you know. Dom James, of course, has to agree with what they say.

Bob, I am sorry I let you go ahead and set the book up. I ought to have said no, because the thing was by no means as certain as I hoped. Still, since they do not reject the whole book as such, and permit the essence of it to be retained, the job is not all wasted. We can hope for something.

Forgive me for all this trouble, Bob. I am terribly sorry to have got you into a mess. We will have to foot the bill, of course. I had better go on bread and water for a while. And hide in a cave. What could be better?

God love you, Bob. I am sorry.

> Devotedly in Christ,
> Tom
> fr. M. Louis /s/

SEPTEMBER 30, 1952

> Our Lady of Gethsemani
> [Letterhead]

Dear Bob:

Thanks for your letter and for the copy of the telegram. I am glad you had all the information. Today you should be seeing Dom James. I doubt if your wire reached him at Citeaux. Anyway, you will arrive at some sort of a decision. Meanwhile, unless you have agreed to drop the whole thing (which I hope you have not!) and unless some better plan has been arranged, I suggest that you write personally to the Abbot General with the following information.

1—Tell him how much the book is being expected and ordered already. Also what book clubs have accepted it and what that means. How much the book has been publicized. What is being said about it and so forth—more or less as in your telegram. It might require a little explanation to show him what this all means.

2—Suggest that the effect of a complete withdrawal of the book will cause consternation as well as bring the Order into a bad light, apart from whatever other effects it may have.

3—Tell him that you went ahead with all this on the understanding that a Journal as such would not be considered unacceptable for publication, but expecting only to make changes within the framework of the Journal itself—which you have already been willing to do from the beginning.

I think if he sees that you are not merely working to protect a <u>hope</u>, a <u>projected</u> book, but a thing that has already been accomplished and practically speaking accepted by the public before publication, and that the present step would be just the same as withdrawing a published book from circulation, I think he will understand the various angles. I myself will meanwhile write to him with emphasis on what is more pertinent to our end, relying on you to give him above all the material details of pre-publication sales and promotion, etc., as well as the sentiments of well-established Catholic critics in this country. I am writing him without waiting for his letter because he may take his time, and delay would be undesirable. I think you are right in offering to withhold foreign rights as a means of meeting the objections raised against the book by the Prior of Caldey [in Wales].[1] I think this is a good idea, and will also mention it. You should mention it too, I think.

Meanwhile, I'll get busy on my letter to him. You know his address—Reverendissime Dom M. Gabriel Sortais, O.C.S.O., Piazza S[an]ta Prisca 12, Aventino, Rome. He is very reasonable and understanding, and whatever his decision is, of course, I have to abide by it in obedience. We are therefore in the position of having to accept his final decision as the will of God for the book and for us. But I think also the points we are bringing out—I feel obliged in conscience to bring them out—also throw some light on what God's will is in the present case. Again, Bob, I am very sorry for having got you into such a predicament. In the future, we will simply have to go very slow, get everything censored in manuscript, and not launch any publicity or go into print until <u>everything</u> is okay. You might tell him you understand that, too. I will. There is no other way.

God bless you, Bob. All this is ultimately for the best. If we get the green light, I'll be looking for the criticisms of the Prior of Caldey and will either send them straight to you or make the cuts here—assuming there may be places where changes are only suggested in a broad way. It might make matters simpler if you sent me a set of page proofs that I could have on hand for the purpose—or for the archives in case everything falls through.

As ever.

In Corde Christi,
Tom
fr. M. Louis, O.C.S.O. /s/

1. Dom Albert Derzelle, O.C.S.O.

Harcourt, Brace & Company, Inc.
[Letterhead]

Rev. M. Louis, O.C.S.O.
Abbey of Our Lady of Gethsemani
Trappist, Kentucky

Dear Tom:

I had a long talk with Father Abbot last night about THE SIGN OF JONAS and the situation, as I understand it at this moment, is as follows:

The Abbot General, Dom Gabriel Sortais, withheld his Imprimi Potest in part due to the fact that two of the censors, Father Maurice Malloy and Dom Albert [Derzelle] of Caldey, withheld their Nihil Obstats. The third censor, an American I take it, had presumably granted his Nihil Obstat. This, at least, was the situation when Reverend Father [Fox] left Citeaux.

In the meantime, Father Maurice Malloy has granted his Nihil Obstat on the understanding that all his suggested changes that you sent us be made. We shall, of course, make all these changes. The granting of his Nihil Obstat therefore changes the vote from two against and one for to one against and two for.

Reverend Father has therefore agreed to the following course of action: I am to write to him requesting that he pass on to Dom Albert my petition for a reconsideration of his Nihil Obstat. If he does, in the end, grant it, Reverend Father will then ask the Abbot General on this basis to reconsider the granting of his Imprimi Potest.

I am now getting up this first petition for Dom Albert. Considering the fact that he is a Belgian, that he is most concerned with your European reputation, and that he was influenced in part by what he referred to as poor reviews by the Dominicans of THE ASCENT TO TRUTH, you could not possibly have a more powerful friend in court than Jacques Maritain. As it happens, I saw Maritain with Dan Walsh a few evenings before I saw Father Abbot. His praise of THE ASCENT TO TRUTH was unstinted, and his interest in THE SIGN OF JONAS, and his conviction that its publication would do great good was very pronounced, and he asked if he personally could do anything to forward its publication. He is an internationally known philosopher, he is a Thomist, and he is a European. If he thinks THE SIGN OF JONAS is as publishable as I think it is, surely Dom Albert ought to think so too—at least if his grounds for objecting to it are what I understand them to be. Since talking to Reverend Father, I have spoken to Maritain on the telephone. He said he was astonished that THE ASCENT TO TRUTH was adversely reviewed in England. He personally has read many favorable reviews (as, indeed, I have). I suppose the difference between Maritain and other "professional" philosophers is that he is also an artist. Interestingly enough, he also said on the telephone that the objection to THE SIGN OF JONAS because it is in diary form is "fantastic." In any event, as he put it, this involves an aesthetic judgment, and it's an erroneous judgment.

The final proofs, with all of Father Maurice's deletions, have now gone off to Maritain and he has promised to send me a long and frank report on the book.[1] I have asked him to write this in French, so that it can be forwarded directly to Dom Albert and perhaps to Dom Gabriel.

Father Abbot also acknowledged that since the main objection to THE SIGN OF JONAS is the effect it would have on your European reputation, perhaps petitioning for its release only in the United States would be in order. In any event, I hope we can convince Dom Albert that the matter is wholly worthy of his reconsideration and that there is already a great deal of evidence—from Catholic bookstores, from three Catholic book clubs, from the censors of the Diocese of Brooklyn, and so on—that it is a book which will do a great deal of good for the Catholic and non-Catholic reading public, and also for your reputation as a writer.

Needless to say, this delay has been a great blow to me, but I understand why it has occurred and maybe in the long run it is a good thing. It certainly cannot help increasing advance interest in the book to have it postponed a little longer. It will also be a real test of its true worth to gather all these testimonies for Dom Albert and the Abbot General. One thing I have learned; henceforth we shall release your manuscripts for galleys only <u>after</u> the <u>Imprimi Potest</u> has been granted.

I shall be in touch with you just as soon as I hear from Jacques Maritain. With all good wishes.

Yours devotedly,
Bob /s/

1. RG wrote to Jacques Maritain, in a letter dated October 3, 1952, explaining Dom Albert's objections to the book and asking for a letter of endorsement (in French) from Maritain, which he wrote (four typed pages, double spaced, on October 12, 1952). It reads in part: "Ce que je pense de ce livre? C'est bien simple: il y a peu de livres dans la littérature contemporaine que me touchent aussi profondément. C'est une œuvre d'une qualité rare et supérieure qui prend place, comme <u>The Seven Storey Mountain</u>, parmi les témoignages les plus significatifs du grand mouvement de renouveau spiritual qui répond, j'en suis persuadé, à un dessin de la providence du Dieu sur ce pays." ("What do I think of this book? It's quite simple: there are few books in contemporary literature that touch me so deeply. It is a work of exceptional and superior quality, which takes its place, like *The Seven Storey Mountain*, among the most significant testimonies of the great movement of spiritual renewal that corresponds, I am sure, to a plan of God's providence for this country" [translation by PS]).

OCTOBER 21, 1952

Our Lady of Gethsemani
[Letterhead]

Dear Bob:

Father Abbot just told me of your wire, and that Dom Albert had withdrawn his objections to the book. It remains to be seen whether this means the <u>General</u> has withdrawn <u>his</u> objections. Please don't rush, Bob, until we hear from the General.

Meanwhile, I have been holding this here. Fr. Maurice in New Mexico wired "no further changes" but actually in granting the nihil obstat he does demand three changes. I send one of them on galley 18. I think the one on Galley 32 ("unarmed" instead of "naked") is already made. The third I beg you to look up and make—it means cutting all reference to the frying and eating of fish.* I enclose Fr. Maurice's letter so that you can see what is involved. These changes have to be made, or else. But there is not much to them. I had, of course, written to the General and Dom Albert promising to make changes if they asked any such. They still might, so we must be cautious. If we get the General thinking that we are a bunch of rebels, there will be absolutely no hope for any cooperation from him in the future. And in any case, Bob, I have no intention of doing anything that is not precisely according to his mind and his ideas, since my profession will not allow me to do so. I am still waiting to find out just <u>what</u> [is on] his mind and [what] his ideas are, on this point. Perhaps Dom Albert's withdrawal of his objections may have been the result of a communication from the General. My letter ought to have reached the General in Asia by this time.

I hope you have been holding up all right. This business has been rather rough on all of us, I suppose. It will certainly teach me to watch my step in the future. We cannot hurry these things. Incidentally, new legislation of the General Chapter demands that books be passed by all the censors of the Order and receive the imprimi potest from the General, in the future, <u>in manuscript</u>, before they are even submitted to a publisher. This was not aimed at Jonas, since the legislation was planned before the issue arose. But it is certainly concerned partly with the American Cistercian authors!

I have been a little under the weather down here, not because of the book: that is only one of my troubles and probably the least. One of my best scholastics [Trappist monks to whom TM gave spiritual direction] cracked up on me at the beginning of the month and has had to go home. I have been getting little or no sleep some nights, and at the root of the whole business is a terrific, obscure conflict about that old problem of solitude, etc., which God alone understands. One thing is [be]coming clear, I have to live much more simply and more radically, cut down on the multiple activities, stop pouring myself out, live very much in silence and humility and interior poverty. That is the only condition which will make any future books possible as far as I can see: but I am not adopting this course for the sake of writing, but for my own sake. If I don't live to <u>a great extent</u> alone with God and in silence, everything is going to fall through very soon. Father Abbot is willing to take off a lot of the pressure down here, but there is still necessarily a lot to be done with the scholastics. What gets me most is giving classes and conferences, for some reason—plus the noise and tension here, with the building program and crowding, etc. On the other hand, if I keep the right tempo, books will come along without strain and without any special hardship and they may even be good books for a change. It will mean, right now, a period of silence until I get myself together.

However, I hope and pray that Jonas is at last going through. The blood we have sweated in the process will certainly do something to make up for any spiritual deficiencies the book may have. I do think there is a solid core of spiritual value in the thing, and still cling to my principle of not writing a professional "spiritual journal." I think the distinction our good censors have not made is between obvious and blatant and forced "edification" and the edification that cannot help coming from a simple and sincere and unpretentious statement of what the monastic life is really like. I am willing to admit, however, that in writing more like a writer than like a monk, I have put in some things that the Order would prefer to have out. If that is so, the passages can be sacrificed. They are by no means important and they all deal with trivialities. In fact, that is precisely the issue. What is and what is not trivial? To me, nothing in the monastic life is trivial—and yet, from another point of view, <u>everything</u> in it is trivial. I hope they will leave us just a little of our original point of view, and the book will be what it was meant to be. Let's keep praying for that. For the rest, I am now convinced that Our Lord is going to use the book for something terrific, although we may never see it. I think it will probably be attacked and discussed just as much after publication as before. Strange that trivialities should cause such a commotion.

Please tell Dan that everything is going all right. Both of you keep praying for me, as I also remember you always, and in my Mass. God bless you, Bob. Sorry the book turned [out] to be such a wild wedding present.

Ever yours in Christ,
Tom
fr. M. Louis /s/

P.S. When I say silence, I do not mean we cannot put together the little books of "Notes" and the "Grammar of Prayer"—but give me time.

*This occurs around <u>December 21, 1948</u>.

OCTOBER 29, 1952

Our Lady of Gethsemani
[Letterhead]

Dear Bob:

At long last a letter has arrived from our Most Reverend Father General in Tokyo. My letter did not reach him until he got to Hong Kong. He has considered the whole situation and has decided that the <u>Sign of Jonas</u> can be published and he grants his <u>imprimi potest</u> for this publication. We must, however, make the corrections of Fr. Maurice and Dom Albert. The former have already been made, I take it. I do not know what Dom Albert wants of us, but as soon as you can find out what his corrections are— make them, or let me make them if they require the author's intervention.

It is with great relief that I see the end of this affair. The delay has not harmed the book, I feel sure, although it may have given us a few sleepless nights. So much the better. The General's letter was admirable, and I am very sorry to have upset him. His kindness will be sufficient guarantee that I will be more prudent in the future. In any case, the General Chapter has come out with a lot of new regulations that will make us watch our step.

He refers to moves that were made in England on behalf of the book. I have been completely in the dark as to what has been going on. What happened? In any case, he indicates that his letter to me covers all the letters to him from various quarters. His grant of the imprimi potest, I take it, is sufficient answer.

The general impression I get is that he wants the books of his monks to appear with a sedate slowness and without great noise. I am sure that any writing I do in the future is going to be with a soft pedal on it!

Will you please change the dedication of the book to read: "Beatissi-mae Virgini Mariae Dolorosae." Sorry to make another change, but I promised Our Lady of Sorrows that, if the book went through. You won't mind. When do you expect to publish the book now?

By the way, I promised this Dr. [Lawrence Sidney] Thompson of the U[niversity] of Kentucky Library that I would ask you again to lend him the ms. of the Ascent for an exhibit there, and also any material you may have on Jonas. I mean material that will make a peaceful exhibit. The censor's correspondence would certainly make a lively one!

With all good wishes and prayers. God bless you Bob. Again, forgive me for letting things get out of hand. I ought to have used my head.

Sincerely, as ever.

> In Christ,
> Tom
> fr. M. Louis /s/

OCTOBER 30, 1952

WESTERN UNION
ROBERT GIROUX
CARE HARCOURT BRACE CO
383 MADISON AVENUE

[ABBOT] GENERAL PERMITS PUBLICATION [OF] JONAS. INCLUDE DOM ALBERT[']S CORRECTION. THANK GOD[.]

> FATHER LOUIS
> TRAPPIST, KY

OCTOBER 30 [1952]

WESTERN UNION
REVEREND M LOUIS
ABBEY OF OUR LADY OF GETHSEMANI
TRAPPIST, KENTUCKY

DEO GRATIAS [THANK GOD]. WHAT IS DOM ALBERT'S CORREC-
TION[?] PLEASE WIRE COLLECT[.]

BOB

OCTOBER 31, 1952

WESTERN UNION
ROBERT GIROUX
HARCOURT BRACE AND CO
383 MADISON AVE

DON[']T KNOW CORRECTIONS[.] BETTER CABLE DOM ALBERT[.]

FATHER LOUIS
TRAPPIST, KY

NOVEMBER 3, 1952

Rev. M. Louis, O.C.S.O.
Abbey of Our Lady of Gethsemani
Trappist, Kentucky

Dear Tom:

I was ready to answer your letter of October 21st when the wire arrived with the news that the General had granted permission for the publication of THE SIGN OF JONAS. Needless to say, I am greatly relieved and very happy.

When do we expect to publish? That, of course, depends on the nature of Dom Albert's corrections, if any. Naomi cabled to Tom Burns on Friday, but he probably didn't get in touch with Dom Albert until today. I am hoping that he won't have many corrections. As I understood it, his chief objection was to the <u>diary</u> form. Surely he can't expect us to change that, at this stage, and in view of the General's <u>Imprimi Potest</u>?

The English story <u>is</u> somewhat mysterious. On October 15th or thereabouts, Father Bruno Scott James wrote Tom Burns as follows: "I am almost sure that the Prior of Caldey is prepared to reverse his judgment on THE SIGN OF JONAS, or rather to withdraw his opposition." The next day there came a telegram to Burns which said: "Prior of Caldey has written to Abbot General to revoke decision and advise publication." On the basis of all this, I rather think there will be no further corrections from England. I do hope that cable comes soon, however, since meanwhile we are holding up the corrections of Father Maurice [which are] already in hand for fear that Dom Albert's might duplicate or supercede.

Is this now the correct way to list the censors:

"Ex Parte Ordinis
Nihil Obstat: Fr. M. Maurice, O.C.S.O., Dom M. Albert, O.C.S.O.
Imprimi Potest: Dom M. Gabriel Sortais, O.C.S.O., Abbot General"

Please wire collect either your OK or emendations, if any.

The new dedication, to Our Lady of Sorrows, is of course made. Also the three final corrections that Father Maurice had in mind, except that on the third, because of space difficulties, I had to hedge somewhat. I did take out the reference to frying and eating of fish, but I left in the reference to the stove and referred to cooked food (when you have macaroni it is, I trust, cooked), so as not to leave a hole in the page.

Maritain's reading, aside from the blessing of his wonderful letter, also found some French typos, accents and such. These changes have also been made.

So all in all the waiting has been very much to the good. Please tell Father Abbot that I have learned a great deal from this experience and we shall not be so hasty in the future. Please thank him for his great patience and tell him I am delighted to know that Maritain's letter has been forwarded to Dom Gabriel. Also, I spoke with Dan Walsh on the phone, and he is delighted with the latest news and said he knew it would all work out well.

With all good wishes.

Devotedly yours,
Robert Giroux

P.S. The manuscript of THE ASCENT TO TRUTH is going to Dr. Thompson of the University of Kentucky. Sorry this was not taken care of sooner. We are also sending him some samplers of THE SIGN OF JONAS and copies of the jacket, and one of the posters. I agree, none of the JONAS correspondence.

NOVEMBER 6, 1952

WESTERN UNION
ROBERT GIROUX
HARCOURT BRACE AND CO
383 MADISON AVE NYK

NIHIL OBSTAT SHOULD READ EXACTLY AS IN ["]ASCENT TO TRUTH["] PLUS FATHER M[.] ALBERT DERZELLES[,] OCSO STOP IMPRIMI POTEST[:] FATHER M[.] GABRIEL [*sic*] NOGUES[,] OCSO[.]

FATHER LEWIS MERTON [*sic*]

NIHIL OBSTAT OCSO[:] IMPRIMI POTEST NOGUES[,] OCSO[.]

NOVEMBER 7 [1952]

WESTERN UNION
REVEREND M LOUIS
ABBEY OF OUR LADY OF GETHSEMANI
TRAPPIST, KENTUCKY

MANY THANKS [FOR YOUR] WIRE[.] ASSUME YOU MEAN FATHER
M[.] GABRIEL SORTAIS INSTEAD OF NOGUES FOR [ABBOT] GEN-
ERAL[.] WILL ADD FATHER M[.] ALBERT DERZELLES TO TWO
AMERICAN CENSORS[.] REGARDS[.]

BOB

NOVEMBER 12, 1952

Rev. M. Louis, O.C.S.O.
Abbey of Our Lady of Gethsemani
Trappist, Kentucky

Dear Tom:
    I had lunch with Naomi yesterday and she showed me your letter about
CISTERCIAN CONTEMPLATIVES. Harcourt, Brace, as I think I have already said, will be very glad to publish this.[1] Despite her recommendation
that the monastery publish this book, Naomi says it's entirely agreeable
with her if we bring it out. We should very much like to do so—to publish,
in fact, all your books from now on—and I hope that this is agreeable to
you and Father Abbot.
    The book should be enlarged somewhat, with different pictures and a
revised text. I know how pressed you are for time, and I also know that you
don't want to undertake any kind of demanding job of writing now. The
question therefore arises, does it have to come out right away? With THE
SIGN OF JONAS and BREAD IN THE WILDERNESS in the offing, why
can't we hold the revised CISTERCIAN CONTEMPLATIVES until the
fall? New Directions have announced BREAD IN THE WILDERNESS "before the beginning of the Lenten season, 1953." Since we haven't yet received Dom Albert's corrections (Tom Burns has cabled: "Minimum
changes inside three weeks"), we cannot schedule JONAS definitely, although we hope to publish in February. I think it would be foolish, even
disastrous, for the books to get in each other's way. Since Jay [Laughlin]
agreed that JONAS could come out first, I hope you will time the proofs
accordingly, or—better still—relieve yourself of a headache by sending
them through Naomi. Since she is your agent, and since she is the only
objective person who has all the facts in this mix-up, you really should
clear through her. Jay Laughlin is, as you know, in India, and [Robert]

MacGregor of New Directions disclaims responsibility for the actions of the firm, though obviously he is the only responsible party on the scene.[2]

I will let you know just as soon as we hear from England about Dom Albert's corrections. I am grateful for the word "minimum" in Tom Burns' cable—but we shall see.

With my very best wishes to you and Father Abbot.

Yours devotedly,

[Robert Giroux]

1. TM, *Cistercian Contemplatives: A Guide to Trappist Life* (Trappist, KY: Gethsemani Abbey, 1948). This short booklet was not revised or republished by Harcourt, Brace.

2. Robert MacGregor worked closely with JL, as editor and general manager at ND.

JANUARY 3, 1953

Our Lady of Gethsemani
[Letterhead]

Dear Bob:

It seems like ages since I have either written to you or heard from you. The first reason for this letter is to enclose a list of names to which advance copies of Jonas ought to be sent, if you will be so kind. I look forward to seeing the book, and rejoice that it is being bought. I rejoice se-cundum quid, wondering whether or not this will be the book I will be most sorry for having written. I am sorry for having written all of them—although I cannot say that quite without qualification for the Mountain, since it appears to have helped a few people. But God could have helped them much better perhaps through some other instrument.

Also if it is not too much of a nuisance or in some way inconvenient to you, I would appreciate it if you would let Dr. Thompson of the University of Kentucky keep the ms. of Ascent. I believe he is eager to get possession of the mss. of the Mountain and Waters, also. Unless you have some special reason for keeping them, perhaps it would be a good idea to let him have them—I mean it wouldn't hurt Harcourt, Brace at all. I haven't heard how his exhibit of the Ascent material went off. As for the ms. of Jonas, we had better keep that on ice, out of sight, Father Abbot thinks.

Bread in the Wilderness is comfortably stalled for the time being. Don't worry.

What plans for 1953? Did you type those illegible "Notes and Sentences?" That is about the only sort of project I can work on right now. I have a lot more—not a lot, some more. I could collate them with the typed material, and put them in some kind of order for next winter. Father Abbot is disposed to let me have longer and more frequent intervals in the shed, which has been fixed up now—stove and all. It is about the only thing that will guarantee any kind of production for the moment.

Here is a list of names,* and one other enclosure.

God bless you this year. You are as ever in my prayers.

In Corde Christi,
Tom
fr. M. Louis /s/

*This is [in] addition to the regular author's copies, which please send [them to me] here. Charge royalty account for others. Oh yes! Please send me a copy of Aelred Graham's article—I'd like to see what it is all about + I won't get excited. Why should I?

FEBRUARY 5, 1953

Rev. M. Louis, O.C.S.O.
Abbey of Our Lady of Gethsemani
Trappist, Kentucky

Dear Tom:

Dan and I have just come from a fine lunch, at which we celebrated the publication of THE SIGN OF JONAS this day. After the vicissitudes of last fall, it is gratifying to know that the book has been launched, and it is even more gratifying to read the fine press it is receiving.

I enclose George Shuster's cover piece in the Times; Charles Poore's review in this morning's edition of that paper (our first notice in a New York daily); Chad Walsh in next Sunday's Herald-Tribune; the piece in Newsweek; and John O'Brien in the Chicago Tribune. There will be more coming: tomorrow's New York Herald-Tribune will carry a review; and other dailies, weeklies and monthlies will follow.

I also enclose Dom Aelred's article in The Atlantic.[1] I met the author and he asked me to tell you of his affection and admiration for you. I wish more of it showed in his article.

New Directions has announced BREAD IN THE WILDERNESS for March, which I hope is a mistake. I enclose their ad.

Yours devotedly,
Robert Giroux

---

1. Aelred Graham, O.S.B., "Thomas Merton: A Modern Man in Reverse," *Atlantic Monthly*, January 1953, 70–74. Dom Graham, a monk from Ampleforth Abbey in England, served as superior of the Portsmouth Priory from 1951 to 1967. In a note to RG dated February 5, 1953, he wrote: "Many thanks for 'The Sign of Jonas,' which I am reading with interest. It seems to confirm both my publicly expressed views of Thomas Merton and my private opinion of Fr. Louis (which anyone is free to announce to the world), viz. that I am not personally worthy to clean his boots."

FEBRUARY 16, 1953

Our Lady of Gethsemani
[Letterhead]

Dear Bob:
The other day I forgot to thank you, in the letter I wrote, for the beautifully bound copy of Jonas. It reminds me that I have been meaning to ask you to get bound both Jonas and the Ascent for the Holy Father. We could present them together. Maybe Clare Luce could present them, or would that start a war? You didn't send him the Ascent already did you?

Anyway please let me know what happens, and when the books are bound.

In haste. With best wishes as ever.

In Corde Christi,
Tom
fr. M. Louis /s/

APRIL 11, 1953

Our Lady of Gethsemani
[Letterhead]

Dear Bob:
It seems like a long time since I wrote to you or heard from you. How is the book going? Someone told me that Atlantic printed a letter or something in reply to Dom Aelred. Are there any more reviews?

Remember I wrote some time ago asking whether you could get copies of the Ascent and Jonas bound for the Holy Father. I still mean to send him bound copies. If it is not too much trouble, could you get it done, or else let us know and we can do it here. You can charge the royalty account.

Thanks very much for the new complete Eliot. It is very valuable to me. I don't know when I shall ever get around to reading the longer plays, but I have been going over Four Quartets and Choruses from the Rock.[1] Last December, I gave the scholastics a talk on Murder in the Cathedral and read them the Christmas sermon. It is very fine for us. Few things could be deeper or more appropriate than his understanding that martyrs—and for that matter contemplatives—are not made by man's own choice.

Then how about those Notes and Sentences? If you send me a typescript and the handwritten notes, I might be able to do a little work on it this year. I have some more stuff here now. Of course there is no hurry, but it would be useful to have everything within reach.

I hope you will settle everything with New Directions about the time for Bread in the Wilderness to appear. Let me know.

Someone sent me Maritain's new book, <u>Creative Intuition in Art and Poetry</u>, and it seems to be very fine.

It does not seem that I will be writing any more Journal.[2] The Abbot General is opposed to it, and I certainly see his point of view. It makes no difference to me and I certainly do not wish to make any representations to him about his decision. After all, the book business is in about the last place, in a life like this. Father O'Brien, with his suggestion that I write a "great religious novel." I take a very dim view of his suggestion.

If I ever do that St. Bernard book it will probably be a collection of disconnected essays. I cannot see my way to struggling through all the activities of his extremely busy life.

Dr. Thompson of the University of Kentucky was after me for a lot of things in connection with <u>Jonas</u>, for an exhibit. If he still comes asking you for anything, I give full permission to let him have all he wants except the manuscript, because I think Father Abbot does not want that to be exhibited.

This afternoon I should be planting pine seedlings. They are all drying up on me. The woods are fine—just at that stage when everything is turning green and the world really looks new: which it is. Old too.

I hope you had a very good Easter—I keep you in the Mass. That <u>is</u> Easter: the real Easter: the unleavened Bread of sincerity and truth [see 1 Corinthians 5:8]. Well, God bless you, Bob. Let me hear from you. Above all, I'd like to get those books bound for the Holy Father.

As ever.

> With best wishes in Jesus Christ,
> Tom
> fr. M. Louis /s/

1. T. S. Eliot's poem "Choruses from the Rock" laments the emptiness of modern society. See the letter dated March 8, 1948.

2. There are no journal entries between March 10, 1953, and July 17, 1956, when TM resumes writing a journal that he will continue for this rest of his life. See TM, *A Search for Solitude: Pursuing the Monk's True Life*, vol. 3 (1952–1960) of *The Journals of Thomas Merton*, ed. Lawrence S. Cunningham (San Francisco: HarperCollins, 1996).

APRIL 30, 1953

Gethsemani

Dear Bob:

I am sending you a copy of a technical study on St. Bernard which perhaps will form one of the sections of the St. Bernard book—but changed, of course, and made more readable.[1] This version is currently appearing in the <u>Collectanea</u>, the magazine of the Order. I don't know whether you will think it at all worth while. However it brings me to a new stage in a line of thought which has aroused some controversy and might create some interest on that account. It is not really a "new position" but a clarified position.

I would very much like to hear from you, if possible, about getting those books bound and about the material for Notes and Sentences— which was to make up a book for which I had devised a title. But now, as I expected, I have forgotten the title.

If you think the Jesuits would take this heavy job on Action and Contemplation in several installments in Thought, they can have it.[2] I'll have to brush up a few details. They can send me proofs in that case.

Are you coming down this summer? I hope you are.

Anyway, do please write when you can. How is Jonas doing?

As ever. With best wishes.

In Corde Christi,

Tom

fr. M. Louis /s/

1. TM, "Action and Contemplation in St. Bernard," *Collectanea Ordinis Cisterciensium Reformatorum* 15, no. 1 (January 1953): 26–31; 15, no. 2 (July 1953): 203–61; 16, no. 2 (April 1954): 105–21. Reprinted in *Thomas Merton on St. Bernard* (Kalamazoo, MI: Cistercian Publications, 1980), 23–104.

2. Published by Fordham University, *Thought* gave its readership a broad range of articles and reviews on topics in theology, philosophy, sociology, history, education, literature, science, and current events.

MAY 1, 1953

Harcourt, Brace & Company, Inc.

[Letterhead]

Rev. M. Louis, O.C.S.O.

Abbey of Our Lady of Gethsemani

Trappist, Kentucky

Dear Tom:

This is just a note to say that all is going well. I am off on a business trip to California (the annual conference of the American Psychiatric Association—quite a business!) and I will be back around May 10th, when I hope to write you the leisurely letter which is long overdue. Unfortunately my plans do not allow me to come back through Louisville this time or I would report to you in person.

The sales of THE SIGN OF JONAS have reached 81,728 copies and it is still pulling its weight three months after publication. There is no indication as yet that the rate of sale is going to follow the pattern of THE SEVEN STOREY MOUNTAIN, although that could still happen before the year is out. All the book clubs have reported that more members have asked for this selection than for any other book they have ever published.

After my return, I will mail you the typed manuscript of the book of "Sentences" which I find quite wonderful. As far as I know New Directions is bringing out BREAD IN THE WILDERNESS this fall in time for the Christmas season.

I had an invitation from Porter Chandler to attend the blessing of Father Gerard [McGinly]'s monastery at the end of the month, and I had planned to attend, but unfortunately it turns out to be May 30th and that is the day I promised to meet Eliot on his arrival from London. I have heard wonderful things about Our Lady of the Genesee [in Piffard, New York] and I hope I may be able to visit the community at a later date.

With all good wishes to you and Father James, I am.

Yours devotedly,
Bob /s/

P. S. Jonas + Ascent are being bound in elegant style for the Vatican + are due shortly from the bindery.

MAY 4, 1953

Our Lady of Gethsemani
[Letterhead]

Dear Bob:

I just got a letter from Clare Luce, written on the way to Italy to take up her diplomatic post at Rome. She promised that if I would send her the bound copies of the Ascent and Jonas she would personally deliver them to His Holiness, so I hope you can do something to procure these. Or at least let me know and I can get a couple of copies bound in Louisville— although I am not certain of getting what we want here.

[Rainer] Biemel, my Editor at Desclée de Brouwer [in Paris] says he has a book about the Soviet Union published in this country under the title of Nightmare. Probably written over a pen name, Jean Rounault. Do you know of it? Is it worth getting? If so, could you procure it for us, on the royalty account?

Translations of Ascent and Jonas are on the way at [the publishing firm of] Albin Michel, Paris. Lots of trouble getting everything accurate in the theology in Ascent but I have a Dominican friend of Jacques Maritain helping with the work.[1]

God bless you, and may all go well with you.

In Corde Jesu Christi,
Tom
fr. M. Louis /s/

1. A revised version of *The Ascent to Truth*, translated as *La Montée vers la Lumière*, was eventually published in 1958 by Éditions Albin Michel, with the assistance not of a Dominican but of the French Carmelite François de Sainte Marie, O.C.D.

MAY 11, 1953

Rev. M. Louis, O.C.S.O.
Abbey of Our Lady of Gethsemani
Trappist, Kentucky

Dear Tom:

I am just back from Hollywood and doubtless none the better for it, although I did acquire a slight tan. It was fun seeing some of the studios with King Vidor, the director, as my expert guide. There was very little "shooting," since Hollywood is quite paralyzed by the rage for three-dimensional films, just as they were paralyzed in 1929 by the talkies.

The bound copies of ASCENT and JONAS are due from the bindery on Friday. They are being bound in the same leather and general style as the special copy of JONAS which you received. I am therefore writing to Mrs. Luce, telling her the books will be soon on the way.

I read the St. Bernard article with great interest and I must confess that your phrase "technical study" is entirely accurate. Just to keep things straight with Naomi, I am submitting it via her office. I will be seeing the editor, Father Lynch, on Friday at a meeting which Jacques Maritain expects to attend, and I will find out whether they can use it in Thought.

The book about the Soviet Union entitled NIGHTMARE was published here by Crowell in 1952. I must have missed it at the time of publication. It's being ordered and will be forwarded to you.

I want to go over the manuscript of SENTENCES before mailing it, and I expect to have this ready next week. The sales of JONAS last week were approximately 250 copies, which is excellent. The total is very near 82,000 copies.

With best regards to you and Father James.

Ever yours,
Robert Giroux

MAY 19, 1953

Rev. M. Louis O.C.S.O.
Abbey of Our Lady of Gethsemani
Trappist, Kentucky

Dear Tom:

The bindery has just delivered the presentation copies of JONAS and ASCENT. The former is bound in red leather in the style of the copy you received; the other is bound in blue leather, and they both look very handsome. I am writing Mrs. Luce about the matter of presentation today.

Meanwhile the Jean Rounault book, NIGHTMARE, has just arrived and I send it to you herewith.

Yours,
Robert Giroux

JUNE 3, 1953

WESTERN UNION
ROBERT GIROUX
HARCOURT BRACE AND CO
383 MADISON AVE NYK

IF YOU HAVE NOT SENT BOOKS FOR HOLY FATHER TO CLARE
LUCE[,] PLEASE SEND HERE FOR [ME TO] AUTOGRAPH[.]

MERTON

JUNE 3, 1953

WESTERN UNION
REVEREND M. LOUIS, O.C.S.O.
ABBEY OF OUR LADY OF GETHSEMANI
TRAPPIST, KENTUCKY

BOOKS FOR HOLY FATHER MAILED TO YOU TODAY FOR AUTO-
GRAPHS[.] REGARDS[.]

BOB

JUNE 20, 1953

Gethsemani

Dear Bob:
   I haven't yet thanked you for the bound volumes of Jonas and the Ascent which are very fine. Nor have I yet thought up the suitable Latin inscriptions which I mean to etch on the flyleaves with my own unintelligible
handwriting, for the Holy Father. At the moment I am waiting for his encyclical on St. Bernard because when I write to him I want to write about
that also.[1] Then also the book Nightmare finally got to me through the iron
curtain and I have read bits of it. Rounault, whose real name is [Rainer]
Biemel, seems like a fairly interesting chap. The one thing I haven't seen
anything of yet is the ms. of Notes and Sentences.[2] I hope you didn't send
it, because if you did it is lost. But I have nothing against you sending it
soon. Though at the moment I am going through one of those phases
when the mere thought of everything I have written or might write almost
makes me vomit.
   I like Rice's new magazine [Jubilee]. He is after me to do something for
it but it is hard to see how I can manage to do so. However, he might be
able to use those cloister-in-southern-France pictures. I don't think I will

ever be able to make a book out of them. What do you think about letting him have them? Or some of those drawings I did last year—although I think they are too bad to be printed. Of course, if you have any use for any of these things, by all means go ahead with them.

I wonder if we could finally decide on a title for N[otes] and S[entences], at least provisionally, so that if I have to talk about the project to Jay for instance (another "next book" question, but with no trouble this time) I will say some words that do not sound anything like N[otes] and S[entences]. I believe the title I once thought up was <u>Words made out of silence</u>. Would you be interested in a little book I could do on the Camaldolese hermits, with some nice pictures? Their P[rior] G[eneral] wants to make a foundation in America and wants me to help out and I would be eager to do so. But nothing can be said very definitely about the prospects.

Are you likely to come down this summer, or did the Hollywood trip use up all your free time?

We are reading the Letters of St. Teresa [of Avila] in the refectory and I like the way she ends all her letters. Before signing, she writes out a definite precise statement of what day it is. The Spanish of her time must have had very concrete minds. They knew just when and where they were. We don't. Today, then, is June 20th, the day before the Fourth Sunday after Pentecost, 1953. May the grace of the Holy Spirit be with you.

Devotedly in Christ,
Tom
fr. M. Louis /s/

1. "*Doctor Mellifluus:* Encyclical Letter of His Holiness Pope Pius XII on the Occasion of the Eighth Centenary of the Death of Saint Bernard" would eventually appear with TM's extensive introduction on Bernard and notes on the encyclical in *The Last of the Fathers: Saint Bernard of Clairvaux and the Encyclical Letter, Doctor Mellifluus* (1954).

2. An early version of what would eventually be published as TM, *No Man Is an Island* (1955).

JULY 17, 1953

Rev. M. Louis O.C.S.O.
Abbey of Our Lady of Gethsemani
Trappist, Kentucky

Dear Tom:

I have sent you the typed transcript of WORDS MADE OUT OF SILENCE (provisional title).

You will find a top copy and carbon, as well as the holograph text. I've become greatly attached to the latter and it would mean much to me to keep it, if you don't have to make other disposition of it. I return it now because there were a few indecipherable words, particularly those which my small Latin could not unravel. Anyway let's regard the top script as the master copy, for the printer; keep the carbon; please let me have the original manuscript if you can.

In my opinion, the manuscript makes a lovely short book. Is it conceivable that we could think of doing this in 1954—the fall perhaps?

Yours ever,
Robert Giroux

JULY 23, 1953

Rev. M. Louis, O.C.S.O.
Abbey of Our Lady of Gethsemani
Trappist, Kentucky

Dear Tom:

A few duplicate reviews of JONAS have come to my desk and I forward them in case they have not reached your notice. You may not have seen Sally Fitzgerald's interesting piece which appeared in, of all places, The New Republic.[1]

What Naomi says of the St. Bernard encyclical project interests me greatly. If you're not going to get to the big biography in the next year or so, this might afford a means of doing a small book on St. Bernard. However, I doubt that even [the publishing firm of] Templegate could get out a book this year. I know it's the anniversary year and it would be desirable to do it in 1953, but it would be just as good a book, from the publicity standpoint, early in 1954. Of course, Father Abbot may think it is out of the question altogether, and we certainly want to abide by his wishes.

Ever yours,
Robert Giroux

1. Sally Fitzgerald, editor of Flannery O'Connor's collection of letters, entitled *The Habit of Being* (1988), published her article "Chesterton on the Idea of Christian Tragedy" in the January 5, 1953, issue.

[JULY 26, 1953?]

Our Lady of Gethsemani
[Letterhead]

Dear Bob:

Many thanks for the reviews of Jonas. I am glad the reviewers like the book, mostly. Here are a few slight corrections that ought to be made. I slipped up on one of those scandalous allusions to fish being served in the refectory, at a great banquet.

Is there anything you can send to Dr. Thompson at the U[niversity] of Kentucky? He wants another exhibit. Maybe some of the pictures, without me in them preferably. I think it would have been better on the whole if the papers had not said who was the monk, in those pictures. I guess they thought it was important to do so. That is just the trouble. Somebody in the world has to affirm that it is not important to have your picture taken. Of course, I suppose, if it is not important to have it taken, it is indifferent whether it be printed. That is true. But if you let your picture be printed people think that means your picture is important. Which it isn't.

Naomi said she would tell you to send me the stuff I gave you from "Notes and Sentences" and when I wrote to her I thought I had a brilliant title but now I have forgotten it again. But in any case it would not be too hard for me to get all that stuff together at present, adding to it what I have written since you were here. That, by the way, is all I have written, but it is fair enough. I feel a great distaste for writing an official biography of St. Bernard, and think I won't. When the time comes for that book . . . well, it will have to be something other than a biography. Perhaps three long essays on important aspects of his thought.

I forget whether I ever wrote you about your painful situation. I don't think I can say much that Father Abbot did not already say. You have the faith to see that these things do not come about by chance. In a sense, this is part of your individual "vocation." Your handling of it is going to be part of your sanctity—which is what you must achieve. But God will achieve it in you. Precisely the incomprehensibility of the situation is what makes this most inevitable, if you will let Him do what He alone can do.

As for Carmen [RG's wife]—since I do not know her at all I should not speak. Medicine cannot perhaps do much and maybe she has found that out by experience. But anyway it doesn't seem much to ask that she try it again. Oh well. The best I can do is to pray for both of you. May the Holy Spirit Who is with you both, as a result of the Sacrament, guide you and heal this division.

God bless you, Bob. If Jonas does well, I am happier about it for your sake than for my own. Thanks for all you have done and put up with.

As ever.

> Devotedly in Christ,
> Tom
> fr. M. Louis /s/

AUGUST 12, 1953

Dear Bob:

Here is the text of my introduction and commentary on the Encyclical Doctor Mellifluus.[1] I still cannot lay hands on an English translation. I do not know if an official translation is being made for the Vatican polyglot press. We are doing one here, but I do not know what it is going to be like. The Encyclical itself is not much longer than my introduction, being about 5,000 words.

The whole book would therefore be quite small—around thirty pages or less. Besides the Encyclical itself and my introduction I have also obtained a prefatory letter from Cardinal Fumasoni Biondi, which is very good. It takes a page. Then I could fill out with two items I have been thinking of: first, the main dates in the life of St. Bernard and secondly, a list of his written works.

There are lots of very nice pictures available now, and with one of them for a frontispiece I think we could make this an extremely nice little book.

Cardinal Fumasoni Biondi (Prefect of the Propaganda [Fidei, or Congregation for the Propagation of the Faith]) highly approves of the project, has seen and approves the introduction. I know Rome would be very happy if the book came out at Harcourt, Brace. It would be of immense help in disseminating the Encyclical. You have already published some Papal documents, haven't you?

Finally, Bob, I have a personal reason for hoping you will be able to do something with this. It is to the interest of Harcourt, Brace also. I think that this encyclical, with this presentation, will put the final touches to the Aelred Graham business.[2] Properly interpreted, the Encyclical supports me and not Graham. I may add that when my own ideas are properly interpreted, the Encyclical is in my favor. If someone else gets hold of it and uses a little imagination, he might turn the encyclical against me on one particular point that Dom Aelred used rather heavily—the misconception that I want everyone to become either a Trappist or a mystic or both.

The title of the book would be "The Last of the Fathers" and the subtitle could indicate that it consists of the Encyclical and Commentary.

I am sending you the carbon of this letter rather than the top copy as the ribbon is getting to be a little faint.

This would be a good appetizer for the future book on St. Bernard don't you think? Or are my hopes too sanguine?

May Our Lady obtain for you many graces on the feast of her Assumption. God bless you always.

As ever.

Devotedly yours in Christ,
Tom
fr. M. Louis /s/

1. *Doctor Mellifluus*, an encyclical of Pope Pius XII on Saint Bernard of Clairvaux, was published on May 24, 1953.
2. See the letter dated February 5, 1953. Dom Aelred Graham, O.S.B., the headmaster of Portsmouth Priory School in Rhode Island, had written a negative article about TM in the *Atlantic Monthly* (January 1953).

AUGUST 24, 1953

Our Lady of Gethsemani
[Letterhead]

Dear Bob:

Here is a translation of the Encyclical which has been made here and which was just read in the refectory. The reading gave me ideas which will lead to some changes in the preface. You can judge from this whether you want to print the job or not. The actual text we would use for publication would be a translation made at the Vatican. The Vatican translation has been turned over to the press of the Order in Belgium and I am impatiently waiting for a copy of it to arrive, together with the Abbot General's permission to use it in this country.

As for the introduction, my picture of it has changed. I think it ought to include three sections: first, a sketch of St. Bernard's life and character, second an outline of his chief works, and third the notes on the Encyclical. In these I would be less pugnacious about the question of mysticism and more practical in my orientation. The introduction might perhaps be a little longer than the Encyclical, at that rate. I have also asked the Abbot General for an introductory letter. The whole thing will be very official.

Now that you have this material in hand I hope you will let us know very soon what you think about it as we want to get busy with the job as fast as we can, if you are not going to do it. I still hope, however, that you will. I do not know why half the words in this letter are divided by gaping spaces. Forgive my hasty typing.

You can see that the changes in the introduction which I propose will make this book more accessible to the general reader. Any other suggestions you may have would be welcome.

I am trying to do a little work on Notes and Sentences. Another alternative title would be "Ashes and Speeches." I liked that the other day. Not now.

With all best wishes, as ever.

Devotedly in Christ,
Tom
fr. M. Louis /s/

SEPTEMBER 12, 1953

Our Lady of Gethsemani
[Letterhead]

Dear Bob:

Before leaving for the General Chapter, Father Abbot gave me permission to try to get a copy of Herodotus from somewhere, and I think you are the logical one to ask.[1] It is probably in the Modern Library, isn't it? In any case can you please do me the favor, and buy us some moderately priced edition of Herodotus—and put it on our account?

I have been able to do a lot of work on "Sentences" and it has turned, as I thought it would, into a full-sized book along the lines of <u>Seeds</u>. So far I have over a hundred typewritten pages, and probably a hundred or so to come. We have had a "vacation" and this has left me a little more in the clear. It did me a lot of good to get out in the fields a little more than usual. We harvested a big tobacco crop—first time I have ever worked in tobacco, and it is a lot of fun. To my horror, one of my students chewed some of it when riding home in the truck, but he received his just deserts—physically as well as spiritually.

Have you come to any decision about that Encyclical? I sent a copy of the preface to Ed, wondering if he could do something with it for Jubilee and I haven't heard anything. I would like to change it before anything more happens. Do you happen to know what is going on with it there, or does Naomi?

Before doing anything with the Camaldoli material I think it would be best to make an illustrated article out of it for Jubilee. That is what I am thinking about at the moment.

<u>Bread in the Wilderness</u> is, so it seems, about to see the light of day.[2] That book has gone through the most extraordinary phases. There has never been more than one original manuscript, and that is a fantastic mosaic of corrections and changes. It has travelled more than anything else I have ever written, been through the hands of two publishers and three printers, not to mention two designers—and all the censors. It is a miracle that the book is coming out at all.

I hope everything goes well with you. I frequently remember you at Mass and hope you can come down here sometime in the not too distant future. God be with you always.

Sincerely in Christ,
Tom
fr. M. Louis /s/

1. Herodotus, considered the "Father of History," was a Greek historian who lived in the fifth century BC.
2. See the discussion of this book starting with the letter dated July 28, 1950.

SEPTEMBER 23, 1953

Harcourt, Brace & Company, Inc.
[Letterhead]

Rev. M. Louis O.C.S.O.
Abbey of Our Lady of Gethsemani
Trappist, Kentucky

Dear Tom:

We want to go ahead and do a small book of THE LAST OF THE FATHERS. It's an amazing encyclical and you've done a splendid commentary and your ideas about revisions make it even more publishable. I think the three parts you suggest—a sketch of Saint Bernard's life, an outline of his chief works, and notes on the encyclical—are excellent. On my first reading, I thought the introduction should begin on page two of the version you sent me, so as to make it more accessible to the general reader, but your second thoughts go in exactly the right direction it needs. It ought, in short, to be a little book on Saint Bernard, with this encyclical as a taking-off point. I talked with Naomi at lunch today, and she is pleased that we want to go ahead.

Inasmuch as the encyclical is dated last May, we naturally want to do the book as soon as possible. I don't, however, want to complicate our lives with the censors again. How should we proceed? Do you want to send us the manuscript after they have seen it or before? Is it conceivable that we could have everything in hand by the end of October, which would allow publication in time for Lenten reading?

I hope it will not be taken amiss if I inquire whether it would be possible to get hold of a British rendition of "Doctor Mellifluus." Can you find out whether Father Ronald Knox has done a translation? I realize the difficulties, and I don't think it should go as far as the secular translations of the Pope's address on psychotherapy (which I enclose for your interest) went. I do think, however, that the version is more literally rendered than it need be. If Father Knox hasn't done an "official" translation, would it be possible to polish this one up somewhat?*

I have got hold of the Modern Library edition of Herodotus and it should reach you shortly. Father Abbot sent me a wonderful card from France and I was immensely pleased to have his good words. The news of "vacation" and the tobacco crop harvest sound all to the good, and I'm delighted to know that your work on "Sentences" is bringing it to a full-sized book. We want to make it a beautiful job of book-making. Speaking of that I append some very fine words of praise for the design of JONAS. This notice appears in "Bookbinding and Book Production" for September, 1953:

THE SIGN OF JONAS is a book which breathes its spirit through every device common to book design which is used here. It is modern without being blatant, clerical without being doctrinal, peaceful without somnambulism. The photographic endsheets of the Gethsemani forest heighten the effect and the handsome open lettering of the title page, reminiscent of carved altar inscriptions, matches the line drawing of the sign of Jonas, derived from the jacket reproduction of the symbol. The lettering is repeated in the chapter openings, an expense well justified by the result. Set flush right 2 picas below the chapter number, it is followed by a few paragraphs of soliloquy set in italics. The leading is just right, the presswork, paper and binding faultless as required. What a happy harmony! . . .

With all best wishes.

Ever yours,
Bob /s/

*When you say "Vatican translation," isn't it possible to get this official version Englished by stylists. Among other things, "Dr. M[ellifluus]" is a literary essay, too!

OCTOBER 3, 1953

Our Lady of Gethsemani
[Letterhead]

Dear Bob:

Here is the only copy of the Vatican translation of the Encyclical I have so far received. We have permission to print it and to change the style as we please as long as we do not tell anyone it is the Vatican translation. This last point is very important and our Definitory would get in trouble with the Papal Secretariate if anyone finds out we are using the official translation.[1]

I am sending you this copy, then, so that you may go over it for style, but I suggest that some Jesuit friend of yours might check your changes with the Latin, and I myself will go over it in proof to coordinate it with whatever I have written in the commentary, so that we all agree. Is this the kind of arrangement that you envisaged? I cannot undertake the work on the Encyclical text myself as I am busy making my additions to the commentary. I will also write to France post haste for some pictures of St. Bernard. I think we ought to print at least one, don't you?

Here, too, is a copy of the introductory letter of Cardinal Fumasoni Biondi, and one of the letters of the Abbot General.

I have finally settled on a title for the Sentences book: "The Wind blows where it pleases." It is better than the others, anyway, and I actually believe I like it.

The Herodotus has not come yet, but I look forward to receiving it. It will help with my study of the Old Testament. Maybe someday we could do a small book on the Prophets. By the way, can this St. Bernard job fulfill my contractual obligation for a book on him? I hope it can. If I ever can write a long one I will, but you know how things are. I'd just as soon get that sword of Damocles off from over my head, although it was very beneficial to the monastery to get the advance, etc.

I close in haste, as I want to get this off fast.

With best wishes, as ever.

Devotedly in Christ,
fr. M. Louis /s/

P.S. I forgot: Dan Walsh was here and made an important suggestion which I liked very much: printing the <u>Latin</u> of the Encyclical to face the English. The Latin is marvelous, and gives the lie to Graham Greene's remarks on Papal Latin in Life ["The Pope Who Remains a Priest: Pius XII," September 24, 1951], so I think it would be a fine idea—and we could remark on this point, too.

---

1. A Trappist Definitor judged, among other responsibilities, the advisability of publishing something written by a Trappist monk.

OCTOBER 9, 1953

Our Lady of Gethsemani
[Letterhead]

Dear Bob:

Here is practically all the material for the <u>Last of the Fathers</u>, at least all that is to be written by me. I am sending copy to the two censors and they will probably come through in about a month or six weeks. Meanwhile, on my own responsibility, and with the permission of Fr. Prior* who is in charge here in Reverend Father's absence, I feel safe in telling you to go ahead and set this material up, provided you are willing to make any changes the censors may suggest. The material is substantially approved since the chief section of it, and the only one about which any difficulty might arise, has received the nihil obstat of our own censors and the imprimi potest of the Abbot General. I refer to the notes on the Encyclical. For the rest, the Preface, Life and Writings ought to cause no trouble.

I am also writing to France to get one or two pictures of St. Bernard to pick a frontispiece from. How about a picture of the basilica of Vezelay or something else like that? I'll try to get a few shots.

Finally, on a sheet of contents, you will notice I plan a list of suggested books to read. If you are in need of a fairly large number of pages we could even slip in some excerpts from St. Bernard, but I think the book is big enough as it is. I'll do an index if there is room—and if I have a fair amount of time with the page proofs.

Many thanks for Herodotus. I have not had time to get into it, having been pretty busy with this. But now I hope to have a chance. Meanwhile I will get back to "The Wind blows where it pleases." How's your reaction on that title?

I am expecting something any day from New Directions about the Psalm book. Have you heard anything?

I hope Jubilee is not printing the earlier version of the article on Doctor Mellifluus that I sent them.

As ever, with best wishes and prayers.

Sincerely and devotedly in Christ,
Tom
fr. M. Louis /s/

*He held it up after all but Reverend Father said OK today, October 16.

NOVEMBER 4, 1953

Rev. M. Louis, O.C.S.O.
Abbey of Our Lady of Gethsemani
Trappist, Kentucky

Dear Tom:

THE LAST OF THE FATHERS has all been retyped and copy edited, and is now being designed. I think it reads very well and, having gone over the "official" translation of the encyclical, I realized that I did the other translation an injustice. I have made a few changes, where the unofficial version is more felicitous to the English ear, so we'll be sure not to call it the "Vatican translation" anywhere. While it would be interesting to have the Latin text, I'm afraid this is a luxury we can't afford; it will make a 128-page book as it is. I hope you have a short bibliography and a short index in mind.

New Directions phoned today and said that the Psalms book is now on press and they expect finished copies in three weeks. I'm eager to see it. I deduced that there was some delay with Monsignor Fearns, who even asked to see the photographs, so perhaps we ought to apply to the Archbishop of Louisville for an imprimatur for this book. What do you think?

I really prefer "Sentences" to "The Wind Blows Where It Pleases." The latter is not only too "poetic," but the [Paul] Blanshard-type mind will take it to mean, "Monks do whatever they want."[1] Perhaps a phrase in the book will provide the title; there's plenty of time to settle this.

Have you any illustrative material on St. Bernard you can rush here? The enclosed photostat was obtained in the library. It's charming in itself, but I don't think it's right for the book. Keep this, if you'd like; we have the original.

With all good wishes to Father Abbot and yourself and my friends in the community, I am.

Ever yours,
Robert Giroux

1. Paul Blanshard was a controversial author, socialist, assistant editor of *The Nation*, and an outspoken critic of Catholicism.

NOVEMBER 27, 1953

Our Lady of Gethsemani
[Letterhead]

Dear Bob:

I have your letter of the fourth, in which you mention the possibility of sending the LAST OF THE FATHERS to the Archbishop of Louisville for censorship. That would be a great mistake, as he takes longer than anyone else I have ever had anything to do with. I think he does not like to get books for censorship, and he always gives a lot of trouble with them. I see no reason why Msgr. Fearns should not deal rapidly enough with this text which is relatively plain sailing. The reason why there was so much delay with Bread in the Wilderness was that New Directions forgot to inform him that I had made some changes demanded by his reader. They had to hunt them up in the printed pages.

Still waiting for BREAD IN THE WILDERNESS. I hope it will look good.

I am about finished with the book of meditations, and since I cannot send it back to you now, according to our new rules, until it has been censored, I shall try to get it decently typed by someone I know. That will save time. In any case, there is no rush.

Perhaps the best thing would simply be to call the book CONSIDERATIONS. A non-committal and prosaic title. Other ideas: DARKNESS AND LIGHT, or another—IN SPIRIT AND IN TRUTH. I don't think the last will do. Considerations seems OK. How about DIRECTIVES?[1] Anyway, "Sentences" no longer fits.

This morning I had a gay visit with Beatrice Lillie who dropped in here to see one of our monks who used to write script for her.[2] A lot of his stuff is in her show "An Evening with Beatrice Lillie," which is running in Cincinnati.

How soon can we expect proofs for LAST OF THE FATHERS?

As ever, with best wishes.

Devotedly in Christ,
Tom
fr. M. Louis /s/

P.S. I sent a letter of recommendation with a certain Father Englebert who may have looked you up.[3] He is very intent on having me write a preface for his book but Father Abbot has gone sour on all prefaces. So, in fact, have I.

1. Presumably other titles for *No Man Is an Island.*
2. Beatrice Lillie, a noted comic actress, was featured in such films as *Around the World in Eighty Days* (1956) and *Thoroughly Modern Millie* (1967).
3. Perhaps Omer Englebert, O.F.M., author of a biography of Saint Francis.

NOVEMBER 30, 1953

Rev. M. Louis, O.C.S.O.
Abbey of Our Lady of Gethsemani
Trappist, Kentucky

Dear Tom:
You are right about not sending THE LAST OF THE FATHERS to Louisville. It certainly should have clear sailing here involving as it does a Papal encyclical, and letters from the Cardinal Protector [Fumasoni Biondi] and Abbot General. We'll send it through Monsignor Fearns at Dunwoodie [Seminary] when the proofs are ready, which doesn't look like much before the end of the month—after Christmas anyway.

Has a picture of Saint Bernard turned up, or do you have anything we can use on the jacket as well as a frontispiece? At the moment, we are trying the drawing I sent you in photostat, but if you have anything better we should very much like to see it.

I like CONSIDERATIONS very much indeed. Let's stick to it for the time being and if I have any inspirations after I read the manuscript, let's see if they meet with your approval. I doubt if we can do better than this, however. I understand that the censors will read the manuscript before we see it, and I think that's an excellent rule.

Beatrice Lillie at Gethsemani! Having seen her show, my mind reels at the thought of a visit from that zany character. It must have been fun. I enclose an interview with Eliot from last week's Times; its description of him as looking like an "abbot of an ascetic order" will amuse you.

With best regards.

Ever yours,
Robert Giroux

P.S. Father Englebert has not looked me up so far but I thoroughly approve the moratorium on prefaces by you.

DECEMBER 3, 1953

Our Lady of Gethsemani
[Letterhead]

Dear Bob:
Here is the picture of St. Bernard I was expecting from Europe. It is a mosaic, from a chapel in the Vatican. Identification is on the back. The other smaller pictures are of the spot where Bernard began preaching the Crusade at Vezelay in Burgundy. I imagine you can find good use for both these subjects. In addition I can send you, if you like, a picture of a page of manuscript of St. Bernard from our vault here. Let me know.

The monk who sent me these pictures from Belgium would like to have them back when we are finished.

I am finishing the Considerations (thought of another title: Viewpoints) this week, by the grace of God. Sister Thérèse has promised to type the book for me while our censors are going over my carbons. Thus you will have a clean copy without too much delay, although there is no hurry.

I close in haste. God bless you.

With best wishes, as ever.

In Christ,
Tom
fr. M. Louis /s/

DECEMBER 7, 1953

Rev. M. Louis, O.C.S.O.
Abbey of Our Lady of Gethsemani
Trappist, Kentucky

Dear Tom:

The photos arrived this morning; many thanks for getting them to us so quickly. The mosaic portrait of St. Bernard is amazing, but we're not so sure that it lends itself to a jacket design. Perhaps we should use the cloister picture on the jacket, and this as a frontispiece. But another thought occurs, and I wish I had remembered about the page of manuscript in your vault, which might make the best jacket of all. Can you get a picture of it? And, if it has color, can you also get a color shot? Meanwhile, we'll hold these pictures from Belgium and return them later.

I'm delighted that Sister Thérèse's typing means we shall have a clean copy with less delay. You have had such good titles on all your books; Viewpoints seems rather flat in contrast and I for one prefer Considerations. Fortunately, there's time to brood about this before we have to make a final choice.

Ever yours,
Robert Giroux

DECEMBER 11, 1953

Gethsemani

Dear Bob:

Here is one picture of a St. Bernard manuscript that we have handy here. It is a little faint, but it could get by on a cover I think. I was rather thinking of the mosaic as a frontispiece. I also hear from this man in Belgium that he has a nice picture of St. Vorles, where St. Bernard was educated. That might serve for your cover. Do you want to write to him directly to save time: Rev. Père Anselme Dimier [O.C.S.O.], Notre Dame de Scourmont, Forges-lez-Chimay, Belgium. He knows English very well. In haste—and blessings.

Devotedly in Christ,
Tom
fr. M. Louis /s/

JANUARY 8, 1954

Rev. M. Louis, O.C.S.O.
Abbey of Our Lady of Gethsemani
Trappist, Kentucky

Dear Tom:

The galleys of THE LAST OF THE FATHERS are all at hand, and I enclose the marked set for the printer herewith. A duplicate set for your files will go off Monday. I will wait for your corrections before sending a set of proofs for the Imprimatur. I don't think there will be any difficulty, since part of the book is after all a Papal encyclical. The letters from the Cardinal Protector and Abbot General ought to have some impact also. As usual, the sooner we can have your corrected proofs, the happier our printer will be.

Jay Laughlin sent me a copy of BREAD IN THE WILDERNESS. I wrote to tell him what a beautiful book I think it is; it was well worth all that time. I also think it is one of your finest pieces of writing; the changes and revisions are excellent. Jay wrote me:

Tom writes me that he hopes still to get around to the commentary on St. John of the Cross one of these days. That would suit me fine, and I trust that you will not raise any objections. He also intimates that he may return to the writing of poetry, which I have long urged on him, and that too would be a cause for rejoicing down at New Directions.

Both items are certainly agreeable to us, since the first is of long standing and since all your poetry has been done by them. Jay seems to be satisfied or at least reconciled to these items alone. I hope that will be all he does.

We ended the year with a sales figure of 86,298 copies of THE SIGN OF JONAS, which is truly amazing. In 1953, five years after publication, THE SEVEN STOREY MOUNTAIN sold 5,000 copies in our regular edition; many books sell less than this in their <u>first</u> year. I hope you will give these figures to Father Abbot, to whom I send my every good wish for the new year, as well as to yourself.

Ever yours,
Robert Giroux

P.S. I'm sending proofs of the THE LAST OF THE FATHERS to Dan Walsh; I spoke to him on New Year's and he is lunching with me soon.

JANUARY 14, 1954

Our Lady of Gethsemani
[Letterhead]

Dear Bob:

I have been over these proofs and everything in the main seems very satisfactory. I did not plan to concentrate on them so intensely as I have done, but today I have been free and I never know what tomorrow may bring, so I thought I had better get this job off my chest while I was able.

You will notice two things: first I made two significant and rather long additions—two and three pages. They were necessary—one on the book De Consideratione, which I had not treated at all, the other on St. Bernard's Mariology. Second, I have gone over the Encyclical text and tried to put it into proper English. I have not done this as completely as I [would] have liked, but I tried to make the text idiomatic at least in the most important passages. I feel as you do that it is a great tragedy that Papal documents are presented to English-speaking people in English worthy of a well-educated Chinese. Protestants who run into the usual formal jargon will always be convinced that the Pope is a foreigner and a spy, and that he has nothing to say anyway.

If these additions mean that I can no longer add a bibliography and index, please let me know. I will gladly sacrifice the bibliography, would like if possible to have at least a page or two of index.

Certainly we should get a new set of proofs with the corrections before submitting it all to the censor.

I was glad to hear the [sales] figure on Jonas. Did you ever give any more thought to that idea of the revised edition of the Mountain. Perhaps we could do the Mountain and Jonas together, boxed. The two might make a good Modern Library Giant, afterwards. I speak as one less wise.

I hope you had a good Christmas. The snow here has been deep and wonderful, and the woods are quiet. I am busy with many things, notably with the Scripture course on St. Paul.

Does Dan have any changes to suggest in the book?

God bless you, Bob. May you have a good and happy and holy New Year—under Our Lady's protection. I keep you in my prayers.

As ever.

Devotedly in Christ,
Tom
fr. M. Louis /s/

Rev. M. Louis, O.C.S.O.
Abbey of Our Lady of Gethsemani
Trappist, Kentucky

Dear Tom:

In seeking a motif to illustrate THE LAST OF THE FATHERS, our designer came across the enclosed picture of St. Bernard, which I am sure you will find as interesting as I do. The question is, would it be suitable to use the coats of arms (particularly the fleur de lis), or the bishop's staff, or the mitre, or the dog (this is new to me; what is its significance?), the heart, or any decorative symbol not shown here which you think might be used typographically? Don't bother to return this photostat; but if you could let us have your counsel and suggestions about the motif, which we need at once before going into pages, I will be most grateful.

Many thanks for getting the proofs back so promptly. I'm delighted with the revisions in the encyclical, and in the text. There was one repetition in the added material, about the Marian writings of St. Bernard being the best things he ever wrote; I inserted a phrase to explain the repetition and, when you see the page proofs, I hope you'll approve. Also, in the encyclical, where the phrase about the "mystical kiss" occurs, you added a parenthetical note signed "Tr."; we've used brackets instead of parenthesis, deleting the "Tr." which will puzzle many readers.

With regard to index and bibliography, I wonder if the former is necessary. In so short a book, won't it be possible to locate almost any subject rather easily? If you feel you want to make an index, by all means do so, but I would think that, from the viewpoint of the general reader, a bibliography would be more useful. There are quite a few references both in the text and in the encyclical which need spelling out in a formal bibliography at the end. Index or bibliography (or both, since there is room for both) we shall require copy just as soon as page proofs are ready.

Dan has not yet sent me any comments on the proofs. Perhaps he has written directly to you. [Rev.] James Pike of St. John the Divine [Cathedral] has a review of BREAD IN THE WILDERNESS in next Sunday's [New York] Times which is a rave notice for him. I enclose it. I wish he could transcend the spirit of condescension which seems so ingrained in him.

With all good wishes.

Ever yours,
Robert Giroux

FEBRUARY 3, 1954

Harcourt, Brace & Company, Inc.
[Letterhead]

Rev. M. Louis, O.C.S.O.
Abbey of Our Lady of Gethsemani
Trappist, Kentucky

Dear Tom:

You are too kind about the Abbot of Villers design, and it was stupid of me not to see that the fleur de lis had nothing to do with Clairvaux, that the mitres were meant negatively, and so on. We shall have to find some other motif, and set the dog free.

Carl Jung's CONTRIBUTIONS TO ANALYTICAL PSYCHOLOGY is out of print, but I've found a copy on my shelves which you may have. I'm sending off a packet of books, including this; several [James] Thurber titles; E. M. Forster's THE HILL OF DEVI, an extremely funny book which is profoundly serious and whose chief character, a rajah, has a deeply religious sense. I'll order the Karen Horney [perhaps *Neurosis and Human Growth: The Struggle toward Self-Realization* (1950)] and J. F. Powers [perhaps *The Prince of Darkness and Other Stories* (1947)] for you. Our list of books in print will go into the package; if you find anything else you want, let me know.

I enclose the revised front matter. Page proofs will soon be ready.

Ever yours,
Bob /s/

FEBRUARY 16, 1954

Our Lady of Gethsemani
[Letterhead]

Dear Bob:

Here are the index and bibliography—in more of a mess than my stuff usually is, even! I did them in a rush. Sorry. I hope they can be figured out.

The proofs follow under separate cover with a few very minor changes. I am very pleased with the whole thing. The only question in my mind is whether we ought not to put something about the Encyclical on the title page. I'd feel better if we could.

As for the bibliography, I leave the form to you: whether you want all the titles in italics or not.

And now to thank you for all the books. I cannot adequately do so. It was a tremendous package. The Hill of Devi looks like the best, but I haven't been into it yet, except for the pictures, which are wonderful.

Then [James] Thurber. Yes, I still think he is very funny. I don't know just how much he will be able to circulate around here. Probably not much. With those who can take him he will, no doubt, operate prodigies. This Karen Horney seems to me to be very lucid and practical and solid. As for your [Carl] Jung—let's consider him a long-term loan. I'll eventually get all I need out of it, and it won't get around in the community much, so when I am through you can have him back. But thanks for everything.

The typed ms. of "Viewpoints" is back, but the censors have not come through. Censorship is greatly prolonged now because everything comes back only through Rome. I hope there is no hitch, and see no reason why there should be. I have new ideas about a title, but you will see.

The other day I got a card from Mark Van Doren saying he would be down here early in March. It made me very happy. He is working on a long poem on Lincoln and, as you so well know, Lincoln's birthplace is barely a bomb's throw from Gethsemani. He is bringing Dorothy with him.

Well, it rains, and I transplant maple trees.

Did I thank you for the review of <u>Bread</u>? I have seen no others. I hope the book is in print again!

As ever, with all best wishes—and God bless you.

Devotedly in Christ,
Tom
fr. M. Louis /s/

FEBRUARY 19, 1954

Gethsemani

Dear Bob:

After sending off the last letter and the proofs, I suddenly thought of two other things I would like to add to the <u>Last of the Fathers</u>. The first is a dedication—

To Étienne Gilson.[1]

After the book is ready we could send him a specially bound copy. I certainly owe him a lot, and since he is one of the best men on St. Bernard in our time, this would be the most appropriate way of showing it. The second thing—I wonder if we could not add somewhere in the preface some such statement as this:

The importance of this encyclical lies above all in its practicality. Pope Pius XII makes use of the doctrine of St. Bernard to bring the highest spiritual perfection within reach of all Christians, whether they be living in the cloister or in the world. And he shows us that the Gospel of

Christ, which was preached to all men by the Savior and His Apostles, must still remain a living reality in the lives of all. Indeed it must be the one Reality upon which our lives are entirely centered, if life is to retain its significance.

Again, forgive the mess. I seem to remember that there was plenty of space on the last page of the preface, and that is why I do not scruple to make this addition.
As ever.

Devotedly in Christ,
Tom
fr. M. Louis /s/

1. Étienne Gilson (1884–1978), a French Thomistic philosopher, wrote, among many other works, *The Spirit of Mediaeval Philosophy* (1936), *Reason and Revelation in the Middle Ages* (1938), *The Mystical Theology of Saint Bernard* (1940), and *History of Philosophy and Philosophical Education* (1948).

FEBRUARY 25, 1954

Rev. M. Louis, O.C.S.O.
Abbey of Our Lady of Gethsemani
Trappist, Kentucky

Dear Tom:
Many thanks for the index and bibliography and the addition to the preface, which arrived in the same mail. All this has gone through and so have the proofs, which arrived this morning. We have made out the dedication to Étienne Gilson. All that's lacking now is the imprimatur and the ex parte ordinis [including the *nihil obstat* and *imprimi potest*]. Can you send me the correct wording for the latter?

I'm delighted to hear that Mark Van Doren, and Dorothy too, are coming down. It's just possible that I'll have to be in Cincinnati in late March. If so, I shall certainly get to Louisville and the Knob Hill country.

Under separate cover I am sending you Father LaFarge's autobiography, THE MANNER IS ORDINARY.[1] It's had a wonderful press with a cover review in the Sunday Times by Jacques Barzun. LaFarge and his story are anything but ordinary; a grand person to work with.

Ever yours,
Robert Giroux

1. John LaFarge, S.J., worked for many years as a parish priest in southern Maryland before becoming editor of *America* magazine. His father was a famous American painter and maker of stained-glass windows.

Gethsemani

Dear Bob:

Just a hasty note to ask two more favors: first, as soon as the corrections are made in the FATHERS, perhaps I could have a complete set of page proofs to file here eventually, and to be shown to a friend, a Passionist Priest [Barnabas Mary Ahern, C.P.] who gives good advice.

Then, having looked over your new booklist, I got Reverend Father's permission to ask you to send the new Stuart Chase book whenever it is ready, and charge to our account. It looks interesting. So does the whole list.

God bless you, and happy Lent.

Devotedly in Christ,
Tom
fr. M. Louis /s/

MARCH 3, 1954

Rev. M. Louis, O.C.S.O.
Abbey of Our Lady of Gethsemani
Trappist, Kentucky

Dear Tom:

Here is a file set of THE LAST OF THE FATHERS, with all the corrections but lacking the index and bibliography which I believe you have in galleys.

Under separate cover Stuart Chase's POWER OF WORDS and T.S. Eliot's new play, THE CONFIDENTIAL CLERK, go off to you.

As ever,
Robert Giroux

MARCH 4, 1954

Rev. M. Louis, O.C.S.O.
Abbey of Our Lady of Gethsemani
Trappist, Kentucky

Dear Tom:

Here is a review by George Shuster in next Sunday's Herald-Tribune.

Mr. Jack Adams, who is a friend of Father LaFarge, and a fine man active in the Catholic interracial movement, has asked if you would autograph some of your books. I hate to burden you with this chore during the Lenten season, but since a Trappistine vocation is involved I thought you might want to do it. Under separate cover you will receive a package of eight books, two each of your books on our list. One set should be autographed to Barbara Howe, "on the occasion of her entering the Trappistine monastery of Our Lady of the Assumption" in Canada. Could those four be mailed to the following address (I don't know her name in the Order):

> Miss Barbara Howe
> Monastère de Notre Dame de l'Assomption
> Rogersville
> New Brunswick, Canada

Perhaps a note should be enclosed saying that these come as gifts from Mr. Adams of New York? The other four books should be inscribed to Mr. Adams and sent to him as follows:

> Mr. John Q. Adams, President
> Manhattan Refrigerating Co.
> 525 West Street
> New York City 14

Please let me know the postage charges for both packages; Mr. Adams wants to take care of this.[1]

Ever yours,
Robert Giroux

1. In three subsequent letters, dated June 2, 1954, June 8, 1954, and June 16, 1954 (not included in this collection because they are of minimal importance), RG and TM dealt with the problem of these books being lost. Thus, additional copies were sent.

MARCH 18, 1954

WESTERN UNION
FATHER LOUIS
ABBEY OF GETHSEMANI
TRAPPIST, KENTUCKY

ARE THE NAMES OF YOUR CENSORS FOR LAST OF FATHERS MAL-LOY AND BOURNE AND IS IMPRIMI POTEST ABBOT GENERAL[?] WE NEED COPY SOON AS POSSIBLE[.] REGARDS[.]

BOB

WESTERN UNION
ROBERT GIROUX
HARCOURT BRACE AND CO
383 MADISON AVE NYK

CENSORS FOR NEW BOOK ARE MALLOY AND BOURNE[,] SAME AS IN JONAS[.]

MERTON

MAY 14, 1954

Our Lady of Gethsemani
[Letterhead]

Dear Bob:

Copies of the Last of the Fathers reached me yesterday. As I expected, it is handsomely done. The print on the cover turned out nicely after all—much better than the one with the hound and the discarded mitres. The close quarters in which the monks are huddled in their monastery suggests a comparison between the cenobitic life led at Clairvaux and that led at Gethsemani.

Father Abbot said, though, it was rather a pity the book had to be so high priced, and I feel somewhat the same way. One can't have everything. I am always happy to see a good-looking book come out, especially if it is one of mine. I was glad about Bread in the Wilderness being one of the fifty books of the year, glad to see some Harcourt, Brace books on the list—the catalogue looked very interesting. I was especially glad to realize that there is a very good printer [Victor Hammer] here in Kentucky, who without a blush dares to print a fine edition of Pico della Mirandola.

Remember I spoke of sending a specially bound volume of the book to [Étienne] Gilson? Can you get one bound, or are you already doing so? I would be glad to get it as soon as possible, if it is not too much trouble. And could you also do me the favor of getting one bound for the Holy Father (this time he really rates a presentation copy) and for Cardinal Fumasoni Biondi (in red)? Then send them here, please, and I will send them both to the Cardinal with all kinds of inscriptions.

I was relieved that you and Naomi decided against the sudden inspiration of a Marian year project that came too late. I would not really have time for it anyway. The Scripture course I am teaching on St. Paul keeps me busy. I have had very little time to write anything.

"Viewpoints" has finally been approved by the censors. I think what held everything up was not the censorship but the fact that the Abbot General's secretary got the two reports under different names, thought there was question of two different books. He was waiting for the second report on each one.

I want to do a little work on it, however, and I presume there's no rush. Next spring was the time we decided on for publication, unless I am much mistaken.

Do you have Karl Menninger's "Man against himself"? I think Harcourt, Brace published it, and I could use a copy. I am also looking for Erich Fromm's "Man for himself" and "Psychiatry [Psychoanalysis] and religion." After that I will keep quiet about psychoanalysis for a while. Karen Horney's books have proved immensely useful to me, however. Can you get me the 3 above mentioned and charge them to the royalty account? I am sorry to ask you so many favors. But here, finally, is another one: I enclose a list of monastic publications and writers who could do with review copies of the Fathers.

As ever, with very best wishes and prayers.

In Christ,
Tom
fr. M. Louis /s/

MAY 28, 1954

Rev. M. Louis, O.C.S.O.
Abbey of Our Lady of Gethsemani
Trappist, Kentucky

Dear Tom:

Many thanks for your letter of the 14th. I'm glad the advance copies have reached you and that you liked its looks. I've sent copies to Dan, Ed Rice, Lax, and your relatives, and review copies have also gone to the ten monastic publications and writers. Incidentally, a new magazine called The Pope Speaks, which is devoted to Papal documents, asked us if they could use your translation of the text of Dr. Mellifluus. I hastily assured them it was not your translation, but you may nevertheless hear from them.

I wish the book had been priced lower myself, but the present price does represent the value of the three-piece binding, the two colors throughout and the other decorations. It could have been issued almost as a pamphlet, but we wanted to make it a permanent and handsome book and I sincerely hope we have done so. The principal item in printing costs now is the binding. Believe it or not, we have to charge $4.00 for T. S. Eliot's FOUR QUARTETS, which is only sixty-four pages. As one publisher said to me recently, "It's getting so we'll soon have to charge $5.00

for the paper and binding of an average-size novel without any text at all—and maybe that's the way to do them."

By the way, the special hand binding takes so long (Father LaFarge's book recently took three months) that I wonder if you wouldn't prefer to send the inscribed copies to the Holy Father and Cardinal Fumasoni Biondi in the present binding? I'll be only too glad to get the white leather binding for the Papal Library and the red leather for the Cardinal's—if you don't think the time element is important.

I hope Karl Menninger's MAN AGAINST HIMSELF has reached you. One of the Erich Fromm books, PSYCHOANALYSIS AND RELIGION, has just come to us and we are forwarding it. I'm also enclosing a catalogue blurb about Karl Stern's new book which we are bringing out this fall on the subject of psychiatry and religion. Dr. Stern takes the position entirely contrary to Fromm's. I find the manuscript fascinating, but it needs a lot of work before it will be ready for the printer.

I am happy to know that VIEWPOINTS has finally been approved by the censors.[1] I shall be eager to see the manuscript when it is completed and, even though we agreed it is to be for next spring, I hope you will have it ready before the end of June. I have not given up hope of getting down to Gethsemani this summer; it would do me good.

Please give my very best wishes to Father Abbot and tell him I am writing separately about the royalty statement on "Jonas," about which he properly raised some questions. We are having the figures analyzed, and I expect them early next week. Just as soon as they are ready I will send them along.

With all good wishes.

As ever,
Robert Giroux

1. Reference is to *No Man Is an Island.*

VIGIL OF PENTECOST, 1954 [JUNE 5, 1954]

Our Lady of Gethsemani
[Letterhead]

Dear Bob:

Many thanks for your letter. I received the Menninger book but not Fromm's as yet. I am extremely glad Karl Stern is writing about the relationship of psychoanalysis and religion [*The Third Revolution: A Study of Psychiatry and Religion*]. Karen Horney is the only psychoanalyst I have run into so far who has the integrity + the balance to see things as they must be—as the very logic of psychoanalysis itself demands. After all, if there are right + wrong ways of acting there must be such things as moral values + the idea of moral freedom must signify something.

Could you please give me Stern's address? I am sure he would not mind if I write to him when I have various questions. The problems of various kinds of neuroses are keeping me busy at the moment + I am becoming convinced that spiritual direction, in our day, presupposes a pretty solid groundwork of analysis in very many cases. You cannot build asceticism on a neurosis—although a neurosis can be negotiated, so to speak, ascetically. Anyway, I'll probably have lots of questions to ask Stern. I hope his book will be very good. If you want to risk sending me a set of proofs I might get a chance to go over it, but I can't absolutely promise.

I quite understand about the Last of the Fathers + I know production costs have gone up.

So far I haven't had a moment to work on Viewpoints. The Scripture course I am teaching slows down writing quiet a lot, although it may someday lead to a book.

I also want to finish that St. Aelred job. The nuns at Seton Hill say they have been holding up an anthology of Aelred waiting for my book to come out. I'd like to print some of their texts right into the biography. We'll see later.

God bless you always. I'll pray for you in a special way at Mass tomorrow. As ever.

Sincerely in Christ,
Tom
fr. M. Louis /s/

JULY 9, 1954

Gethsemani
Trappist, Kentucky

Dear Bob:

Here finally is the manuscript of Viewpoints, with a new title. The prologue explains the title, the quote from [John] Donne (which might be put on the title page) also shows its source. Perhaps you could also add a dedication: "To the scholastics at Our Lady of Gethsemani" or words to that effect.

I have made a few additions which the censors will check, but the book as a whole is approved by the censors of the Order. You have only to get it approved by the diocese. I wanted to get the manuscript to you as quickly as possible to have it off my hands. I presume you are planning publication for next spring.

If the title still is not good enough, I also thought of another fragment of the Donne quotation: "A Piece of the Continent." But all my titles have "of" in the middle of them, and I am sick of that.

This book has been cooking for a long time, and that is the way I think it ought to be. I am glad of it.

Did you ever get a letter from me asking for Karl Stern's address? If you answered it and I never got the answer, that would be nothing unusual. By the way, the books all went off to your friend's friend in Canada, etc. At least, they started into the monastic machinery that leads to the post office, duly signed by me. So I suppose they are well on their way.

I have been having an awful time with the French censors and the Abbot General. "Ascent to Truth" was all printed and everything when they stopped publication on a purely editorial consideration—the book was not "opportune" (the English version had been criticized by a bishop in some Dominican magazine of which our Order is evidently terrified) and then immediately after that the General forbade any more work on the French translation of Jonas. Two contracts torn up. I am waiting to hear the reaction of the publisher—a Protestant, and a guy with a high reputation for treating his authors well and observing contracts . . .

Have there been any reviews of the Fathers? Or is it doing anything? Not much, I suppose. I sent copies to the Holy Father and Gilson and Cardinal Fumasoni but haven't heard anything back.

I am not satisfied with the ending of the present manuscript and will probably add a couple of pages on the silence of Our Lady.

I am still thinking of building up that pamphlet What is Contemplation into a small book, as I once promised.[1] If I get a chance to do it during the students' vacation, it will be done. If not, then no one can tell what happens to the idea.

Hope everything is going well. I still wish you would drop by Gethsemani sometime. Naomi may have told you of a letter I wrote her about an article, which would involve the new Stern book.[2]

God bless you, and all best wishes—as ever.

Sincerely in Christ,
Tom
fr. M. Louis /s/

1. Eventually TM will revise *What Is Contemplation?* into a full-length book: *The Inner Experience: Notes on Contemplation*, ed. William H. Shannon (San Francisco: HarperCollins, 2003).
2. TM, "The Neurotic Personality in the Monastic Life," *The Merton Annual* 4 (1992): 3–19 (not published in TM's lifetime).

JULY 23, 1954

Harcourt, Brace & Company, Inc.
[Letterhead]

Rev. M. Louis, O.C.S.O.
Abbey of Our Lady of Gethsemani
Trappist, Kentucky

Dear Tom:

The manuscript of NO MAN IS AN ISLAND arrived safely, and I am now reading it with pleasure. The title is so much better than VIEWPOINTS and the whole arrangement of the text seems an improvement. I have two weeks' vacation from the office beginning today (I'm typing this letter myself after hours) and that will give me a chance to read the ms. in leisure. If you write me (and I hope you will) during that period, the address is 219 East 66th Street, NYC 21.

Forgive me for not having passed along Dr. Karl Stern's address. It is Ottawa General Hospital, Ottawa, Ontario, Canada. He was visiting New York recently, and we spoke of you. He admires your books very much, and would be delighted to hear from you. He is a good, humble, brilliant man. He probably will protest my showing you the tentative table of contents of his new book THE THIRD REVOLUTION, which I find fascinating and which to my great joy has received the imprimatur of the Archbishop of Ottawa. It has also been taken by the St. Thomas More Book Club. It is not yet in proofs, but I'll send you an early set; I realize you may not have the time, and this is not of course for a quote; it will simply be an extra set which will be available if you are free to consult it, like the Menninger, Horney and Fromm (I hope this has reached you) books.

I really don't believe that the Order appreciates the seriousness of permitting a contract on the business level, and then withholding permission on the censorial level. It has every right to do the latter (and no one would question this right in itself), but when it <u>follows</u> the former a serious situation of scandal develops. I wonder if the Abbot General is entirely aware of this?[1] Naomi is justifiably upset, and so am I—particularly in the wake of our original experience (which would not have caused scandal because Naomi and I would see that it did not). But with a French publisher the matter is beyond our control; and with the state that poor country is in, just having sold out millions of Catholics in Indo-China . . . Surely that extraordinary letter of Jacques Maritain about JONAS could not have failed to impress the General, coming from so thoroughly French a writer. As for the Dominican review of ASCENT TO TRUTH, I am amazed that the British point of view (which is quite peculiar about <u>all</u> books by American writers) should wield such influence in France. I know this must be an ordeal and that you do not criticize any of it; I hope and pray they see the wisdom of permitting French publication of works which, in fact, now have existence in print with the Abbot General's <u>imprimi potest</u>.

Please pray for me and my personal intention.

As ever,

Bob /s/

P.S. In case <u>Jubilee</u> did not send you their review, I enclose it with some others. Fr. [Raymond Leopold] Bruckberger (that French viewpoint again) surely could not have thought you <u>intended</u> such a little book as THE LAST OF THE FATHERS as full-length study! Perhaps the <u>Times</u> first asked Maritain to review it and he had to refuse because of his ill health.

1. NB wrote to Dom Gabriel Sortais, in a letter dated July 19, 1954, expressing her dismay that neither *The Ascent to Truth* nor *The Sign of Jonas* could be published in France. In his reply to NB, dated August 3, 1954, Dom Sortais noted that *The Ascent to Truth* needed to be revised to be acceptable to a Latin temperament; he was aware that TM did not have the time to do the necessary revisions. The second book, in his opinion, gave at times an unfavorable impression of Cistercian life.

OCTOBER 11, 1954

Gethsemani

Dear Bob:

Many thanks for the books—Judson, Mumford and Coffin.[1] I am already greatly enjoying the anthology. Suddenly liking W. H. Auden much more than ever before, glad to have so much Emily Dickinson. It is a fine collection. However, by mistake you sent two packages, the same order twice over. We are keeping the second copy of Judson and sending back the extras of the other two books.

Existential Communion is about finished in the first draft but it will take some going over.[2] I got a nice letter from Gilson about the Last of the Fathers, and I enclose it.* Will you please return? How comes No Man Is an Island?

Best wishes, as ever.

Sincerely in Christ,
Tom
fr. M. Louis /s/

*I imagine it is not for quotation!

1. Horace Judson, *The Techniques of Reading: An Integrated Program for Improved Comprehension and Speed*; Lewis Mumford, *In the Name of Sanity*; Charles Monroe Coffin, *The Major Poets: English and American*. Subsequently, RG sent TM the following books by Franz Kafka: *The Great Wall of China, Parables, The Metamorphosis, The Castle, Amerika, The Penal Colony*, and *Letters to Milena*.
2. This is the working title for what would become *The New Man* (1961).

NOVEMBER 4, 1954

Gethsemani
Trappist, Kentucky

Dear Bob:

The Kafka books have all arrived—Penal Colony, Metamorphosis, Amerika, Castle, Great Wall, Parables, Letters to M. It all looks very exciting, and I have been enjoying some of his brief meditations (Advice to gentleman jockeys, etc.).

However, the package of typewriter ribbons and carbon paper never arrived. I was waiting around for it, and the letter from your secretary finally came asking about them. I just cannot account for what happens to packages that are sent. It seems strange that two from you have gone astray in six months. But they never reached Father Abbot's office. I checked there several times. Do not replace them, please. I have got some ribbons from Louisville finally.

Thanks, in any case, for all your kindness. I am especially grateful for the Kafka books and will get a lot out of them. They will pep up the writing too.

By the way, what is coming of No Man Is an Island? Are you doing anything with it?

I was glad, too, to get the new Stern book. I have not begun it yet but will be reading it shortly. It looks very interesting and well done. I got into a correspondence with Erich Fromm who is teaching psychoanalysis at the University of Mexico. He is an interesting person, and amenable to discussion anyway. I think a certain amount of correspondence will be fruitful. I will write Stern when I have finished the Third Revolution.

Finally, a French [Benedictine] monastery—La Pierre qui Vire [in Burgundy]—is putting out a gift book on the monastic life, mostly fine pictures (I have not seen them yet, but I know the kind of thing they do).[1] I am to write the text I mentioned that I would like to offer you the book for an American edition. I will send you the pictures when they come. However there is one catch. They want to have both editions (if there is to be one here) printed in France (as far as the pictures are concerned). They say they have a very fine gravure firm they are dealing with in Alsace, and I believe them. Would you be willing to accept the book on that basis? Anyway, I'll show you the photographs.

Did the Last of the Fathers get anywhere?

How have you been? I hope you are well—and I still urge you to take a little vacation down here sometime, if you can. Would be very glad to see you again. I keep you in my prayers.

In case I don't write again before Christmas, I wish you a holy and happy feast with all blessings.

Devotedly yours in Christ,
Tom
fr. M. Louis /s/

1. The reference is to TM, *Silence in Heaven: A Book on the Monastic Life* (New York: Thomas Y. Crowell, 1956), originally published in French as *Silence dans le Ciel* (1955).

NOVEMBER 8, 1954

Rev. M. Louis, O.C.S.O.
Abbey of Our Lady of Gethsemani
Trappist, Kentucky

Dear Tom:

I'm glad to know that the Kafka books have all safely arrived, and I am dismayed to learn that you have not received the typewriter ribbons and the carbon paper. They should have been in your hands long ago. In any event we are making up another package today and it will go off to you without fail by first-class mail. If there are any other supplies of this kind which you need, please don't hesitate to let us know.

I have returned from a big editorial swing around the country—Chicago, San Francisco, Los Angeles, Dallas, Gambier [Ohio]—and I very much regret that I did not have the time to stop off at Gethsemani. I am grateful for your renewed invitation to pay a leisurely visit and I mean to do so when I have the time.

I have read the manuscript of NO MAN IS AN ISLAND through twice, and I think it is magnificent. I have a few editorial queries which I am getting together and will send off to you shortly. Am I right in assuming that the manuscript has been cleared by your censors and by the Abbot General? If not, will it nevertheless be possible to publish in time for Lent? Dan Herr of the Thomas More Book Club was in this week and is very anxious to have it as the Lenten selection if at all possible. THE LAST OF THE FATHERS, about which you ask, has done very well indeed and has now reached the eight thousand mark—which, considering its size, its nature, and the price, is a very healthy trade sales record.

With regard to the picture book on monastic life which you are doing for La Pierre qui Vire, their desire to have both editions printed in France raises several complications. If the text appears under the pictures, or even on the reverse of the pictures, we shall be unable to add it to the French gravure. In this case, the English text will also have to be printed in France, which means a meticulous job of reading proofs set up by the French compositors and a lot of mailing back and forth of proofs. If, on the other hand, the pictures are all to be done in one section with a full text proceeding in another section, it may be possible to take their gravure work. I don't see why the American edition has to be printed in France at all, and I think you ought to consult Naomi on the handling of this, because it can lead to royalty complications on your work and she may be able to avoid this. But, meanwhile, please send us the photographs so we can consider the possibilities of the book and, if possible, indicate the kind of layout that they have in mind, the amount of text which you will write, etc.

Did I tell you that the Thomas More Book Club has taken Karl Stern's THE THIRD REVOLUTION? Though there have been few reviews so far, it has got off to the excellent start it deserves. I hope you will let me know what you think of the book when you have read it and I know that Dr. Stern will be anxious to hear from you.

Yours ever,
Robert Giroux

P.S. What a wonderful letter of Gilson's on THE LAST OF THE FATHERS! As you requested, I return it herewith.

NOVEMBER 16, 1954

Our Lady of Gethsemani
[Letterhead]

Dear Bob:
The ribbons and carbon paper arrived. Alleluia. I ought to have enough to keep me quite busy for a few weeks now. Many thanks.

Everything is clear with the censors. NO MAN IS AN ISLAND can go ahead to the printer whenever you feel ready. But you are left with the job of sending it to the bishop. I do not know who the censors of the Order were. Just put Imprimi Potest and Dom Gabriel [Sortais]'s name as in the last one. I'll check and see if there is a date.

As for the name: I have thought of this one, which seems to me to be fairly good:

ROADS TO A FRONTIER

Other suggestions: Beyond Solitude; Pathways; Highways and Hedges; Wine from Libanus; Beyond Joy and Sorrow. When I see so many titles for one book, it occurs to me that perhaps they are all completely meaningless. I did not think them all up myself. Maybe in the end, you will have to discover a title. I'll keep thinking. (Between us, Bea Lillie's gag man and I thought up "Emeralds and Ashes," which I really like but it probably has nothing to do with anything.)

Many thanks for the THIRD REVOLUTION. I am half-way through it and I will comment and write to Stern when I have finished, but even now I think it is remarkably good—a clear survey of the whole question, in its context. I like the wide-angle lens with which he views it all. From that point of view the book has a unique value.

I'll check with La Pierre qui Vire about the picture book. Still have received nothing. I will let you know as soon as I do.

More when I get your editorial suggestions. Best wishes.

In Christ,
Tom
fr. M. Louis /s/

NOVEMBER 29, 1954

Rev. M. Louis, O.C.S.O.
Abbey of Our Lady of Gethsemani
Trappist, Kentucky

Dear Tom:
There are only a few editorial points to make about the new book. The front matter is fine, particularly the Prologue "No Man Is an Island." However, it's not true that this phrase was written on [John] Donne's deathbed,

as you state, because it was written in 1623 and he died in 1631. I have therefore changed "on his deathbed" to "during a serious illness," which is true.
The chapter entitled "In the Wilderness" is missing. Did you delete it,
pages 206–211? The manuscript now jumps from 205 to 212, from "The
Inward Solitude" to "Silence." The transition is fine, but since you made
no mention of the deletion and the old chapter still appears in the Contents, I thought I'd better mention it. We are proceeding on the assumption that the chapter stays out.

I'm glad you transferred "The Wind Blows Where It Pleases" from the
beginning. In some ways, it is the most "poetic" chapter, and quite moving, but it was not right to open with. Incidentally, you use the title "Remembering God" in the contents, but "My Soul Remembered God" in the
text and I've made it the latter in both places. OK? The chapter I like best
is "Freedom, Conscience, and Prayer."

Father Abbot sent the censors' names, and we'll send the proofs to the
archbishop's readers here. Do you want to insert a formal Latin dedication to the scholastics, or will the mention in the Author's Note suffice?

Let me know about these small points and meanwhile we shall go
ahead with production.

Yours ever,
Robert Giroux

DECEMBER 5, 1954

Our Lady of Gethsemani
[Letterhead]

Dear Bob:

It was good to get your letter and to learn that everything is simple and
satisfactory with the new, as yet nameless, book. About that name. I still
keep clinging to NO MAN IS AN ISLAND, although Naomi objected and
quoted you as an ally. I sent you a couple of alternatives the other day. Of
these, as I think them over, the only one I still like is BEYOND SOLITUDE.
Finally, reading over the prologue just now, I remembered an idea that
once occurred to me: to use the words WILD FIGS from the Amos quote.[1]
Though it sounds a little queer. Incidentally, thank you for changing the
statement about Donne's deathbed. I am no longer up on everything I
ought to be up on.

Yes, the chapter "In the Wilderness" is definitely missing. The censors
of the Order went up in flames over it because I said it was better to be a
hermit than a cenobite. So I took it out, and sent it to some Benedictines
who loved it and are now planning (with the hopes of permission from
French censors???) to print it in a magazine of theirs. I was happy that
they understood the ideas in it so well, and said such good things about
them in their letter. These are the monks of La Pierre qui Vire—I'll tell
you about the picture book in a minute.

Your other notations are quite ok with me. About the dedication, I enclose a Latin text. I have yet to send the prologue and one or two late additions to our censors. I am enclosing two or three pages added to the chapter Freedom conscience and prayer. I wonder if you received these additions yet. If you have them, will you please send this copy back and I will tussle with the censors over it.

Now about the picture book. The photos have arrived. Bob, they are absolutely marvelous. I have never seen such wonderful stuff anywhere. It is going to be a tremendously effective job. Of course, I will write them that they should forget about the American edition with their printer and go ahead by themselves. For us at this end, I think the only possible way to get organized is for you and me to get together and talk about the book, over the pictures. There may be changes, etc., you would like. There are 100 fine pictures, most of which they intend to run full page, in groups of four pages with, in between, four pages of special text material—quotes from Scripture and ancient monastic rules. As I figure it, I get about thirty pages of text to write myself. I am busy with that now and love the job.

But do you think you could come down? Meanwhile, there are one or two pictures that might need replacing for the American public and I will try to get them to send us a pile of stuff they rejected. I'd also very much like to get some pictures of the Camaldolese into the book. Did Jubilee ever come out with an article on Spanish hermits? That would fit nicely. When I get everything together here, perhaps you could find some way to fly down and talk it all over.

Glad you are going ahead with production on the book, anyway. I'll be waiting for proofs.

Very best Christmas wishes to you, Bob. Tell Dan hello and wish him a merry Christmas from me in case I do not get a chance to write, which is very likely.

God bless you always.

In Christ,
Tom
fr. M. Louis /s/

1. "And Amos answered and said to Amasias: I am not a prophet, nor am I the son of a prophet: but I am a herdsman plucking wild figs" (Amos 7:14, Douay-Rheims Bible).

DECEMBER 13, 1954

Rev. M. Louis, O.C.S.O.
Abbey of Our Lady of Gethsemani
Trappist, Kentucky

Dear Tom:

Several omissions have become apparent during the copyediting of NO MAN IS AN ISLAND. There are three places, which escaped my notice, at which you indicate inserts and have failed to provide copy. The first two are in Chapter II, "Sentences on Hope," both on page 18; the third is in Chapter XI, "Mercy," page 179, the last page of the chapter. Perhaps in the end you changed your mind and decided to leave these pages as they are. In any event, will you let me know whether more copy is coming and, if so, whether we could have it in time to send to the printer with the manuscript itself?

Yours ever,
Robert Giroux

DECEMBER 17, 1954

Our Lady of Gethsemani
[Letterhead]

Dear Bob:

There is no further copy coming for NO MAN IS AN ISLAND. I decided to leave those spots unfilled. I presume you got a recent letter of mine with some additions for the chapter on Freedom Conscience and Prayer.

By the way, is there any remote chance of a second edition of the Last of the Fathers? I made a few important additions in the French version and they would add much to the English one. Also, I received a nice note from the Vatican of which I will send you a copy when I get time. If possible, I would like to see a new edition in a moderate, popular priced, pamphlet edition . . . What do you think? Is it at all feasible?

I finished the text for that monastic picture book, had a good time writing it. Still wish you could come down and talk about the pictures. But anyway let me know what next. I don't think I can send the text, under present legislation, until it is past the censors.

Again, holy and happy Christmas.

In Christ,
Tom
fr. M. Louis /s/

[DECEMBER 1954]

Dear Tom:

Forgive my long silence. This is just to send you a rather large Christmas card in the form of Illustration. It has the best color photos of the Matisse chapel at Vence [France] yet printed. And isn't that cover of Jean Fouquet's "Saint Stephen" incredible? It took me a long time to note the connection between the rock and the back of his head: a perfectly composed martyr. I have much to write to you and Father James [Fox] about, and I shall when our sales conference (which has swamped me) ends on Friday. I saw Jay Laughlin at a party Monday, and we are lunching next week. THE ASCENT TO TRUTH has sold 45,000 copies so far and is still going strong. What a wonderful and amazing sale for a book which must present many difficulties to readers! Tom Burns is expecting to do well. Please tell Father Abbot I am writing about my English trip and the tax problem (which looks gloomy) early next week.

Bob /s/

JANUARY 7, 1955

Rev. M. Louis, O.C.S.O.
Abbey of Our Lady of Gethsemani
Trappist, Kentucky

Dear Tom:
The jacket sketch for NO MAN IS AN ISLAND has just come in and it is one of the best yet by [Enrico] Arno, the artist who did THE WATERS OF SILOE and THE SIGN OF JONAS. We shall have color plates later this month and I am sure you will agree with us that it is the best jacket we have done here.

We should like to have an endpaper illustration similar to those in the three big books. A good cloister shot, or an outdoor scene, or an archway, or an ornamented column—anything with the quality of those Sauvageot photographs—is what we're looking for. By lucky coincidence, Ed Rice was in the office today and he thought he might have something in his photograph file that we might use. At the same time, I'd be grateful for anything you can send us.

With best wishes,
Robert Giroux

JANUARY 10, 1955

Our Lady of Gethsemani
[Letterhead]

Dear Bob:
The galleys came today. I am writing to say that I will get busy on them as soon as possible and that I may have to make slight additions to the text here and there. I will try to keep them down to a minimum.

I notice that you do not begin with the prologue. Did you ever get it? I thought I had sent it to you. Or perhaps there is some other reason why it is not set up. Please drop me a line to let me know.

I finished the text for the book of monastic photographs which I still think you will like very much. It will be typed and then censored. Then you can have it.

I close in haste—I am far behind with correspondence.

God bless you always—best wishes and prayers.

Devotedly in Christ,
Tom
fr. M. Louis /s/

JANUARY 12, 1955

Dear Bob:

I am sending two shots from the monastic collection from France, for the book Silence in Heaven. I think the procession is by far the best one for NO MAN IS AN ISLAND. In fact, it seems to me to be ideal. The other one is nice too. Will you send back whichever one you do not use?

Working slowly on the proofs, I have made a lot of changes in the first galley, but the rest is normal. I want the beginning to be good, and especially I want it to be clearer than it is, so I hope you will bear with me.

All best wishes—God bless you.

Sincerely in Christ,
Tom
fr. M. Louis /s/

JANUARY 15, 1955

Our Lady of Gethsemani
[Letterhead]

Dear Bob:

I have finished the galley proofs and am sending them back today. As I told you, I made a few changes in the first galleys and the rest are relatively clear. However, at the end of chapter 8 I thought I ought to add a few pages. I am sending them with this letter. I hope you don't mind. It seems to me that they are worthwhile and practical in the context. I hope you will agree. However, if they present any special difficulty in the present plan, treat them as you see fit. But I hope they can be fitted in.

Another thing: I thought it would be better to <u>number</u> each separate paragraph, and I have done so throughout. Look it over and see what you think. I like to have the paragraphs clearly separated, and I think most readers would prefer it that way too. However, suit yourself.

Finally, I thought perhaps a short index would be a good idea. Will you give me the go sign on this sometime between now and the page proofs?

Or at least let me know what you think. And again, I am still worrying about the prologue and—I think—there was even a preface wasn't there?

We are going on retreat next week, but I will be accessible for this work, I think.

As ever, with best wishes and blessings.

Devotedly in Christ,
Tom
fr. M. Louis /s/

JANUARY 15, 1955

Our Lady of Gethsemani
[Letterhead]

Dear Bob:

After the 8 extra pages that went off with the proofs yesterday, I am sending 3 more herewith. I hope this is not too much of a nuisance, but I feel this is all worthwhile, especially as the last three are about that old "active contemplative" routine that has been so much discussed. I hope this one will make the Franciscans feel happier.

Also I think I ought to reconsider my passing thought about an index. Surely this book needs no index.

Are we going to stick to this title? If so I am happy.

With best wishes.

Devotedly in Christ,
Tom
fr. M. Louis /s/

JANUARY 28, 1955

Rev. M. Louis, O.C.S.O.
Abbey of Our Lady of Gethsemani
Trappist, Kentucky

Dear Tom:

We have moved forward on the book with great rapidity, and the page proofs are already at hand.[1] I want to thank you and Father Abbot very much for your help in dispatching the galleys so promptly. We were able to include all the extra material, including the pages at the end of Chapter Eight which you mailed on January 15th. We have also numbered the separate passages. I don't know why we did not think of this before; it is absolutely right. Under separate cover today I mailed the corrected page proofs and all the front matter in revised—that is, final—form. On the page proofs, we've indicated corrections which have been brought to the printer's attention. In other words, for all practical purposes the book is finished and you will next see it in bound form—in about four weeks, I believe. I thought you would want to have the final proof for your files.

I enclose a photostat of the jacket design by Enrico Arno. I think it is one of the most successful we have done and it is even more handsome in color. The proof of the final plate should be ready on February 3rd.

Finally, I thought you would be interested in a supplement of books on psychiatry which Dr. Rudolf Allers prepared for the Thomas More Book Club. It includes Karl Stern's book which they mistakenly list as THE FOURTH REVOLUTION!

With all good wishes.

Yours ever,
Robert Giroux

1. By mid-January 1955, *The Seven Storey Mountain* had sold 337,010 hardback copies (in all, including reprint editions, book club editions, and paperback editions, it had sold nearly 900,000 copies); *The Waters of Siloe*, 94,032 copies; *The Ascent to Truth*, 46,052 copies; and *The Sign of Jonas*, 84,578 copies.

JANUARY 31, 1955

Our Lady of Gethsemani
[Letterhead]

Dear Bob:

Following our phone conversation just now (the closest I have been to New York for a long time!), I am sending you the pictures for "Silence in Heaven" [in French, *Silence dans le Ciel*] together with my own text. I want to summarize as clearly as possible the position of the French monks who are putting out the book, their plan, the format, etc. I enclose herewith the two sheets of instructions they sent me, with the titles of the photos, etc.

The book consists of 101 photographs, 224 pages. It begins with some thirty pages of text written by me. The photographs are grouped in sections of 4 or eight pages, separated by four pages of texts from ancient monastic rules, from Scripture, etc. The titles to the pictures will also be on these pages.

The format of the book is 21 x 25.5 centimeters.

The Monks of La Pierre qui Vire, who are bringing out the book, publishing it themselves, are having the whole thing done in "heliogravure" by Braun et Cie of Mulhouse, who are apparently very good at it. But the situation in France does not permit them to print a big enough edition to sell the book at a reasonable price. Therefore, unless they can get us to come in on it with them, they will have to cut down on the text and the photographs, or else they will charge us a 7% royalty for the use of the pictures in our edition.

Furthermore, the collection of pictures which I am sending you to look at is incomplete. One of the photographers they are working with is a temperamental ex-Carmelite nun, who is very good as photographer but is temperamental in business. She ignores our requests for further copies of the pictures we want from her. It will be easier to get a complete set of the pictures if we simply let the original set be printed over there, and import the sheets. Also the prints that were sent us are imperfect in some respects, and their set is the only complete and perfect one.

If there are some other aspects of the monastic life we would like to see covered, they can get pictures for us. I, for one, am asking them to get some pictures of the hermits of Camaldoli in Italy.

The idea of the book is this: it is <u>not</u> to be in any sense journalistic. No "reporting." The whole idea is to maintain a strict monastic reserve, and simply present the monastic life and ideal in pictures. The pictures are numbered on the back, and the list of titles (which are more or less arbitrary) will show you that they are grouped according to a certain plan. The first section "L'appel du desert" leads one in to the atmosphere of solitude and seclusion, then come the sections on manual labor, prayer, vows, liturgy. Finally, the last sections are "symbolic."

If you have any editorial suggestions that you would like to make, they will consider them certainly. They are very attached to the ideas of discretion, and of "evocation"—atmosphere or what you will. The "helio" process will admirably bring out the character of the pictures.

However, you know far better than I what the problems are to be. But for my own part, I am very interested in getting the complete book out in France as well as here, and also it would be very important for the monastery not to have to pay that 7% royalty for the pictures. If we go in with them, we can have the pictures without any further charge, only the cost of our share of the processing—which will probably be low by American standards. To me the thing seems simple enough to be quite safe. I leave the rest to you, and hope we can work out something. I would really like to help those monks and also keep the book as complete as possible.

Since my text has not been censored, I am submitting it to you in a totally "unofficial" way.[1] It was good to talk to you, Bob. I should have urged you strongly to come on down. God bless you.

As ever.

Devotedly in Christ,
Tom
fr. M. Louis /s/

---

1. *Silence in Heaven* prompted a series of lengthy letters in French, dated February 3, 1957; February 9, 1957; April 11, 1957; April 16, 1957; May 14, 1957, between the abbot general and TM. The abbot general had initially been told by one of the censors that the book did not give a balanced view of monastic life in the Western Church as a whole. TM dealt with this problem by adding new material, which was not translated into the Italian edition. The abbot general was not able to figure out what happened. Was TM at fault or was the Italian translator? In his reply to the abbot general, TM said that he was not responsible for this problem; he mentioned that Abbot Fox had suppressed at that time all communica-

tion between himself and his agent and the various editors concerned. In fact, TM knew nothing about the Italian edition at all—which firm had published it or who had contacted the censors. TM tried to explain the situation as best he could. In 1954, one of the monks of La Pierre qui Vire had asked him to write a text entitled "Silence in Heaven," destined, at the same time, for the Camaldolese hermits. Abbot Fox then cut off any correspondence between the Camaldoli and TM. The problem: Abbot Fox put up a wall that prevented any communication—and this was the basis of the problem. In 1955, TM reworked the material to be called *The Silent Life*. He subsequently wrote three new chapters on the Benedictines, Cistercians, and Carthusians. La Pierre qui Vire then went on to publish this material under various titles. TM had never seen the final version of this book. The abbot general, after reading the translation done by Madame Marie Tadié, *La Vie silencieuse*, sent TM a list of corrections to be made, since he expected TM to be more prudent in his judgments than a layman writing about these subjects. He suggested that the problem might be that TM wrote so hastily that he did not reflect sufficiently on the manner of his expression. The abbot general, however, wanted to assure TM of his understanding and affection for him.

MAUNDY THURSDAY [1955?] [APRIL 7, 1955]

Farrar, Straus & Cudahy, Inc.
101 Fifth Avenue
New York 3, N.Y.

Rev. M. Louis, O.C.S.O.
Abbey of Our Lady of Gethsemani
Trappist, Kentucky

Dear Tom:

I deeply regret the misunderstanding which occurred during my last weeks at Harcourt, Brace and which resulted, despite my promise to you, in the final corrections not being made in the first printing of NO MAN IS AN ISLAND (save for twelve specially made copies).[1] I think now that the firm probably acted in good faith, though they still question mine.

However, this afternoon I telephoned Monsignor Fearns and explained the entire matter in detail. He was extraordinarily kind and said his main concern now was only that the second printing be held up until you had read the Censor's report yourself and were satisfied that all the changes were included to your personal satisfaction.

I enclose a copy of the Censor's report together with the nine pages of the book on which his points occur.[2] Please send the corrections to Naomi to transmit to Harcourt, Brace, so that her records are complete.

I told Monsignor Fearns, and I give you my word, I shall never again entrust a matter of such importance to a printer, a production man or indeed anyone, without having conclusive proof before my eyes that the conditions implied in the granting of the imprimatur have been faithfully fulfilled.

I am grateful to Harcourt, Brace for having released you from their contract, and I know that their doing so is due mainly to Naomi's skill and tact in an extremely difficult situation.[3] Her conduct in the Monsignor Fearns matter was none the less admirable.

Ever yours,
Bob /s/

P.S. Cable from T.S. Eliot confirming his leaving HB + coming here too!

P.P.S. I went to solemn Mass this morning at St. Ignatius Loyola with Dr. [Gregory] Zilboorg, a recent convert. He admires the new book enormously.

1. RG was hired by Roger Straus in February 1955 on a five-year contract. The firm was called FSC from March 1955 to November 1962. RG had talked to NB about the possibility of joining FSC. She introduced him to Sheila Cudahy, who arranged a dinner meeting with Roger Straus and RG. Among the seventeen authors who followed RG to his new firm were TM, T.S. Eliot, Jean Stafford, Robert Lowell, Randall Jarrell, and eventually Bernard Malamud and Flannery O'Connor.

2. RG wrote to Monsignor Fearns, in a letter dated February 21, 1955, thanking him for the reader's comments, dated February 14, 1955, which were quite minor, certainly from a theological point of view, at least in the opinion of PS. The comments began with high praise: "This is a splendid, outstanding treatment of asceticism." In a letter to RG dated April 4, 1955, Monsignor Fearns noted that the changes were not made in the book, and thus it had no right to bear the *nihil obstat*. NB's letter to TM dated April 7, 1955, said that this situation infuriated John McCallum. TM, too, wrote to McCallum, in a letter dated April 12, 1955, apologizing for all the confusion that had occurred. By mid-March, advance sales were close to 20,000.

3. In a letter dated March 29, 1955, NB informed John McCallum that TM wanted to be released from his contract with HB because he would like to continue having RG as his editor. The release was signed on April 4, 1955.

JUNE 23, 1955

Farrar, Straus & Cudahy, Inc.
[Letterhead]

Rev. M. Louis, O.C.S.O.
Abbey of Our Lady of Gethsemani
Trappist, Kentucky

Dear Tom:

This is not the long letter which I have been wanting to write you about a great number of matters, but merely a short "interim" note to show you the jacket sketch for THE LIVING BREAD. It's based on a Third Century mosaic which the jacket artist, Enrico Arno (who did NO MAN IS AN ISLAND), found with the title "The Eucharistic Victory." I hope you like it as much as I do. The only revision I have to suggest is a "v" which looks less like an "o." I'll be most anxious to know how it strikes you and I enclose a return envelope because we need the artwork as soon as you have finished with it.

Yours ever,
Bob /s/

P.S. T.S. Eliot has just returned to England after a month's visit. As usual, his presence and his advice have done me a world of good. He is preparing a new book of essays for us on the art of poetry. Also, he has found a young Canadian poet whose work I think we may take on here. I think you will like him and I'll send you a set of proofs later on.

P.P.S. I think I overstated my reservations about the photographs in "Silence in Heaven." Their quality is obviously superior; I'll be eager to see the kind of reproduction job which comes from the French press.

JUNE 30, 1955

Farrar, Straus & Cudahy, Inc.
[Letterhead]

Rev. M. Louis, O.C.S.O.
Abbey of Our Lady of Gethsemani
Trappist, Kentucky

Dear Tom:

Many thanks for returning the jacket so promptly. I realize that you still wish to work on the manuscript. As a matter of fact, Naomi showed me Father Thibodeau's editorial comments.[1] It was obvious that he had made an extremely careful reading. Naomi had also told me about the censors, and, of course, the text must be as right as it can be made.

I had also heard about the complications over SILENCE IN HEAVEN. I think the additional chapter on the Cistercians and Benedictines is all to the good.

I have been seeing quite a bit of Frank dell'Isola [TM bibliographer who lived in Brooklyn, New York], who is quite excited about the prospect of visiting Gethsemani. He's an awfully nice guy, and I find his "deez 'n doze" Brooklyn accent amusing in a bibliographer who is so meticulous. He learned a lot from the T.S. Eliot bibliography compiled by Professor [Donald] Gallup of Yale, which I gave him, and from which he got some excellent ideas. He has certainly done an amazing job and I have told him that we will want to publish it after THE LIVING BREAD comes out.

With all good wishes.

Sincerely yours,
Bob /s/

1. In a letter to TM dated December 6, 1955, NB talked about receiving instruction from Rev. Wilfred Thibodeau, S.S.S., Superior of the Congregation of the Blessed Sacrament, and how she anticipated being conditionally baptized twelve days later.

SEPTEMBER 14, 1955

Farrar, Straus & Cudahy, Inc.
[Letterhead]

Rev. M. Louis, O.C.S.O.
Abbey of Our Lady of Gethsemani
Trappist, Kentucky

Dear Tom:

Naomi's office sent over your letter about the delay on THE LIVING BREAD, since she is now in Europe (I see her in England next week!).

The substitution of SILENCE IN HEAVEN is fine with us, since there is little likelihood of rushing the two theologians and the Cardinal in Rome even if it were thought desirable to do so (and I am sure it is not). Publication in January 1956, would be perfect from our point of view, and the expanded ms. on the monastic life, with sections on the Benedictines, Cistercians, and Carthusians, as well as Camaldolese of the original, sounds marvelous to me.

Is there any chance of keeping the original title? I prefer SILENCE IN HEAVEN to THE SILENT LIFE or the other alternatives you suggest. So does Sheila Cudahy, my associate here, who is a great admirer and reader of all your books. Incidentally, since I leave for London tomorrow, could you write to Sheila (Mrs. Pellegrini) in my absence? Also, since it will take a little time before the ms. is typed and ready, could you send us a few paragraphs of description—500 words at most—that we could send out as an announcement, and perhaps a table of contents? I hate to bother you for this but it too will be needed in my absence.

I'm delighted to hear that Jubilee is doing TOWER OF BABEL [October 1955]. Ed Rice and his people are certainly doing a fine job, and the current Negro issue is a great credit to them. I'm anxious to build up our poetry list here. At present it is scant, but with Eliot and [Robert] Lowell coming over, it ought to get going in a year or so, and I hope your poetry can be part of the list. I am also eager to see SOLITUDE. Is this related to the book of notes which you let me have in ms. a few years ago, and which you at one point called SENTENCES?

The pictures of the Swiss monastery which you sent were first-rate, particularly the one of the cloister. I am also grateful for the well-designed card containing your translation of the Hymn of the Eucharistic Congress at Rio. I hope you received the additional copy of the Dom Aelred Graham review (he certainly made amends for past mistakes) of NO MAN IS AN ISLAND.[1] The Art Directors Annual is soon going to press—1955 edition—mostly prize ads and designs chosen by the experts; a copy has been earmarked for you.

Give my best to Frank dell'Isola if he is still visiting. My long delayed visit may be possible after my return from Europe; if not then, I will definitely be down in the spring.

Yours ever,

Bob /s/

P.S. Your translation of the hymn, and your knowledge of Latin, makes me bold to ask whether you could help me out on a St. Thomas More letter in verse which I can find nowhere in translation.[2] It's addressed to his son and three daughters and, aside from "V" for "u" and vice versa, his Latin poetry is beyond my elementary grasp of the language. I have been reading a great deal of St. Thomas this summer; what a truly great saint and patron of men of letters. If I may say so, that is so obviously part of your vocation, too—man of letters, I mean. I'm sure the decision about a temporary respite is all for the best, but I hope and pray the temporary part doesn't last too long!

P. P. S. Curtis Brown just phoned to relay your message about sending my letters to Mrs. [Ann] Skakel.[3] I'm grateful for your letting me know, and for personal reasons I'm sorry I can't say yes. She's a marvelous person and it has nothing to do with her—but with Harcourt, Brace. If you have to clear your files, I'll take them gladly and indeed anything you may decide to entrust to me.

1. Aelred Graham, O.S.B., *Commonweal*, May 13, 1955, 155–59.
2. For the prose translation of this poem, see "Thomas More Greets His Beloved Children, Margaret, Elizabeth, Cecilia, and John," in Thomas More, *"The History of King Richard III" and Selections from the English and Latin Poems*, ed. Richard S. Sylvester (New Haven: Yale University Press, 1976), 159–60.
3. See the letter dated August 27, 1952.

NOVEMBER 15, 1955

Farrar, Straus & Cudahy, Inc.
[Letterhead]

Rev. M. Louis, O.C.S.O.
Abbey of Our Lady of Gethsemani
Trappist, Kentucky

Dear Tom:
   I am very happy to be back from Europe, even though I can say that it was the best trip I have ever made abroad. I am delighted to find that the galleys of THE LIVING BREAD are already at hand, but the usual emergency situation has again arisen. As I wired you today, the material on galleys 6 and 7, about the Priests' Eucharistic League and the People's Eucharistic League, needs considerable revising. Because Naomi also had the impression independently that there were errors in this material, I went in person to see Father Raymond A. Tartre, S.S.S., National Director, Priests' Eucharistic League. He not only thought there were errors about his organization, but he was puzzled by the material on the Society for Perpetual Adoration of the Blessed Sacrament. You say that this Society came into existence during the Second World War, and "soon spread to every part of the world." The fact is that the Priests' Eucharistic League was founded in 1879 and now numbers (1955) 31,411 members. Father Tartre, who would seem to be in a position to know, doubts that the European group has grown quite as fast as you indicate.

Under the circumstances, wouldn't it be better—at least in the American edition—to start with the two American groups—the Priests' Eucharistic League and the People's Eucharistic League? On galley 7, Father Tartre does not know what you mean by the "Eucharistic Legion."

I am sending herewith by airmail special delivery the booklet which Father Tartre was good enough to give me. Surely you will want to put in something about the history of Blessed Peter Julian Eymard, their founder, as well as the statistics on page 12 and any other information you consider important. I think it's fine to give the address in Rome of the European group, but wouldn't it also be tactful to give the address of the American headquarters also?

I have just today been able to get in touch with the office of Father [Robert] Rousseau [S.S.S.], Director of the People's Eucharistic League. I expect to have some literature tomorrow which I shall rush to you. Naomi and I both feel your material on this organization needs to be amplified also. After all, the great number of your readers will be lay people. In this connection, I strongly urge that you change the initial sentence of paragraph 4 on galley 7. To say that the book was written "primarily for priests" is to give a great number of reviewers a good excuse not to review it in the secular press. Naomi agrees completely on this point.

There is another reason—which is also very good news: the book has already been accepted by the Catholic Literary Foundation and by the Thomas More Book Club. This is, of course, a tremendous start and it is indicative of the fact that the book is going to reach a very wide audience. I am momentarily expecting to hear from Father [Harold] Gardiner [S.J.] of the Catholic Book Club in New York. They may be added too.

There are a number of small editorial points which are noted on the enclosed page of queries. As you can understand, I am particularly concerned that the <u>censor librorum</u>, Monsignor Fearns (who already has the uncorrected galleys) be given no reason to delay sending us the <u>nihil obstat</u>. The book clubs want to publish in March, which is Catholic Press Month, which means that we shall have to have a green light by December 1st. If you can give me some indication of when you expect corrected galleys, we will prepare the way to expedite matters at this end.

I had a fine talk with Frank dell'Isola here the other day. His visit to Gethsemani was a tremendous experience and I was delighted to have personal news of you. The "Tower of Babel" which I read in <u>Jubilee</u> is a magnificent job; congratulations!*

With all good wishes.

Yours ever,

Bob /s/

*I'm sending it to Eliot.

P.S. Please translate <u>all</u> Latin—as on galley 25 (the <u>first</u> one, I mean).

Farrar, Straus & Cudahy, Inc.
[Letterhead]

Rev. M. Louis, O.C.S.O.
Abbey of Our Lady of Gethsemani
Trappist, Kentucky

Dear Tom:

The plate changes have all been made in THE LIVING BREAD and I enclose corrected plate proofs herewith. One "correction" resulted in a real beaut, which has been changed: you wrote "who have enrolled in them" and it came out "who have enrolled in Arom"!

I like the new opening chapter to LIVING IN SILENCE very much. And there's something extraordinary about that photograph you gave Naomi for the jacket. I knew it was the monastery of Le Reposoir in the Savoie [France] from another book we are doing, on the life of Mother Mary of Jesus who reconstituted it as a Carmel [monastery]. What a life she had! I'm sending you the book THREE WHITE VEILS FOR SANDRA under separate cover.

I hope you received the additional reviews of THE LIVING BREAD. The press on the whole has been marvelous—deservedly, of course.

Yours ever,
Bob /s/

Rev. M. Louis, O.C.S.O.
Abbey of Our Lady of Gethsemani
Trappist, Kentucky

Dear Tom:

I am awfully glad that you agreed to let us show your paper on "The Neurotic Personality" to Dr. Gregory Zilboorg. He called to say that he had some important points to take up with you, and he wants to get in contact with you directly. Will you drop him a line at 33 East 70th Street, New York City 21?

As I understand it, he thinks the subject important enough and your treatment of it provocative enough to warrant your exploring the bibliography much more deeply. There are French sources in particular, psychiatric and theological, which he feels you should consult before releasing the piece. Also, unless you already have them, I want to send you two books of his—A HISTORY OF MEDICAL PSYCHOLOGY, a fascinating survey of the subject from the earliest times to the present, and MIND, MEDICINE AND MAN. Will you let me know if it's all right? He has some further points about improper terminology. He also said the subject is such that after we got a <u>nihil obstat</u> and published, the paper would be

jumped on by French critics especially and their criticisms can be anticipated and liquidated. Zilboorg really gets around; he is a close friend of
Father [Agostino] Gemelli in Milan [one of the founders of the Catholic
University of the Sacred Heart in Milan], he's been consulted by Vatican people following which the attacks on psychiatry by a well-known TV
preacher ceased and desisted. He has been giving a course on pastoral
psychology at Woodstock [College in Maryland] under Fathers John
Courtney Murray [S.J.] and Gustave Weigel [S.J.]. He is, as you may know,
a convert. He thinks you ought to attend a course the Benedictines are
giving at St. John's [Abbey]; he will participate in this.

He told me an astonishing story; he visited Gethsemani in 1924 when
the Abbot was a Frenchman and so were most of the monks! He is a
scholar, a linguist, a classicist, a wit, an ex-Menshevik, a Freudian, a psychoanalyst, and a Catholic. You couldn't find a better or wiser adviser in
his profession.

Yours ever,
Robert Giroux

MAY 26, 1956

Our Lady of Gethsemani
[Letterhead]

Dear Bob:

Many thanks for your letter of the other day. I wrote Dr. Zilboorg yesterday afternoon. I would indeed be very glad to get the books of his that
you named. I have not read either of them.

He suggested that I attend a sort of summer school session they are
having at St. John's Abbey, but I cannot get permission to go. You know
how our rules are on these points. I hope Dr. Zilboorg will someday stop
by here and then I can have the pleasure of meeting him. Incidentally,
don't forget that it is quite some time since you have been down!

I shall be very interested in his comments on the Neurotic Personality.
This requires a lot more work and thought, and study. I will give it a little
time to mature. That will not harm it at all. Besides, I am thinking of new
aspects of the question. I am sure you are not in a hurry for it.

How about the new monastic book? Any reactions for a new title?
Proofs coming sometime soon? I am eager to know all about it—it is one
of the books I have written that I actually like, which is more than I can say
of some of the others.

Bob Lax was down and we had a wonderful visit and he is trying to get
[Adolph ("Ad")] Reinhardt to do a cover for a pamphlet I am getting
printed for us here—I think you saw it, Basic Principles of the Monastic Life.[1]

What are some good new books on your catalogue? I am trying to fill in the holes in our novitiate library. It is rather a problem to get some of them to read intelligently.

As always, with very best wishes—and God bless.

Devotedly in Christ,
Tom /s/

1. TM, *Basic Principles of Monastic Spirituality* (Trappist, KY: Abbey of Gethsemani, 1957).

JUNE 23, 1956

Our Lady of Gethsemani
[Letterhead]

Dear Bob:

One of the Zilboorg books you spoke of has arrived, <u>Mind, Medicine and Man</u>. Did you say you were sending another? Should I check to see what became of it?

This one is fine. I am reading it with the greatest interest and, I hope, profit. It will be very helpful. One of the things I fear as religious begin to interest themselves in psychiatry is that we may fall into oversimplification, superficiality and, at last, quackery. We are not above looking for easy ways out—we love nostrums. The slogan that solves everything, etc.

I just heard from a boy who applied for admission to the choir here. He took tests which showed him to be quite neurotic, and I said we could not accept him. I now learned that after "treatments" for a month or so he is allegedly all right . . .

Zilboorg has written and I am in contact with him all along.

What I mainly want to know is when to expect proofs for the new book—it has had so many names I forget what to call it. What name have you decided upon? What about my last suggestion which was, I think, IN SILENT HOUSES?[1] I forget what the others have been. No signs yet of the Thames & Hudson Picture book. What happened? And again, I do hope you will not let me down with the pictures—hopefully we can fit in as many as possible.

About proofs then: I'd like very much to get them very soon, as at the end of July and early August I expect to be too tied up to touch them. Later may be too late.

Thanks again for the book. It is splendid.

All best wishes and blessings.

Devotedly in Our Lord,
Tom /s/

1. Evidently a working title for TM, *The Silent Life*, which was published on January 3, 1957.

AUGUST 4, 1956

[Postcard]
Chapel Interior
St. John's University
Collegeville, Minnesota

Robert Giroux
Farrar, Straus, + Cudahy
101 5th Avenue
New York 3, N.Y.

Dear Bob:
My two weeks here have been immensely profitable, + of course, I have seen Zilboorg, who has many ideas for me.
Meanwhile thanks for the specimen page, + I look forward to seeing proofs. I am most anxious to have pictures. You should have a collection of some 20 or 25 I have sent—many Benedictine, Camaldolese, + some Cistercian. I can get Carthusians. Would like to talk it over indeed. Can you come?

[Thomas Merton]

AUGUST 7, 1956

Rev. M. Louis, O.C.S.O.
Abbey of Our Lady of Gethsemani
Trappist, Kentucky

Dear Tom:
I want to assure you at once that there will be photographs in THE SILENT LIFE. I'm not sure whether it will be 8 pages or 12, but I'm sure you agree that all four Orders should be represented.
That brings up the problem. I have 25 photographs here, but the greater part of them—13 in fact—are exterior shots of Le Reposoir. Since we are using the biggest and the best on the jacket, I doubt if we would want to use more than one other of the building (interesting though its appearance and location are) inside. The other 12 break down as follows:

4 nature shots of Le Reposoir (snow, icicles, water, trees)
1 architectural shot of arches
5 photos of Camaldolese (by Marconi of Genoa)
2 photos of Benedictines (at least I assume "Benedikt Rast, Fribourg" means that)

Now the first 5 probably won't be used, not unless we want to make this a Reposoir book. The five Camaldolese are all good photos and should be used; I'll probably need your help on captions. But what about the Benedictines, Carthusians and Cistercians? We can't represent the first group solely by two shots of a German community (or can we? They are both good). What about St. John's Abbey at Collegeville, have they anything? For the latter two groups, I shall have to rely wholly on your help—and the sooner we can get pictures the better. Will you let me know about this at the first opportunity?

John Peck of this office sent the galleys to you, and I trust they are now in your hands. I was delighted with your card. Mark Van Doren wrote that he saw you and that you are writing better poetry than ever. Which I believe, having read the three you sent Naomi. I'd give anything to publish THE SILENT POEMS.[1]

Yours ever,
Robert Giroux

1. Evidently a working title for TM, *The Strange Islands* (New York: New Directions, 1957).

AUGUST 18, 1956

Our Lady of Gethsemani
[Letterhead]

Dear Bob:

About the photos: I am absolutely certain that I sent either to you or to Naomi, a year ago, a collection of over thirty excellent shots of Benedictines and Cistercians, of the same quality as those in <u>Silence in Heaven</u>. They may have arrived at Farrar, Straus & Cudahy at some time when you were absent, in fact I seem to remember something of the kind. Anyway, it was a big batch, the best I had, and was sent <u>before</u> the items you mention which were sent in small groups afterward. I do hope you can track down that big group. As I say, I am convinced it was sent to you, and arrived when you were away, but it might have been sent to Naomi, though I think she would know if it had been. But it is at least a year ago. I do hope they can be found. They are superb.

These are nothing but leftovers I have around here, but one might use a couple of Fontenay cloister [in Burgundy, France] (again!) and some of our American monks. I like the old shepherd—he is one of our best old brothers.

The sessions at Collegeville were splendid, and, of course, I had several talks with Zilboorg, which were very helpful. They may develop into something later. Meanwhile, however, he assured me that the piece on Neurotics in the Cloister ought not to be published.

The galleys of the new book ought to be back by now, and I hope page proofs will come through real soon; I would like to get them out of the way. If by chance, you can come down to talk over the picture situation, it should not be later than September 12, as after that I will be off on a special job somewhere.

I am so glad you are using the big Reposoir shot for the cover.

Best wishes, as ever, and all blessings.

Devotedly in Our Lord,
Tom /s/

SEPTEMBER 3, 1956

Our Lady of Gethsemani
[Letterhead]

Dear Bob:

Here are some excellent Carthusian photos, all from La Valsainte in Switzerland. I think you can certainly use these, or some of them. I particularly like the snow shots. The closer air view showing all the cells is also a good one for the book. I believe the one of the monk working in his cell may already have been used by David McKay in White Paradise. Better check.

Did you find anything of the great bunch of Benedictine and Cistercian pictures I sent you a year ago? Let me know at once if you want me to write for more. It may be hard to get some. I do hope you have found the older ones.

I am looking forward to seeing page proofs soon.

Oh, by the way, if we are really in a pinch, Ed Rice might be able to let us have some Benedictine pictures. I know he once did an article on Saint Benoît du Lac in Canada.

I never got the Berryman book [*Homage to Mistress Bradstreet*] you announced. I'll check again with Reverend Father. It may have been stopped by someone as profane material. Thanks anyway for thinking of me.

How is the Bibliography coming along? When do you expect it to appear?

I hope all is going well with you. Remember me to everybody. God bless you.

Devotedly in Our Lord,
Tom /s/

SEPTEMBER 5, 1956

Farrar, Straus & Cudahy, Inc.
[Letterhead]

Rev. M. Louis, O.C.S.O.
Abbey of Our Lady of Gethsemani
Trappist, Kentucky

Dear Tom:

This is to thank you for the Carthusian photos which arrived by special delivery today. They are all good, particularly the snow shots and the cell-workshop (I don't think it matters that it may have appeared in another book).

Your galley proofs arrived while John Peck was on vacation, and I went over them myself. The Epilogue which you added is really fine; I'm delighted you decided to write it. The corrections, and particularly the long insertions, are first rate. I do not know whether we will have page proofs ready for you much before September 15th. If they do arrive after that date, I hope arrangements will be made at your end to forward them to you, or can you give me your forwarding address now? There's not the remotest chance of my getting away from New York before that day, I am sorry to say.

I talked with Naomi, before she left for California, about the large collection of Benedictine and Cistercian pictures which you sent a year ago. She says she does not have them. My recollection is that I looked at them in her office; as a matter of fact, we phoned you from her office that day and I remember saying that I was "disappointed" in the pictures (which shows you how blind I was). However, I also connect these pictures with LE SILENCE DANS LE CIEL—close-ups of monks in choir, saying Mass, etc.—some very fine faces. I honestly do not recall a batch of pictures separate from the ones which came in connection with La Pierre Qui Vire. I have searched through everything here and Curtis Brown assures me they will do likewise in their office.

However, I now think we have almost enough to go on. I think it might be good to have some other American photos. Would it be possible to get any of the Primitive Observance Benedictines at Elmira [New York]; of the Trappist Monastery at Geneseo [New York]; or Dom [Thomas] Verner Moore [O.S.B., M.D.]'s American Carthusians [in Vermont]? I don't think that would be overloading the book with American photos, or if it is I don't see the harm for a book being published in this country. Do you?

With best wishes.

As ever,
Bob /s/

P.S. Let me know if there was any slip-up on the Berryman, which was sent to you. Today I am mailing T.S. Eliot's poem, THE CULTIVATION OF CHRISTMAS TREES. I hope the Dell'Isola bibliography has reached you; I think it looks marvelous.[1]

---

1. *Thomas Merton: A Bibliography*, comp. Frank dell'Isola (New York: Farrar, Straus & Cudahy, 1956). In a barely legible letter, probably dated sometime in early October 1956, TM informs RG that he likes the pictures and the layout in *The Silent Life*. He requests that RG pay for the permission to reprint the photographs. After looking at the Dell'Isola bibliography, TM comments that he has certainly written too much.

OCTOBER 2, 1956

Rev. M. Louis, O.C.S.O.
Abbey of Our Lady of Gethsemani
Trappist, Kentucky

Dear Tom:
I enclose the final layout of the photographs in THE SILENT LIFE. In a few instances, I had no identification for the pictures and I am entirely dependent on you for copy (see number 8 for example). In other cases, I am not always sure that I have said exactly the right thing. I am most anxious to have your OK on this as soon as possible. The printer and the designer are breathing heavily and, of course, I am anxious not to lose the scheduled press time which they have reserved for us. I enclose a stamped return envelope and I hope you can get it back to me at once. I will send you proof copies as soon as they are run off.
    With all good wishes.

Ever yours,
Robert Giroux

DECEMBER 16, 1957

Rev. M. Louis, O.C.S.O.
Abbey of Our Lady of Gethsemani
Trappist, Kentucky

Dear Tom:
    This is my Christmas letter to you, to accompany a package containing Georges Bernanos' DIALOGUES DES CARMELITES and some pictures of Our Lady in sculpture, which I thought beautiful. The Bernanos is, believe it or not, the libretto for an opera by François Poulenc which opened at La Scala [in Milan] last year with rave reviews. NBC had the imagination to do it on TV (in English), and it is superb! Imagine, an opera by a

modern composer based on a story of the martyrdom of a group of Carmelites at Compiègne during the French Revolution, with a libretto by Bernanos. I liked the story so much that I rushed out to get the text at a French bookstore on Madison Avenue. What gives dramatic force to the very moving story of the community's fate is the characterization of Sister Blanche. The final scene, the execution, is a grand chorus of <u>Salve Regina</u>. No dialogue; just voices singing as one by one the nuns ascend the guillotine scaffold, until finally Blanche's voice alone, that of the final victim, is heard. Another first-rate musical scene is that between the Mother Superior and Blanche. NBC found some excellent singers and actors for the parts, including a Negro soprano in the role of the new Prioress. I understand that Angel Records recorded the opera in France, but were not satisfied with the result and withdrew it. As soon as it is available, I'll send it to you. I hope you'll be able to hear it—indeed the whole community should hear this modern religious opera.

Under separate cover, I'm sending a packet of FSC books: T. S. Eliot's new collection of essays, ON POETS AND POETRY; Edmund Wilson's CLASSICS AND COMMERCIALS; Elizabeth Bishop's translation of THE DIARY OF HELENA MORLEY (highly praised by Bernanos); and THE SELECTED WRITINGS OF JOHN JAY CHAPMAN, an American writer you should know. I hope these all get to you in good order.

We all of us here—Roger [W. Straus, Jr.], Sheila [Cudahy], and myself— send you our best Christmas greetings. We are most eager to hear about the fate of the <u>Secular Journal</u> with the fourth censor, and we do hope that he has the grace and insight to see that its publication will do much good. If you can, I hope you will drop me a line soon—and please remember me in your prayers.

As ever,
Robert Giroux

DECEMBER 28, 1957

Our Lady of Gethsemani
[Letterhead]

Dear Bob:

It was wonderful to hear from you and to get the books. I was intrigued to hear about the [Georges] Bernanos play being set to music ["Dialogue of the Carmelites"]. I knew it had been rather a successful French film. I had read it a couple of years ago in English and was much impressed. I will try it again in French. I think at times he lays it on rather thick, with Blanche, but then you have to I guess. Things like that have to be spelled out real simple, if they are to register on large audiences. I am sure that with music it is admirable.

I was also very happy to get the other books. Edmund Wilson I respect implicitly and I think the reading of Classics and Commercials will be most salutary. I am finally waking up to the fact that in a monastery one tends to lose a sense of perspective, though God forbid that a monk should want to see, in all things, through the eyes of the average even intelligent New Yorker. Modus in rebus [there is a proper measure in all things]. Taste is taste. One needs to retain a certain stimulation, and one needs to be challenged. The Morley Diary is particularly interesting. I am getting very interested in everything to do with South America, am starting to learn Portuguese—one of the novices is an ex-Benedictine from São Paolo, just made his solemn profession. We are getting lots of South American postulants. I read Spanish and talk it fortunately—that is probably the providential reason why these postulants started to apply shortly after I got into the job. Anyway, I am keenly interested in all South American literature; I think it is important that the many good poets down there, for instance, should be better known in America (North, that is).

Chapman looks very interesting, and, of course, the Eliot book is very welcome. In fact, I had been debating in my mind whether to try to bum a copy. So I am most grateful.

In exchange for that, I am afraid I can only come across with an official disappointment, on the Secular Journal. The fourth censor was no better than the other two. The lineup is roughly this: First censor—nothing wrong, good book. Second censor picks up a hundred little straws he doesn't like, and after 13 pages concludes: nothing against faith or morals, not opportune to publish the book since it is "inferior to anything thus far published by the author"—and would stir up adverse criticism, would offend "priests. Catholics. Protestants and others." All the unfavorable opinions are substantially the same. Nothing against faith or morals, the book would just antagonize nice people. So that is the story. The General asked that I write personally to Catherine de Hueck stating it to be my wish that the book not be published. I told her he had asked me to do this. In my opinion, the book can hardly be as bad as they think, and also I believe their objections to the passages that would "stir up" righteous folk could be allayed by elimination of key sentences here and there where I lash out too wildly. However, they are all against the book and I don't think there is much that can be done about it now. The General is down on it one hundred and ten percent. Father Abbot says he will reimburse you for the advance paid to Catherine, so she will get something out of the transaction anyway.

You have by now received the "Thoughts in Solitude" which I believe to be the more honest and original version of Thirty-Seven Meditations. I wonder what you think, and I am anxious to hear about it. Also I wonder if by now Naomi has sent you the series of studies on medieval theological subjects, St. Bernard, [French Cistercian] Adam of Perseigne, Blessed Guerric [of Igny] and what not. I think this will make a useful but somewhat restricted book along the lines of some of the more scholarly things that sometimes appear. I do not think it will have a very wide appeal, or can be made to have such an appeal, but I think it has definite possibilities. It is serious and probably a lot deeper than my other stuff I have done without being for all that too hard to follow. I think it would break nicely into the series of things that has been coming out. Certainly no one will ever object that the book is not "fitting," coming from a monk. I think you would be able to get rid of eight or ten thousand [books] over a period of time. The biggest chunk of the book has appeared in French, and the English ms. has not come back from France yet. Naomi is expecting it.

Finally, the future will bring the possibility of combining into one book two short things I have put out here, on Monastic Spirituality. I will send you Monastic Peace in a couple of months if the printer ever gets the lead out of his shoes, and I think you will like it.

With all the varied reading I am doing now (Einstein, etc.), I think maybe in the long run I might be able to get together a collection of essays over a much wider field than anything so far—science, philosophy, even history, even politics (?), anyway something beyond the strict limits of pure spirituality.

As Novice Master I don't have time to do much sustained writing, but the bits of things that are needed get themselves written without difficulty, and there is certainly much material piling up in the form off conferences and so forth. Did I ever send you the mimeographed "Notes on Genesis"? Let me know, and if you do not have them I will send you a copy. I think I still have a copy.

Things are going along fine. I really like the work and, of course, it is interesting and rewarding. I am anxious to get out and get our forest into some kind of shape too, but there ought to be thirty-six hours in the day.

God bless you, Bob, and Happy New Year to all of you, Roger, Sheila, and all. Thanks again for everything. What about "Thoughts in Solitude"? I suppose there is no longer any question about this being "the next." I like it all right now that it is back in its original shape.

As ever, in Christ,
Tom /s/

FEBRUARY 14, 1958

Farrar, Straus & Cudahy, Inc.
[Letterhead]

Rev. M. Louis, O.C.S.O.
Abbey of Our Lady of Gethsemani
Trappist, Kentucky

Dear Tom:

The proofs of THOUGHTS IN SOLITUDE have just come in, and I rush them to you at once. You will find in this package a set of marked galleys and the manuscript, both of which you must return, and an extra set of galleys to keep.

I was very happy to hear through Naomi that you now feel the revised version has merits over the original. I think so too, and—after all—you created those merits. I was bothered and disturbed by your first reaction and was ready to say, look, we can be wrong and if you still think so when you see the proofs, change it. I am relieved to know that you have changed your mind and I hope that a fresh look at the book in type will confirm your impression.

The front matter is not yet ready, but I'll send it along shortly. I took the liberty of using some of the latest prefatory material and some of the early. Again, if it doesn't seem right, change it. We have a handsome jacket sketch by Enrico Arno, which will soon be ready in proof and which I'll send.

I sincerely hope that these proofs get to you before Ash Wednesday, and that—if for some reason they do not—Father Abbot will allow you to finish with them nevertheless. Printers do not observe Lenten regulations and we have a very tight printing schedule to meet (when do we not?). Correcting proofs, as you and I know, is work and surely work is an appropriate Lenten chore?

> As ever,
> Bob /s/

FEBRUARY 26, 1958

> Farrar, Straus & Cudahy, Inc.
> [Letterhead]

Rev. M. Louis, O.C.S.O.

Dear Tom:

Thanks very much for getting the galley proofs back so quickly. I am much relieved that, having given the text a fresh reading in print, you find it satisfactory. I think it's a very good book indeed. I don't actually think the rearrangement of chapters makes a bit of difference, so I agree with you that we should leave them as they are. I will send you a set of page proofs "for information," as we say. That is, we will not expect you to return any corrections unless through some mischance we have goofed somewhere. In that case, I suggest airmailing only those proofs containing errors, rather than the complete set.

Meanwhile, I enclose the galley proofs of the front matter in duplicate, one set of which should be returned to us almost immediately. You will note that we need the Order's nihil obstat with names of censors, and so on. The little drawing on the title page is also being used as the jacket decoration, much in the style of NO MAN IS AN ISLAND, which Arno also designed.

I certainly do think that the book of essays containing the "Martha, Mary and Lazarus" piece has book possibilities for later on.[1] I've only read that one piece (and the one on "Contemplative Life" which appeared in one of the quarterlies) and I think it's fine.[2] I'll be in touch with you and Naomi again as soon as I've finished reading.

I'm sure that at some point sooner or later the Secular Journal will take its place with your other work. I'm delighted to know that the Abbot General is willing to give it another chance. But whether it passes the censors this time around, or whether it later works out as the complete journal (with the part, that is, now at St. Bonaventure's [College]), it will be worth waiting for. I'm writing Naomi about this too.

As ever,
Bob /s/

P.S. It was somewhat unexpected to find the Camaldolese in the N.Y. Times (see enclosed clipping), but I'm not quite convinced about New York's being ideal for hermits.

1. See TM, *Marthe, Marie et Lazare* (Paris: Desclée de Brouwer, 1956). This is a French translation of a somewhat expanded version of TM's essay "Action and Contemplation in St. Bernard."
2. Presumably a reference to "Action and Contemplation in St. Bernard."

MARCH 3, 1958

Our Lady of Gethsemani
[Letterhead]

Dear Bob:

Here are the proofs of the front matter. I have taken care to insert the Nihil Obstat, etc., as you desired. I think everything is in order now. The preface is just as I would have it. It contains all I really wanted to say as an introduction to the book as a whole. I too am satisfied that it will turn out to be a good book. In fact, I am inclined to think it is in many ways better than both Seeds of Contemplation and No Man Is an Island, as far as concerns the content of part two, and perhaps even part one. Or again, it is more truly what I wanted to say, anyhow. I think No Man Is an Island was really too long and I reduced its effectiveness by inserting too much. That was one of the things I was afraid of here, but certainly this book is not too long.

Working on the Secular Journal the last few days has been rewarding. Fr. Irenaeus sent photostats from St. Bonaventure's and a lot of them are illegible. But I think the judicious addition of about twenty pages taken from key spots will make the book more interesting and will at the same time perhaps help the censors to see the light. I have had another spontaneous very favorable judgment from one of the novices, a Nicaraguan poet, who was very eager to read it and liked it all very much, especially the Latin American section. I have no difficulty in believing that the censor ear all wet [*sic*]—except, of course, Fr. Paul, who used to be a book reviewer anyway and seems at least to have some vague notion of what really constitutes a good book! So we can always hope.

I like the little Assyrian character Enrico Arno has turned up with this time. The novices, looking at it as a portrait of the author, have given way to a certain merriment over it.

Thanks for the clipping! I know that for some time they had been thinking of a foundation in this country and they have finally got around to it. Three years ago I would have been on my ear over the whole affair. Now, alas, I am older and more tepid, I suppose. But no, the status quo as far as I can see is not only God's will, but, as is always true with His will, contains unlimited possibilities for the future. I am just beginning to grasp what immense possibilities are buried in my vocation, once one can break through the surface of conventional rigidity and get down into the real life of it— a thing which is seldom done and which most monks unconsciously seem to regard as dangerous. Some day we are going to wake up and discover that the Old Testament was tied up and put away two thousand years ago. For the moment, we still prefer it to the New.

Well, that's all for the moment. We still aren't fasting—the place has been swept with the flu. I have mercifully escaped for once, except that I had a couple of colds. Three novices who didn't go down were awarded a prize—they had a full day off, slept late, got a lot of cookies and—a glass of wine. They are very proud of themselves.

God bless you in Our Lord.

As ever,

Tom /s/

MARCH 5, 1958

Farrar, Straus & Cudahy, Inc.
[Letterhead]

Rev. M. Louis, O.C.S.O.
Abbey of Our Lady of Gethsemani
Trappist, Kentucky

Dear Tom:

Just a note to let you know that the proofs of the front matter arrived safely—and very quickly, too, for which I am most grateful.

I'm pleased that on rereading you find that the Preface contains all that you wanted to say about the book as a whole. I feel that THOUGHTS IN SOLITUDE will stand with your best work. I'm glad to know that you like the little title-page drawing by Arno. And what you say about the material from St. Bonaventure's that you are working on interests me very much. Perhaps the new material will make a difference to the censors next time around.

   With all good wishes.

As ever,
Bob /s/

SEPTEMBER 12, 1958

Farrar, Straus & Cudahy, Inc.
[Letterhead]

Rev. M. Louis, O.C.S.O.
Abbey of Our Lady of Gethsemani
Trappist, Kentucky

Dear Tom:

   I was delighted to have your inscribed copy of the Prometheus: A Meditation, for many reasons.[1] First, it is among your very best writing. Second, it is such a beautiful job of book design. And third, since we had already decided to run the SECULAR JOURNAL with uneven right margins, I was mighty pleased to see this feature of the special edition. I am thankful for the book, and happy about the inscription.

   As I write, proofs of the SECULAR JOURNAL come to my desk so I'm sending a set off to you at once with this letter. The marked set has so few queries, and the manuscript is so clean, that I see no need for you to do that kind of proofreading job. In other words, there's no need to return these proofs. If there are changes or corrections which you wish made, however, send them in a letter (the sooner, the better) or just return the galleys on which they occur, if that's easier.

   Incidentally, I hope you intend to include Prometheus in a collection of your essays at some date. A very interesting suggestion has come in, that you do a book which could serve as a guide to meditation, discussing the various methods such as the Ignatian, Sulpician, and so on—in short, a "how to" book for modern readers. I think it's an excellent idea. I haven't had a chance to discuss it with Naomi yet, but I'll be interested to know how it strikes you.

Yours ever,
Bob /s/

P. S. I'm sending AN AMERICAN AMEN by Father [John] LaFarge and THE SECRET NAME by Lin Yutang by separate cover.

---

1. TM, *Prometheus: A Meditation* (Lexington, KY: King Library Press, 1958).

OCTOBER 1, 1958

Farrar, Straus & Cudahy, Inc.
[Letterhead]

Rev. M. Louis, O.C.S.O.
Abbey of Our Lady of Gethsemani
Trappist, Kentucky

Dear Tom:

I was delighted to get the proofs back from you so promptly. Mrs. [Baroness Catherine de Hueck] Doherty had a few minor corrections in the Preface, which arrived yesterday. I have made all the changes you indicated, but the correction in the entry for November 1, 1941—you changed the past tense to the present—seems to be incomplete. It reads: "Friday morning before we drive up to Buffalo to meet Catherine de Hueck" (that's what you changed to the present tense): "Riding to Buffalo was like any other ride." You start this paragraph in the past tense, but the conversation with the Baroness which follows is in the present tense. It seems to me that the paragraph starting "Riding to Buffalo" should be a new entry. I have changed it as indicated on the enclosed proof. Let me know if this meets with your approval.

Having just finished Boris Pasternak's DOCTOR ZHIVAGO, I agree with you that it's a masterpiece.[1] It makes me think that your idea of a book of "Letters from My Cousin Trofim [Lysenko]" is a very intriguing one. It's a perfect medium for getting down informally a lot of the ideas you've had in mind for your study of Religion and Revolution. I don't know what Naomi will think of the project. As you say, so much depends on how it "writes." I understand about the book on Ignatian and other modes of meditation; it's best to put this idea aside and turn to something which appeals to you. I like your other suggestion, too, but I think you ought to do them as individual essays for magazine publication as the occasion arises. (Neither [Brazilian poet] Jorge de Lima nor [18th-century Brazilian architect and sculptor] Aleijadinho are known to me; are there any books in English I can get on either figure?)

Jay Laughlin just sent me the beautiful limited edition of THE TOWER OF BABEL with Gerhard Marcks's excellent woodcuts. I am delighted to have this. I'm sending you a copy of the Arthur Goodfriend book [*Rice Roots*] under separate cover. It's a useful miscellany but perhaps somewhat dated (1950) now. However, there's an advance copy of a book called EASTERN EXPOSURE by Marvin Kalb also on its way. This is right up to date (1956) and it confirms a great deal of Pasternak's picture of Russia. [Vladimir Nikolayevich] Petrov's SOVIET GOLD is out of print; I'll see if I can get a second-hand copy. I understand that the new Alan Morehead book on the Russian revolution [*The Russian Revolution*] is a good popular account. Have you read it?

THOUGHTS IN SOLITUDE has been going very well indeed, and I am getting together a collection of reviews to send you. I was going to send them with Frank dell'Isola, but decided not to. I hope you do not get too involved with him. He told me he was going to write a journal, "Gethsemani Revisited" which he hopes to publish. He's a well-meaning person, but he just doesn't have any sense, common or otherwise. I had a good meeting with Bob Lax and Ed Rice at the publication-day party for Father LaFarge. Ad Reinhardt, whom I hadn't seen for twenty years, also turned up.

My mother, age 81, is now in the hospital, and I hope you will keep her in your prayers. The death from cancer of my oldest brother this summer was a great shock to all of us, particularly to her. Please give my warmest regards to Father Abbot and ask him to pray for me. I'm dictating this letter at home, and it will be signed and sent in my absence.

As ever,
Robert Giroux

1. On October 29, 1958, TM wrote to Aleksei Surkov of the Soviet Writers' Union in Moscow about *Doctor Zhivago*: "It was, therefore, with great joy, and deep respect for Russia, that I and so many like me were able to hail the recent work of Boris Pasternak, which burst upon us full of turbulent and irrepressible life, giving us a deeply moving picture of the heroic sufferings of the Russian nation and its struggles, sacrifices and achievements. That his work received the Nobel prize certainly cannot have been a merely political trick. It is the expression of the sincere and unprejudiced admiration of the world for a Russian genius worthy to inherit the preeminence of the great Tolstoy. . . . Are you Communists unable to see how this great book has glorified Russia? Can you not understand that this book will make the whole world love and admire the Russian people and nation, and venerate them for the superb heroism with which they have borne the burdens laid upon them by history? If you punish Pasternak, it is because you do not love Russia, do not love mankind, but seek only the limited interests of a political minority." TM concluded by saying that he writes to Surkov as a friend, not as an enemy—and then suggests that Surkov might even consider publishing this letter in *Pravda*.

OCTOBER 23, 1958

Our Lady of Gethsemani
[Letterhead]

Dear Bob:

As you may remember, we have been working down here on a book about sacred art. It is called ART AND WORSHIP. I have written the text, collected a lot of pictures, and have been busy with a man [W. Terrell Dickey] in Louisville, a friend of mine, who has been helping to design it. We have already got the type set up, and we are preparing to go ahead and get our 88 pages of pictures done, perhaps, in flat bed gravure. It is Fr. Abbot's wish that the thing be done right, even if somewhat expensively. It has also been my idea to keep it from being specially profitable and keep the price down as low as possible so that a lot of people might buy it. I thought if a few Bishops could get interested in it, it might be taken as a sort of informal textbook on art for seminaries and colleges. A good Christmas book, too.

I want you to take a look at the proofs, Bob. It is just possible that this book might be interesting enough to you to warrant a place on your list, and if you really want to have it, I would like you to have it. Yet, of course, as we have gone so far with it, there would have to be some kind of arrangement, if you were going to publish the book. I mean, it would seem that if you do want it, we should still go on following the line we have taken, in regard to its production. (Not flat bed gravure necessarily, I know it is expensive).

The fact is, now that we are getting to the end of the job, it is clear that the book would do much better if it were launched in New York, and it has grown into something that, I feel, ought to be given the best possible chances, and not just lie around the gatehouse here gathering dust. I think the book is provocative enough to be very interesting.

The news about the book clubs and the Secular Journal makes [me] happy. I am glad above all for Catherine [de Hueck Doherty].[1] For me too.

Thanks for EASTERN EXPOSURE [by Marvin Kalb]. It is a very interesting book and I am reading along with a lot of pleasure. Mark Van Doren sent me his beautiful AUTOBIOGRAPHY. Isn't it fine?

Well, here are the proofs. I can't send pictures for the moment, but will when the censors have returned their copies. The proofs of the captions, etc., will tell you enough in the meantime. I am planning to eliminate a few pictures that are not worthy of the book so that only the best will be used.

With very best wishes, as ever.

Faithfully in the Lord,
Tom /s/

1. All royalties from *The Secular Journal* went to Madonna House, the community founded by Catherine de Hueck Doherty.

NOVEMBER 22, 1958

Our Lady of Gethsemani
[Letterhead]

Dear Bob:

Naomi tells me you are favorably considering Art and Worship and I am glad. I look forward to hearing from you soon about it, and we will undoubtedly have to get together on it. I am still hoping to get some more pictures and, meanwhile, the censors are going along as usual and holding on to the copies they have. I hope the work on the book will bring you down here. If you cannot possibly get down, there is a faint possibility that Reverend Father might let me go to N.Y. as it is essential that we go over the material together at least once, otherwise it will be all mixed up and cannot possibly come out right.

Meanwhile I am writing to ask if you would mind sending a copy of Frank dell'Isola's <u>Bibliography</u> to a man in Mexico who is bringing out a Spanish selection of my verse and wants a lot of bibliographical background. His name and address:

> Ernesto Mejía Sánchez
> Apartado 25229
> Mexico 20, D.F.

Would you please send him a copy and charge it to me?

As soon as I hear from you and all is settled, I will have the whole box of material for <u>Art and Worship</u> expressed to N.Y. The only thing we worry about here is Fr. Abbot is absolutely set (and I am of course) on the pictures being well reproduced. If necessary we can scrap anything that will not reproduce very well.

All the best—God bless you.

> Faithfully in Christ,
> Tom /s/

NOVEMBER 26, 1958

Rev. M. Louis, O.C.S.O.
Abbey of Our Lady of Gethsemani
Trappist, Kentucky

Dear Tom:

Thank you for your good letter of November 22nd. I like the text of ART AND WORSHIP enormously, and we certainly want to explore the book possibilities thoroughly. It would make an ideal gift book for Christmas 1959 publication.

This makes the matter of timing somewhat urgent. As you can appreciate, we cannot come to a final decision until we have all the pictures in hand. Without them, it is impossible to estimate costs. I hope it is the pictures you are referring to as the "whole box of material to be expressed to New York." I am in absolute agreement with Father Abbot about the necessity of good reproduction. This again is a matter of time; the sooner we have the pictures and the longer we can work with them both here and at the printers, the better the reproduction will be.

It does not look as if I can get away for the time being, with our sales conference coming up. I therefore leap at the "faint possibility" that Reverend

Father might let you come to New York to go over the many complex details which require personal attention in a production job of this magnitude. With kindest regards.

As ever,
Robert Giroux

P.S. A copy of the BIBLIOGRAPHY has already gone to Señor Sánchez.

DECEMBER 4, 1958

Our Lady of Gethsemani
[Letterhead]

Dear Bob:

Many thanks for your letter of the other day. Today I have finally got back from the censors the copies of the photographs, or most of the photographs, that we wanted to use in Art and Worship. I am sending them off to you right away. They will give you some idea of the illustrations. Next week I will try to get in to Louisville and see the man we are working with on the designs, layout and so forth. We will get everything into a big box and send it off to you by express so that you can see the technical problems involved. I have everything now, practically. The only problem is that perhaps some of the pictures will not be easy to reproduce and for these we might have to seek substitutes.

The way the illustrated section goes is this: it is planned to be very large, and is divided into sections or groups, depending on the point I want to discuss.

Group I—pictures illustrating what I mean by Hieratic Art.
Group II—The Human Face in Sacred Art (perhaps the largest and most detailed).
Group III—Sacred Art in Brazil (Colonial and Modern. I have a few new pictures of things by [Candido] Portinari, not provided for in layout).
Group IV—Sacred Space—Architectural shots.
Group V—Sacred Simplicity—all kinds of primitive, etc., things.
Group VI—Kitsch (corn)—Only two pages. We might add to this if you see fit. It might be interesting.

Together with all the pictures I will send the rough layouts we have been working with. In the envelopes of the copies, there are lists identifying the photographs. On the back of the pictures, the places assigned to the pictures in the layout are usually but not always in red. When there are several marks, one of which is red, then the red one is to be followed. This will be one of the things we will have to go over together, obviously.

Now here is a question: please let me know as soon as possible whether you plan to use the type we have had set up in Louisville. I am keeping my proofs and the original copy here, together with a few additions I have made to the copy in proof. I will hold on to this until I hear from you further.

About my going to N.Y. I asked Father Abbot and he refused me permission to do so. So I am afraid that unless something further develops, I cannot come there. The reason I said there was a "faint possibility" is that quite often the laybrothers go out on business trips and it is not absolutely forbidden; it depends on the will of the Abbot. In my case, it seems to be no. He says he will gladly pay your way down here when you come. I told him that it was not the money that provided the difficulty but the time. If you want to get in touch with him directly on the point, go ahead. But I shall assume that sometime in January you may be able to get down, or later on. Our retreat is in February so that is out. Naturally, I must admit it would be much more satisfactory for me if you would come down here and I look forward to a good visit. But I do hate to put you to a great deal of trouble. However, things will work out somehow.

Now to get this in the afternoon mail. By the way, would there be any chance of getting half a dozen advance copies of the Journal to use as Christmas gifts?

In haste and with every blessing—and best Christmas wishes,

Tom /s/

DECEMBER 13, 1958

Our Lady of Gethsemani
[Letterhead]

Dear Bob:

Yesterday I went in to Louisville and saw the man who was doing the layouts for ART AND WORSHIP. I arranged with him to have all the pictures sent to you by express, and because I left the package at his place to be called for, not knowing what the charges would be, I had it sent to you collect. So you will know the meaning of a large package that comes collect. You can charge us for whatever it costs. Practically everything is there, mainly only layouts of the illustrated sections—+ front matter, arranged in envelopes according to the groups I described in my other letter. The only thing now lacking is the rough layouts and I am sending them by mail from here. Thus, you will have everything except the complete copy. This I am keeping here, in the form of proofs to which I have made written additions. I will be waiting to find out what we are going to do about the type, and whether you will be using it. Then if you are, I will send the proofs in to Louisville so that the new material can be set up and all can be sent to you.

I do hope you will be able to use our type. As we will have to pay for it anyway, we will donate it to you if you can use it. I think it is very suitable, myself, and don't think the book will be inordinately large for an art book.

Today is the seventeenth anniversary of my entrance into the monastery here and a trip in town yesterday certainly did nothing to make me feel sorry that I have left "the world." It was so good to get back to the silence and the clean air of the country and the peace of the cloister. I know it is something of a cliché to say that existence out there seems meaningless, and yet it certainly does. I know, of course, that it is not necessarily so, but for so many people it really seems that way: and for me, I am afraid, it would not make much sense. Which is only another way of saying I am grateful for my lot in life, and hope I can repay God by using it fruitfully.

One thing did strike me: the <u>enormous</u> number of books and magazines and other things that are published. A lot of it is very good, too. I really think that publishing has gone places in the last seventeen years, especially with the better class of paper backs. (I brought home a load of them). Still, it is a sobering thought for any author to find himself indeed a drop in such a tremendous ocean. And that is the way it ought to be. The fact that everybody is now reading, or at least buying, Pasternak, is a fine thing in a way, but it does not mean anything like what it might seem to mean: and probably to Pasternak himself in the long run it will mean almost nothing. This is just to say, then, that though I am happy to be a writer and will be happy to go on writing whatever God gives me to write, I cannot really take it with all the seriousness of a "Vocation" with a capital V, or a life or a "Career." Without a thought of moving anything much, I can continue to talk quietly to anyone who wants to listen, and that is enough if the situation thus created makes room for the action of the Holy Ghost.

With these and other devout thoughts, I wish you a happy Advent and a very Holy Christmas: and, of course, am very eager to hear any further developments on ART AND WORSHIP.

Faithfully in Christ, Our Lord,
Tom /s/

DECEMBER 19, 1958

Rev. M. Louis, O.C.S.O.
Abbey of Our Lady of Gethsemani
Trappist, Kentucky

Dear Tom:

I owe you at least three letters, I am sure, but this is simply to let you know that all the materials for ART AND WORSHIP are now in our hands—the big package of pictures from W. Terrell Dickey, the rough layouts, the proofs, and finally the copies of the photographs. We like the pictures very much, but it will take a little time before we know whether we can use the type which has already been set up. My guess is that we cannot, but I am not certain. Can you hold it for a few weeks until we have a final answer? We feel that this type and layout will make a book which is too thin and oversized. The other first reaction is that this layout does not give full value to the artwork, bunching it together in one section. We rather think that the André Malraux approach of spreading the pictures throughout the book will make a more attractive and more saleable book.[1] Your main text, of course, was not written as Malraux's to illustrate works of art. Yet, ART AND WORSHIP is, in a real sense, an art book and it will sell in the art book market, which is a special one. As I say, we have not reached final decisions, and, of course, we shall do so only with your full knowledge and consent. I would like to send down some alternate layouts, or perhaps bring them down in the latter part of January. I'd also like to get some layout ideas from Ed Rice—and I don't mean the "manifesto" approach he used for your article in Jubilee.

The first copies of THE SECULAR JOURNAL arrived from the printer today. I have sent one copy off to you by first-class airmail, and I hope it reaches you at the same time as this letter. Ten additional copies are going to you by book post, and I hope that these too are in your hands before Christmas.

I was deeply moved by your letter of December 13th. I can only wish you a happy and holy Christmas and say that I will, if I possibly can, visit the monastery in January. It's been much too long since my last visit, and it will, I know, do me much good.

Yours ever,
Robert Giroux

1. André Malraux, a French author and art historian, wrote several art books, including *The Psychology of Art* (1947–49) and the three-volume *The Imaginary Museum of World Sculpture* (1952–54), as well as edited a series entitled *The Arts of Mankind*. Malraux became a minister of state in President Charles De Gaulle's government (1958–59) and later served as France's first minister of cultural affairs (1959–69).

JANUARY 3, 1958 [1959]

Our Lady of Gethsemani
[Letterhead]

Dear Bob:

Many thanks for your letter and for the books. It was good to hear from you and I shall look forward to seeing you at the end of January. Did I warn you that we are having our retreat in the middle of February and that if you are delayed, you should not come then but in March. I hope you will be here at the end of this month and we can fight out the problems of <u>Art and Worship</u> [this book was never published]. Would you believe that the incomparable censor (the same one who is always making all the trouble—or one of the two) has now objected to the illustrations. Fr. Abbot wrote I think asking for the duplicates of the pictures. Thank heaven this book is in no great hurry, but knowing the censors we may still be waiting for a nihil obstat in September. I think that all my sins as a writer have been suitably purged by these gentlemen and their untiring efforts. I certainly hope so. And I do not refer to their criticisms of the manuscripts as purifications either.

It was good to see the <u>Secular Journal</u> coming out after all the obstacles and problems it had to meet. And I am glad it promises to do well.

Don't think me fussy if I say that I was not happy with the pictures. I honestly think they were a bad idea. They did not come out well (naturally with the screen) and what is more I am convinced that they may cause trouble with our General in Rome. The thing is they may have made it difficult if not impossible to propose the publication of further volumes of the Secular Journal, for there is still a lot of usable material in manuscript at St. Bonaventure's [College]. I hope it will not turn out that way, but the General is almost certain to raise a stink about those pictures. Anyway, I think that all the curiosity about how I may look is silly and irrelevant and I think it would be smarter to keep my face unknown as far as possible.

Then, again, I wasn't happy with the "At last after twenty years full revelation" approach. Not that there isn't truth in the words, the book has obviously had to wait, but I don't like the implication that there is anything special to be released or revealed. I suppose I can blame the censors and the Order for unconsciously producing this reaction in the publishers, because it is definitely a matter of record that the censors acted as if it were that kind of a book and opposed "release after twenty years" as long as they could.

I am not mad or irritated, and I don't hold anything against anybody, but just wanted to put in my monastic two cents' worth. And I think this is only logical, because, after all, the chief appeal of the stuff I write derives from the fact that I am a monk, and the more monastic one is about the books, the better one can hope to keep up the appeal—if that is what matters, which from my point of view it is not. I know you will probably think I am too extreme about all this, and I admit that I can hardly be expected to see things precisely from the New York angle. But, in any case, thanks for taking so much trouble to present the book attractively, because it is attractive and I am very pleased with the design, the printing, etc. You have certainly done all you can to make something out of the material, and I am proud and happy about the result, except for the two points I mentioned.

More later. Meanwhile, Happy New Year to all of you, and blessings.

Faithfully in Christ,
Tom /s/

JANUARY 8, 1958 [1959]

Our Lady of Gethsemani
[Letterhead]

Dear Bob:

When I wrote the other day, I forgot one important question you asked, which was about trying new layouts. By all means, I should like to see some. I think the others are too crowded, and would like to see things fixed so that there would be no more than two on a page at any time, and mostly only one picture on a page. I would like to see as much space as possible.

Have you considered the various pictures yet from the point of view of reproduction? I could get something else to replace ones that will definitely not reproduce well. This is one of the things the censor was worried about apparently, though I should think it was hardly his business. It is amazing how a book can get held up on the slightest and most irresponsible whims of someone who knows nothing about publishing and appoints himself as an uninvited editor, the way these people do. Do they think publishers don't know their business? Or can't take care of their own interests?

We can talk about all this when you come down.

And about SECULAR JOURNAL—I wanted to send a copy to Aldous Huxley, but I don't know his address. Could you get one to him, please? And one to Gregory Zilboorg, which might perhaps count as a review copy (if not charge it to me).

I thought too various Latin American publications might like to see it since it is so largely pro-Latin. Do you still have the address of Mejía Sánchez, to whom you sent the bibliography? He is editor of Revista de Literatura Mexicana, published at the National University of Mexico.

Other places to whom review copies might be sent:

Origines, Trocadero 162, Havana, Cuba.
Casa de la Cultura Ecuatoriana, Quito, Ecuador.
[Ediciones] Mito, Apartado Aereo 5899, Bogotá, Colombia.
Asomante, Apartado 1142, San Juan, Puerto Rico.
Panoramas, Reforma 18, Mexico 1, D.F.
La Prensa, Managua, Nicaragua.
Abside, Plateros 76, Mexico 19, D.F.

And if they come through I'd like to see them if possible.
When you come down we can talk about the reactions, etc.
All the best—as ever.

In Christ our Lord,
Tom /s/

JANUARY 16, 1959

Rev. M. Louis, O.C.S.O.
Abbey of Our Lady of Gethsemani
Trappist, Kentucky

Dear Tom:

I have just learned that Eliot is arriving in New York at the end of January, in connection with his play, THE ELDER STATESMAN, which we are publishing. This means that I shall have to be on hand for a while, and since your February retreat follows, I should like to plan on coming down after Easter, instead.

The decision to submit the illustrative material to the censor naturally freezes all consideration of production plans. The later date also makes more sense for a discussion of these plans; I hope that it will be possible for the new censor to clear matters up by the end of March. I've sent the duplicates to Father Abbot, together with a note about my change of plans. The photos had been with Ed Rice, with whom I had been consulting on layout problems, which he's so good at. We both agree that the quality of the pictures is superb. The originals, which are here, are so much better than the duplicates: if the censor is concerned about reproducibility, I hope someone points out to him that the duplicates are to the originals as ink is to water.

I was distressed to learn that you do not feel happy about the pictures in THE SECULAR JOURNAL. I think one reason they occurred to us was to accentuate the "secular" part of the title. They do illustrate, approximately in some cases and precisely in others, the period covered in the journal. The fussy screen was used deliberately to emphasize the this-is-another-era idea. It's no consolation to me that all the reactions so far have been excellent. The three book clubs are delighted with the book; <u>Publishers' Weekly</u> for the first time has given us a good advance notice. I consulted with Naomi, of course, and her reaction was so favorable that I never thought of consulting with you. I apologize, and I hope you will forgive me.

The copies listed in your letter of January 8th (mostly Latin American addresses) are going out with a card saying "Compliments of the Author." [Aldous] Huxley moves around, so we are sending his copy in care of Harper & Brothers.

I hope to see you either the weekend of March 28th or the following one.

As ever,
Robert Giroux

JANUARY 24, 1959

Our Lady of Gethsemani
[Letterhead]

Dear Bob:

Good, I will be expecting you at the later date, after Easter. But meanwhile I would like to liquidate the question of the type that has been set up here. I don't want to keep the printer waiting indefinitely. Have you got far enough with the plans to be able to tell me definitely one way or the other whether you will want to use this type? If the chances are so largely negative that there is no real hope, let me know and I will get him to break it up. Or have you some other suggestion? Could you please help me resolve this one problem now? The rest we can take up at leisure when you come.

Reverend Father has been away and has probably seen one of the censors at the monastery in [Conyers] Georgia but I have no news from him. We will probably not have anything definite for a while, but I can hardly see how they would continue to object strongly to <u>this</u> of all books.

Many thanks for sending the copies to Huxley and to Latin America. I wrote to Huxley about his theory that drugs promote mystical experience and since last writing to you received an interesting letter in reply so that now, for the moment, I have his address—until he makes the next move.

I had not thought of your point that pictures would emphasize the "in illo tempore" aspect of the Secular Journal. I will offer that as an explanation if the General decides to take me to task on the business. Of course, I can see your side of it also. And naturally I hope you don't think I didn't like the design of the book as a whole, which is very fine indeed. Many thanks for again taking so much trouble. I know we both agree on the matter of making the book a work of art in every respect: it is something important.

I am glad to hear we got good advance notices and continue to hope the book will do very well. No doubt, you will have much more to say about that when you come down. To this, then, I look forward. It will be nicer after Easter anyway. Early February can sometimes be quite dreary here.

With all good wishes—God bless you.

Faithfully in Christ,
Tom /s/

JANUARY 30, 1959

Rev. M. Louis, O.C.S.O.
Abbey of Our Lady of Gethsemani
Trappist, Kentucky

Dear Tom:

To answer your question about the type problem—I doubt very much that it would be possible to use it. However, it might be wise, before the printer breaks it up, to have a carefully proofed set of reproduction proofs made on good paper. These should either be shipped to us flat or kept by you for future possible contingency. My guess is that an entirely new re-setting job will have to be done, but it will be nice to know that we have not irrevocably distributed what is after all a well-designed and expensive typesetting job.

Father Abbot wrote me that the duplicate photographs had arrived. I hope the censors have now approved this aspect of the book.

The first reviews of THE SECULAR JOURNAL are excellent. First of all, the Publishers' Weekly in their "Forecasts" call it "a delightful book." Second, we've received an advance proof of the Chicago Tribune review, which is full of commendation. Nothing in the New York press as yet, but, of course, we do not officially publish until Monday. As soon as I have du-plicate copies, I'll send you a batch.

Looking forward to seeing you in April.

Yours ever,
Robert Giroux

MARCH 18, 1959

Our Lady of Gethsemani
[Letterhead]

Dear Bob:

I wrote to Naomi the other day with the news that the Censors had fi-nally passed Art and Worship, requesting only a couple of minor changes in the text. The new censor found nothing wrong with the pictures or with the idea of the book as a whole. Just that one other censor who I think is getting cantankerous in his advancing years maybe.

And now, what about you? When can we expect you? Easter week is bad for me, but the week after is all right. Then the second week after Easter (in fact from the 10th to 18th about) is bad again, and after that is all right. It would be ideal for you to come sometime like the evening of the 4th or 5th, better still the 6th, and stay over a few days. After the 18th any time is good. I hope to see you soon.

When you come, we can talk over getting together a book of things re-cently written, some of which Naomi has been handling for magazines, in-cluding the Prometheus, the article on Pasternak I have been working on, and a few other things like an article on Christianity and Totalitarianism and a long one on the Power and Meaning of Love. I have a couple of ideas that might be added to this, and I think it would make a good book of <u>recent</u> work. Since I really haven't been writing anything much for the last three years, this material will be in many ways quite new, and I think it would do well. There is no hurry with it, and more might come up while we are planning the thing. I will show you what we have anyway.

Naomi said she had sent the little Desert Fathers' translation to you [*The Wisdom of the Desert* (1960)]. I did not think of it as being up your alley really—it is quite slight, though I like it.

If and when you come, I would be very interested in seeing late issues of things like Encounter, Dissent, and perhaps better ones I may not have heard of, if it is not too much of a bore to bring them. I have a paper back of Dwight Macdonald [perhaps *The Responsibility of Peoples, and Other Essays in Political Criticism* (1957)], which I like fairly well. Did any of those South American reviews come through? You might bring them too if any. I don't know if you sent clippings on the Journal, but if you did they did not get through.

It is very nice here now and I hope it will be even nicer in April.

Are you going to this thing for Mark Van Doren by the way?[1] I wrote a screwy poem for the memorial volume, which he might like though perhaps the others won't.[2]

I still need more pictures for Art and Worship. One sensible thing the negative censor said was that the best modern stuff was not represented. That is fair enough. Can you lay hands on any?

With best wishes for Easter, and all blessings.

Faithfully yours in Christ,
Tom /s/

P. S. Yes—I have the bronze [Christopher Award] medal. Pity they didn't hang it on you + Naomi, with fanfares.

---

1. See the letter dated April 10, 1959.
2. See "Message to Be Inscribed on Mark Van Doren's Hamilton Medal," in TM, *The Collected Poems of Thomas Merton* (New York: New Directions, 1977), 800–801.

APRIL 10, 1959

Rev. M. Louis, O.C.S.O.
Abbey of Our Lady of Gethsemani
Trappist, Kentucky

Dear Tom:

How would the weekend of Saturday, May 2nd, work out for a visit? I'm sorry for the delay in not having written sooner, and I won't trouble you with the complications and difficulties which prevent my leaving New York earlier. The fact is that the first week in May is really free from my point of view, and I hope there's nothing against it from the monastery's point of view.

I'll probably get a plane Friday morning, May 1st, and arrive sometime late in the afternoon. I have to go on to Atlanta on Monday—that is, unless [fiction writer] Flannery O'Connor wants to see me before I go on to Louisville. It doesn't matter whether I make this leg of the trip before or after I see you. Let's just count on May 1st through 3rd.

I look forward to talking over the collection which you describe in your letter of March 18th and I will bring down the very beautiful layout which Ed Rice has done for ART AND WORSHIP. I'll also bring the magazines along and the reviews of the JOURNAL. We have not, however, received any of the South American reviews. I definitely intend to be present at the Mark Van Doren dinner on April 29th. Under separate cover I am sending you copies of THE ELDER STATESMAN by T.S. Eliot and Robert Lowell's LIFE STUDIES, which we are publishing this month.

Yours ever,
Robert Giroux

P.S. I'm sure Pantheon sent you a copy of Pasternak's "I Remember," but I'll bring that along too if they haven't.

MAY 26, 1959

Farrar, Straus & Cudahy, Inc.
[Letterhead]

Rev. M. Louis, O.C.S.O.
Abbey of Our Lady of Gethsemani
Trappist, Kentucky

Dear Tom:

The staid old Times Literary Supplement has an excellent review of SECULAR JOURNAL. It more than makes up for the rather silly reviews of ELECTED SILENCE in England.

I had an excellent meeting with Father Paul [Bourne, O.C.S.O.] at Conyers [Georgia], after great trouble in locating the place. When my driver got lost, he stopped a car full of Negroes and said: "Where's this yere monastery?" Dead silence. He tried again: "You know, where the monks are." Big smiles, faces brightened up: "Oh, you mean the monks' monastery! Why that's just down the road a little piece." Father Paul and his associates are certainly putting the principles of modern art into practice at Conyers. I hope you see it one day, for it is quite beautiful. The stained glass alone, which I saw them laying out, is superb—abstract, Matisse-like swirls of color. The only represented figure in the whole Church (in glass, that is) will be an enormous Byzantine figure of Our Lady over the main altar. The cloister is not only open, with traditional columns and arches, but has a pool. The effect they are getting on the stone by rubbing it by hand and applying some kind of finish is astounding. The effect is completely non-concrete. Father Paul is tremendously interested in ART AND WORSHIP, liked Ed Rice's layout as much as you did, and wants to help in every way. He was misled by the terrible photostats, and realizes they gave a false picture. I think you are lucky to have him as a censor.

Yours ever,
Bob /s/

JUNE 20, 1959

Dear Bob:

I am finally getting around to drawing up that list of articles for the book.[1] Forgive me from taking so long, I have had a lot of other things to do and wanted to find a clear space in which I could move freely before starting to dig up all this. I think almost everything on the list would be easy to come by, and some of it you already have. I am checking with a pen, the things I think you have on file. Please let me know if you do not.

The way this material shapes up on the list seems to me to balance out pretty well. It seems to me that the early book reviews will help a great deal. They will give variety, and there will be a certain appeal to curiosity in the fact that there is a review of an early book [*Laughter in the Dark*] by [Vladimir] Nabokov, as well as books [*The World's Body* and *Enjoyment of Literature*] by [poet and critic] John Crowe Ransom, etc. Can you get these from the papers in question? I have added one Columbia Review article [November 1939], which is really not a "juvenile" since it was written when I was a graduate student and was working for the papers downtown. It is on [novelist] Richard Hughes.

I don't think I have any of the Part Two articles around here. I would like you, if possible, to get copies of all of them and send them down to me. I will go over them and revise, correct and do what I think ought to be done, and then we can type them up here and send them back nice and tidy.

The third part (longer studies) will bring in a lot of bulk. I think that to include Basic Principles of Monastic Spirituality might make the whole thing too long. I leave that up to you, if you like it.[2] The thing I have marked "[Blessed] Paul Giustianiani on the hermit life" is a preface to a book that appeared in French. I don't know if I can still find an English text of it, but if I can I think it should go in. I would like to include the piece on St. John of the Cross, which was in the book Saints for Now (ed. by Clare Boothe Luce). You took the Feast of Freedom when you were here. Monastic Peace will be about the longest thing in the book. You have a rather messy carbon of the material for Action and Contemplation in St. Bernard, which I would like back as soon as possible so that I may go over it and get it typed out for you.

About the fourth part, there should be little trouble: get them from the magazines as they come out. Ed is just bringing one out in Jubilee now, and Naomi can get the others for you. This will bring the book well up into the ninety thousands, so I am leaving aside things like Prometheus, which have an entirely different character, and the Liturgical essays, which, with the addition of others, will someday form a book in their own right, unified and simple.

I hope there is no mix-up on the material in Part III, which I once sent you. These are in some cases the only copies of the essays that I have left. Still, others can perhaps be found.

There are one or two small things which I might be able to dig up and which are not on this list. Now that I see the material lined up, I am rather hopeful about it. It ought to make a fairly good book. At least a big one. And there will be variety in it, and finally it has a kind of chronological interest.

I have not yet thanked you either for the books that J. Laughlin brought down. The Sleepwalkers is a real acquisition and I very much enjoy [Bernard] Malamud. The Djuna Barnes I have not cracked into yet; it looks a bit cryptic. Many thanks for these and so many other things: I am glad you had a good visit with Father Paul; I am sure it was worthwhile in many ways, and it is good to hear that the Georgia monastery makes sense.

Let us hear from you soon about these articles.[3] I'd like to clean up the revision work as soon as possible, as in August I am to be swamped by a bunch of kids who come to spend two weeks here. Best to all—God bless you.

Faithfully in Christ,

[Thomas Merton]

1. This was a preliminary list of possible articles in what would eventually become *Disputed Questions*.
2. TM, *Basic Principles of Monastic Spirituality* (1957).
3. TM listed seven articles for part 1; nine articles for part 2; nine articles for part 3, and six articles for part 4.

NOVEMBER 25, 1959

Farrar, Straus & Cudahy, Inc.

[Letterhead]

Rev. M. Louis, O.C.S.O.
Abbey of Our Lady of Gethsemani
Trappist, Kentucky

Dear Tom:

I feel that I have been out of touch for decades. I do not like the feeling, and I hope to prevent its reoccurrence particularly in view of Naomi's departure from Curtis Brown. She always seemed another way of being in touch, and I am appalled at her leaving the agency to go to Doubleday. I still cannot believe that she will have gone as of December first.

Book of Essays. We have collected almost everything here except the Columbia Review piece on Richard Hughes, which Bob Lax has promised help on. It all makes quite a collection—more than one book, I think. It's fascinating going over some of the early things. In the light of the current bruhaha over [D.H.] Lawrence, it's refreshing to read the opening of your review [in the *New York Times Book Review Section* (January 14, 1940)] of [William York] Tindall [*D.H. Lawrence and Susan His Cow*]: "Lawrence sincerely condemned [James Joyce's] Ulysses as obscene." The writings on the contemplative life alone come to 40,000 words; with preface and other customary material this makes a fair-sized book. The long studies come to 72,000 words or a substantial book.

What appeals to us most, right now, as the timeliest possibility is a book combining the recent pieces on the Russian Orthodox, Eastern Rites, Mount Athos, Pasternak, St. John Climacus and so on. Do you think there is enough for a book here? If so, we wonder if it could be ready to bring out before the next book on the agenda:

Art and Worship. While Ed Rice is still working on the layout of this, I am beginning to think that the text ought to be longer—particularly the latter section on modern religious art, which is almost perfunctory. There is so much interest in this that it ought either to be dealt with more fully (which is what we hope you will agree to do) or be dropped altogether, which would be regrettable. The press work and manufacture of ART AND WORSHIP is going to take care and time, and while we keep it moving along in the works, it would be wonderful if the Russian book took shape in the meantime.

I enclose an article in Encounter by Edmund Wilson on DOCTOR ZHIVAGO which you may not have seen. Also an article in Life, which seemed worth saving, on Russian Orthodoxy. The color photos are excellent.

Did the paperbound copies of THE SILENT LIFE reach you with the other material? I hope all goes well with your health. Pray for me.

Yours ever,

Bob /s/

NOVEMBER 28, 1959

Dear Bob:

I wrote you a letter yesterday, but it had not gone out when yours arrived today, so I am going over it again, saying much the same thing because I was about to suggest what you yourself suggested. Precisely, what seems to be called for is a book of essays consisting of the more recent material, and I was reaching the conclusion that the whole list I sent you in June was much too much for a single book.

In a few days, therefore, I am sending you a full length book ms. comprised of two essays on Pasternak, Mount Athos, St. John Climacus, A Renaissance Hermit, Four Liturgical Essays (Time and Liturgy, Nativity Kerygma, etc.), Power and Meaning of Love, Christianity and Mass Movements and, finally, a study of 25,000 words on the Christian Life of Prayer. It will total up to quite a long book. This is called <u>Disputed Questions</u>. (I spoke of it to my new agent, Perry Knowlton, under the title <u>A Contemplative Point of View</u>. The first seems to me shorter and better.)

Regarding the rest of that material on the June list:

1—I suggest a book of <u>Early Essays</u> made up of the early book reviews, etc., and the spiritual essays, listed as Part II of the June list. That could be put off for another couple of years however.

2—Monastic Studies: this would contain what I have in Part III of the June list, especially <u>Monastic Peace</u> and <u>Basic Principles</u>. And all the medieval studies on St. Bernard, etc. But as we still have a lot of the booklets in stock in the bookstore, we will have to wait at least two more years for this also. Just as long as you have the material there, there is no problem.

3—As for the timing, I agree that <u>Disputed Questions</u> should logically go right into production. I will get it up there as soon as the last part is retyped. <u>Art and Worship</u> can wait, above all as I am in no mood to do any work on modern sacred art now, since I know too little about it. About how many more pages do you want? Can you send me something to look at, to go on?

The other thing I wanted to say in my letter was that a very good book in French has been written by a young girl, a dancer, who was for a while in a Trappistine convent. <u>Trois ans à la Trappe</u>, by Marina de Berg. I recommend it to your interest as a fine possibility for translation. Very lively and interesting, and utterly true.

Harcourt, Brace has been making suggestions to Curtis Brown about a Merton Reader. Nothing is being done about it at the moment, but if I remember correctly Frank dell'Isola, God bless him, suggested that to you long ago. In any case, it should wait until the three above volumes are out, namely another four or five years. In addition to those, I will probably have at least one other book for you, about 45,000 words. This ought to keep us happy and busy for awhile. Having done quite a bit of work since late summer, I am ready for another layoff. That is the way I seem to have been going: intense work for four months and then layoff for a year. But I think this time it will be a rather longer layoff.

I am glad we are getting back into action with a <u>new</u> book, and this one represents all my latest thought and work. That is the way it ought to be. With best wishes for Advent.

> Faithfully in Christ,
> [Thomas Merton]

DECEMBER 24, 1959

> Farrar, Straus & Cudahy, Inc.
> [Letterhead]

Rev. M. Louis, O.C.S.O.
Abbey of Our Lady of Gethsemani
Trappist, Kentucky

Dear Tom:

I have been going over the manuscript with great pleasure, for I think it has some of your best writing. I particularly like "Vocation to Solitude," the new version of which arrived last Friday.

You are right in keeping all this new material, with new slants and approaches, apart from the older stuff. But I really think, Tom, that there is enough here for more than one book—for three quite unified books, in fact. The first is the Russian and related material (would "The New Man" fit in with that?); the second, with some additions, is "Time and the Liturgy"; and the third is "The Christian Life of Prayer" plus most of the others. (I wonder, also, if "Christianity and Totalitarianism" wouldn't fit in with the Russian and Eastern Rite book?)

Of course, you have indicated all this yourself by the ordering of the contents. But I really think that lumped all together as DISPUTED QUESTIONS they make too rambling and chunky a book. After discussing it with Sheila [Cudahy], I can tell you that the book we'd all like to see you concentrate on first is the Russian one for the fall of 1960. Ed Rice mentioned an essay called "Orthodox Spirituality"; is there any chance of this being ready soon? To cite a straw in the wind, <u>Thought</u> has just come out with your Pasternak article and the New York Times had a little note mentioning your piece alone (enclosed). I also recall our talking last May about the Christian theme in Dostoevsky; have you ever considered doing a piece on his work, or does Dostoevsky come into "Orthodox Spirituality" in some way? Finally, Bob Lax mentioned a piece on Zen.[1] There's tremendous interest in this among the younger people, and it would be wonderful if this too could go into a book concerned with eastern thought. I don't think the four essays we now have make a long enough book, though they are all good. But if "Orthodox Spirituality," and perhaps the Dostoevsky, Zen, and "Totalitarianism" pieces were added, it would be long enough and unified too.

The Christmas, Easter, Ash Wednesday pieces, together with "Time and the Liturgy" would also make a beautiful, unified book, but we'd feel happier if you could add to its length somewhat. The contemplative pieces will easily make the third book.

I hope we can start with the orthodox and eastern one. Please let me know how all this strikes you, and just what the possibilities are. In any event, we have several books in sight and it will be good to move ahead on them.

With all good wishes for a holy Christmas and for the New Year.

> Yours ever,
> Bob /s/

P. S. For some reason, I never got a copy of "Nativity Kerygma" + Ed has loaned me his, which I am having recopied for the ms. But I'd love to have it for myself.

P. P. S. Lax has also mentioned an essay on [William] Blake. Am I crazy to think it will go in the first book?

1. Perhaps a reference to the forthcoming "The Recovery of Paradise: Wisdom in Emptiness; A Dialogue: D. T. Suzuki and Thomas Merton," *New Directions in Poetry and Press* 17 (1961): 65–101.

DECEMBER 29, 1959

Dear Bob:

The ideas about the new book are in general perfectly acceptable to me. And they make good sense. The liturgical material really ought to be in a book by itself and I have a lot of notes that can easily be worked up to complete what I sent you. I don't have any of the original Kerygma left; I thought I had sent you one last year, but perhaps I did not, for they came at the last moment before Christmas and I hardly sent out a dozen of them then. This year the monastery sent out the rest of them.

The title the "New Man" belongs with the ms. I have not yet sent you. We had better keep it that way—you'll see.

All right, let us proceed with what can provisionally be called the Russian book. But actually I would like to make it a little broader than that. It would include the following:

Two Pasternak articles (I am sending <u>Thought</u> offprint)
Mount Athos
St. John of the Ladder
Renaissance Hermit
St. Bernard, Monk and Apostle
Sacred Art and Spiritual Life
Absurdity in Sacred Decoration

Power and Meaning of Love
Christianity and Totalitarianism
which have already been written
~~The Spirituality of the Eastern Church~~
~~Le Douanier Rousseau~~
The Primitive Spirit of Carmel

These last three are only waiting to get on paper.[1] One final suggestion, which interests me now, is an article on the former Shaker colonies in Kentucky.[2] Centered on the one near here, it could be called simply Shakertown. These four are ready to be written, [and I] could get them to you in a couple of months if I am able to get down to work on them soon. In fact if things go normally, I could have them there much sooner.

I think also that Power and Meaning of Love could and should be in this book. If you think so, and if it would take up enough room, perhaps I could put off the one on Le Douanier Rousseau to a later date. Let me know.

The Zen article—well, it will be coming along one of these days but not in a hurry. It requires a lot of thought. I hope to do something though. Blake, I have done nothing about lately. Dostoevsky, still cooking. I haven't had time to read him in the leisurely way that would be required for this type of thing, but we can keep it on the agenda.

So the Russian book will end up by not being so Russian. Do you like Disputed Questions as a title? I do in a way, but no doubt there is a better one to be found.

The three books I think should be: first, this one, then Christian Life of Prayer, etc. (easy to add other essays). Then the Liturgy one—unless by that time you think the New Man should come in between.

Look, the Harcourt, Brace people are being very fussy and insistent about the stupid idea of a Merton reader consisting only of selections from Harcourt, Brace books. My idea is that no such reader should appear unless it contains selections from everything and should in any case be put off for at least two more years. Why don't you get in on this with a counter suggestion, and bewilder Perry Knowlton [TM's new agent at Curtis Brown] with it.[3] After all, the idea was first brought up by Frank dell'Isola a long time ago and was proposed to you, I think. What is your opinion of the whole thing? I personally am not eager to let Harcourt, Brace do it, though if they meet requirements, they can, for all I care.

Do you think Frank dell'Isola can handle it adequately? If he can, he should be in on it, as he first brought the thing up. Let me know soon what your reactions are, and I can tell Knowlton what I think too. I already have, of course.

Have you seen Bob Lax's wonderful Circus poem [*Circus of the Sun*], now in a book of its own? I understand you are publishing Salvatore Quasimodo

[Nobel Prize Laureate in Literature for 1959]: you remember me for a copy when it comes out?

I am sending you the book of the Christmas sermons of a medieval Cistercian, Guerric of Igny, which we brought out. The essay of mine will eventually form part of another of those books of yours. I don't think I have already sent you this, but if you get two, so much the better.

Best New Year wishes, and all blessings.

Faithfully in Christ,
[Thomas Merton]

1. TM wished to exclude the two titles that are crossed out.
2. TM, "The Shakers," *Jubilee*, January 1964, 36–41.
3. See the letter dated May 26, 1960.

FEBRUARY 12, 1960

Farrar, Straus & Cudahy, Inc.
[Letterhead]

Rev. M. Louis, O.C.S.O.
Abbey of Our Lady of Gethsemani
Trappist, Kentucky

Dear Tom:

I'm sorry that we are in such a pickle over the Reader. I think you are absolutely right in insisting on representation of <u>all</u> your writing, not just the Harcourt stuff. I think Naomi is right in proposing to edit it and in proposing her own firm [Doubleday] to break the deadlock.[1] The trouble is, no one else seems to agree with me. Sheila Cudahy thinks it is inappropriate for Naomi to edit a collection of your writing, and she also thinks it won't go down well with bookstores or readers. Roger Straus thinks there is no reason for Doubleday to enter the picture at all; he feels he can break the deadlock with William Jovanovich of Harcourt, with whom he is on friendly social terms. After all, Harcourt and Knopf got together on E.M. Forster's COLLECTED STORIES, one-half of which each had originally done (Knopf did the collection); we got together with New Directions on THE COMPLETE WRITINGS OF NATHANAEL WEST (half of which Jay had originally done; we split royalties on the collected edition).

Perry Knowlton is a nice young Princetonian, but my personal impression is that he is more interested in the main chance [*sic*] than in the author's welfare. I've already been told that he intends to ask all the Curtis Brown authors to sign an agreement with the agency. I hope this is an unfounded rumor. Your only protection as an author is that you have a working relation with the agency based on mutual trust, not on a signed paper. It really grieves me that Naomi is no longer there. She was right to leave, and she is obviously happier at having left—but I no longer feel that your best interests are now paramount at Curtis Brown. I must tell you this in confidence, but I would feel wrong in not reporting this to you. Knowlton was all confused about a writer named Thomas MacDonald [*read* McDonnell, the book editor at *The Pilot* (Boston)], who proposed himself to Harcourt as editor of the Reader; and Father Kilian McDonnell, who was in correspondence with him over some of your writing in <u>Sponsa Regis</u> [a journal devoted to Catholic religious women published in Collegeville, MN]. This confusion is perhaps understandable, but it's symptomatic of his remote feelings about things Catholic.

I feel deeply that it is in your best interests to bring out a <u>new</u> book of writing this fall. We definitely have one here in these essays, and I want to do a little more thinking and editorial work on the contents. I would prefer a substantial book, as I suggested at our last meeting (I hope we can soon have another), but I think it is just as desirable to achieve as unified a feeling as possible. I don't have an alternative title to DISPUTED QUESTIONS yet, so let's use that for purposes of discussion. I would like to sign contracts for four books:

1. ART AND WORSHIP (this was never listed in an agreement)
2. DISPUTED QUESTIONS
3. BOOK OF FEAST DAYS
4. COLLECTION OF ESSAYS

The worst thing right now would be to announce a Reader of already published things. A <u>new</u> book is paramount, and we have two in the works in DISPUTED QUESTIONS and ART AND WORSHIP. On the latter, Ed Rice is still working at the layout and he has just asked me for captions for the pictures. This is going to take longer on press work than DISPUTED QUESTIONS because of the half-tones.

Assuming that the essay on the "New Man" is going to be part of DISPUTED QUESTIONS, and that I will be receiving a typescript soon, I will send you my idea of the table of contents and, if you approve, go right into print. If you wish changes, we'll arrange them quickly and proceed into galleys. If you think it would help for me to come down before Lent, to get this editorial work completed, I'll be very happy to do so.

Ever yours,

Bob /s/

1. In a letter to John McCallum at HB, dated January 22, 1960, NB said that she would be "very happy indeed" to edit a Merton reader, with a guaranteed advance of $5,000. In a subsequent letter, dated March 7, 1960, Roger Straus wrote to William Jovanovich at HB that it was his understanding that such a reader would not appear for a number of years and that FSC and HB might collaborate in its publication. He suggested that either Jacques Maritain, Christopher Dawson, or Evelyn Waugh might write the introduction to this volume.

FEBRUARY 16, 1960

Dear Bob:

Thanks for your letter of the 12th, which I received this morning. I think it would be a good idea to go ahead with the contract for the four books as you mentioned.

And, above all, I am for proceeding at once with <u>Disputed Questions</u>. You already have <u>all</u> the material for this book, if you have received the "Primitive Ideal of Carmel," which I sent, I think, with the letter which you answered. <u>The New Man</u> is not an essay but a complete book, though a short one. It is 135 pp. in ms., but the type is small and there are quite a few words per page. I would say it adds up to 45 or 50 thousand words. I advise including this book on a contract, either in place of the second book of essays, or in addition to it, making a five-book contract.

I believe that the situation is so unclear that you really should come down and we really should hash out our affairs. I want to make some small changes, including one I think of especially in the <u>Mount Athos</u> piece.[1] I have a copy here and I can be working on it. Also, there should be some modifications on one of the Pasternak articles. We should talk these things over and get straight on what we are going to do with this book.

At the same time, I can be proofreading the ms. of the <u>New Man</u>, which was finally finished, (typing) yesterday, and can give that to you when you get here. You can give it a preliminary look and we can decide what to do from then on with it.

Finally, and most important, I believe it is quite urgent that we all discuss together the matter you brought up concerning Curtis Brown. I do not see things very clearly, and Father Abbot even less so, from this distance. I know Naomi agrees with you and has made some positive suggestions which we can discuss. I can tell you frankly that I have never been at all satisfied with the way Curtis Brown has handled foreign rights, and if that same situation is going to get into the regular American contracts, it will be very disappointing. I would therefore very much appreciate it if you could get down. Any time, between the time you get this letter and Quinquagesima [last Sunday before Ash Wednesday] weekend (last days of Feb.) would be fine. Perhaps you could break away for a day or two next week. Just send us a wire to let us know when to expect you. Naturally, it will be a pleasure to see you again. But quite apart from the human side of it, I believe it is important that we get together on these various editorial problems, because I can see that the picture is not at all clear.

Then we can go right ahead with <u>Disputed Questions</u>. And I believe that only in a meeting can we finally settle just what is still to be done with <u>Art and Worship</u>. You said Ed [Rice] wants captions: in the proofs I sent, there were lots of them. I hope they have not been lost. The pictures followed a definite scheme, and I was making all kinds of comparisons. If he has changed the order in the layouts we are liable to be up a tree, as far as this aspect of the book is concerned. But in that case, if only I have his layouts and dummy, I can get the captions done. Best to let me know how many words wanted in each case.

P.S. (not quite) if the only time available for you is Quinquagesima, (Sat[urday] 27 and Sun[day] 28) all right, don't hesitate. But it would be a bit better for us if you came during the previous week, or the weekend before (21st).

All best wishes and blessings—see you soon I hope.

In Xto Jesu,

[Thomas Merton]

1. See TM, "Mount Athos," *Jubilee*, August 1959, 8–16.

FEBRUARY 17, 1960

Farrar, Straus & Cudahy, Inc.

[Letterhead]

Rev. M. Louis, O.C.S.O.
Abbey of Our Lady of Gethsemani
Trappist, Kentucky

Dear Tom:

I'm delighted to have your letter of February 16th and I will be down to see you next week. I plan to arrive on Tuesday, the 23rd, for a three- or four-day stay. I will probably reach your doorstep around one o'clock on Tuesday afternoon.

I will bring all the manuscripts with me, both DISPUTED QUESTIONS and ART AND WORSHIP, and I hope we will be able to have a number of meetings during the week to discuss these as well as the Curtis Brown problem.

I very much look forward to seeing you. Unless I hear from you to the contrary, I will assume the date of my arrival is okay.

Yours ever,

Bob /s/

APRIL 12, 1960

Dear Bob:

Here is the final and complete version of one of the essays for the new book as it has appeared in Worship [a liturgical magazine]. There have been significant changes.

An orthodox priest in Paris wants to publish my Mount Athos article in a magazine there. But I do not have a corrected version to send him. Could you get me, real quick, a copy of the version you have there, so that I could pass it on to him? Any expense involved can be taken from our account.

The uncensored articles are painfully going through their rebirth. The Solitude one has been rewritten and enlarged and the all-round impression seems to be that it is improved. Fr. Paul [Bourne] is all for it, anyway. I hope plans for the book have been going forward.

Fr. Abbot has not yet signed the last contract with Curtis Brown. The New Directions one. He has it here but, again, is waiting for the censors finally to approve something. <u>Then</u> we will inform them of our new decision.

I am sorry I have not yet got around to giving you that list of foreign publishers, but I guess there is no great rush.

A special messenger from the Holy Father, an architect, bringing me a present of a stole from Rome blessed by John XXIII, was here yesterday, and has some ideas for the Art and Worship book. I am hoping that suggestions will come from you also. How is Ed doing with the new captions, etc.? Are his layouts taking shape?

This is just a brief note to wish you a happy Easter. I hope to write more at leisure later. Have been rather pressed lately.[1] I like the little E.M. Forster thing on Mt. Lebanon, and have received a touching letter from one of the surviving Shaker eldresses in New Hampshire.

All best wishes.

God bless you,
Tom /s/

---

1. Indeed, TM was preoccupied by other matters. In a letter dated April 8, 1960, he wrote in French to Jacques Maritain about a problem he encountered with the abbot general. TM had asked Daisetz T. Suzuki to write an essay concerning paradise and Buddhism, which he did, and because TM felt that this essay needed a counterpart written from a Catholic perspective, he wrote one. TM hoped to publish both essays in some journal. Permission to do so was granted. When TM wanted to invite others to contribute essays, such as Erich Fromm and Paul Tillich, the abbot general opposed the publication of such interreligious dialogue in book form. In TM's view, "Un tel dialogue pourrait, semble-t-il, faire du bien parmi les intellectuels" ("It would seem that such a dialogue would be beneficial among those who are educated" [translation by PS]). Thus he asked for Maritain's advice, which he would send to the abbot general, and then abide by the general's decision. As TM indicated in his letter to the abbot general, dated April 21, 1960, Maritain encouraged TM to put together such an interreligious book, and TM was willing to continue, aware of the obstacles he might face from censors. The abbot general's fraternal response to TM, dated April 28, 1960, was negative, which TM graciously accepted, in a letter dated May 20, 1960. TM even went one step further: "Si vous voulez que je cesse entièrement de contacts ou de dialogues avec les non-catholiques, vous n'avez qu'à me le dire" ("If you would like me to cease completely my contact or dialogue with non-Catholics, you have only to tell me this" [translation by PS]).

Farrar, Straus & Cudahy, Inc.
[Letterhead]

Dear Tom:

Many thanks for the final version of the essay in <u>Worship</u>. Actually Father [Kilian] McDonnell [O.S.B.] had sent me the corrected proof of this, and it is now at the printer's with the rest of DISPUTED QUESTIONS. I will, nevertheless, proofread against this printed copy.

We are expecting galleys around April 28th. I had hoped to have sample type pages to send you earlier, but they have still not come in. Perhaps next week will turn them up. We have a jacket sketch based on the classical idea we discussed; it needs a few little revisions, then I'll send it on to you.

I'm sorry I won't be able to provide you with the revised Mount Athos piece until the proofs come in. I could ask the printer to stop press and send us the article to photostat for you, but this would be disastrous to our position on their printing schedule, and I'm sure you would agree this does not make sense. I'll rush an extra galley proof of this essay, so you can forward it to Paris shortly after April 28th.

It's a little awkward about Curtis Brown, but we'll just wait until Father Abbot releases the New Directions contract and formally gives notice of the decision. I have told Tom Burns (of Burns & Oates) who is here from England; he likes the contents of DISPUTED QUESTIONS very much and wants to do it. We shall not come to any agreement until Curtis Brown is notified, of course.

Eloise Spaeth is very much interested in ART AND WORSHIP and has some good ideas on the modern art section, which she wants to discuss with me when she returns from the Caribbean at the end of the month.[1] Ed Rice was relieved to learn that the makeup and caption problem was unraveled, and as soon as I get together with Mrs. Spaeth, we'll proceed with the job. I'll consult you about her recommendations and suggestions just as soon as we've gone over them. At that point, you can decide on the final list of plates and so on.

With all good wishes for the Easter season.

Yours ever,
Bob /s/

---

1. Eloise Spaeth spent considerable time collaborating with TM on *Art and Worship* and eventually advised against its publication. For his part, TM felt that he lacked sufficient expertise about modern religious art.

APRIL 22, 1960

Farrar, Straus & Cudahy, Inc.
[Letterhead]

Rev. M. Louis, O.C.S.O.
Abbey of Our Lady of Gethsemani
Trappist, Kentucky

Dear Tom:

Here is the sketch by the jacket artist for DISPUTED QUESTIONS. They are unusual colors, but very striking, don't you agree? The drawing on the Greek vase is apropos and seems to show a master and a scholar and perhaps a scribe. The inscription is not clear to me and perhaps should be omitted, or made decorative. The whole thing is rather unusual and somewhat different from the idea you originally proposed, but the artist was unable to find a single figure that worked. Let me know if you think we should go ahead with this and please return the sketch as quickly as possible. I like it.

Your letter enclosing the revised version of the essay on Solitude has just arrived. Having proceeded with the galleys at our own risk, we shall have to make the changes in proof. Please let me know about The Primitive Carmelite Ideal and the Renaissance Hermit as soon as you have an okay. I will send you copies of the Mount Athos article under separate cover.

I hope that letter to Curtis Brown can go off in the near future.

Yours ever,
Bob /s/

P.S. I enjoyed your new typewriter!

APRIL 30, 1960

Abbey of Gethsemani
[Letterhead]

Dear Bob:

Please excuse the red ribbon; I have to use it up somehow.

The cover design is very fine, though it is not exactly what I was thinking. I like the colors. I think it will be effective; the only thing I wonder about is the vase. If I can find a drawing of the thing I thought of, I'll get it to you. But this is fine, very pleasing.

Still, Fr. Abbot has not signed that last contract with Curtis Brown. Probably when he does the letter saying good-bye ought to go with it. But meanwhile that Reader has come up again. What is the feeling about it at your end? Has Roger Straus come to an agreement with [John H.] Mc-Callum [of HB and Company] or whoever it is that one is supposed to agree with over there?

Where the Reader is concerned, I suppose Curtis Brown had better handle the contract. But we'll tell them this is the exception, unless you have some other idea. Personally, I think it would be simpler to let them carry on with the Reader. It has been Perry Knowlton's main concern anyway since I have dealt with him, so he might as well carry it through.

I received the Mount Athos article and I have revised it fully, for the French Byzantine rite magazine (orthodox, I mean). I am sending you the new version in case you would want to put it in the book. It is considerably improved and should go in if it is still possible at all.

Still nothing from the censors. Honestly, I think something ought to be done to make the process more rational. We have been waiting <u>months</u>, and the Lord knows what they will come up with anyway. Notes on Solitude, Primitive Carmelite Ideal and Ren[aissance] Hermit are still not fully approved, but I certainly hope they will be with nothing more than minor changes.

Will have more interesting news next time I write—this is a hasty note, as things are rather busy.

All best wishes, and God bless you.

Cordially in Christ,
Tom /s/

MAY 26, 1960

Farrar, Straus & Cudahy, Inc.
[Letterhead]

Rev. M. Louis, O.C.S.O.
Abbey of Our Lady of Gethsemani
Trappist, Kentucky

Dear Tom:

The galley proofs of DISPUTED QUESTIONS are now here. I am not sure whether you want me to send them now, or wait until the final Imprimi Potest arrives (for "Renaissance Hermit," I believe). Please let me know whether I should send them.

We have revised the jacket, removing the vase motif and using the drawing on a fragment or shard of pottery. The same colors have been retained, and all in all I think it's a handsome job. We tried hard to find a ruminative figure such as you proposed, but none was right. The drawing has been revised to eliminate the boy; it's now two scholars or sages who are not teaching or gossiping or bull-sessioning, but simply (we insist) disputing questions.

Could you tell me a little more about "Problems and Pardons," the New Directions book?[1] This, I take it, is different from "The Desert Fathers." I'm concerned, because the title seems to echo "Disputed Questions" somewhat. I think it's important that publication of the two books be kept far apart; it would be detrimental to both books unless a big gap and perhaps other titles (like "Art and Worship" and "The New Man") intervene. Incidentally, you did give me the manuscript of "The New Man," and we shall not act on it until you have the Imprimi Potest. I like it enormously and hope it can be the next book. Mrs. Spaeth is at work on "Art and Worship" and I'll send on her comments as soon as she turns them in.

My life with Curtis Brown has become quite unreal, and I do think that in fairness to everyone the situation should be clarified. I am writing Father Abbot by this same mail, asking him to notify them officially.[2]

Because of Roger Straus's personal relations with William Jovanovich [President of HB] (they share posts on the Publishers Council), the two firms have been very much in accord on the Reader. WJ's most recent letter to Roger said: "Clearly we would all do well, as you say, to take time and reflect further. I am most pleased by the personal cooperation you have extended in this, and I hope indeed that <u>when the time is appropriate</u> we can work together."

What puzzles me is Perry Knowlton's insistence on a contract now, before a table of contents has been agreed upon by you, New Directions, Harcourt, and us. Technically speaking, a letter of agreement between the three firms is all that is required, not a new contract. We did this with New Directions on THE COMPLETE WORKS OF NATHANAEL WEST. They controlled "Miss Lonelyhearts" and "The Day of the Locust," and we controlled "A Cool Million" and "The Dream Life of Balso Snell." We simply exchanged letters with each other and the West estate. I don't think Perry Knowlton has ever handled an omnibus volume like this. I feel strongly that he is pushing for something that needs no pushing.

I have been assuming that you wanted <u>all</u> your published books represented in the Reader, and that publication of the Reader would be several years off—after DISPUTED QUESTIONS and ART AND WORSHIP and THE NEW MAN and perhaps others (parts of which would be represented in the Reader). I also understood from our talk during my visit in March that there would be no editor, that you would choose the contents, and perhaps do a special preface. At the proper time, since Harcourt, Farrar and New Directions are in accord, we can accomplish publication by an exchange of letters. We have agreed to pro-rate the royalties to you on the amount of material used from each book. In other words, if we each have one-third or whatever proportion, we pay that fraction of the royalty. As for imprint, we might make it a joint imprint, as Knopf and Harcourt did for E. M. Forster's stories, and as we and Burns & Oates do for the Vision books.

Please do not make a contract for the Reader a condition of the Curtis Brown wind-up. This will be put us in an impossible situation. I assure you that the Reader will be published: Harcourt and Farrar are not asking for a contract now; they are already in accord. Not until the contents are agreed upon or settled by you will the exchange of letters, constituting the contract, be necessary.

I am going abroad on July 15th. It is imperative in my opinion that the Curtis Brown decision be made known to them at once, so that we can proceed with publication of DISPUTED QUESTIONS according to the new contract which Father Abbot signed during my recent visit. If, for any reason, you would like me to come down again, I could do so shortly after our sales conference, which is scheduled for June 13th. Or, as I am suggesting to Father Abbot, if there is any aspect of the matter which he wishes to discuss by telephone, if he will let me know by letter the best time to call him, or if he would simply pick up the telephone and call me collect, I am sure we could quickly straighten out any difficulty there might be.

With all good wishes.

Yours ever,
Bob /s/

P.S. I enclose a sad dispatch today from Moscow about Pasternak's illness: two heart attacks.

1. This was the working title for *The Behavior of Titans* (New York: New Directions, 1961).
2. Abbot Fox wrote to Perry Knowlton, in a letter dated June 1, 1960, that the abbey wished to discontinue Curtis Brown as its agent. On June 3, 1960, RG wrote to Father Abbot acknowledging that Knowlton was no longer TM's agent.

JUNE 3, 1960

Farrar, Straus & Cudahy, Inc.
[Letterhead]

Rev. M. Louis, O.C.S.O.
Abbey of Our Lady of Gethsemani
Trappist, Kentucky

Dear Tom:

I'm sorry I missed your phone call, and no doubt this letter will cross yours. I assumed you knew that the manuscript had gone to the printer before the revised version of "Solitude" reached me. The essay is now being set up. Do not hold the galleys for it, however. Let me have whatever corrections there are in the remainder of the book as soon as you can, and I will send separate galleys of "Solitude" the moment they come in.

There is an interesting account of Pasternak's funeral in today's paper which I enclose, since you may wish to refer to it in the book. They state that he was a Christian convert. Now that he is dead and beyond the State, can you not cite one of his letters to you in the book? It would be a wonderful thing. I also enclose a tardy but interesting review of THE SECULAR JOURNAL in The Catholic Worker.

Father Abbot's letter to Curtis Brown arrived this morning. I think it covers the ground admirably, and I have written to tell him so.

Proofs of the jacket for DISPUTED QUESTIONS are due next week and I'll get it off to you.

As ever,

Bob /s/

JUNE 6, 1960

Farrar, Straus & Cudahy, Inc.

[Letterhead]

Rev. M. Louis, O.C.S.O.

Abbey of Our Lady of Gethsemani

Trappist, Kentucky

Dear Tom:

Just a note to acknowledge receipt of the replacement for galleys 64 through 69, with the changes on pages 16, 28 and 29. I have forwarded these changes to the printer, and the proofs which you receive will contain them.

I honestly do not think that the line to Pasternak is needed, for the simple reason that the opening pages of the book are a profound tribute to him. Since sending you the obituary, I saw a film of the funeral on TV. Crowds of people surrounded his house in the country, and they even filmed [Sviatoslav] Richter at the upright piano. There were strains of Chopin's "Funeral March," but since they continued even out by the grave, I imagine that these were studio-dubbed. I hope you have decided to quote from Pasternak's February letter in the post-script. (Second thought: why not head this note "In Memoriam"?)

As ever,

Bob /s/

JUNE 8, 1960

Abbey of Gethsemani

[Letterhead]

Dear Bob:

I have copied out the Pasternak letter, complete with the first section which is in Greek, I mean just the opening sentence. I think if you are going to print it, it would be good to print the whole thing and not just an excerpt, including this Greek, which will make it more individual I think.

It is presented in the form of a postscript. For a while, I have debated about using this. From a certain point of view, it does not seem to be useful or justifiable but I am aware that there are arguments on both sides. In so far as the letter shows something of what Pasternak was like and the wonderful depth of his character, I think it ought to be printed as it might never be printed in any other place. (A collection of his letters in all languages would be impossible!) So perhaps, with reserves, this can be done. I trust you to handle it with all discretion.

I am glad there is no complication about the Solitude section of the book. I will be looking for the proofs, and meanwhile you will be going along with the proofs I have corrected.

J. Laughlin writes to me that the new title of their book, THE BE-HAVIOR OF TITANS, is acceptable and, in fact, he likes it better than the other, so that is straightened out. I suppose you have ironed out with him the problem of timing of the two books. I look forward to seeing the proof of the dustcover.

The other day, I got a letter back from Perry Knowlton acknowledging mine and closing our association with Curtis Brown. (I have made that same misprint a hundred times in the last years, though I hope it is not significant!) To tell the truth, I wouldn't have minded him going on with the READER if this could be done without haste or enthusiasm. But Father Abbot put an end to that too. I have said nothing about it.

If, however, the whole thing has started with an editor, this Thomas McDonnell, who I hear is a young Catholic poet, I am willing to have it continue that way. It will save me a lot of trouble, and still I will have all opportunity to make the suggestions I want. In any case, there is no hurry.

I hope everything else is going along smoothly.

Many thanks for the piece about the Pasternak funeral. It came too late to be included in the additions I made to the text. Do you want me to add anything more from this? Just let me know. I got back one of the copies of the NEW MAN which the censor had, which means at least that one of them is finished with it and we ought to be getting a decision fairly soon. I am glad you agree this should be the next book.

With every best wish, as ever, and with all blessings.

Cordially yours in Christ,
Tom /s/

P.S. How about using somewhere, in P.S. or Appendix, the letter to [Aleksei] Surkov? Here is a copy.

JUNE 9, 1960

Farrar, Straus & Cudahy, Inc.
[Letterhead]

Rev. M. Louis, O.C.S.O.
Abbey of Our Lady of Gethsemani
Trappist, Kentucky

Dear Tom:

Just a note to acknowledge receipt of the proofs, and your letter of June 8th. I like the Pasternak insert very much, particularly the ending. I have a few minor changes which you will see on page-proof, including the change at the beginning of "Prologue" to "In Memoriam."

I will deal with the style points as you allow me, including the new numberings. I prefer just white space in most cases—a break—because of the use of numbers for other sub-divisions as in the revised "Solitude."

As ever,

Bob /s/

P.S. I expect new jacket proof tomorrow + will send.

JUNE 17, 1960

Farrar, Straus & Cudahy, Inc.
[Letterhead]

Rev. M. Louis, O.C.S.O.
Abbey of Our Lady of Gethsemani
Trappist, Kentucky

Dear Tom:

I had a very good meeting with Eloise Spaeth today about ART AND WORSHIP. One of the things which has prevented her from writing you directly is that she is in the middle of bringing out an art book herself for Harper's. It's called AMERICAN MUSEUMS AND GALLERIES: An Introduction to Looking. It is due to come out November 9th and she is now floundering around in proofs. She likes the text of ART AND WORSHIP very much in a general sense, but she feels that the section on modern art is inadequate. She has a great deal of material which she'd like you to see, and my first suggestion would be that you drop her a line at her summer address (Mrs. Otto L. Spaeth, Box 518, East Hampton, L.I., New York) just to say that you've heard from me and are getting in touch at my suggestion. This will give her the opportunity, after she gets through her proofs, to go into details. I think she also feels you should devote a little more space to the 19th century; her point is that so many books have been written about Byzantine art, the Middle Ages, and the Renaissance, but so little about the 19th century (your point about [Spanish painter Bartolomé Esteban] Murillo she considers an excellent one). As for the modern period, she is not certain that it is really a renaissance, but so much is going on that she knows about and can tell you about that she feels it would be a shame to bring out a new book and not cover this. If your exchanges develop into a real collaboration as far as the modern section of the book goes, I am going to propose that she receive a small royalty for her time and expenses. However, we will cross that bridge when we come to it.

DISPUTED QUESTIONS had already gone back for paging on Monday when your letter of June 8th arrived. I will wait for page proofs to see how and if we can work in Pasternak's letter, which is delightful. As for the letter to [Aleksei] Surkov, it is a truly noble document. I cannot help feeling it may even have had something to do with the let-up of pressure on P[asternak]. I know you will understand when I say in the same breath that I don't think it should appear in this book for reasons of tact.

I spoke with Jay the other day about THE BEHAVIOR OF TITANS and everything seems to be okay. I'm glad we have settled the Curtis Brown matter and this now frees our hands on the five books we have contracted for. I have had some correspondence with Thomas McDonnell; he's done some magazine pieces on children's books and other subjects but I did not know he wrote poetry, nor do I think, although he proposed doing a Reader to Curtis Brown (when Perry Knowlton told me about it he called him Kilian McDonnell), that he started this project. Anyway, I'm glad the pressure is off to settle the matter immediately.

I enclose a proof of the revised jacket. There are many changes from the original sketch which you saw but the colors and the basic concept remain the same. Everyone here seems to like it, and I hope it meets with your approval.*

With all good wishes.

Yours ever,
Bob /s/

*We are making textual corrections as indicated.

JULY 13, 1960

Farrar, Straus & Cudahy, Inc.
[Letterhead]

Rev. M. Louis, O.C.S.O.
Abbey of Our Lady of Gethsemani
Trappist, Kentucky

Dear Tom:

Under separate cover I have sent you an information set of page proofs of DISPUTED QUESTIONS. It is all in order now with the new text of the piece on Solitude and with the Pasternak letter (every time I read it I like it more) as an appendix, since it was too late to get into the essay itself. The appendix proof will reach you a little later and I particularly want you to see it to make sure that the Greek text is correct. I know just enough Greek to realize he's referring to your Christmas book but I am curious to know the meaning of the whole thing.

We are making the jacket change you suggested, quoting the part of the Preface which you prefer. I am glad you like the cover design; the comments here have been very good.

First reactions to DISPUTED QUESTIONS "in the trade" have been extremely good. Both the Thomas More Book Club (Chicago) and the

Catholic Literary Foundation (Bruce) have chosen it for their October selection. The Catholic Book Club (New York) would also have done so except that they wanted it for December and the action of the other two
clubs made this unfeasible. I think the book will have a great success.
    ART AND WORSHIP. Mrs. Spaeth has written a very interesting and
helpful memo on the illustrations which are to accompany your text. She
feels primarily that modern art is not in focus. She really has excellent
standing in this field, and I think you will agree from her memo that she
will be extremely helpful. She is a friend of Ed Rice, a patron of Jubilee,
and, as I believe I told you, is about to publish a book on museums with
Harper's. If you like her enclosed comments and feel as I do that her help
will be useful, please drop her a line (Mrs. Otto L. Spaeth, Box 518, East
Hampton, L.I., New York). Don't be put off by her spelling; she is original
rather than accurate—"phylosophy" is really ingenious.
    I am off on Friday for vacation abroad, my first in five years. I'm going
to the Glyndebourne Music Festival with the Eliots (Don Giovanni) and
then to a music festival at Aix-en-Provence. This is a part of France I have
never seen and I know it is one of the most beautiful. I'll be back on August 28th.
    Anne Murray [RG's secretary] will forward the Pasternak proof to you
in my absence and will see that it is properly Greeked.
    With all good wishes.

Yours ever,

Bob /s/

P.S. If in the appendix proof you wish to add the details about Pasternak's illness, it's the perfect place to do so.

SEPTEMBER 16, 1960

Farrar, Straus & Cudahy, Inc.
19 Union Square West
New York 3, N.Y.

Dear Tom:
    I am finally back not only in New York but in our new offices at 19 Union
Square West. (The soapbox orators in the park across the way do not seem
to be Reds so much as people with strong religious convictions, including
that of atheism.) I saw more of Europe than ever before and enjoyed every
minute of it, especially the outdoor opera in the Roman arena at Verona.
    We publish DISPUTED QUESTIONS on September 26th, and already
there is every sign of keen advance interest. I have just received a proof of
the review by William Michelfelder in The Saturday Review, which I enclose. I like the review on the whole and I am especially glad that he re-

views it as a book and not "a group of essays." I agree with you about the jacket; it's not what we envisaged, but it will amuse you to know it has had nothing but praise. This is <u>exactly</u> the right time for the book in the U.S. in the middle of this crazy Presidential campaign.

I'm sending all the review copies you suggest plus one to [theologian] Reinhold Niebuhr. (On TV the other night he introduced Kennedy as follows: "Senator Kennedy is blamed by Norman Vincent Peale for things which have been done by the Archbishop of Madrid. Well, he is <u>not</u> the Archbishop of Madrid; he is not even the Archbishop of New York.")

On foreign rights, we are working out a contract with Tom Burns, of course, in London, and the German, Dutch, Italian and Danish publishers you mention. I have a few questions, however, about some of the others.

<u>Spanish</u>: Are you sure you want Editorial Sudamericana in Buenos Aires, who have done most of the previous books? I thought you preferred a house in Spain, and I note that Ediciones Rialp of Madrid did THE LAST OF THE FATHERS.

<u>Portuguese</u>: Is Sor [Emanuel] da Virgem [a nun] a translator and do you simply want her to have a copy of the book, or does she have contact with a Brazilian publisher? I note in Frank dell'Isola's invaluable book that a publisher in Rio did SEVEN STOREY and JONAS, and another in Porto did SEEDS OF CONTEMPLATION. Which of these do you prefer?

<u>French</u>: We are certainly agreeable to Marie Tadié acting as agent-translator on a split commission, but we have our own representative in Paris and I think it is important that the contract with Albin Michel or whoever it is be signed by FSC rather than Mme. Tadié. I'm sure we can work this out to her satisfaction as well as ours. Will you let me know if this is agreeable to you and I will write to her directly?

Thanks for sending me those letters from London, which are fascinating. I have taken the liberty of passing them on to Tom Burns.

I expect to see Eloise Spaeth next week, and I think if you let her know that you want to wind up the modern section by the end of October, say, she will be cooperative. She's probably leaning over backwards out of a sense of courtesy, and I think if you simply tell her what you want and need, or don't want and need, she'll understand. I shall be writing regularly now that I'm back and settled and I expect to have more news for you as we near publication. (You know, I think, that the book is an October selection of the Thomas More Book Club and the Catholic Literary Foundation.)

As ever,

Bob /s/

SEPTEMBER 17, 1960

Abbey of Gethsemani
[Letterhead]

Dear Bob:

The author's copies of the new book have arrived and I am very grateful.

I have thought of a few more ideas for review copies: I think one ought to go to this Jesuit magazine in Paris,

Études, (P[ère] Jean Daniélou [S.J.])
15 Rue Monsieur, Paris 7.

And one to Jaques Barzun at Columbia.

And some to the better Protestant magazines too.

Is this all ok? Bob Lax is probably coming down October 12th, and if you have anything interesting lying around in the way of books or magazines, perhaps he could bring them. Reviews too, if they will be available by then. Probably will, won't they?

Harper's Bazaar is doing a double spread of some stuff of mine on the Desert Fathers in December (from a little book J. Laughlin is doing, I think you saw it).

I wish Eloise Spaeth would send more material. Just one little driblet came. This morning a thing arrived in the mail and it was an enormous chromo of St. Joseph, which nearly slew me on the spot. I looked again at the label, which I thought was in her writing. It was some good soul in England. I thought she was really getting very humorous. She will pardon the rash judgment.

Hope you had a fine time in France with Eliot.

All best wishes as ever. God bless you. Dan Walsh is here.

In Xto Jesu,
Tom /s/

P.S. I am sending a book in French about a young Yugoslav Catholic killed by the Reds. It might go for your kids book series, which I vaguely remember. I promised them I would send it. I mean some Yugoslavs in a refugee camp who sent it to me.

SEPTEMBER 26, 1960

Abbey of Gethsemani
[Letterhead]

Dear Bob:

No better date than this to write about the new book, since today is the day scheduled for its appearance. (Both in our bookstore and in the biggest bookstore in Louisville it has been on sale for a week.) (No rules in Kentucky.)

Thanks for the review. If there are more, Bob MacGregor of New Directions is to come down next week and he can bring them, together with anything else of interest that is lying around.

About your questions:

Editorial Sudamericana: This publisher has contracted to do my Collected Works in Spanish. The contract included the proviso that they would get all my books as they came out. Curtis Brown continued to balk and flub over this matter and the contract was signed that way when I gave up in despair of ever doing anything straight about it with their little man in BA [Buenos Aires] whom I never directly contacted. The impression I got was that the air of general inertia and denseness in the NY office made it impossible for anything but a contract processed mechanically and obstinately according to the desires of the little man in BA or the other men in other cities like that. Anyway, Sudamericana has it. I don't mind. Let 'em.

Sor Emanuel da Virgem is as a matter of fact the best kind of contact. She is a nun, a Brazilian aristocrat, knows all the writers, publishers, etc., is in close contact with two of the best Catholic houses which have been falling all over themselves to get my stuff and have been selling it well. She wants to handle it and has permission of her Superiors. At least, she can go ahead with this one, no? But we might perhaps arrange separate rights for Brazil and Portugal. I don't think this is important. The Porto publisher is ok.

French: what you say about Marie Tadié is ok with me. You work it out with her. Her address is 1 Square de Padirac, Paris 16, Left Bank I guess. Union Square. Lawd.

The other day twenty newspaper reporters from all kinds of African and Asiatic nations blew in here by surprise, on a visiting course at U. of Indiana. I gave them a talk on spiritual life and it seemed much appreciated, especially by the Hindus among them, and the Koreans. Got a very fine reaction, though Kenya and Tanganyika did not seem to get it too good. I don't know if there will be any repercussions in their home base. Might be some good contacts though, we'll see.

I haven't written to Eloise Spaeth again, but she owes me a letter and a hundred new pictures and I hope you have stimulated her. Did you ever get that Van Eyck picture of Jan Arnolfini and his wife from the National Gallery?

All the best as ever, all blessings.

Yrs. in Christ,
Tom /s/

OCTOBER 25, 1960

Dear Tom:

I enclose some reviews of DISPUTED QUESTIONS, including (for them) an unusually intelligent notice from the Kirkus Bookshop Service, which goes to many bookstores. The Library Journal quote is important for all those overworked and underpaid librarians who order books. I was delighted to find a quote from the book at the bottom of Marquis Childs' political column in the New York <u>Post</u>.

Eloise Spaeth told me how much she enjoyed meeting you, and of the possibility of Bishop [John J.] Wright's doing a preface for ART AND WORSHIP. Excellent idea, which I've followed up by writing him and sending proofs. I'll let you know what he says.

I've been rereading THE NEW MAN and I think it's one of your best books. I understood you to say that it had already been cleared by the censors. If so, do you see any reason why we should not do it in the fall of 1961 if ART AND WORSHIP is not ready? It seems to me that THE NEW MAN is particularly timely and ought to be available soon. The art book, if it is to be as handsome a book as Ed Rice intends and as we would like it to be, will probably be slower in production because of the half-tones and make-readys; and the subject is going to be right no matter when it comes out. I don't want to imply that we intend to stall on the art book; I know you want to get it behind you and so, believe me, does Eloise Spaeth. (Her chief point now seems to be that Eric Gill, who was radically needed in the 30's, is over emphasized today through the Ade-Bethune-water-down school and that good modern artists have gone much beyond Gill's very important, necessary, but now dated influence.) In any event, I want to know if you see any disadvantages in scheduling THE NEW MAN before the art book.

I'm enclosing a new Lowell poem, which I think you will like. Sunday evening I heard the great Russian pianist Sviatoslav Richter at Carnegie Hall in a sensational all-[Sergei] Prokofiev recital. You may remember I spoke of him that afternoon when we heard the [Dame] Edith Sitwell's <u>Façades</u>. He is the man who played the piano at Pasternak's funeral. I have sent him a copy of your book.

Yours as ever,
Robert Giroux

NOVEMBER 15, 1960

Farrar, Straus & Cudahy, Inc.
[Letterhead]

Rev. M. Louis, O.C.S.O.
Abbey of Our Lady of Gethsemani
Trappist, Kentucky

Dear Tom:

I am delighted to report that Bishop John J. Wright of Pittsburgh has written a prefatory note for ART AND WORSHIP. I enclose a copy herewith. It does not include any reference to art courses for seminarians, as Mrs. Spaeth hoped it would; obviously the Bishop has no intention of touching on that. I think his endorsement of the book is valuable, and I have written to thank him. Mrs. Spaeth's address is 120 East 81st Street, NYC 28.

I'm also happy to hear that you feel THE NEW MAN will be all right for 1961. The only reference to clearance I can find in our correspondence is this; in your letter dated June 8th: "I got back one copy of THE NEW MAN which the censors had, which means at least that one of them is finished with it, and we ought to be getting a decision fairly soon. I am glad you agree this should be the next book." Presumably you still have to hear from the second censor on this. Is there anything I can do about this, other than my inquiry serving as a basis for raising the question? I find no record either of changes to be made in the manuscript or the imprimi potest.

That's wonderful news about the book of SPIRITUAL PERFECTION. There is plenty of time for publishing, of course, and I'll await your own good time on this.

I haven't heard from Richter yet, and he's not due back until December 10th. The [Sol] Hurok office tells me he will not be in the Louisville area, alas. He's being kept from "alien influences" even in New York, or perhaps I should say particularly in New York. I'm still going to try to get to him personally and I'll give him your best.

Even though the election is over, there are "Viva Kennedy" signs still around the office. Flannery O'Connor just wrote from Georgia to say that the Baptist ministers now have nothing to talk about.

With warmest regards.

Yours ever,
Bob /s/

P. S. I enclose reviews from Texas + <u>The Catholic World</u>.

DECEMBER 1, 1960

Farrar, Straus & Cudahy, Inc.
[Letterhead]

Dear Tom:

I am grateful for your two letters of November 28th, the first because it speaks out about things which with reason have given you much concern, and the second because it expresses concern about my feelings.[1] The last thing in the world I want is for you and me to work in anything but complete accord. With regard to Sudamericana, I thought I was being the big brave hero in taking the bull by the horns. Your previous letter seemed to give me this cue, and I acted on it in good faith. I honestly cannot see how in law or in anything else they can have a claim on all your books in perpetuity forever and ever amen. If they had paid fifty thousand or a hundred thousand or a million dollars down, they would have a pretty good claim. The arrangement seems to me not only to be unjust but untenable; and I would still like to rework it with your permission. If you feel it can be explored, it would be extremely helpful to have a copy of the agreement which Father Abbot signed. I cannot believe that this agreement would contain the quid pro quo necessary for an enforceable contract. Even if Sudamericana publishes DISPUTED QUESTIONS under this agreement, it's worth exploring to change for future books. Apparently, I've already done enough damage and I will, of course, do nothing further until I hear from you, but I really do think that the change from Curtis Brown to FSC offers you the chance to have your works published in Spanish translation in Spain and subsequently in South America.

However, if it is your wish that nothing further be done in this matter, then that is that as far as I am concerned and you have only to tell me so. I think I understand the difficulties perhaps more completely than any of your friends and the last thing I want is to add to them. I'm sorry I have already done so in the usual blundering manner of a well-meaning friend.

As for Marie Tadié, I have had a very pleasant letter from her this morning. She has received the book and she will act as agent as well as translator, receiving the regular agent's commission as well as payment for her translation. The contract will be drawn up between Albin Michel and FSC incorporating Marie Tadié in the agent's clause. I hope that this is all agreeable to you. It simplifies the problem of collecting your foreign income; we will now be doing it instead of Curtis Brown and we will not expect an agent's commission.[2]

The contract with Hollis & Carter is now being drawn up by our London agent, Laurence Pollinger. The book is under consideration in Italy, Germany and Scandinavia. I will keep you advised of all developments as they occur.

With all good wishes.

Yours ever,

Bob /s/

1. The two letters of November 28, 1960, have not been located.
2. In a letter to JL, dated November 28, 1960, TM said, "[I am] getting some funny impressions, indirectly, from certain actions of Bob Giroux at FS & C. He will not play along with this situation at all [TM wanted Madame Tadié to be both his French agent and translator] though he knows my promises and obligations. He doesn't answer questions and he is busy finagling around with other people: I don't [know] what he is doing, but I think he simply wants to dispose of the books according to his own ideas. He even spoke of very kindly taking care of the foreign rights for books published by you. He seemed quite willing to do this. Well, if the question arises, I want you to know that I am not willing, and that I am beginning to see you were right in having doubts about my leaving Curtis Brown."

JANUARY 25, 1961

Farrar, Straus & Cudahy, Inc.
[Letterhead]

Dear Tom:

I hope it is true that the contract with Sudamericana limits their rights to Latin America only, and I have written to their agent, Mr. Lawrence Smith, in Buenos Aires asking about this.[1] You are right about Spain wanting a different translation, and I see no reason why this should not be done. The crux of the matter is whether Sudamericana would object. Clause 14, which you cite, seems to give hope, and does seem to limit it to "the Spanish language throughout Latin America," but the previous clause granting to them "the sole license" may blur this. It all depends on what position Sudamericana takes; if they get stuffy, it's hard to see what can be done. In any event, I'll let you know what reaction I get. That provision giving them "all future works" is beyond belief! I can't imagine what was in Curtis Brown's mind; even on the basis of the clauses you cite, they have the right to publish all your books, but not the obligation. Some one-way street!

Incidentally, an inquiry for DISPUTED QUESTIONS, BREAD IN THE WILDERNESS, and THE BEHAVIOR OF TITANS came to us the other day from another Barcelona firm than the one you cite. This one is Editorial Juventud, S.A. Does this name mean anything to you?

I enclose three reviews of DISPUTED QUESTIONS in The Christian Century, America, and a diocesan paper. Also some recent and rather sad news corollary to Pasternak's death, including an editorial in the New York Times.

Did you hear about Robert Frost at the Kennedy inauguration? He was asked to read a poem, and had written a long rhymed preface but couldn't get past the second line (he kept repeating it like a stuck needle). Then he muttered in a very clear voice on the air, "There's not enough damn light," finally dropped the preface, and recited the poem from memory.[2] Anyway it was refreshing to have poetry honored in some way by a President. At the White House next day Frost is supposed to have given Kennedy this advice: "As President use power with poetry. Be Irish, not Harvard."

I'm having a meeting with Eloise Spaeth and Ed Rice on Thursday, prior to their departure for Gethsemani. I've got the three art books you wanted and will give them to Ed. Eloise has obtained a good many prints from the Metropolitan Museum of Art—at least ordered them, since the bill came to this office. I hope they're ready for her to bring along. I wish I were driving down with them.

We are now all set on England, France and Italy with DISPUTED
QUESTIONS, and we are working on Germany and Scandinavia.
With all good wishes.

Yours ever,

Bob /s/

P.S. I enjoyed "Classic Chinese Thought" in Jubilee [January 1961], and
learned a great deal from it. Pray for Doctor Tom Dooley, who died this
past week at 33.

1. In a letter dated November 11, 1960, RG wrote to Lawrence Smith: "First of all, it is
a fact that Curtis Brown is no longer agent for Father Merton's works. This decision was
made by his monastery who turned to me, as his friend and former classmate, to arrange
contracts for all his subsequent work, beginning with *Disputed Questions*."
2. As inauguration day approached, Frost composed a new poem, "Dedication," which
he planned to read as a preface for "The Gift Outright," the poem Kennedy had requested.
Frost worried, however, that the poem, typed on one of the hotel typewriters the night before, would prove difficult to read even in good light. When he started reading the poem,
the bright sunlight made reading the poem impossible. Thus he recited "The Gift Outright" from memory.

FEBRUARY 13, 1961

Farrar, Straus & Cudahy, Inc.

[Letterhead]

Dear Tom:

I've been in correspondence with Mrs. Lydia Pasternak Slater, sister of
Boris Pasternak who lives in London. She has just written me as follows:

> Dear Mr. Giroux: Very many thanks indeed for Thomas Merton's beau-
> tiful book. It is such a relief to read a sensible and deepfelt article
> about my brother, after all the trash and gabble one has to swallow.

She then goes on to speak of the collection of his letters she is compiling.
Apparently, it won't be ready for quite a while. Incidentally, they found a
letter in Boris's handwriting clearly absolving Lydia of the Soviet charges
against her. Not that that will stop them.

The reviews of DISPUTED QUESTIONS continue to appear, and the
book is holding its own on several best-seller lists. I enclose a review in the
Chicago Sun-Times.

Ed Rice and Eloise Spaeth arrived home at the height of the blizzard,
and had to abandon their car in Newark and mush on to New York by dog
sled. They said they had a wonderful visit with you, and were full of ideas
for the book. I'd love to be able to do a full-color insert, and I'm going to
explore the possibilities with Ed. If we can do it without raising the price

to $15.00 a copy (Ed thinks we can), we'd be delighted. It's not the cost of color plates, it's the cost of make-readies and proofing. Skira [World Publishing Company], who does the best color in the art book field, has the books manufactured in Europe. We may have to do that too. It means that we are unlikely to have finished books in time for 1961 publication, but I think the better-looking the book is and the more time we take, the better it will be for the whole operation.

Do you think THE NEW MAN will be released in the meantime for next October? The fall would be an excellent time to bring it out.

With all good wishes.

Yours ever,

Bob /s/

FEBRUARY 13, 1961

Abbey of Gethsemani
[Letterhead]

Dear Bob:

There are hundreds of things to be said, I have to stick to the most important ones.

First of all, there have been unending headaches about the French translation of Thoughts in Solitude. Entitled in French Sur les Chemins de la Joie, translated by a Benedictine nun, handled by Dom Jean Leclercq, O.S.B., who turned it over to Éditions d'Histoire et d'art, J. et M. Wittmann, affiliated with [Éditions] Plon.[1] They have had it over five years and nothing has happened. They have stalled about sending a contract; we have no record of a contract here; they claim they sent one and it was never returned. I told them two months ago to send a contract and we would sign it. Nothing has happened. I told Dom Leclercq to get the ms. back from them, and they replied that the book was in production and that they planned to bring it out in "April or September." I am highly suspicious of everything these people say, and I wonder if your Paris man could get after them and get a signature on the dotted line, and a time limit in the contract too. I do hope that you can smooth this thing out for us and prevent it from becoming intolerably complicated.

Marie Tadié says you have been very kind about letting her work for us and dispose of some of the books I send over for her to translate, in fact all of those I send her to translate. That is fine. I think she will do all right, and she has a good head and is energetic and devoted to our interests. She says you want to sign the contracts at this end. I have mentioned this to Father Abbot and I think he seems to want things to go on just as they did before, and that the contracts should be signed here. Will you please take that up with him? I have spoken to him about it, but he is now tied up in a big tangle with the Abbot General coming here and probably won't write to you for sometime. This matter is to me entirely indifferent as I don't give two hoots who signs the contracts, but to him it is important, so please don't go ahead with anything until you have found out what his mind is on the question. There just seems to be no way of keeping this d— book business from being utterly complicated. I should tell you of this discovery, I suppose, as if you didn't know from way back.

Eloise and Ed had a fine visit and we did what seemed to me to be a lot of work, but I guess to you city slickers it was nothing but a drop in the bucket. I was bushed. But anyway we certainly got the Art book lined up right and we know exactly what other pictures we need. I hope we will have them; Ed can lay them out any way he likes and send the stuff down to me and I will write the captions. The art books you sent were super and I found several things in them I absolutely want to use myself. Including the fine picture of [Alfred] Manessier and his Catholic family gathered under a solid abstract picture. I mean painting. Eloise said I mustn't say "statue" either. A statue is always of Lincoln.

Happy to hear you are bringing out Leclercq's Alone with God. It will be very worthwhile I believe, though I don't expect it to break into the best sellers in the first week.

I was really gratified by the sensible and friendly review in Christian Century. A little magazine called New University Thought wants to do a review and I am very much in favor; I want to reach that kind people. They will be writing you for a copy, and I hope you will gratify their desires in this matter.

I believe Fr. Abbot has signed the contract for both Spain and Argentina for Disputed Questions. On this you must check with him when you write, but I think it is all sewed up and in the bag. They do seem to want to claim Spanish rights for themselves too, perhaps not as strictly as they do South American rights. I agree that it is a completely screwball contract and I protested when it came, but the thing was signed and now we are stuck with it. I didn't put up a death struggle over it as I knew it was no use.

Frank dell'Isola has written a really stupid article about my work, and had it published in some little new Catholic magazine.[2] Did you see it? He has no perception of what I am really after or good for, and thinks No Man Is an Island is my best book or some such rot. That everything since then has been going down hill and is of minor relevance, etc., etc. He is talking about coming down here and finishing the bibliography. For one thing, I don't think there is any point in him coming down this year, and I certainly don't think this is the time for the bibliography to be finished. I am certainly well disposed for the reception of the ashes the day after to-morrow and I would welcome an early demise, if by God's grace, I might sally forth with the consolations of the sacraments. Still, it seems to me to be more practical when an author is still hanging restlessly around his typewriter and giving evident signs of life, to assume that the bibliography of his works will not need to be wound up immediately. Not that I intend to write a vast amount of things right away. This is to be a year of study and thought and reflection, or absorbing, etc., etc. But there are things to be published nevertheless. I intend to make the required corrections in the New Man in a day or two and will send you the ms. ready to go into production. I presume the best time for publication would be possibly the spring of 1962. The only possible conflict will be a rewritten edition (with considerable new matter) of Seeds of Contemplation, which I am sending New Directions about the same time, I think it would make sense to work out a schedule that would keep these two books a few months apart.

Happy Lent and all best wishes, thanking you again for the wonderful art books, which are a joy and an inspiration. All blessings, always.

Cordially in Christ,
Tom /s/

1. Dom Jean Leclercq, O.S.B., a monk of Clairvaux Abbey in Luxemburg, was one of the founders of Monastic Interreligious Dialogue, begun in 1978. An authority on medieval monasticism, he is the author of *The Love of Learning and the Desire for God* (1961). His correspondence with TM is collected in a volume entitled *Survival or Prophecy? The Letters of Thomas Merton and Jean Leclercq*, edited by Patrick Hart, O.C.S.O. (2002).

2. Frank dell'Isola, "Thomas Merton: Outlines of Growth," *Catholic Book Reporter*, February 1961, 8–10.

FEBRUARY 21, 1961

Abbey of Gethsemani
[Letterhead]

Dear Bob:

Here is the New Man—all released, corrected and everything. It is all set to go whenever you want it to go. I think it really is cut out, above all, for a Lenten book since it speaks so much of "illumination" and culminates in the Easter Night Liturgy. However, I leave that up to you. As I said before, it will be for you and New Directions to work out the timing so that this will not be fallen over by, or will not stumble upon, the new edition of Seeds of Contemplation, which is really a new book, containing all of the old but having much more in it.

Thank you very much for the quote from Lydia Pasternak Slater's letter. It is certainly very encouraging. Ed Rice brought a couple of records she made of Pasternak's poems, and I am delighted to have them. I am only waiting for an opportunity to write and thank her. It is wonderful to have so authentic a version of Pasternak's poetry, which is so deeply moving.

The other day I was writing to Laughlin about Quasimodo. Now I remember that you are the ones who published him. I am going to get in touch with him too. His poems are to me superb, full of pathos and intensity and strength. He is a very, very great poet. Though I admire Saint-John Perse tremendously, I think there is something more sinewy in Quasimodo, more human reality. I want to read Quasimodo's translations of the Gospel of St. John and of Aeschylus. As I say, I will probably be writing him; I managed to dig up his address in the Louisville Library. If you would see fit to let us have a copy of your really remarkable selection from him, I would be able to have him at hand all the time. I think I may write something about him eventually.

At present, I am pitching at a mystical theology course I have to give here for the next three months and it is pretty well taking up my time.

I am glad Ed and Eloise made it safely back to New York. I was really worried about them, and apparently Ed did do some very fancy skidding.

I presume Lydia Slater Pasternak [*sic*] would like copies of the letters of Pasternak that I received, directly or indirectly. I will take that up with her. I am very glad she is collecting them.[1] It will be a marvelous collection.

As ever.

> All best wishes and blessings in Christ,
> Tom /s/

---

1. See *Six Letters: Boris Pasternak, Thomas Merton*, ed. Naomi Burton Stone and Lydia Pasternak Slater (Lexington, KY: King Library Press, 1973).

FEBRUARY 28, 1961

Abbey of Gethsemani
[Letterhead]

Dear Bob:

I don't know if you are yet back from Jamaica [where RG vacationed with Mr. and Mrs. T. S. Eliot], but I have to get this letter off to avoid complications in the business over the French contract for THOUGHTS IN SOLITUDE. Remember I wrote you that we had given it to Wittmann, and that I wanted to get a contract with them definitely. Since writing you on that, I received a tentative contract, which nobody signed; it was not meant to be signed, but I made the changes which seemed to be necessary, esp. regarding Abbey of Gethsemani as proprietor, etc. I returned it to them. I told them to take it up with Marie Tadié.

When I wrote to you I unthinkingly said "tell your man in Paris to get after them." But, of course, our man in Paris is a woman and is Marie Tadié, so I hope you remembered what I forgot, if you did anything at all about it.

The contract as far as I could see was otherwise satisfactory, except there was no time clause in it. I expect it will go along all right, with

Marie Tadié. Meanwhile you will have figured out with Fr. Abbot who signs what.

I hope you have had a good time in Jamaica. Here we have been in and out of snowdrifts, but I hope now we will level off and get some lasting spring.

By now you will have seen the NEW MAN. I am grateful for Anne Murray's letter and for the Quasimodo [*The Selected Writings of Salvatore Quasimodo*] she is sending. When I get a breather, I am going to try to get in contact with Quasimodo. There are so many things one wants to do, and there is so little time in which to do them: especially if one has a way of deliberately letting a hole open out in the midst of the day in order to do and be nothing, which is proper to the contemplative. On the day when we cease to run into contradictions we will know that we are dead.

The Abbot General just left us. He had a very nice visit of about ten days. Everything here seems to be smooth for the time being.

More and more I realize my almost infinite capacity to get into hopeless tangles in business. I forget everything. Let's hope we can all keep out of jail in spite of my confusions.

As ever, all blessings and good wishes.

Cordially in Christ,
Tom /s/

APRIL 14, 1961

Farrar, Straus & Cudahy, Inc.
[Letterhead]

Dear Tom:

This letter is long overdue and there is much to write about. To start with THE NEW MAN, which we very much want to publish this fall, I hope you will let us keep the original title. It's a good one, and a very appropriate one, and I don't think any of the other suggestions are nearly as good. SEEDS OF CONTEMPLATION, on the other hand, is a well-established title, but as I discussed with Bob MacGregor the other day, the usual publishing practice is simply to put the words "New Edition" or "Revised Edition" on the cover, and to retain the old title even if it is rewritten and keeps the best that was in the old edition. There is a copyright problem, too, in that New Directions will have to run the old copyright dates to protect the original parts of the book as well as the new date (1962, I hope!) for the new material. Please don't let's give up THE NEW MAN in any event.

I am expecting galley proofs in May and, of course, there will be plenty of time to insert additions or to make any changes you wish.

Frank dell'Isola called last week and asked if I would do a book of his essays grouped around his writings about Thomas Merton, principally the one which recently appeared in the Catholic Library Journal. I'm afraid I really let him have it on all counts, starting with my opinion of the most recent article, which is plainly stupid. I'm afraid the fellow is a light weight and he is certainly not a writer. I told him we would not publish his essays and for the sake of literature I hope no one else does.

My stay at Ocho Rios with the Eliots was wonderful. It was a very British corner of the island complete with carefully manicured lawns practically down to the ocean side. The woman who ran it was so British that she wore rubber slippers into the ocean; she also swung a mean croquet mallet, so heavy (compared to the ones I've handled in the U.S.) as to feel like a sledge hammer. It's a technicolor island, and the average daily temperature was 80 wonderful degrees. It was good to get away from the longest and dreariest winter I've ever known in New York. Eliot said the climate there was too perfect for work. He said he could not think and felt like a vegetable, but I noted that it did his bronchial condition a great deal of good.*

I'm really confused about the foreign rights situation on the four books we have under contract. I'm writing to Father Abbot to explain what I think should be the procedure. Perhaps I was at fault in having the contracts signed here instead of by you, but I forgot that agents don't sign contracts and I was following the usual publishing practice whereby, when we place an author in England or France or wherever it may be, we sign the contract, not the author, though, of course, the publishing rights continue to belong to the author. However, the point as to who signs the documents is a mere detail, and I will be glad to follow whatever procedure you and Father Abbot want. The protection you get from a publisher signing the document is a closer check on royalty statements from abroad.

The possibility that you might develop your course in mystical theology into a book interests me very much. There is a real need for a good overall view of the subject and if this works out it could be a wonderful book indeed.

I'm sending you a couple of books by a wonderful writer we acquired with the Noonday list, Isaac Bashevis Singer.** You'll get his books by separate cover, with Lowell's translation of PHAEDRA.

With all good wishes.

Yours ever,
Bob /s/

*He also told about an old duffer who, on hearing his name, said: "A writing chap named Eliot? Any relation to that horse-faced woman novelist [George Eliot (Mary Ann Evans)] my mother knew?"

**<u>Gimpel the Fool</u>, <u>The Magician of Lublin</u>, <u>Satan in Goray</u>. To come in fall: <u>The Spinoza of Market Street</u>.

Farrar, Straus & Cudahy, Inc.
[Letterhead]

Rev. M. Louis, O.C.S.O.
Abbey of Our Lady of Gethsemani
Trappist, Kentucky

Dear Tom:

I think we have created a problem about the title of THE NEW MAN where one does not exist. Why should any reader confuse NEW SEEDS OF CONTEMPLATION with the new book? I do not really think they will. We like THE NEW MAN very much, as a title as well as a book, and unless you now feel it is not right in itself we would like to retain it.

As a book, I am convinced it is one of your best. The writing is crystal-clear in its concentrated economy; the book has wonderful unity and structure. The passage at the beginning of "Image and Likeness" about the world in its newness is poetry, man, sheer poetry. We are expecting type pages this week, and I'll send them along. The designer has done a simple but very effective jacket: the title in big severe type against a white background. I'll send this with the sample pages.

I think that for my peace of mind, if no one else's, we should withdraw from the foreign rights picture. Neither Sheila nor Roger feels we should take a commission on anything we have done, nor do I. As you know, we made contracts with Hollis & Carter and with Garzanti [Editore] for DISPUTED QUESTIONS, asking for (and getting) better terms than you had before. If this has helped, all to the good. It will be embarrassing to withdraw from these contracts. As long as we both understand that they are your contracts, not ours, even though we signed them, will that be all right with you? We will continue to check statements and royalties, and remit them to you semi-annually, but we shall take no commission.

Our friendship and association are much more important to me than foreign rights. We have had a long-standing relationship, and one of constancy, and I wish it to remain so always. I'm distressed and disturbed at what seems to be the implication that we want to appropriate the foreign rights. They are a headache and a worry and need looking after. My only worry is that I'm taking an easy way out, and not fully protecting your interests. But I want to lessen your problems, not add to them, and that is why I suggest this course.

With warmest regards.

Yours ever,
Bob /s/

MAY 13, 1961

Abbey of Gethsemani
[Letterhead]

Dear Bob:

Thanks for your last good letter and for the first paragraph about the title.

I have not yet worked out the possibility of a new title with New Directions, but certainly there is no problem about THE NEW MAN for you, and I think, too, that I can come out with something better for the second edition of SEEDS. I just haven't heard from them about the various suggestions that occurred to me. So let's not bother any more about the non-existent problem.

I am glad you like the book. At this end, since it is something I wrote several years ago, and actually did not fully finish according to my own ideas, I have the uneasy feeling about it that one with a few perfectionistic drives might have. I wish that I could do it all over again, but that is nonsense. If it is all right as it stands and if I can make a few judicious (I hope) additions, then that will certainly be quite enough.

And now for the foreign rights problem, or situation. This is due entirely to our confusion and obtuseness down here, our lack of experience of publishing. I am sorry we made the whole thing unpleasant for you, and I am very sorry indeed that you want to drop the whole thing. At the same time, I certainly sympathize with you. I can see that you want no part of a thankless task. And dealing with a monastery is, one way or other, ultimately like that. It is like dealing with the Pentagon, or God knows what organization with its own rigid forms. And that is why most of all I regret and dread the situation that is now going to arise when Fr. Abbot's secretaries and what not start trying to handle foreign publishers. We have reached all kinds of impasses just buying books in the retail market. There are booksellers in France who simply won't have anything to do with us.

I spoke to Father Abbot about this, and he certainly has no complaints at all, on the contrary, and he thought that everything was settled to our mutual satisfaction, with regard to commissions and so on. Since this is the case, and since it is just a matter of some confusion and incomprehension down here in the correspondence, do you really think the situation is impossible for you? I am not trying to talk you into doing something that will be difficult and disagreeable to you, and if you think that really it is not going to work, then I for one will fully accept your decision, because I know what you mean and we all understand.

So let me put it to you this way: assuming that the situation has already reached the hopeless stage, do you think we might be able to function through the men you have as agents in foreign countries? Do you think we could make it dealing with them, and not direct with publishers? If we can, we might give this a try. If, for some reason, you cannot put us in touch with them, would you be willing to hold on to the unpleasant responsibility, of course <u>with</u> commission (I know that is not the issue for you and it is not for us either, please believe me).

If we cannot make it any other way we will probably have to go back to Curtis Brown, which is unsatisfactory, but at least workable.

I am sorry all this came up, and I have no hesitation in saying that I understand your position perfectly. You are quite right.

The Singer books have come and I am in the midst of one of them, Gimpel, which is fabulous, literally. I think he is tremendous, powerfully religious, haunting.

He has a wonderful mythical, archetypal quality that really fascinates and shakes you. Some of his stuff is, I am sure, in a broad sense prophetic. The Lowell translation of Phaedra is beautiful clean verse, really excellent.

Thanks for all these things.

I look forward to seeing the samples of what they hope to do with the NEW MAN. And when Ed gets the layouts done we can move along with ART AND WORSHIP, but that will evidently be sometime yet, though Eloise is patiently collecting material.

All best wishes Bob, and every blessing.

Cordially yours in Christ,
Tom /s/

JUNE 2, 1961

Farrar, Straus & Cudahy, Inc.
[Letterhead]

Rev. M. Louis, O.C.S.O.
Abbey of Our Lady of Gethsemani
Trappist, Kentucky

Dear Tom:

The proofs of THE NEW MAN have just come from the printer, and I am sending them to you under separate cover. Please return the master set with your corrections; the other is meant to be kept.

Incidentally, I don't think you've sent me the names of the censors in this case. We are submitting proofs here to the diocesan people, of course.

I enclose a copy of the jacket, which has what I hope is a New Look for us. It's a straight type job, and I hope you approve of the way it has turned out.

Your letter about the foreign rights problem touches the heart of the matter, and it moved me very much. The crux of the matter is that whoever handles foreign rights should do so in totality, whether that agent is FSC or whoever. In other words, <u>all</u> your books (New Directions, FSC and so on) have to be under one central American control, or there will be no control. This American representative will have to have absolute responsibility as well as control, no matter what other agents in the various countries are used. I really do not see how the monastery could be expected to keep track of the various payments, advances, royalties, commitments, and so on. It's a tricky and demanding job even for experts. Someone at Macmillan recently went abroad and collected $15,000 owing on foreign royalties for years back—to a big house like Macmillan!

Unless there is continuity and an understanding of the publishing history (that's where I goofed on Sudamericana), chaos is sure to come again. I've asked Paula Diamond, our foreign rights expert, for her advice and counsel, and she agrees with the above. Would the monastery be willing to turn over all the details to an agent whom they could trust completely? Unless they are willing to do so—and that would mean directing all inquiries to the agent at once, and not trying to arrange details unilaterally—no agent, however good could succeed at the job. I think she's inclined to feel we are not right for the job. She has some ideas about possible agents, but the other question has to be settled first.

Yours ever,

Bob /s/

JUNE 30, 1961

Farrar, Straus & Cudahy, Inc.

[Letterhead]

Rev. M. Louis, O.C.S.O.
Abbey of Our Lady of Gethsemani
Trappist, Kentucky

Dear Tom:

This is just to thank you for returning the galley proofs of THE NEW MAN so promptly. They are now being corrected; I'll send your page proofs after July 15th. We've made the jacket change, and I enclose a corrected copy.

There was an excellent review of THE BEHAVIOR OF TITANS in Commonweal, which I hope Jay sent you. Deservedly excellent, in my opinion, for I think it an extraordinary book and a historic one in your whole body of work. You will be amused to hear that the reviewer compares it to [Henry David] Thoreau's book on the importance of civil disobedience.

I'm off to the Jersey shore for the Fourth [of July]. Ed Rice is back from London, Paris and Dublin, and I lunch with him and Eloise Spaeth on July 6th to discuss ART AND WORSHIP.

With warmest regards.

As ever,

Bob /s/

AUGUST 18, 1961

Rev. M. Louis, O.C.S.O.
Abbey of Our Lady of Gethsemani
Trappist, Kentucky

Farrar, Straus & Cudahy, Inc.
[Letterhead]

Dear Tom:

The alumni magazine arrived today with a picture of Mark [Van Doren] accepting your medal at the commencement exercises.[1] I thought you might like to see it. I passed through the [Columbia University] campus the other night, and it hasn't changed much except for the filling in of 116th Street (no traffic within the campus, which is a big improvement).

I have not thanked you for the page proofs. Your invented lines to fill in the short pages (and why these occur, I never understand; the <u>printer</u> creates them) read as if they always belonged.

It's very hard to find a New York agent who will handle only foreign rights, for the reason that they all have to use opposite numbers in the countries involved. I've talked it over with Naomi, and she thinks her friend at Curtis Brown <u>London</u> (Molly Waters) might be good. I believe she heads the foreign rights department there, and being closer to the continent, and doing only foreign rights, might make sense. But would she want to share with the people you already have lined up, like Mme. Tadié? If you and Father Abbot agreed, FSC would be willing to handle all the foreign rights, but for technical reasons we would have to sign the contracts on your behalf. (I don't really think this last should make any difference to Father Abbot. It is necessary because we make agreements as a publishing corporation, not as an agent. It does not change your role or the monastery's as author and proprietor.)

I feel as if I ought to be coming to see you soon. Maybe I could get Ed Rice and Eloise to make a junket, and we could really finish the art book on one concentrated weekend. One thing I am not clear about: will you be rewriting any of the text, or adding to it in any way?

I'm sending you the new (for us) [François] Mauriac novel, THE FRONTENACS; an off-beat campus novel by Bernard Malamud called A NEW LIFE; and a jazz musician's story called NIGHT SONG by John Williams.

With kindest regards.

Yours ever,
Bob /s/

P. S. I also enclose an interview with Pasternak in <u>The Paris Review</u>. I meant to send it long ago; perhaps this is a duplicate. Anyway, it's very interesting.

1. University Medal for Excellence at the Columbia University commencement, June 6, 1961.

SEPTEMBER 1, 1961

Farrar, Straus & Cudahy, Inc.
[Letterhead]

Rev. M. Louis, O.C.S.O.
Abbey of Our Lady of Gethsemani
Trappist, Kentucky

Dear Tom:
I am stunned by that poem ["Chant to Be Used in Processions around a Site with Furnaces"].[1]
Is there any reason why it could not also be published in Commentary Magazine? I know the editor very well, but I would not wish to send it to him without your permission. I did not see it in the Catholic Worker.
As ever,
Bob /s/

1. Published in the *Journal for the Protection of All Beings* 1 (1961): 5–7.

OCTOBER 18, 1961

Abbey of Gethsemani
[Letterhead]

Dear Bob:
The new books have arrived. I am delighted to get to [Nikolai] Leskov at last, he has long been on my list. Have you published The Cathedral? I think that is supposed to be his great novel. The tales are wonderful, with that great, creative, nineteenth-century Russian love of the imaginary world they found they could make. It is exhilarating to read, and I love the book.
I am also very happy with Lowell's Imitations. Without trying to evaluate where it stacks up in Lowell's whole production, I just want to say it is a book I particularly enjoy. I love it; I keep going back to it. It is fascinating, because of the unique way in which the poems are like the originals and yet not, take liberties, go into a montage, blend and exclude as they please. It is a fascinating way to render foreign verse. I haven't begun to think all I would like to say in comment. The [Charles] Baudelaire is in ways unique, makes me shudder less than the French, is a little more urbane, has something of an eighteenth-century English note about it. Lax compared Lowell to [Jonathan] Swift the first time he ever spoke to me of him. He is good at [Arthur] Rimbaud, wonderful with Pasternak. These are the best renderings of Pasternak, in many ways. Though I like the "faithful" versions his sister sent also. [Eugenio] Montale, wonderful. [Heinrich] Heine too. I haven't yet steeled myself to read the [Victor] Hugo. Probably I am going to find myself liking even Hugo.

But he cannot imitate [Paul] Valéry. There, I think, he stops. Valéry is absolutely inimitable. And here, too, he is closest to just translating, though I don't have Valéry at hand to compare.

In any case, it is a marvelous book.

Have you seen this Suzuki dialogue with the Latin American poets I did for the New Directions anthology?[1] I know you will like a copy. It had strange fortunes especially with the censors and in the end they stipulated that it had to be published in an anthology or magazine with lots of other things, so as to be partially buried.

Incidentally, they have new and even more strict censorship regulations explicitly designed to make the writers of the Order miserable and encourage them to stop writing. With the way my time is eaten up, I don't need much encouragement. But I do have a manuscript half done, for you. It needs a third part on humanism, which will be a little while in gestating. If the Lord leaves us a little while to think of things like <u>humanism</u>. Quixotic, really.

With best wishes always and all blessings.

Cordially as ever, in Christ,
Tom /s/

1. "Recovery of Paradise." Daisetz T. Suzuki (1870–1966), a Japanese-born practitioner of Zen Buddhism and author of the three-volume *Essays on Zen Buddhism* (1927–34), had an extensive correspondence with TM, collected in *Encounter: Thomas Merton and D.T. Suzuki* (1988). TM honored him in his *Zen and the Birds of Appetite* (1968).

OCTOBER 25, 1961

Dear Bob:

In the last few days, I have been cleaning up some work with the man who has been editing the MERTON READER. He is doing a good job, and I have been able to have a more or less free hand in it too, which is gratifying. On the whole, I think the book will turn out to be a good one and will be of benefit to all of us, bringing many of the Farrar, Straus books into focus also. I hope everything will go along smoothly in the business end of this project, and presume that it will.

One thing I have done: in editing it, or helping to do so, I have made sure they did not include several essays that would make the nucleus of a good little book on their own. I want to propose that to you now as a project for one of the books on our contract. Provisional title, let us say NEW ESSAYS.

I don't know how much of this material you have, but I will send you a couple of the things I have at hand. I am including one or two things on the Liturgy you have seen. It was previously decided that these would go in a special book on the Liturgy, but I just haven't the time to get at this now, and if I do I am going to want to remodel all existing material. Hence, I think these few essays should go in as they stand, with other material. Here is the lineup.

Classic Chinese Thought (Jubilee)
Two Chinese Classics (coming Jubilee next year)[1]
English Mystics (Jubilee, Aug[ust] [actually published in September 1961])
Liturgy and Spiritual Personalism (Worship, 1960)
Easter, New Life (Worship, 1959)
Theology of Creativity ([American] Benedictine Review, 1960)
Time and Liturgy (Worship, 1957? [December 1956])
Ash Wednesday (Worship, 1960 or 59?)
Nativity Kerygma (Worship, 1960?) Also privately printed.
Good Samaritan (not yet printed, supposed to be priv[ately] printed next y[ea]r [*Seasons of Celebration*, 171–82])
Machine Gun and Fallout Shelter (Cath[olic] Worker, coming? [November 1961])

This should total about thirty-five or forty thousand words, and I could add a couple of things that may get written in the next month or so, or else we could end up with Monastic Peace [see *American Benedictine Review*, September 1962] and/or another longish study called the Feast of Freedom which you have or should have; this would bring it up to 60,000 words.[2]

I think you will like this idea. The only possible catch is the liturgical essays, but for my part I think a sprinkling of them in with the others will be a good idea, and I just have no hope of doing a whole book on that material now.

Please let me know if you are missing some of this. If I have it, I can send it along.

With best wishes always.

Cordially yours in Christ,
Tom /s/

1. See TM, "Christian Culture Needs Oriental Wisdom," *Catholic World*, May 1962, 72–79; also TM, "Two Chinese Classics," *Chinese Culture Quarterly* 4 (June 1962): 34–41.
2. See TM's introduction to *Letters of Adam of Perseigne* (Kalamazoo, MI: Cistercian Publications, 1976), 3–48.

NOVEMBER 14, 1961

Abbey of Gethsemani
[Letterhead]

Dear Bob:

The NEW MAN has arrived and, of course, I am very pleased with it. The striking simplicity of the cover is most satisfying. It is the most attractive job you have done for me at Farrar, Straus & Cudahy, except perhaps the Secular Journal.

Could you possibly send review copies to the following? Perhaps you will have done so or planned to do so already, but I might mention a few names just in case:

Worship, Collegeville, Minnesota
Sponsa Regis, Collegeville, Minnesota
The Christian Century (and some other notable Protestant Magazines)
Dr. John C.H. Wu, Seton Hall University
Graham Carey, 16 Gray Gardens, Cambridge, Mass. (Editor of Good Work)
Rev. Fr. John Correia Afonso, S.J., St. Xavier's College, Bombay 1, India
Rev. H.A. Reinhold, 1625 Lincoln Ave., Pittsburgh, Pa.
Dom Jacques Winandy, Bellefontaine, Martinique, F.W.I. [French West Indies]
Dom Damasus Winzen, Mount Savior Priory, Box 3066, Elmira, N.Y.
The Catholic Worker, 175 Chrystie St., NY 2

And, of course, Hudson Strode would probably like one. He has written me a letter or two lately.

Did I tell you how much I liked and admired the splendid job Ed Rice did with his Church History? If not, I make up for it now. It is excellent. I don't know if you ever saw this thing on the Bomb which Bob Lax got out for me.[1] Probably you have seen it.

With cordial good wishes as ever.

Yours in Christ,
Tom /s/

1. TM, *Original Child Bomb* (New York: New Directions, 1962).

NOVEMBER 20, 1961

Farrar, Straus & Cudahy, Inc.
[Letterhead]
Robert Giroux
Editor-in-Chief

Rev. M. Louis, O.C.S.O.
Abbey of Our Lady of Gethsemani
Trappist, Kentucky

Dear Tom:

I'm happy to hear that you like THE NEW MAN. The only review so far—an advance notice—could hardly be better; I enclose it herewith.

We have sent out all the copies on your list, as well as a rather wide coverage based on our own review mailing lists. Technically, publication day is January 4th, but the bookstore practice of displaying books the moment cartons arrive is something we cannot control, and, of course, shipments are made as soon as stock is available.

We have had a letter from Thomas P. McDonnell regarding material from THE NEW MAN for the Merton Reader he is preparing. From his letter, I would gather that he has little, if any, conception of the thorny contractual and permission problems involved. I think he needs some expert advice and counsel, and I'll be glad to give it to him. In order to do so, however, I need to know a great many facts—namely, the precise contents of the Reader; whether it is intended to include New Directions and other FSC titles, as well as Harcourt, Brace; the publishing house with whom the contract for the Reader has been made; whether there is an agent; what royalty arrangements are proposed for each of the contributing publishers; and so on. It just took me a year to work out an agreement on a Djuna Barnes anthology with New Directions, with whom we have always had very friendly relations. Where previous contracts are in existence, there is bound to be a complex situation. It can be worked out if one knows the ropes and has all the facts, but it takes doing, and judging from Mr. McDonnell's letter about THE NEW MAN, he is proceeding in a manner so full of bliss and innocence that a ton of bricks is bound to fall on him. Thank God, he isn't Frank dell'Isola anyway! Please tell him what he is up against and ask him to get in touch with me directly.

I spoke to Jacques Maritain the other evening at the Campion Award Dinner in honor of Father [John] LaFarge. Maritain was in surprisingly good form and health. He asked about you, and he remembered in detail the circumstances surrounding the publication of THE SIGN OF JONAS. The only flaw in the evening was the ungracious appearance of a representative of the Legion of Decency, which no one could explain. Maritain asked, "Do you think he was sent here because of me?"

I got most of the Pax releases from Bob Lax, but I had not seen the "Original Child Bomb," which I would not have missed for anything. Thank you for letting me have it. I'm afraid I've had no luck with the reprinting of the death-furnace poem in the Reporter or anywhere else. The reason given is prior publication by the Catholic Worker, sincerely given, I think.

I'll be writing a little later about the essays and other material which you sent me, as well as the art book, which I hope that Ed Rice and Eloise and I can finish next month with your approval—the pictorial part, that is.

I'm glad you liked THE CHURCH. Ed is really one of the best designers alive.

With all good wishes.

Yours ever,

Bob /s/

P. S. Next spring we are publishing a book by a Protestant teacher, Friedrich Wilhelm Foerster, called THE JEWS, which I think is extraordinary. I enclose an English review from The Tablet, and I plan to send you an early copy of the book when it is ready.

DECEMBER 8, 1961

Rev. M. Louis, O.C.S.O.
Abbey of Our Lady of Gethsemani
Trappist, Kentucky

Dear Tom:

Dr. Abraham [Joshua] Heschel, whose books we have published—MAN IS NOT ALONE, THE SABBATH, and GOD IN SEARCH OF MAN: A PHILOSOPHY OF JUDAISM—has just returned from Rome, where he met several people in publishing circles who thought there might be a chance of getting his books published in Italian. He was told that it would be helpful for this plan if he had one or two quotes from "eminent American Catholics." Dr. Heschel suggested that you had been complimentary in the past and that you might be willing to give us a quote for this worthy purpose. If you wish to refer to his books again before doing so, and if they are not at hand for any reason, I can get them to you quickly.

I know you will be frank with me if you prefer not to send a quote, or if the rules of the Order make it difficult or imprudent for you to do so.

As ever,
[Robert Giroux]

DECEMBER 18, 1961

Abbey of Gethsemani
[Letterhead]

Dear Bob:

First of all, I am really anxious to help in any way I can to get Abraham Heschel's books known and read. I think he is one of the finest religious writers of our time, and what impresses me most of all about him is the reality and substance of his religious understanding. What he says springs from deep meditation on the revelation of God's plan in the Old Testament. His perspectives are, in general, valuable for everyone, and in a very special way for Catholics.

This having been said, I must immediately add: "Don't quote me in Italy at least until I can find out how much of this would be understood and accepted." Even in America, what I think of Heschel would have to be qualified and would not be appropriate for a blurb, and in the long run it would do him more harm than good if I just came out with an irresponsible statement.

I have asked for some counsel from someone who ought to know the situation, and will act according to his advice, in order to help Rabbi Heschel in any way that will be normally possible for me, in Italy. The situation there, I imagine, is rather delicate. It is humiliating to have to go into all these diplomacies, instead of simply speaking one's mind. However, when it is a question of entering into the world of publicity, then one cannot be altogether simple and I take it this is one of the spheres where the prudence of the serpent is recommended.

Another such is doubtless the realm of editing and publishing Readers, I have been hoping all along that things would not be too difficult with the one being edited by Tom McDonnell, but, of course, with more than three publishers involved (presuming he might even take something that was put out by the Benedictines in Minnesota, for I have vetoed the Bruce books), it is inevitable that there may be all sorts of strange hitches.[1] McDonnell is a guileless and simple man, but for that very reason I think he will appreciate advice. He does not pretend to know too much about the business end of this. I have written to him and urged him to get in touch with you, and he has replied that he will come to New York and see you as soon as he can after the holidays. I am sure you will like him and approve of his plan, which I think is rather well thought out. There is no doubt at all that the Reader will be of great use to all the three "main publishers" and I don't imagine any one of them will raise serious objections to the project as such.

Here are the pertinent facts as far as I know them:

1) The publisher of the Reader is to be Harcourt, Brace & World.

2) Perry Knowlton is acting as agent, on my suggestion, as I thought this would be one of the best ways to keep everything straight. Knowlton is a neutral, and stands above the smoke of combat (if there is to be any such). This does not mean that all the advice and help we can get from all quarters will not be very welcome.

3) I don't know what are the royalty agreements for the contributing-publishers, but it is my personal wish to insist that they all get what is coming to them. I don't want any nonsense about the money end of this, because I do not regard it as a money-making proposition and am not eager to get even excited about who gets what, as long as all get what is right and just. I would just as soon say that if at this end we got nothing, it would be no concern of mine. Unfortunately, I am not the one who collects and the monastery interests are involved. But since we are a monastery and since we have a thriving cheese business, I think I can speak for us all when I say we would hardly care less about the money that may or may not come from this book. What matters to us is rather the book itself.

Hence, with your experience and that of Perry Knowlton, new as he is, and with the presumed good will and experience of the other ones involved, I am sure everything can be kept fairly smooth. If, for some reason, you foresee any trouble and have any special suggestions to make upon which I may reasonably act at this end, please let me know at once. As I say, I am sure McDonnell will be most cooperative.

As to the people at Harcourt, Brace & World, I have had practically no contact with them and do not know what they are thinking about. With New Directions, I anticipate no trouble at all.

Do you have Jacques Maritain's address in New York? I cannot make out whether he is staying in this country or returning to France. But if he is going to be here for a while, I would like to write to him. The story about the Campion Award dinner was very funny. As a matter of fact, one would expect almost anything from the Legion of Decency. I am sure it would have disapproved of the demonstrations of spiritual enthusiasm that took place on the first feast of Pentecost: a drunk is a drunk, no matter what may have been the source of his inebriation.

The Auschwitz poem turned up in many places, including a Mennonite magazine. Also a Jewish paper in Boston. Thanks for your efforts to get it into those various magazines.

About the Art book: here I really ought to do teshuvah [in Hebrew, "return" or "repentance"]. I wrote to Eloise about it finally the other day. I have completely lost heart over the part that I am supposed to add, concerning modern sacred art. The motives for my change of mind are not altogether unreasonable. I am simply not qualified to speak about modern sacred art, which I know only through reproductions. What little experience I have had in looking at originals tells me that there is all the difference in the world between the two experiences. If I am going to make statements about modern sacred art, they will be, it seems to me, little more than bluff.

My solution to the impasse is to let Eloise carry the ball from here on, and we can co-author the book. I will simply touch up the text I wrote several years ago and do the captions for the pictures we have already lined up. This I will do when Ed has done the layouts. Eloise can do the rest, and I will go over it afterward. It seems to me that this is the only practical way to complete this difficult job. Otherwise, we will go on forever. Material will be sent down here and then while I am fretting over it, new material will appear, changes will be in order, and we will never settle on anything.

I hope you will agree that this makes a little sense. But I cannot tackle the modern sacred art or take responsibility for definite statements about it. I really am not too sure where I stand with regard to a lot of it. I do like Bill Congdon's recent stuff, but then I wonder very much whether he is not going to get exploited in a very hardnosed sort of way for a "good cause," indeed the best of causes.[2] But has art a cause to serve in that scnsc? Certainly art should serve the faith as it did in the middle ages, but in the twentieth century we have other and less edifying ways of using the arts, and maybe with more of the serpentine prudence than the Gospel would deem right. The woman who found her lost groat [coin] was looking for the groat because she wanted it. We are certainly glad to find the lost groat, but it would seem we like to emphasize the fact that we are champion groat finders.

I hope this will reach you in time for Christmas, and bring you my very best wishes. May God bless you always. These are not very cheering times, and Advent has never made more sense to me than this year, when it has been darker, perhaps, for me than any other. One thing I think we have to learn in our present predicament is to distinguish between a faith that is faith and one that is simply a disguised despair. Paradoxically, the true act of faith sets us back on our feet in this world, instead of carrying us out of it into some vague beyond. For if God is not in our turmoil with us, where can we find Him? Yet it is because we look for Him elsewhere that we are in turmoil.

Anyway, a happy Christmas and new year, and again, God bless you.

Cordially in Christ,

Tom /s/

1. The Benedictines in Minnesota ran the Liturgical Press, Collegeville, MN. Note that the Bruce Publishing Company published TM, *Exile Ends in Glory: The Life of a Trappistine, Mother M. Berchmans, O.C.S.O.* (Milwaukee: Bruce, 1948), and TM, *What Are These Wounds?* (Milwaukee: Bruce, 1950).

2. See William Condgon, *In My Disc of Gold: Itinerary to Christ* (New York: Reynal & Company, 1962).

MARCH 1, 1962

Abbey of Gethsemani
[Letterhead]

Dear Bob:

Perry Knowlton has sent me his letter to you, and also, since I last wrote, I dug into the files and found your letter to me of a couple of years ago that dealt at some length with the question of the Reader. I wish I had thought of doing that earlier. I had completely forgotten your wish not to have a contract made. If I had given myself a chance to be reminded of it, things would perhaps be less complicated.

All that I had remembered of that earlier letter was that you said something about Roger Straus getting together with Jovanovich and that the Reader could be worked out between you and Harcourt, Brace. I had forgotten your desire to have this done in some special way, the implications of which I do not quite understand as I do not know anything about business. But, at least, I do want you to know that I am not trying to be fussy or unpleasant, but simply acting according to such lights as I have in these matters, which are admittedly very dim, and could be turned on better if I had a better memory.

If by my mistake, I have made the Reader complicated, then I will have to philosophically assume the difficulties which result and go on from there. But I want you to know that I was not deliberately causing confusion and that I am sorry if confusion has been caused.

One reason why this strained situation is unpleasant is that I have some business to talk about regarding other books and it is rather hard to do that with everything else hanging in the air. I may as well proceed with simplicity and say what is on my mind.

First of all, someone is after me to do a book on peace, and is offering a substantial advance for such a book. I do not feel that I have time to sit down and write a special book on this subject, but I do have a kind of Journal in the works, called THE CONJECTURES OF A GUILTY BYSTANDER and this deals in large measure with nuclear war and the present crisis.[1] This I am sure you will want to see and you will probably agree that it ought to be the next (new) book.

Second, I have been asked by the Benedictines out at Collegeville to do a book for some series they are putting out with Helicon Press in Baltimore. If I do a book for them, it would probably be around 50,000 words on Cassian.[2] How would you feel about such a project?

Third, have you any interest in the essays I sent tentatively some time ago as a possible nucleus for a book, which could come out sometime in 1963? I would be interested to know what you think about that.

Fourth, if you took the Conjectures (referred to above) what would be the possibility of my scraping together some other stuff on peace for the publisher who has asked for a book from me?

If there is anything you want me to do about the Reader, or anything you think you ought to tell me about it, please do so. And do not assume that I am very clear about the situation at this end, or that I have the impression that I am running things. Perhaps, where I went wrong was that I ingenuously accepted a proposal, which happened to be good, when it was dumped in my lap, and did not give all the angles enough thought. But I do think the idea of the book is good, anyway. That much.

With best wishes, as ever.

Cordially yours in Christ,
Tom /s/

P. S. Thanks for the good reviews.

---

1. TM, *Conjectures of a Guilty Bystander* (Garden City, NY: Doubleday, 1966).

2. Saint John Cassian (ca. 360–435) was a Scythian monk and a "Desert Father" noted for his mystical writings. This suggested book was never written, but see Merton's novitiate conferences on Cassian: TM, *Cassian and the Fathers: Initiation into the Monastic Tradition*, ed. Patrick F. O'Connell (Kalamazoo, MI: Cistercian Publications, 2005).

MARCH 22, 1962

Abbey of Gethsemani
[Letterhead]

Dear Bob:

I hear you have been in Jamaica, and hope you had a nice vacation there. While you were away, I wrote you a longish letter with several questions. No doubt you will get around to them when you are in the clear. But there is one point that I would like to clear up now if possible.

Macmillan has offered a ten thousand dollar advance for a short book on peace. I would like very much to follow out their suggestion and do the book for them. It would not even be a full-length book, certainly not over 50,000 words, probably only 40,000. I feel that since they are very serious about this and are taking a special interest in the idea, it would be a good idea for me to go along with it.

As I have other material practically ready, and better, and longer, for Farrar, Straus & Cudahy, I feel that there is no objection to my doing this book for Macmillan.

If you have any objections or suggestions, I hope you will please let me know of them soon.

Our friend Frank dell'Isola has come out again with a repetition of that same article, this time a longer version, in Cross and Crown [March 1962], saying substantially the same things as before. I <u>don't</u> advise you to read it.

All best wishes, as ever.

Cordially yours in Christ,
Tom /s/

MARCH 28, 1962[1]

Rev. M. Louis, O.C.S.O.
Abbey of Our Lady of Gethsemani
Trappist, Kentucky

Dear Tom:

My stay in Barbados (not Jamaica—that was <u>last</u> year) was a little longer than planned, and I am sorry not to have answered your long letter of March first and your second letter of the twenty-second sooner.

There are aspects to the Macmillan situation I don't want to go into here. I'll write you about these in a personal letter from home, as well as about many other things I have not been able to discuss ever since the <u>Reader</u> problem arose.

This is simply to state formally that we do not feel that we can release you from your omnibus contract with us, and from the option therein, to do the short book for which Macmillan has offered you ten thousand dollars. I have discussed the matter fully with Roger Straus; he points out that the present contract with us commits this firm to a minimum of twenty-five thousand dollars, and we do not think it fair to accede to a side release under these circumstances. Macmillan has not written us directly; they know we are your publishers, and they must think that by approaching you directly they will succeed in getting you to obtain the release. I am sorry that we cannot agree to it.

I'll be writing soon about all the other matters in detail. Meanwhile, I hope you will understand the reason for our contractual position. I know you don't like "business matters," but this is a business decision which the Company has made.

With kindest personal regards.

Yours ever,
[Robert Giroux]

1. According to the letter dated August 22, 1963, TM never received this letter.

MARCH 30, 1962

Farrar, Straus & Cudahy, Inc.
[Letterhead]
Robert Giroux
Editor-in-Chief

Dear Tom:

You have told me so often that you don't want to get mixed up in business matters, that you don't understand business, that it really doesn't interest you, etc.—all of which I understand and sympathize with—that I have been paralyzed about writing you. The fact is that I am in such a business pickle with my colleagues here, all of which is probably my own fault, that I hardly know how to unravel the knot.

To start with the last thing first, Crowell-Collier. This big mass merger of a magazine empire with an old publishing house (Macmillan) is one of the most depressing recent developments in publishing. They are putting on a big campaign to capture "name" authors, and they are throwing large sums of money around (they have an inexhaustible supply) to get them. They don't care what the books are particularly, as long as they get the names. Jean Stafford, for example, tells me that they asked her to retell the Arabian Nights for children! Believe it or not, they are committed to a paperback program of 600 books a year—imagine, 50 every month! Columbia friends tell me they are deluged with tons of letters and printed forms, asking them to fill in "suggested titles" and then "suggested authors"! I tell you all this because it is the background against which the suggestion of a short book on peace was sent to you. I feel that this background constitutes a serious objection to your doing the book for them. It just isn't the kind of list you should be on—for your own sake as an author. You have been writing on this subject yourself, and the idea of a book on peace or on pacifism is hardly unique to Macmillan. I'm grateful to you for asking if I had any objections or suggestions; any other publisher, knowing of our options on your work, would have asked us before they even wrote you. I've stated my objections; my suggestion is that you go ahead and do the book and let us publish it. We could not pay ten thousand for one book alone, but if this is a consideration from your point of view, we can raise that amount with a three- or four-book contract, including GUILTY BYSTANDER.

Second, I'm in a terrible spot on the Reader. [Thomas] McDonnell has done an interesting selection from your published books. I know you weren't intending to cause confusion in signing that contract, but I'm afraid that Perry Knowlton (who knows all about business) has. Legally speaking, the contract is meaningless because two-thirds of the contents of the Reader belong by contract to New Directions and FSC. If the Reader were confined to the Harcourt titles, Knowlton would have been justified in asking you to sign an agreement with them for a re-presentation of their books. Neither Roger Straus nor Sheila Cudahy can understand how Father Merton and Father Abbot could sign a publishing agreement involving rights they had previously sold to two other publishers. I have explained that your concern was with editorial content, not with contracts, and that if anyone had the obligation to point this out to you, it was Knowlton. I'm sorry that McDonnell has done so much work before this was cleared up. As Roger and Sheila point out, the publication of the Reader will compete with the sales of the most recent books (that is, not the Harcourt ones). I hate to have FSC put in the position of dog in the manger, but I think it is only fair to suggest that FSC publish the Reader and Harcourt yield on releasing the titles which, after all, have been in print the longest time.

Your last two letters made it easier to write you the above, and I am grateful to you. I hate the feeling that I am trying to run things just as much as you do. You are an artist concerned with creating. That's a tough enough job in itself, and no one knows better than I what special obstacles and road-blocks you have to surmount. Nothing pains me more, in my relation to you, than the feeling that I am adding to your problems or causing frustrations or holding things up. The irony about the Reader is that it goes back to the time when I was at Harcourt; it is my idea, though naturally then it was limited to Harcourt titles and McDonnell was nowhere in the picture.[1]

The book on [Saint John] Cassian for the Benedictines at Collegeville is certainly in order, especially if it is part of a series. I also feel that the essays are a possible nucleus for a book in 1963, but I had hoped that they could have more unity of theme along the lines we discussed when last I saw you—a book of meditations on Feast Days and Holy Days [published as *Seasons of Celebration*]. Does this still seem feasible to you? However, since

THE CONJECTURES OF [A] GUILTY BYSTANDER deals with nuclear war and the present rigid crisis, this seems to me above all to be the most timely and top-priority book. The subjects of Christian pacifism and peace are so closely allied that I would hope you could work this into the GUILTY BYSTANDER book. I think it's scattering your shot to do another separate short book on this, and I hope you can combine them. As for the Art book, if you have lost heart over it, you are absolutely right to put it aside for the time being. Everyone agrees about this—Eloise, Ed Rice and [me].

Yours ever,
Bob /s/

P.S. I enclose some more reviews of THE NEW MAN, including a hard-nose one from The Catholic World, which annoys me. Jay has done a marvelous job on ORIGINAL CHILD BOMB.

P.P.S. Forgive the lousy typing—mine own.

P.P.P.S. I saw Mark [Van Doren] at the National Book Award (he was a poetry judge + picked [Alan] Dugan) + we talked of you.

1. TM followed the production process of *A Thomas Merton Reader* at HB. As he wrote to one of the editors, Julian P. Muller, in a letter dated October 8, 1962, he found this firm "wonderfully cooperative." In a letter to Muller dated January 11, 1963, he said that the *Reader* "represents the best kind of editing and publishing." In a letter dated February 26, 1963, Muller tells TM that he would be glad to publish TM's future books if TM felt constrained by FSC. In his reply, dated April 19, 1963, TM says that he has been worried about his relationship with FSC; his anxiety stems from his desire to have NB take him again under her wing and "watch over [his] complex activities." In an act of pure bravura, Roger Straus wrote to William Jovanovich at HB stating that he would be willing to release selections of FSC's TM books for the proposed *Reader*, provided that HB agree to release to his firm Robert Lowell's *Lord Weary's Castle* and *The Mills of the Kavanaughs* on a pro rata basis and also selections from the prose writings of T.S. Eliot for a proposed volume he had in mind.

APRIL 3, 1962

Gethsemani

Dear Bob:

Many thanks for your good letter. I certainly have been reading light on this thing [that is, the <u>Reader</u>], because it is way beyond me. I repeat that I am very sorry about the contract. From where I stood at the time, I thought it was a normal, reasonable, accepted way of doing things. When you get a book published, then there is a contract. When the book posits a problem, then there is an agent. Naïve.

I enclose the letter I have just written to Perry Knowlton. I don't think the letter gets anywhere much because I don't see that there is much I can do at this point. It seems to me that the whole thing is between FSC and Harcourt. Since I got involved with Knowlton, I think also that I ought to stay with him in this case. I mean I don't see any reason or sense in dropping all the pieces and starting over. That would be absurd at this end, so it seems to me. The complications would be without end. From where we are, can't we go along and hope seriously that you can all work this out together in some way that suits all of you? There must be a simple way of doing this. After all, if the problem were so great, New Directions would be much more concerned than they are. It seems to pose no difficulties for them.

It seems to me that the key men in all of this are Roger Straus and [William] Jovanovich and if they want to they can work it all out to the satisfaction of everybody. For my part, I am certainly willing to do everything in my power to help things along. But I hardly know what is in my power now: I am only the author, and authors hardly have a decisive say in matters like this.

Thanks for the briefing about Macmillan. I knew nothing about the big deal, except Ed Rice vaguely said something about it when I inquired of him. Elizabeth Bartelme [publishing agent for Macmillian] seemed to me to be OK and their suggestion seemed to indicate a genuine and sensible interest.

However, I am going to think the whole thing out seriously on the basis of your suggestion.

There is one other factor: there is in the GUILTY BYSTANDER quite a lot of material on nuclear war in an informal vein. The stuff in the Peace book is in essays and they are more or less lined up in continuity. Just after Macmillan wrote, Justus Lawler at Herder & Herder said he wanted some of my peace articles for a series they are doing and which would be specially directed to Catholics, who need it.[1] This also is a possibility. I don't see any real need or sense in FSC doing both these books, especially since they would come in close succession. I do think though that one of them done by Herder & Herder, in a paperback theology series, might make sense. (As for the ten thousand advance, I am not concerned with that one way or the other.) There was certainly no real conflict between a Peace book by Herder & Herder and the GUILTY BYSTANDER at your end.

I think the best thing would be to let the Art book simmer for a couple of years and then we'll see.

On the Essays: the book of various Feasts could be done later when I get time. One or two liturgical essays like the Christmas and Easter ones could go in a volume of essays now as they are so general as to cover all the Christian life. I am sending you also one on St. Ignatius of Antioch, which is another possible inclusion. Hope we can get out of the woods on this READER thing, really.

And again, sorry for my obtuseness.

> Best wishes and blessings, in Christ,
> Tom /s/

---

1. This was a book that the Trappist authorities told Merton not to publish, but that finally appeared years later: TM, *Peace in the Post-Christian Era*, ed. Patricia A. Burton (Maryknoll, NY: Orbis, 2004).

Dear Bob:

Naturally I keep thinking about this Reader business, and also, of course, I asked for the agreement about it, from the files. Having consulted this, I find it to be a letter to Jovanovich, to McDonnell and to Dom James, and signed by these and by Perry Knowlton. The letter is not a contract. It contains the following clause which I believe is relevant to the objections you have stated.

It is understood that the contract <u>to be drawn</u> will provide for the usual publishing terms in connection with secondary publishing rights in so far as they may not be in conflict with agreements already in force, regarding the material . . .

In other words, there has certainly been no violation whatever of any rights of Farrar, Straus & Cudahy, and it is not a question of a contract valid or not valid. Obviously, nobody considers that the existence of this letter somehow gives us a legal title to material in books published by F, S & C. Even in my dim mind, it never assumed that character. On the contrary, all that I ever thought was that since relations between me and F, S & C were friendly ones, it would be easy to work out some kind of agreement.

Now the situation has arisen that some cutting is to be done. That cutting will most probably be done in material that was selected from F, S & C books. This I believe will bring the amount of material from those books down. In fact, I presume that it will be a question of four or five thousand words each from books like Disputed Questions and Secular Journal, and less from Thoughts in Solitude, probably little or nothing from the others.

In other words, it seems to me that there is hardly any reason to think that such selections would do anything but good for F, S & C and for the books published by them. Indeed it might bring those books to the attention of my non-Catholic readers who do not appear to have heard of them, and I am sure this will be to the advantage of F, S & C.

I will be naturally hoping that on this basis an arrangement can be made without too much complication. If such an arrangement still seems to be impossible, I will conclude that the relations between myself and F, S & C are no longer amicable. This has nothing to do with you personally, Bob. But it is the way I see the situation from here. I know that you cannot do too much about it yourself. I would not want this in any way to affect our own personal friendship.

With best wishes, as ever.

Cordially yours in Christ,
[Thomas Merton]

MAY 11, 1962

Farrar, Straus & Cudahy, Inc.
[Letterhead]
Robert Giroux
Editor-in-Chief

Rev. M. Louis O.C.S.O.
Abbey of Gethsemani
Trappist, Kentucky

Dear Tom:

As Perry Knowlton may have told you, Roger Straus is now trying to work out with William Jovanovich the modus operandi for the READER. You could not have known that much more is involved than granting permission to Harcourt to reprint extracts from our books. We have wanted to publish a collected volume of Robert Lowell's poetry for some time, and Harcourt has refused to release LORD WEARY'S CASTLE—in fact, they warned Lowell when he took his third book to us that they would never release it. There is also a question of a collected T.S. Eliot volume of prose, part of which they have and part of which is under our imprint. If Harcourt agrees to the principle involved—namely, that we both have to make concessions—then there will be no problem. If they do not agree, there will be a great problem, indeed, and I am afraid it is beyond my control, or anyone's. I am sorry that you are involved in this because of the READER through no fault of your own, and I am sorry that I am involved in it. Roger expects to hear from Jovanovich next week and I will write you at once.

Meanwhile, we would like to draw up a contract for GUILTY BYSTANDER. Do you think we could agree on a length of not less than 50,000 words? Also, could you give me some idea of what deadline you would like?

I do not know whether you happened to see the most recent issue of THE CRITIC, which is published by the Thomas More Book Club of Chicago. They ran a symposium to which I am a contributor and I am enclosing a copy.

I can't tell you how grateful I was for the concluding sentences of your last letter. Nothing will ever affect our personal friendship—certainly not any publishing technicalities or intra-mural difficulties. I am hopeful that Harcourt will come to realize that it is not a one-way street and, in a way, we are fortunate that the READER problem arises at this juncture, making them face up to something which is hardly to their credit.

With warmest regards.

Yours ever,
Bob /s/

AUGUST 27, 1962

Dear Bob:

Thanks for your good letter and the enclosure from the TLS [*Times Literary Supplement*], which was bracing. I am glad the book has gone over well and is getting reviewed here and there.

I have not answered your letter from the office for various reasons, but it is not because I do not want to publish CONJECTURES. The fact is, I cannot. It is no longer possible for me to publish material (at least new material) on the war question, as I have been asked by the Abbot General not to do so. As there is so much about this question in CONJECTURES, it comes under the ban. I have therefore dropped the book, at least until such time as I can think over various other possibilities: for example, revising it so that the war stuff is in the background or purely "incidental." I don't know if that would do the trick, even.

This explains why I have not responded in any way to your request. And, of course, the whole business about the READER makes me loth to start out anything new with F, S & C, though, of course, I can see why they took the stand they did, being what they are, namely a money-making proposition.[1]

I suppose, however, we had better try in some way to finish out the old contract, if we can do so without too much tearing out of hair. But two things have me stopped. I cannot see my way to adding material on modern art to the Art book, since I am not competent to do so, and I would be much happier trying to combine the liturgical stuff with the other essays, rather than writing a whole book on feasts, unless you want to put that off indefinitely into the far distant future. I do wish Eloise would do the modern stuff for the Art book: or else let's finally drop it.

We have had a few hot stuffy spells here, with fairly cool weather in between. I have been tied up with several batches of visitors and haven't been able to get much done. But things go on more or less as usual. I hope you are well, and that you have enjoyed your vacation.

All the best always.

Cordially yours in Christ,
[Thomas Merton]

---

1. In a letter to Julian Muller, dated July 8, 1962, TM showed great displeasure with his relationship with FSC: "My feeling with regard to Farrar, Straus has been that they have been content to sell my books to nuns. Mr. Jovanovich, who probably formed the same opinion, made a point of saying that Harcourt, Brace would not be following that policy. As a matter of fact, it is still the books published by Harcourt, Brace that people associate with my name, in many cases they have not even heard of the others, except for <u>Seeds of Contemplation</u>." Similarly, in a letter to NB dated November 25, 1962, TM wrote: "But since my relations with them [FSC] have been quite strained, and I think they will continue so, because I have totally lost confidence in them. I cannot deal with anybody who seems to me to be doing a lot of absurd, underhand maneuvering all the time."

SEPTEMBER 17, 1962

Abbey of Gethsemani
[Letterhead]

Dear Bob:

The new book on Yoga has not arrived, but it sounds very interesting. I shall certainly consider writing the preface, and am pretty sure there will be no difficulty about this. However, it is hard to say what the censors may do. They keep clamping down on me for things which they consider "not fitting for a Trappist." As you can imagine, this is such a vague and arbitrary category that it can cover almost everything. If one of the censors imagines that Yoga is scandalous, then I will not be able to get anywhere. But I will certainly do my best.

Could you please send two copies of the Dell'Isola Bibliography (charged to our royalty account) to:

> Rev. Joseph O'Dea
> Librarian
> Monte Cistelle
> Via Laurentina 471
> Roma EUR[OPE]

Fr. Abbot is still away at the General Chapter, and the Lord only knows what they are deciding this year. Rumor has it that there is to be a second magazine of the Order for the monasteries of the so-called English language, and though I don't think I will be the goat, I am liable to be very close to whoever is the goat.[1] This will be at once painful and frustrating, and will involve much useless work.

As ever, with the very best wishes.

Cordially yours in Christ,
Tom /s/

1. *Cistercian Studies* (now *Cistercian Studies Quarterly*) began publication in 1966, joining the *Collectanea Ordinis Cisterciensium Reformatorum*, now *Collectanea Cisterciensia*, the French-language publication of the order since the 1930s.

NOVEMBER 21, 1962

Farrar, Straus & Cudahy, Inc.
[Letterhead]
Robert Giroux
Editor-in-Chief

Rev. M. Louis, O.C.S.O.
Abbey of Gethsemani
Trappist, Kentucky

Dear Tom:

I can't tell you how glad I was to hear from you, and to read the piece you wrote as a preface to Dom Denys Rutledge's book, IN SEARCH OF A

YOGI. I think it's excellent, and I've sent it to the printer. When proofs come, you can make any further changes you wish to and also, by then, you may have the censor's release. (In view of the present Ecumenical climate, it ought not to be difficult to get!)

Speaking of that, did you see the piece in the <u>New Yorker</u> ["Letter from Vatican City," by Xavier Rynne, October 20, 1962] on the opening of the Ecumenical Council in Rome? It's such an extraordinary piece that I'm sending it to you herewith. I hear talk of it, especially in Catholic circles, wherever I go. There ought to be talk; it's one of the best written pieces I've read on the subject, and much better written than most things in the Catholic press. In any event, I've been in touch with the pseudonymous author (who really does know his stuff) and he is going to do a book for us on the Council later on.

I saw Ed Rice at the Catholic Book Club dinner, a dreary affair except for [author and publisher] Frank Sheed's wonderful talk; Bob Lax I've not seen in a coon's age; Naomi I never see now because she's an editor instead of an agent. I'm keeping busy, however. I agree with you about the J. F. Powers novel [*Morte d'Urban* (1962)], it's a honey, and I'd love to see your review when it comes out.[1] The amalgamation sounds like a real problem, as far as the novitiate goes, but I know you will work it out. The good news of the let-up on the Cuban thing [Cuban missile crisis], and the cease-fire in the India-China war, makes me feel a little cheerful for the first time in months.

With warmest regards.

Yours ever,
Bob /s/

1. See TM, "J. F. Powers—*Morte D'Urban*: Two Celebrations," *Worship* 36 (November 1962): 645–50.

DECEMBER 1, 1962

Abbey of Gethsemani
[Letterhead]

Dear Bob:

This is just a quick note to let you know that the censors came through bravely with approbation for the Preface. I am glad they did so, because I am not as sure as you are that the "ecumenical climate" has penetrated as far as the Cistercian censorial mind. In fact, I know it has not in many cases. But anyway, we are in the clear. Will I see a proof? When do you plan to publish the book?

Your New Yorker piece on the Council was really lively and good. But I note that fortunately one of his main predictions has been contradicted by the facts: they have really got down to business in the first session, instead of just sparring around. What I have heard, and that is not much, sounds encouraging. Pity that political feeling messed up the Greek observers' being present. I know the man who engineered a special meeting between

Archbishop Nikodim [Metropolitan Nikodim (Rotov) of Leningrad and Novgorod] and Cardinal [Eugène] Tisserant, which led to the sending of observers from Moscow. But this was what antagonized the Greeks. Well, you can't have everything.

Lax, incidentally, is in Greece, and has applied for a Guggenheim: I have to fill out the forms saying he is the prince of scholars. Naomi has sent me a very good translation she did of a French book, "Vigil in the Sun" by a Finnish dancer [Marina de Berg] who was for some time a Trappistine, and got in several fine rows with the Abbot General for saying too much in a book she wrote about her experiences in the Order.

All best wishes, as ever.

Most cordially in Christ,
Tom /s/

DECEMBER 6, 1962

Farrar, Straus & Cudahy, Inc.
[Letterhead]
Robert Giroux
Editor-in-Chief

Rev. M. Louis, O.C.S.O.
Abbey of Gethsemani
Trappist, Kentucky

Dear Tom:

I am delighted to know that the censors have O. K.'d the preface for IN SEARCH OF A YOGI. The proof of your copy is due next Wednesday and I will get it off to you at once. We plan to publish the book next April. You will probably not be surprised to know that Dom Bede Griffiths wrote a good review of it in one of the British papers.

In a couple of weeks I'll be sending you Xavier Rynne's sequel, summarizing the first session of the [Vatican] Council [II]. It's full of interesting sidelights. Eloise Spaeth, who is just back from Europe, tells me that there was much speculation as to the authorship of the first article, but nobody seems to have cracked his identity.*

Under separate cover I am sending you Elizabeth Hardwick's A VIEW OF MY OWN and THE NOVELS OF SWINBURNE with an introduction by Edmund Wilson, the latter will be sure to amuse you; leave it to Wilson to discover that Algernon [Swinburne]'s prose is superior to his poetry.

With warmest regards.

Yours ever,
Bob /s/

*Everyone is convinced it's a Jesuit. [Xavier Rynne was a pseudonym for Rev. Francis X. Murphy, C.Ss.R. (1915–2002).]

DECEMBER 12, 1962

Dear Bob:

I can't guarantee that this typing is going to be very good. I have been walking around in the zero cold and the snow with a Jewish Hasid talking about the problems of the world and more besides, and my fingers have not thawed out, though I think my mind is nimble. I hope.

Thanks for sending the books, which have not yet come, but I look forward to them: especially the one of Elizabeth Hardwick, about which I had heard.

Also, I forgot to enclose my review of J. F. Powers, which I had promised. I meant to send it along with the last letter. At the same time, as a Christmas present, here is the little thing of Clement of Alexandria I did with J. Laughlin.[1] It is supposed to be out early next year.

Thinking of future books, and of the contract which I have with F, S & C: I think it would perhaps be a good idea to look over the situation and see what you want to take next. The problem is a little complicated by the fact that over the past couple of years I have sent you stacks of separate essays and articles, not to mention lists of essays and articles, which might possibly be material for a book of essays on the contract. And then there are other essays that were earmarked for a liturgical book.

Do you think, to clarify matters, you could let me have a list of this material, and perhaps a suggestion of yours as to how you may want to use some of it?

Would you prefer to take first the book of "Essays" or the "Liturgy" book? I think the last time I wrote I was still stalling about doing any more work on the latter: but I do not think it would be too hard to fill it out as I have two more pieces, like, for instance, the Advent one (enclosed, adding to the general confusion).[2] If you wanted to take the Liturgy book next, I think I could manage it.

Since Macmillan was asking for a book I gave them one, not full length or especially good, on Prayer, which they want to bring out in early fall, so whatever book of mine you want to do would be affected by that, and put off until winter or until the spring of 1964 perhaps.[3]

I am not trying to rush this thing at all, but I do think we ought to perhaps consider it, as I am not happy about that pile of miscellaneous essays cluttering up your office, and would like to tidy up at least that.

So will you please send me a list of the essays and other things of mine you may have, and offer any suggestion you may think practicable about which ought to be the next book?

With very best Christmas wishes, always.

Cordially yours in Christ,
[Thomas Merton]

1. *Clement of Alexandria: Selections from the "Protreptikos"* (New York: New Directions, 1962).
2. TM, "The Advent Mystery," *Worship* 37 (December 1963): 17–25.
3. The projected book, *Prayer as Worship and Experience*, would lead to the threat of legal proceedings against Macmillan by FSC, as subsequent correspondence details.

DECEMBER 17, 1962

Abbey of Gethsemani
[Letterhead]

Dear Bob:

Here is the preface. I look forward to the Xavier Rynne article. Actually, I think the first session [of the Second Vatican Council] was exceptionally hopeful. Tremendous good was done by the discussions + exchanges of views, from all I hear. [Jean] Daniélou [S.J.], who was there as an expert, wrote that he was more than happy with the results so far.

It is possible that the questions of peace will eventually be discussed. I hope so. If you can think of anyone who ought to receive the mimeographed thing on Peace I sent, I will gladly send a copy. Several bishops have it, + I think some theologians may look it over. So far I have no reactions from any of them, though laypeople have been very vocal in favorable reactions. At least it is a point of view!

All best wishes for Christmas once again.

Cordially yours in Christ,
Tom /s/

FEBRUARY 1, 1963

Farrar, Straus & Cudahy, Inc.
[Letterhead]
Robert Giroux
Editor-in-Chief

Rev. M. Louis, O.C.S.O.
Abbey of Gethsemani
Trappist, Kentucky

Dear Tom:

Ed Rice tells me that he wants to use an excerpt from IN SEARCH OF A YOGI in Jubilee, with perhaps part of your preface. I'm delighted he wants to, and I hope this has your approval.

We have been offered François Mauriac's short book, CE QUE JE CROIS, which strikes me as excellent.[1] Unfortunately his translator, Gerard Hopkins (a relative of the poet), has died. Is it too much of an inspiration to think that you might want to undertake the Englishing of it? If I'm entirely out of order, forgive me for asking. But please read it anyway, for I'm sure you will agree that it's an extraordinary document.

I'm working on various combinations of the essays, Tom, but I really don't see any way of unifying them by groups. They represent your thoughts on a wide range of topics over the years, and that's perhaps the best way to present them. Have you written on any other feast days or on the liturgy? That group does form a unit.

I would also like to discuss new book ideas with you. The whole movement of renewal which the Council has engendered suggests a host of subjects. Behind it all looms the basic subject of peace on which you have written so fervently and well. I wish your next book would somehow sum all this up. I even have a working title for it: GOOD NEWS.

Eliot's illness and consequent change in travel plans has knocked my winter plans awry. I feel as if I haven't seen you in decades and I'd like to come down in March or April. It was the London smog that did Eliot in, and it's a series of colds that have almost sunk me.

With warmest regards.

Yours ever,

Bob /s/

P.S. The Xavier Rynne material, now coming in, is even better than the New Yorker stuff. I hear Yves Congar [O.P.] is doing a book on the Council too.

1. François Mauriac, a noted French author, received the Nobel Prize for Literature in 1952.

FEBRUARY 5, 1963

Dear Bob:

It was good to get some news from you and to know that we can go ahead at least tentatively with the question of the next book. I gather that you prefer that it should not be the book of essays, but another new one.

There is a certain amount of difficulty in my getting right down to a whole book starting from scratch at the moment. I do not think I will be able to do anything of the kind for another year, because I am in the midst of a whole reorganization of the formation program here and I am more or less the one who is doing it. I have not only both the novitiates, choir and brothers, but also a whole lot of the junior professed in conferences. This is a rather complex situation and just about all I can handle. What time is left me for writing is pretty scarce and I have been giving it to poems and stray pieces, if anything.[1]

Translation would be easier than writing a book, and really I am tempted by the Mauriac proposal. But I am afraid it would be unwise for me to attempt even this. It would be much better for you to go ahead with someone who can get the book to you more or less certainly in a reasonable time.

It might be possible to write up a few pieces on liturgy, before the end of the year.

Actually, since we do have material for a book of essays, I think it would probably be smart to proceed with that. Remember in my last letter, I kept the distinction between the book of essays and the book of liturgy pieces. Finally, there is just a bare possibility that I might be able to go ahead with CONJECTURES OF A GUILTY BYSTANDER and this is what I would like to do. It will mean cutting out a lot of nuclear war stuff (which is now absolutely *verboten*) and hiding your "good news" in the midst of journalism stuff, which would nevertheless be readable and be read, I think, with interest by many. I think this is the best idea, but again, I would like to take it slowly and we would have to plan on delays with censors, etc.

The essays are all censored, and there are certainly enough for a good variety in one book. My idea is let's take the essays first, and I can meanwhile work at CONJECTURES in a spirit of hope and abandonment to providence!!

Coming down is a good idea. I hope you will. Here are the best dates: Easter time is busy ([Rev.] Hans Küng is coming down, I hope). March 27th is all right, unless you prefer right at the beginning of March, but that is pretty bad as I will just be recovering from a heavy ecumenical week, a Josef Smolik, Protestant minister from Czechoslovakia is stopping by and I have a peace seminar with some Presbyterians.

I would be more in the clear in April than in March, but March 27th is good enough. April 24th is better still. Do let me know which will be best for you. Thanks, then, for Mauriac, which is terrific. I like it very much. May I keep it at least until you come?

Certainly all right with me for Ed to use anything from the preface in Jubilee. I am sending you a copy of a book of mine which was supposed to be a pamphlet. I gave it to Justus Lawler at Herder and their New York office made it into a book, which is natural enough, but it was not my original intention. We were actually going to do it here, then the Benedictines at St. Meinrad's might have taken it: and so on.

Looking forward to hearing from you.

All cordial good wishes in Christ,
[Thomas Merton]

1. TM published his sixth book of verse, *Emblems of a Season of Fury*, in 1963. In a letter dated January 11, 1963, TM wrote to Julian Muller stating, "[My] publishing situation is still a bit confused and I am having a hard time finding out what comes off next. Farrar, Straus & Cudahy have me in a position where by simply keeping silent they can make things very uncomfortable and even block all movement. I don't know what the future holds in store, but there again everything will work out for the best."

MARCH 16, 1963

Dear Bob:

Maybe the Lenten fast clears the head. Maybe also a few remarks in a letter from Tom Burns helped me to see a little light: but, in any case, I have finally realized that I have been owing Farrar, Straus & Cudahy some explanations. This did not occur to me until just now, as in the past I had taken it for granted that all the world operated much the way we used to operate when it was a question of full-length books for you, short books and poetry for New Directions, and Naomi Burton taking care of the proper clearances, to which I never gave a thought.

Now it dawns on me that there are such things as clearances and that they have been my responsibility. I have neglected the responsibility, and am very sorry, indeed, for my thoughtlessness. Hence, I beg you to convey my sincere apologies to Farrar, Straus & Cudahy.

Obviously, now that I am aware of this situation, I promise you that as long as our contract lasts, I will not make any further moves to sell full-length books of prose or even books such as that recently brought out by Herder & Herder, which I considered only a pamphlet, without first consulting you. Naturally, it is understood that I go on with poetry and things like Original Child Bomb, with New Directions.

I am in no great rush about the next book, presuming that you are still interested in a next book. But I wonder if it makes sense to tie myself up with contracts which extend far into the future? Perhaps they just involve more difficulties. At any rate, I promise to respect the option agreement at present in force and which, I think, fits the description I outlined above. If there is anything I have misunderstood, I hope you will set me right, so that there will be no more complications in future.

With cordial good wishes always.

Yours in Christ,
[Thomas Merton]

MAY 10, 1963

Dear Bob:

The Xavier Rynne book [*Letters from Vatican City: Vatican Council II, First Session; Background and Debates*] arrived this morning. Thanks very much indeed. It looks great. Is there much beside what was in the New Yorker? I will soon see. And now I confess a secret temptation: I am convinced that YOU are Xavier Rynne. But I guess not. Still, I think you would have looked great sitting there with a mitre on, and concealing a tape recorder under your *cappa magna* [large cape].

And now back to business, as if I were capable of talking sense on the subject. Really, Bob, I do want to get things in order. You have not yet answered my last letter in which I acknowledged my monumental blunders. It is clear, whatever the causes, that as I have been going along these past few years, such blunders become inevitable. I cannot continue like that. It is essential that some new arrangement be arrived at.

One thing that came home to me was that I am simply in no position here to manage such complicated affairs as mine so easily get to be. It is utterly impossible. This is not news to you, of course.

That being the case, I was wondering if after all there was not some way of getting back into a team with Naomi. I mean, as agent. That was the way the idea first struck me. However, I also realized that it would be asking an enormous amount to have her work for me as agent while still working for another publisher. Yet I think she would even be willing to do this, to some extent, if she could get things fixed the way she wants them, with three days a week only, in N.Y. Really, though, the fairest thing would be for me to wind up my affairs with Farrar, Straus and move over with her. It is not that I have any special attraction for Doubleday or anything against Farrar, Straus, still less you. It is not a personal matter at all. It is purely and simply a question of fact: that I am in a mess the way things are now, and this is the only way I can see to get out of the mess and restore some kind of order and reason.

You have been very patient with me, and taken a lot of nonsense, which I assure you I have not intended. I have no doubt that you will heave a sigh of relief yourself when this is all fixed up. I am asking you, then, if you wouldn't please come to an agreement about winding up our affairs, in the way you feel to be most just and equitable. Please let me know what you think would be the best way of doing this. And again, I repeat, this is not a personal matter between us. My friendship for you has not and will not change in the least, and I am not blaming you for anything. Please do not interpret anything I have said in such a light. The motive for my decision has been, chiefly, that in the last five or six years, I have never at any moment felt that I really knew where I stood and that I was in a position to really understand what was going on. This led me to make some rash moves on my own, and I cannot afford to repeat the performance. So that, to the best of my ability, is where I am now.

Please let me hear from you on this. I assure you of my warmest personal regards.

Ever cordially yours in Christ,
[Thomas Merton]

MAY 13, 1963

Farrar, Straus & Company, Inc.
19 Union Square West
New York 3, N.Y.
Robert Giroux
Editor-in-Chief

Rev. M. Louis, O.C.S.O.
Abbey of Gethsemani
Trappist, Kentucky

Dear Tom:

I'm glad you like the looks of the Xavier Rynne book. If you've read the preface, you know that it's a multiple author. I am not one of them, though

I'm involved as editor. I like to think that if any one of the present authors disappears, another will rise to take his place. Like the Scarlet Pimpernel, somewhat. I enjoyed your picture of the tape-recorder beneath the cope. Anyway, the "debate" chapters have fascinating sidelights on the deportment and varied mental powers of the participants. The Holy Ghost was sorely needed. Nobody has guessed that X.R. is one of the oldest shorthand symbols for a Christian; if "X," what more obvious name than Xavier, and the nearest thing to "Rien" for R is certainly Rynne (there are two priests of that name in the Catholic Directory, I'm afraid!). I hear that Msgr. [John Tracy] Ellis has written a good review for The Critic already.

I am grateful for your frankness and directness about the contract problem. I have not been happy, either, and I've felt constrained and confused and embarrassed about the whole thing. I feel that I've been at fault, to a great extent, and I know the difficulties under which you labor and feel guilty about having added to them.

We have two sets of problems, Tom—legal and moral. The latter we can easily work out between us, with Naomi's good help. The former may be a bit more difficult. I was given hell for standing aside on the Herder book, and preventing a suit. Herder would have had no legal defense whatever, but I knew that they must have proceeded because they thought that if you sent them a manuscript it must be free. A similar legal situation exists on the Macmillan book, but this time it's a bit different. In that case, I warned Al Hart, their editor-in-chief, of your prior, contractual commitments. I do not know the editor to whom you have sent a manuscript (at least Naomi tells me so), nor do I know whether Al Hart has explained the legal situation to her. But this seems to me a good place to begin to straighten out the snarl. (What Tom Burns reported as having been said by Roger Straus might have applied to Herder, since it's water over the dam, but not to Macmillan. Far from giving them permission, we advised them that the rights were not clear and that the contractual agreement they may have signed is invalid.)

There are six books in our contract. We have published THE NEW MAN and DISPUTED QUESTIONS. You have submitted a book of essays. That leaves ART AND WORSHIP, the book of feast days, and the "next work" after that, covered by the option clause. If you withdraw the Macmillan book, and we substitute that for the book of feast days, we have only ART AND WORSHIP and the option book to work out. This should not come as a surprise to Macmillan as such, and I hope it does not come as one to your editor there. I am amazed, in one sense, that someone at Herder or Macmillan did not call here; it is fairly common practice to approach an author under contract elsewhere, but the existing publisher is always consulted, either by the editor or the author.

It seems to me that Naomi is the ideal solution for you. We have talked over the whole problem, and I phoned her today specifically about the Macmillan problem, and she agrees that that is where we should start.

It is generous of you to write as you did, and I want to respond in the same spirit. Your affairs are so complicated that a person of Naomi's vast experience and patience and firmness is needed to order them. With all the demands made on you, it's a wonder that there has not been worse trouble.

Beyond that, I have the feeling that a tremendous sea change is now occurring in the Church, a renewal more than a revolution. My old friend Father [John] LaFarge wrote me this morning, about the Rynne, saying not only that he considers it a real achievement, but adding: "It is difficult to grasp the extent and variety of all that is going on at the present time." The fact of the Council itself has been enough to start all this. I am trying to say that this is going to affect all writing, and writers, in this field. You have been always in the forefront, way ahead of all your contemporaries. I know you will continue to be, and I hope to remain your friend and well-wisher always.

> Yours ever,
> Bob /s/

MAY 29, 1963

> Abbey of Gethsemani
> [Letterhead]

Dear Bob:

It was a comfort to get your letter and I am happy at the clarity that it has brought into the situation, even though my own mistakes show up in its light. But, at last, I feel that we are more or less together in considering it. Before, it seems, we were pretty much at cross purposes and thinking in different terms.

It seems to me that it should not be too difficult to work out our problem. I am under contract to furnish you with certain books, and I feel that I can give you what may be needed to fulfill my obligations. And, of course, I am not just trying to "do my duty." For a long time, I have been wanting to get the essays under way.

Naomi, who has been getting me straightened out, thinks it would be much simpler for all of us if you sent me all the essays and related materials that you have on file, and I will then go over them carefully, working over them where necessary, getting the whole thing retyped so that it will shape up into a workable ms., which you can go over without too much perplexity. That will doubtless take care of one book, and I think there is lots of material for a good one.

I also have enough material for "Feast Days," including new stuff that you have not seen and perhaps one or two more things which I am planning to write. I will also get this all together and in shape as one unified manuscript, as I hope to do for the essays.

About Macmillan: I have written them that I felt it was my fault that I gave them a book which I did not have a right to give, and that Farrar, Straus was insisting upon their rights to this book. I said that Farrar, Straus had that right and that they were probably in a position to sue for it, as far as I knew. However, Macmillan replied that they felt that their contractual position was solid and that they meant to hold on to this book. This leaves me in a position which I do not quite understand, but Naomi says you will all try to work it out among you in New York. I certainly want to do whatever justice demands that I do, but it seems that Macmillan intends to defend what they consider to be their right.

As to ART AND WORSHIP, I still feel quite strongly that it would not be right for me to try to add material on modern sacred art. I would be largely bluffing if I did, as I never see the actual paintings, etc., only reproductions. But I repeat that I am perfectly willing to have Eloise Spaeth, or Ed Rice, or anyone else you like, fill in that gap if you feel it is necessary. We can work out any details as to how this could best be managed.

These seem to me to be the four essential points. The only thing I can add is that I would be very sorry to see you and Macmillan get into a lot of unnecessary and probably fruitless litigation over my mistakes. I hope it will all work out and [followed by lines missing from letter].

It was good to have Naomi come down here and help me to understand something of this tangle. She is really putting a great deal of work into it, and for that reason it is only right, I think, that I should eventually go over to Doubleday when I have finally settled everything with Farrar, Straus.

One more point: about the essays: do you think of this as a book of Selected Essays covering the whole span of my work? That would seem to be the right approach, and it appeals to me. Let me know what you think.

The Rynne book is full of new material. I find it fascinating. And guess what: who was here but [Cardinal Edigio] Vagnozzi, the Delegate. I was afraid he would be very unpleasant about something, but he was quite cordial. However, I did not quite pluck up the courage to ask him what he thought of Xavier Rynne. It would have been an interesting experience. We talked mostly of the missions in Asia in the sixteenth century, a safe topic, I think.

Again, Bob, it is a relief to feel that we are getting this thing straightened out gradually, and I am very sorry for the obtuseness and thoughtlessness on my part which led to such complications.

> Very cordially yours in Christ,
> Tom /s/

P.S. Bob—Helen Wolff asked me to do a preface to a dissertation of [François] Fénelon's letters for Harvard Press + London [*Fénelon: Letters of Love and Counsel* (1964)] + for her—not Harcourt—but she is distinct from them, I think. Anyway—is this something I need to clear with you, + if so, is it all right?

JUNE 21, 1963

Farrar, Straus & Company, Inc.
[Letterhead]
Robert Giroux
Editor-in-Chief

Rev. M. Louis, O.C.S.O.
Abbey of Gethsemani
Trappist, Kentucky

Dear Tom:

I am getting the essays together from several sources—my files here, at home, and in Jersey—and I'll send you a list of everything. As I recall, most of them were mimeographed, but if there are any you don't have, I'll send them on. I wasn't really thinking of it as a Collected Essays, but was hoping we could find common themes or an overall theme around which to build one book. Perhaps there are several books in the material, and in a way, just from the viewpoint of length, there should be.

Macmillan are being tiresome and I find it difficult to proceed with anything until this matter is settled. Their people are saying that you have written to tell them that you decided to leave Farrar, Straus. As I told Naomi, they are also saying you want to publish all your work with them. Roger Straus wrote to their president, Warren Sullivan, about our prior contractual right, at the advice of our lawyers.[1] He replied: "We are studying all of the information that we have," which strikes Roger as double-talk. I'm sorry this is such a mess, and I hope we won't have to get a court injunction. It seems to me that we deserve an honest answer. I also feel that our exchange of letters is predicated on this matter being cleared up first. Naomi thought I knew what state the book had reached, but I am not certain whether it's beyond galley proofs or what.

It would be fine if we could avoid a law suit with Macmillan, but I don't see how it can be avoided if they are determined to publish a book whose contract we know is invalid. Only a court can settle such a matter, as far as I can see. Unfortunately, it is out of my hands and—depending on Macmillan's next step—that is where the matter is headed. I certainly hope it is not going to mean a lot of bad publicity and nonsense.

The election of [Pope] Paul VI this morning is marvelous news. His statements at the Council—and two bishops, reviewing the Xavier Rynne book in _America_, call its contents "uncannily accurate"—show a real affinity with Pope John's policies. What a wonderful thing it was that Pope John made so many good men Cardinals!

With kindest personal regards.

Yours ever,
Bob /s/

P.S. I enjoyed your story of Cardinal Vagnozzi's visit to Gethsemani.

1. Roger Straus, as president of FSC, wrote on July 24, 1963, to Warren Sullivan, stating that TM did not approve of Macmillan's plans to publish his work. According to a letter from Straus to Sullivan dated May 21, 1963, FSC had entered into a contractual arrangement with the Abbey of Our Lady of Gethsemani, on behalf of TM, on September 15, 1960, to publish six of his books, only two of which had actually been published. TM, according to Straus, had entered into an agreement with Macmillan not fully realizing the conflict with his prior commitments. Straus asked Sullivan to withdraw from what Straus believed to be an untenable situation. Sullivan subsequently wrote to TM, in a letter dated July 11, 1963, indicating that he planned on meeting with FSC for a "full-fledged discussion" of the matter.

JULY 17, 1963

Farrar, Straus & Company, Inc.
[Letterhead]
Robert Giroux
Editor-in-Chief

Rev. M. Louis, O.C.S.O.
Abbey of Our Lady of Gethsemani
Trappist, Kentucky

Dear Tom:

I am very much concerned about the whole Macmillan situation, following a meeting here with their Executive Vice President, Jeremiah Kaplan. He stated that their Company has copies of my letters to you, including the very personal one I sent you from home on March 30, 1962, after the one I sent from the office on March 28th. I am appalled by this for many reasons, for the letters could only have come from you or Naomi, and I am also puzzled and depressed. On the legal level, Mr. Kaplan thinks that our only recourse is to sue you. All Macmillan has to do, he said, is to sit back and watch the fun. In this, he is mistaken, because our lawyers see the matter differently. However, I must get several matters straight before we proceed further. Since Macmillan has been provided with our documents, without our consent or knowledge, we feel that in fairness we are entitled to full information on their side. Legal fights are never very pleasant, but it's particularly unpleasant to be told to fight with one hand tied behind one's back, and to learn that one is in this position because of the action of one's friends. May I therefore request the following:

1) A list of all the correspondence between us made available to Macmillan.
2) Copies of all your correspondence with Macmillan.
3) Precise information as to the status of the book. Mr. Kaplan would not inform us how it stood. ("I'm not up on production schedules," he said.)
4) A set of proofs of the book, if this is possible and if it is indeed in proofs.
5) A copy of your Macmillan contract.

This material is essential if we are to proceed on an equal level with Macmillan on the legal path they seem to have chosen.

My puzzlement about this whole matter stems from my assumption that you wanted to clear the Macmillan matter up as a preliminary to solving our problems. I wrote you on May 13th last: "It seems to me that Naomi is the ideal solution for you. . . . I phoned her today specifically about the Macmillan problem, and she agrees that is where we should start." You replied on May 29th: "It was a comfort to get your letter and I am happy at the clarity it has brought into the situation." Perhaps I have simply not understood you. Mr. Kaplan stated that you told Macmillan you would destroy the manuscript you sent them, if they did not publish it. In other words, he implied that you have decided that Macmillan and Macmillan alone are to publish the book on prayer—not Farrar, Straus and not Doubleday and not anyone else. Can he be telling the truth?

I am sick at heart about the whole matter. I have certainly been at fault many times in our long editorial and publishing relationship. Perhaps I'm at fault again here—in insisting that the Macmillan matter be cleared up. Your letter of May 29th also said: "About Macmillan: I have written them that I felt it was my fault that I gave them a book which I did not have the right to give. . . . This leaves me in a position I do not quite understand, but Naomi says you will all try to work it out among you in New York. I certainly want to do whatever justice demands that I do." I never would have concluded from this that you and Naomi were providing Macmillan with what they consider ammunition, without telling me that this was so.

Perhaps you feel that Macmillan has a moral right to the book, as well as a legal one. You were approached by an editor of that firm who knew very well that Farrar, Straus was your publisher and had options on your work. This is the basis for our suit of damages against Macmillan. They are well aware of this, and their lawyers hope that instead we shall sue you. This we would never do, as they really know, but that is their "legal" position. It is ironic that the basis for their position is that I failed to give proper notice to you, when you decided to replace the book on peace they originally asked for (something I never understood until quite recently when Naomi told me) with a book on prayer.

I am sorry I have to request the data above, but I am doing so under new circumstances and in a situation which is now moving into a critical stage.

Yours ever,

Bob /s/

JULY 20, 1963

Dear Bob:

Your call yesterday was most helpful, and it has really thrown some light on the situation.[1] I hope that it will be possible to get the book PRAYER AS

WORSHIP AND EXPERIENCE back from Macmillan, and that in this way we can clear up our difficulty. I am sending you the Macmillan contract, in what seems to be a legible copy.

Recapitulating my position:

It is definitely my intention to withdraw this book from publication. I had already returned the advance and asked them to dissolve the contract and return the ms. They refused to do this, but we will try again, Fr. Abbot writing the letter next time.

I note from clause 2 that I have absolutely nothing to gain if Macmillan wins a lawsuit against Farrar, Straus over this book: it appears that, in effect, such a suit would be one between Farrar, Straus and the Abbey, and that we would be held to foot Macmillan's bill for all expenses, etc. Nice mess. I admit that today is the first time I have read this clause with any degree of understanding, and probably the first time I have read it at all. But I have never in any way done anything that I could construe as deliberately helping Macmillan to gain the advantage in litigation with you. They may, of course, without realizing it, have made shrewd use of things I have said, but I am sure that nothing in my letters gave them even a <u>basis</u> for reconstructing our correspondence, except the one point that I had not heard from you definitely, in a way that I could understand, about the exact nature of the obligation in which I found myself and which I was not meeting properly. I mean about the option on the book.

It certainly seems that our interests coincide in every way, at this point, and that you and I both want the book to be withdrawn. I hope that this can be brought about, and it will be a big relief if it can. The only question that remains is the possibility and advisability of letting Tom Burns publish the book in England. The last line of clause 1 seems to leave this open. I have no intention, of course, of letting the book get published in America after the termination of this contract.

So much for that. I don't see what other stand I could possibly take in this matter of conscience, with so many angles which I cannot understand.

I really want to get on with the Essay material, and am planning at least two books to be made out of this. One on the liturgy and the other on material that can be related to form a coherent whole. About the articles on peace and race, there may be difficulty: but I see no real reason why the articles already permitted for magazine publication on peace should now be stopped. But I had better not commit myself, because our censors are likely to do anything.

The main reason why I would like to have a list of the essays you have is that you may have something I have forgotten about and do not have here. This might help me to plan a better book. Otherwise, I can perfectly well go ahead with the material I have on file: but my files are not complete, I know, especially when we go back a couple of years.

I do hope we are finally getting out of this mess, Bob. I offered Mass for all of us who are involved in it this morning.

All best wishes always.

Most cordially in Christ,
[Thomas Merton]

1. In a letter to JL dated July 19, 1963, TM explained his views about this potential law suit: "Farrar Straus is still talking of suing Macmillan. I tried to get the [*Prayer as Worship and Experience*] ms. back from Macmillan and sent them their advance back, but no soap. I see no point publishing a book on prayer if everyone is dragging it through the courts. I can't get much sign of action out of Giroux, he won't answer questions or tell me what's next. I am supposed to do some more books for them, on contract, but don't get any cooperation. I am really fed up with them and want to get out. I suppose they realize this by now and want to do everything they can just to block me and hold everything back, simply by being inert."

JULY 24, 1963

Farrar, Straus & Company, Inc.
[Letterhead]
Robert Giroux
Editor-in-Chief

Rev. M. Louis, O.C.S.O.
Abbey of Our Lady of Gethsemani
Trappist, Kentucky

Dear Tom:

I'm most grateful to you for sending a copy of the contract, which has been of great help to our lawyers. They feel that the most immediate step is to proceed as you stated in your letter of July 20th, with Father Abbot sending the letter to Mr. Warren Sullivan. I know the enclosed wording sounds peremptory, but our lawyers insist that you must make it very clear that the book is not to be published, and that this is your and Father Abbot's idea, not someone else's. I'm sure Father Abbot will want to phrase the letter in his own way, but all the legal points here should be included and put to Macmillan as decisions, not requests. Be sure to send me a copy of the final letter! Our lawyers need them for their file.

With all good wishes.

Yours ever,
Bob /s/

AUGUST 2, 1963

WESTERN UNION
FATHER M. LOUIS
ABBEY OF GETHSEMANI
TRAPPIST, KENTUCKY

OUR LAWYERS URGENTLY NEED [A] COPY OF YOUR LETTER [TO]
MACMILLAN RETURNING [THE] ADVANCE [$5,000.00] AND COPIES
[OF] WARREN SULLIVAN['S] LETTERS TO YOU[.] BEST REGARDS[.]

BOB GIROUX

AUGUST 7, 1963

Dear Bob:
Your telegram reached me this morning. I am asking the Abbot's secretary to make the copies you want and insert them in this letter. I hope
Fr. Abbot already sent you copies of his letter returning the check. I have
had only one letter from Warren Sullivan.
I hope no one is in any doubts as to my very definite wish to withdraw
the book PRAYER AS WORSHIP AND EXPERIENCE from publication. I
have no intention of getting it published anywhere. I do not feel that it is
really a first-class book. But with the present difficulties about it, I have no
desire to see it in print.
I am not sure whether a piece of it is being printed in a small magazine, but in any case that was decided a long time ago and I think it was in
print before. I came to the conclusion that I did not want any of the book
printed anywhere.[1] I don't think this exception will make any difference.
I will check with the editor, but have been expecting copies of the magazine from day to day.
It has been fiercely hot here, at times. I am very busy; the postulants are
coming in and there are a lot of retreatants. I am sure we would all be very
happy if this affair could be settled once for all. I cannot understand why
Macmillan feels that the publication of this book is worth so much bother.
They know how I feel, and they know that I have good reason to be sick of
the whole business which is largely my fault; one would think that they
would be glad to let the book go. However, I have had no further contact
with them since we talked on the phone.
Best wishes always.

Most cordially yours in Christ,
[Thomas Merton]

1. Material from the third and fourth sections of *Prayer as Worship and Experience* was eventually included in TM, *The Climate of Monastic Prayer* (Spencer, MA: Cistercian Publications, 1969).

AUGUST 9, 1963

Farrar, Straus & Company, Inc.
[Letterhead]
Robert Giroux
Editor-in-Chief

Rev. M. Louis, O.C.S.O.
Abbey of Our Lady of Gethsemani
Trappist, Kentucky

Dear Tom:

I am most grateful for your letter of August 7th, enclosing Father Abbot's letter of July 27th to Warren Sullivan, along with Macmillan's letter of July 11th and your letter of July 3rd.

I am especially glad that you sent me the last, because as your version of what happened originally, it shows me why Macmillan are acting as they are. It also makes my head swim. How can you say, in view of my letter of March 28, 1962 that "somewhere along the line it would have been helpful if someone at Farrar, Straus had told me clearly what the problem was."

You do not seem to realize that your letter, in Macmillan's eyes, seems to them an encouragement from you to uphold their legal position, despite your statement that you do not intend to publish the book with any publisher. I am enclosing copies of the crucial correspondence during March 1962, on which our lawyers are resting our case. They are puzzled by the contradictions between what I wrote you, particularly the strictly "business" letter of March 28th, and your summary of July 3rd last. I simply don't understand how you can say you got no reaction from us. I am also sending Naomi a copy of this and all the other correspondence.

Our lawyers are most anxious to have a copy of Macmillan's reply to Father Abbot's letter of July 27th as soon as it arrives. On July 26th, Macmillan had their lawyers write us a letter which indicates that they intend to proceed with publication. I am sorry that you have been caught in the middle of this legal fight. In signing two contracts directly conflicting with each other, and in giving the second publisher reason to think that we not only had no objection but, in effect, had released you, it isn't too surprising that they are taking their assertive position. No one will be happier than I if Macmillan accepts Father Abbot's proposal. I wish our lawyers were more sanguine about the prospects of their doing so.

With kindest regards.

Yours ever,
Bob /s/

AUGUST 11, 1963

Abbey of Gethsemani
[Letterhead]

Dear Bob:

Well, thank heaven this Macmillan thing seems to have been settled. Father Abbot yesterday received a letter from Sullivan and I am sending you the copy they passed on to me. That looks pretty final, doesn't it? So I hope we are not going to have any more trouble about this.

I have been pretty busy the last week or two. There have been a lot of visitors of various kinds: Anglican priests, Benedictines from San Anselmo in Rome, and so on, all people that I have to deal with, so my time has gone into that and I haven't been able to think about work. But I would really like to get down to business on the essays that we, or at least I, have been talking so much about.

Naomi has been sick, I understand. Fr. Abbot has sent her a copy of the Macmillan letter and so I hope that will hasten her recovery, if she is not back on her feet already.

Best wishes to you always.

Most cordially yours in Christ,
Tom /s/

AUGUST 22, 1963

Abbey of Gethsemani
[Letterhead]

Dear Bob:

I wonder if you have any idea what happens to mail when it arrives in a Trappist monastery, for one of the monks. It is always opened by someone else, and it always passes through several hands before reaching the one to whom it is addressed. Sometimes, when the Superior is especially interested, it remains for a long time in his office. At times, it never reaches its destination at all, either through carelessness, or through some arbitrary or fantastic design.

Three or four times, at least, in my time here I have <u>known</u> of letters of very serious and urgent importance that have been withheld from me for one reason or another. How many scores of others have been withheld without my knowledge remains a mystery. I have also known fantastic problems to arise when mail has not reached other monks in certain cases. Only the other day, an important letter from Ed Rice failed to reach me and "nobody had seen it."

It does not seem to me that your letter of March 28, 1962, an important letter if ever there was one, would have been withheld from me by design.

Doubtless, it was only some accident. But whatever the cause may have been, this letter never reached me until I received your copy along with the others you sent August 9th.

The copy of my letter of April 3, 1962, is obviously concerned with your letter of March 30th of that year, and it is clear—or should be once one has the whole picture—that my paragraphs about the Macmillan book (at the time the peace book, not the one on prayer) were written in total innocence of your official decision, which I had never seen. I speak, for example, of thinking seriously of your "suggestion" which refers obviously to the second paragraph of your letter of March 30, which I was interpreting as friendly advice, and which I could not possibly understand correctly not having the background of the other letter. Bob, it would have been simply insane for me to try to push through the Macmillan project if I had received your letter of March 28th. What on earth would have been the point, even if I had wanted to? Nothing could possibly have come of it, since I was, according to that decision, unable to move. This I did not know, and all the trouble goes back to the fact that I never received this letter.

I think this finally clears up the enigma of the bind we have got into over this book. It is perfectly clear to me now that you could not possibly understand my reactions and letters, and my attempts to act independently with the book I offered Macmillan later that summer. I was convinced I was still clear and in a position to do this.

However, the whole thing is fortunately settled by Warren Sullivan's acceptance of my demand that the manuscript be returned. If it has been returned, I do not know. It may be withheld from me. But in any case, that is the situation.

In the monastic life, one is accustomed to receiving a series of mild, aimless and rather absurd kicks in the teeth, and the vow of obedience with its attendant graces does something to make the blows less important. It is sickening to me, though, to learn (as I not infrequently do) that the fallout has entered the lives of some of my friends, through no fault of theirs or mine. I am very, very sorry that you have had the privilege of participating in one of my professional monastic traumas. I hope it will never happen again.

With all best wishes.

In cordial friendship in Christ,
Tom /s/

SEPTEMBER 6, 1963

Rev. M. Louis, O.C.S.O.
Abbey of Our Lady of Gethsemani
Trappist, Kentucky

Dear Tom:

I always seem to be away when important letters come; this time I was brought low by a bad virus which really hung on, but I have now pulled out of it. I was very much cheered by the fine news that Macmillan is returning the book to you, and even more by getting to the source of what to me was a very perplexing and depressing problem. I suspected something of this sort when Naomi came back from her visit to you and asked me why this firm hadn't taken a clear and unambiguous position when you first raised the question. I told her that our business letter could not have been clearer, even though my personal letter displayed more complicated feelings. She said she had seen the correspondence and could remember no business letter and this is when I began to wonder if perhaps it had never reached you. For some reason, I was under the impression that our correspondence had special treatment and was given expedited handling because it involved writing and editorial problems, which are certainly an important aspect of your vocation. Apparently, I have been wrong. Although the loss of this letter is a mystery to me, it is a great relief to know about it and it explains many things which have hitherto baffled me. I feel as if a great cloud has been lifted and I hope we can have a mutually happy and productive future.

I am completing the list of essays, which I will get off to you just as soon as I return to the office.

With kindest personal regards.

Yours ever,
[Robert Giroux]

FEBRUARY 7, 1964

Farrar, Straus & Company, Inc.
[Letterhead]
Robert Giroux
Editor-in-Chief

Rev. M. Louis, O.C.S.O.
Abbey of Gethsemani
Trappist, Kentucky

Dear Tom:

I was delighted that Naomi forwarded the two manuscripts, and I'm happy to report that we have decided to go ahead with one of them this fall—that on the Negro problem and the bomb. In searching for a title which would cover both topics, we have come up with SEEDS OF DE-STRUCTION. The trouble with your proposed title is that we have just brought out a book called THE COLD WAR AND THE INCOME TAX by Edmund Wilson and we don't feel too happy about following with THE COLD WAR AND THE BLACK REVOLUTION. Everyone likes SEEDS OF DESTRUCTION not only for itself but as a contrast and echo of SEEDS OF CONTEMPLATION. Please let me know if this new title meets with your approval.

On ART AND WORSHIP, I would like, with your permission, to work with Eloise Spaeth at this end. If she takes on the art job, it might mean the splitting and sharing of royalties, but I won't put this matter to you and Naomi formally until Eloise makes up her mind about going ahead with it.

I am happy beyond words to have a book of yours on our forthcoming list. It has been much too long between books and I hope to have proofs for you in the coming weeks.

With warmest personal regards.

Yours ever,
Bob /s/

P.S. Hope you've received paperback edition (NAL) of The New Man, which I sent you.

FEBRUARY 10, 1964

Abbey of Gethsemani
[Letterhead]

Dear Bob:

Your letter of the 7th reached me this morning. I am very glad you are going right ahead with setting up SEEDS OF DESTRUCTION. I like the title and as soon as Naomi mentioned it, I got the interesting resonances set up between it and Seeds of Contemplation. Good!

As I wrote Naomi on Saturday, there is no censorship problem. The Letters in the last section have not received formal approval, but I know unofficially that the censor is passing them. That probably goes for the preface too. The other pieces have all been printed before with approval. By the way, you will need to know the magazines where each thing appeared.

Black Revolution was in Ramparts [actually published in *New Blackfriars* (November–December 1963)]
Tucker Caliban in Jubilee [September 1963]
The first Nuclear War essay, Commonweal [February 9, 1962]
The second, Jubilee [May 1962]
The Third, Blackfriars, (England) [June 1962]

I don't remember the precise titles of the war essays; they have changed so often.

When Eloise Spaeth came down here she had a lot of fine ideas about illustrations and as I am completely paralyzed when it comes to getting around and gathering up that kind of material, I think the only way to do the illustrations properly is to have someone like her handle them. I would just like to suggest a few at this end. She probably remembers which ideas I was most attached to. I have a couple of new things I want to get hold of too: some Shaker prints, for instance. So I do hope she will be willing to help out on this end of the book. I will be most grateful and, of course, I want to split royalties and have her as co-author to the extent that this is acceptable to you. I mean, making it clear what part of the book is hers.

We are working on the Liturgy book here, typing it up, and I will get it to you through Naomi perhaps around Easter, maybe before. In my opinion, this should wait until after the Art book, which is aimed at the chapters on art in the [Second Vatican] Council Constitution on [the Sacred] Liturgy. I should rather say focused on those chapters.

Thanks for the New Man in the Mentor edition. It is very nicely done, and I am glad the book is in paperback now. I had been wondering about that. Has anyone taken the reprint rights on Disputed Questions? Returning to the New Man, I am afraid the cover doesn't get the idea at all, but I don't think there is any point in making a fuss about it or remarking on it (as a matter of fact, some of the Mentor Omega covers have been simply awful. I am glad my book came out better than Karl Adam's Christ of Faith).

With best wishes always.

Ever cordially in Christ,
Tom /s/

MARCH 5, 1964

Abbey of Gethsemani
[Letterhead]

Dear Bob:

As you remember, in writing from time to time about the material in SEEDS OF DESTRUCTION, I have been trying to make adequate guesses about the possibility of a hitch with the censors. My only worry was with the "Letters," but these have been cleared and can be used. That is quite definite.

If I did wonder at all about the three articles on peace, I did not have really serious worries about them, since they had, after all, been approved and published once in magazines and hitherto I have always understood it to be the regular practice that once a thing has been published it can be published again. Unfortunately, the new Abbot General, in a decision which seems to me completely arbitrary and unjust, has prohibited the publication of these articles in any form, and they must, he says, be taken out of the book.[1]

This, coming on top of all the trouble we have had in the past year or so about various problems, is something I find quite crushing and not for myself particularly, but also for you. This means another material injustice which you have to suffer in your dealings with us here. This is absolutely sickening: and I suppose that after the fact I can say that I could have been "more prudent," but, at the same time, I wonder how prudent does a wretched Christian have to be in dealing with the arbitrary fantasies of his canonical superiors. I won't go into this any more, as I might say a few things that would fall short of the temperance expected (how reasonably?) of a monk. Needless to say that I am sorry. I have said that so much that it probably sounds a bit hollow to Farrar, Straus & Co. by this time. I honestly don't think that I took an unreasonable risk in this matter, but perhaps I did.

Cutting out so many pages will seriously hurt the book, but perhaps it may be possible to make the following substitution.

The long introduction I wrote to the Letters of Father [Alfred] Delp [S.J.], published by Herder & Herder, can stand by itself, and though it is a clumsy way to go about it, I think it can replace the material that is lost to us now. In fact, it is a better piece of writing, I think, and has not become as dated as those essays of 1962. In a way, this might even be better. I will mail a copy of the Delp book to you immediately, and if you like it, I will send another copy and will also make sure that this is not suddenly *verboten*, but really it cannot be as there was no controversy about this piece with the censors—since I had the good sense to get it censored in England.

This essay on Delp was published in their Magazine Continuum with a rather good title, "Spirituality for the Age of Overkill." I think the essay with this title would fill the bill, and I hope you think so too. As for Herder & Herder, I am sure I can persuade them to let us have this.

I hope that we can iron this one out. Naturally, the expense of setting up the section on war devolves upon the monastery.

One piece of good news: ART AND WORSHIP has been passed by the censors. There are a couple of very minor corrections.

Best wishes always,

Tom /s/

P.S. I am pretty certain I could also add quite a few pages to the "Letters" without objections on the part of the censors who passed them—these two are on my side.[2] Should I try this?

---

1. Dom Ignace Gillet, O.C.S.O., served as abbot general from January 16, 1964, until after TM's death.
2. Reference is to "Letters in a Time of Crisis," part 3 of *Seeds of Destruction*.

Rev. M. Louis, O.C.S.O.
Abbey of Gethsemani
Trappist, Kentucky

Dear Tom:

Naomi phoned me yesterday and I was prepared for the shock, but I do think it is awfully unjust and shortsighted on the part of the Abbot General to suppress the chapters on peace.

We are particularly concerned here for several reasons:

1. In good faith, we submitted the book to the Thomas More Book Club and they have taken it as their June selection <u>with</u> the peace chapters, of course.

2. The entire book has been set up in type. Proofs will soon reach us from the printer and, of course, I will send your copies to you.

3. If a dependable house with a distinguished Catholic list thinks the book is publishable, and if an outstanding Catholic book club with a wide membership feels that it merits selection, should not these two factors be part of the Abbot General's consideration?

4. I cannot help remembering that the very same action was taken on "The Sign of Jonas." The Abbot General [Dom Gabriel Sortais, O.C.S.O.], at that time, ruled that the book was not to be published, even though it was already set up in type. After Jacques Maritain wrote a letter in French, the decision was reversed. I can't help thinking that common sense and further consideration might not work in the same way once again.

Would it be of any point for us, as a publisher, to address a petition to the Abbot General directly? If it were simply a matter of our considering a manuscript about which there were some question of censorship still unresolved, I would not feel that we had the right to question the Abbot General's decision, but, under these circumstances, when the material had gone so far beyond that stage, into print, and read by qualified judges of a fine Catholic book club, it seems to me that these facts ought at least to be made known to the authorities. I do hope that further consideration will be given to the matter and again I cannot help feeling that the French language is somehow a crucial matter here. (Americans are such barbarians and don't really understand what it's all about.)

With kindest regards.

Yours ever,
[Robert Giroux]

MARCH 11, 1964

Abbey of Gethsemani
[Letterhead]

Dear Bob:

Thanks for your letter, which I received this morning. Since I last wrote to you, I think I have worked out the real reason for the misunderstanding with the Abbot General. I had asked the old Abbot General for permission to publish a book on peace which, I told him, was based on three articles on peace, with rewriting + additions, which he had allowed me to publish in magazines. He refused permission for this book. This is on file, and the present Abbot General thought it meant that the republication of these three articles was forbidden, which may well have been the mind of the former General, Dom Gabriel Sortais. I, on the other hand, thought that since the three articles had been permitted once, I would be able to republish them as long as I did not change anything. This is the misunderstanding. I have written to the General explaining this and apologizing in case I myself was at fault.

There is certainly no reason why you should not write to him, though I do not hold out much hope. As to the fact that this material is in print, he will say that, as far as a matter of justice is concerned, this can be taken care of by our Abbey paying the bill for what is suppressed. He can say this without a tremor as we will be the ones to pay. So this argument will not move him.

On the other hand, it seems to me, looking at it objectively, that one could advance the following: the harm that will supposedly be done by the publication of articles of this nature by me has already been "done" since the articles have been published in magazine form. Is it then worth while to go to such great trouble to prevent their republication? Is their republication really such an evil? If it were a question of a new book with entirely new material, I could see their objection. But since this material is thought by you to be worth while and by the Book Club and so on, and since from the expressed point of view of the Abbot General the harm to be avoided is the impression that a monk is interested in war and peace, and since this impression already exists anyway, is it really not out of all proportion to suppress material already set up in type, bought by the Book Club, etc.?

One must, however, avoid the impression that his arm is being twisted or that something has been put over on him. He is new in authority, probably a little touchy about his authority, and apparently has a reputation of being scrupulous and extra prudent, in other words, afraid of making mistakes and lowering the august front of the Order, losing face in a word. This should be taken into account.

On the other hand, just thinking out loud, I wonder if it would not be better to try and replace these articles with something else? Of course, the problem is that the something else cannot be about war and peace. Except in so far as it is touched on in the Delp article, which has some punch, and is probably better than the others.

My solution would be to propose a compromise: ask him if the material that must be replaced could not be replaced as follows: one of the three war articles was originally passed by the censor without any difficulty. This is the one called Christian Ethics and World Crisis (was censored under this name, for Blackfriars is the third of the three).* We could drop the two other peace articles to which he objects. Replace them with the Preface to Prison Meditations of Fr. Delp (passed without difficulty). Perhaps in the circumstances The Book Club might agree. I think the General might buy this. Résumé: instead of the Three Peace articles, drop two of these, keep the third, Christian Ethics and World Crisis (about which no difficulties were raised by the censor in the first place, and which no one has ever criticized) and then the Delp piece, which has been very favorably received. To fill up the other space, I could send more letters for the Letter section and, in fact, these are already being typed.

It seems to me that this solution has the advantage of being face saving for him, as well as feasible. I admit that the first Peace essay has a lot of directness and punch, but then I have added footnotes from [the encyclical of Pope John XXIII] Pacem in Terris [*Peace on Earth*] and I think that if we kept it, these would probably have to go to maintain the position that "nothing has been added."

I think that if you write to him in this form and with a lot of tact, he might be willing to consider it, since it is a question of material that has already been published anyway. I think, above all, that if you drop two of the articles which the censors objected to, though other censors permitted them eventually, he would let down his guard a little. The point is that the material has to be replaced because of the Book Club, and the material we are suggesting is entirely unobjectionable from all points of view.

I hope this will be a solution.

Please let me know what you think. The General is:

Reverendissime Père Dom Ignace Gillet, O.C.S.O.
Monte Cistello,
Via Laurentina, 471, Rome, EUR[OPE] Italy

Best wishes always, and I will pray over this.

Ever yours in Christ,
Tom /s/

P.S. The essay Christian Ethics and World Crisis has been published only in England, and that is an added argument, as it might well be made known in America. (In case he says, "Well, it has been published once, why publish it again?") A repeat, to clarify the point about his objection.

He objects that I should not write about war and peace because it is a kind of scandal for a contemplative monk to be known to follow world events. But, for better or worse, this is already well known and the re-publication of known articles will not in any way create a new impression.[1] On the other hand, you might say that we all understand, of course, that I had to write no new material on the subject.

*We could possibly use this one.

1. On March 21, 1964, Abbot Fox wrote to RG acknowledging FSC's dilemma, as well as offering several solutions of his own. Behind the scenes, the abbot and TM had worked together to get the book approved by the abbot general by omitting the essays on nuclear war, so that the finished book would include three parts: (1) an introduction already approved by the abbot general; (2) "Black Revolution: Letters to a White Liberal"; and (3) "Letters in Time of Crisis." The abbot then suggested lengthening the "Letters" and writing again to the abbot general asking that two essays, previously approved, might be added to the book: "Christian Action in World Crisis" and the preface to "Meditations of Father Delp." The problem the abbot was having with obtaining the permission from the abbot general to publish certain essays vexed TM greatly, as he wrote in a letter to NB dated March 13, 1964: "I am always grumbling about solitude and this is one of the forms it takes in my own life: a progressive alienation from people with whom normally I ought to live in perfect understanding and agreement. Having to get along without too much support in an area where no one is either very sympathetic or very interested in my ideas. Above all, it means having to figure things out in a somewhat long and insecure way, and this brings out the fact that I have always been more dependent than I realized. But, at the same time, that being 'dependent' is just totally useless and even dishonest in this kind of situation. The next result is having to face things alone before God and hope for the best, and to go on with this even though other people may not quite like it or understand it. . . . But there is only one answer, that is to get my own Cross on my shoulder and carry it, whether others think I am making sense or being heroic, etc., etc., or not."

MARCH 24, 1964

Abbey of Gethsemani
[Letterhead]

Dear Bob:

This may not be the smartest thing to do, but I am returning the corrected galleys minus the articles on war. You will see that I have added a great deal to the section of letters, and this has a twofold purpose: to liven up the book as well as replace some of the material that had to go, and also to introduce variety that will give the book a broader perspective and thus, I hope, placate the Superiors.

I am a little worried at the possible reaction to your request, but if you have asked for what I suggested there cannot be reasonable objections at least to the asking. They may or may not grant what you want. It is unfortunate that they should get the impression that I am trying to force something they do not want. This might mean a notable lack of cooperation on their part on the next book. The trouble is that the secretary of the previous General is still in there and is at once very officious and inclined to suspicion. So this does not make things any easier.

At the same time, though the articles on nuclear war might arouse attention, they have the disadvantage of being out of date, and as I look over them I find them quite superficial.

In any event, I hope that we can come up with a reasonable solution. With best Easter wishes.

> Cordially yours in Christ,
> Tom /s/

MAY 28, 1964

> Abbey of Gethsemani
> [Letterhead]

Dear Bob:

Some time ago, I sent Naomi two new pieces to replace the matter that we were not able to publish in SEEDS OF DESTRUCTION. One of these was the result of a considerable amount of rewriting and new thinking, as you will note if you happened to read the piece "Monk in the Diaspora" in Commonweal [March 20, 1964].

The main purpose of this letter is to say that I have heard unofficially from the censors that this material is passed and approved, with a slight change asked for which is entirely accidental. Under normal circumstances, I would announce this as definitive good news; however, before we finally take this as the solution, perhaps the official word should come from Rome, and I expect it will quite soon.[1]

As this material is not about war, it may affect the title you chose. If so, perhaps we might reconsider it, in terms of some such title as SEEDS OF CHANGE or even SEEDS OF REVOLUTION. That's a nice hot one.

I still personally believe that the book would be much helped if we could include the piece on Fr. Delp. I know this has already appeared elsewhere, but has not been too widely read and, in any event, if there is question of money, I would be glad to pay for it out of my own royalties. I do believe this inclusion would be a help. Furthermore, it has been explicitly permitted and in very friendly terms by the new Abbot General.

You will remember I also sent some extra letters when I returned the galleys. With all this, there is now somewhat more material than we had in the first version, and it has involved quite a lot of work.

Hoping you are well, and wishing you all the best.

> Cordially yours in Christ,
> Tom /s/

1. In a letter dated May 15, 1964, RG wrote in English to the abbot general asking that the essay "Christian Action in World Crisis" be included in *Seeds of Destruction*. The abbot general replied to RG, in a letter in French dated May 27, 1964, stating that he would not authorize the publication of this essay in *Seeds of Destruction*, and certainly not in the form in which it appeared in England, unless it was revised and reevaluated. Once the essay was revised, the abbot general finally gave his approval on July 21, 1964.

JUNE 8, 1964

Abbey of Gethsemani
[Letterhead]

Dear Bob:

The letter from the General to Dom James is not exactly what I would call a new magna carta of tolerance, etc. I am told that it is all right in this case for me to write about peace, provided I don't deal with nuclear war. This calls for some interesting acrobatics, which I am currently trying to perform.

It also affects your title, again. There is not going to be much about destruction in this revamped article, but it will be all right as an article. However, to get the original idea in, I think really the best idea would be to include the Delp piece, as I suggested before. This is one of the things with which I am myself most satisfied and it really belongs in this book to make it the fullest statement of what I have to say on this whole subject. And the difficulties are not too great. I do hope you will go along with me on this.

The new material ought to reach you in a couple of weeks. It is beginning to get hot here, and I am glad to get this out of the way before the real heat sets in.

Best wishes always in Christ,
Tom /s/

P.S. I found a copy of the Gandhi article in case you did not get one from Naomi.[1] I forgot the most important thing. Will you please let me have the "Monk in Diaspora" piece back? Someone wants me to contribute to a kind of *Festschrift* volume for Fr. [George] Ford and this piece will do nicely for it. I don't know who is publishing it. I hope this is ok with you.

1. TM, "Gandhi, the Gentle Revolutionary," *Ramparts*, December 1964, 29–32.

JUNE 19, 1964

Rev. M. Louis, O.C.S.O.
Abbey of Gethsemani
Trappist, Kentucky

Dear Tom:

Is it agreeable to you to change the title of "The Monk in the Diaspora" to "The Christian in the Diaspora"? That is really a more accurate title, and, of course, part two of the essay bears the original heading anyway. Our reason for wanting to do this is to give the essay more general application, as indeed it certainly has. I think it's excellent, and so is the tribute to Gandhi, which I now have.

We want to retain the book's title, SEEDS OF DESTRUCTION, too. It is written in a period of crisis, and discusses various aspects of it, negative and positive, including the black revolution. It seems to me the title is more than justified. We do not want to include the preface to the Father Delp book, for the simple reason that it has already been published in book form. The Thomas More Book Club people also are justified in their objection to it on sound grounds.

We would object to your printing the "Diaspora" piece in the Father Ford book if it appeared before SEEDS OF DESTRUCTION appeared. Surely, we have the first moral claim on this article, after the mess we've got into with this book. Here we are in galley proofs for months, one-third of which have to be destroyed, still trying to bring the book to completion. All honor to Father Ford, whom I admire greatly and who is a great personal friend of Roger Straus, as he was of his father. But the publisher of that book should know we are using it in a book this fall or maybe January (we hope). The only way to keep this item from becoming a tearing headache for everybody is to direct the editor of the Father Ford book to write me personally. I'll work out the dates with him, but you should let him know that first publication by us is a necessary condition because of our contract.

I'll send a copy of the essay directly to him after we work out the date bit, with other technical details like credit line, etc. OK? And I assume the new title is OK for that volume too.

What about the Blackfriars' article? Have you been able to double-write it, as [George] Orwell might say? As soon as we get the approved version, I believe we have a book and can go into pages—that is, provided the "Diaspora" and "Gandhi" pieces have been censored and passed. Are these clear, and the additional letters?

We're raring to go with the book. The whole thing is becoming Orwellian. We have a jacket (enclosed) for a book that does not exist (blurb written to cover all eventualities). We even have a review (Library Journal) of a book that will never be published! The reason is that galley proofs always go to the Library Journal. I enclose a copy for your memory book.

I met Bishop [Ernest John] Primeau of New Hampshire the other night with a group of laymen, and he was great. If there were more Council Fathers like him, what a wonderful session the next one would be!

With warmest regards.

Yours ever,
[Robert Giroux]

P.S. I sent you Xavier Rynne's THE SECOND SESSION and Michael Serafian's THE PILGRIM by separate cover. Also Carlos Fuentes' THE DEATH OF ARTEMIO CRUZ.

JUNE 19, 1964

Abbey of Gethsemani
[Letterhead]

Dear Bob:

Here is the new material ["The Christian in World Crisis"] for the book (*Seeds of Destruction*). What I have done is really a compilation of a lot of material from the ms. of the peace book, which I was not allowed to publish, with a commentary on Pacem in Terris, which I have now written. I think it all works together pretty well, but it remains to be seen to what extent it meets the not-too-precise standards set by the Abbot General. I have a feeling that he ought to let most of it through, but that he might want to cut a few paragraphs and, perhaps, demand a lot of corrections of detail. We shall see. Meanwhile, I am sending the stuff to you, so that you will have it.

I hope this is the last of the trouble with this particular book. How are you? The hot weather has finally begun in earnest down here, and it has been pretty sticky. One expects that in June, in Kentucky.

Best wishes always.

Most cordially always in Christ,
Tom /s/

JUNE 22, 1964

Abbey of Gethsemani
[Letterhead]

Dear Bob:

Today you should be receiving that long rewritten essay on peace, which I hope will get by the General all right. It is a shame the Delp piece cannot fit in, but I understand your objections. I was hoping an exception could be made, because it really fits the theme of the book. However, that is your affair. I certainly go along with your judgment.

I would not have suggested the Monk in the Diaspora for the Fr. Ford book at all, if I had not got the impression that you did not want it in this book. However, I have not heard from the editor of the Fr. Ford book about it either. Naturally, the objection works both ways, because if it appears first in this one, it is less of a tribute to Fr. Ford. However, you certainly have a right to it if you want it. And if you want to change the title, that is quite all right with me.

The editor of the Fr. Ford collection is no pro as far as I can gather, but a seminarian. His name is Vincent McGee, and his address is 501 West 122nd St., N.Y. By all means, contact him and find out what is going on. I have no idea who his publisher is, or if he has one yet. It would simplify matters if you were the publisher, I must say! However, that, too, is something I don't know about. I will, in any case, write to him about the essay.

On censorship: Monk in Diaspora and Tribute to Gandhi are both approved by the censors. So are the Letters and the Black Revolution. One thing remains, the long essay on peace, Christian in Crisis. This is not yet approved by the General.

I am happy with the jacket, and the all-purpose blurb and the review of the book that wasn't.

Someone suggested that I ought to send the enclosed poem ["Picture of a Negro Child with a White Doll"] to Commentary (a magazine for which I have the highest respect) and I would like to. Since you have a friend there ([Norman] Podhoretz?), I thought I would send the poem along to you to see what you think about it.

Hope we are going to soon be out of the woods with this book, and able to move on with the others. Any news on ART AND WORSHIP?

All the best always, in Christ,
Tom /s/

JUNE 23, 1964

Rev. M. Louis, O.C.S.O.
Abbey of Our Lady of Gethsemani
Trappist, Kentucky

Dear Tom:

Many thanks for the long essay, which arrived yesterday, and for your letter of the 22nd, which has just come in. I think the essay is splendid and I hope that Father General gives it his blessing. By using <u>Pacem in Terris</u> as the framework, you certainly provided him with a very good reason to approve it.

I think it would be a mistake, however, to send the long essay to the printer before you have approval. Don't you agree?

I can't really send back the proofs until this matter is solved, because the paging of the whole book would be affected by an essay of this length. Since the Gandhi, the Letter, the Black Revolution, and the Diaspora are all approved, this essay is the last lap of a very long race. I will await your further word, and I know you will let me have it as soon as you hear from France.

I am writing to Vincent McGee today and will try to straighten out the matter of the essay in the Father Ford book. I sent the poem, which I liked very much, to Commentary. Eloise Spaeth is writing a report on ART AND WORSHIP and I will get back to you as soon as I have it.

With all good wishes.

Yours ever,
[Robert Giroux]

P. S. Just arrived: next Sunday's cover review of the New York Times Book Review [reviews of four books on the Second Vatican Council].

JUNE 25, 1964

Abbey of Gethsemani
[Letterhead]

Dear Bob:

Your letter came this morning, many thanks. I do not expect an answer from the General for a couple of weeks, at least. It would be madness to send the peace essay to the printer before that. By all means, let us be cautious. I quite agree.

W.H. Ferry of the Center for Study of Democratic Institutions, has seen the peace essay and when it is cleared would like to use it in a pamphlet, or rather part of it. I told him he could if it were ok with you and on your terms, and will see that he gets in touch with you if and when the material is cleared.[1]

The Gandhi piece is to appear in Ramparts, by the way. I forgot to tell you this. Some of the Letters will be in Motive, a Protestant magazine, Nashville. And some may be in the Critic; they have asked for some. I assume this is all to the good.

I have also forgotten to send you a quote from St. Paul that makes a good impression on a title page of a book like this, no? Here it is:

What if God, desiring to show His wrath and make known His power, has endured with much patience the vessels of wrath?

(Romans 11:22)

Food for thought, hah? At least, I think so.

Many thanks for sending the poem over to Commentary. I hope they will like it.

Best wishes always, in Christ,
Tom /s/

1. Wilbur Hugh Ferry collected TM's letters to him in *Letters from Tom* (Scarsdale, NY: Fort Hill Press, 1968).

JUNE 29, 1964

Rev. M. Louis, O.C.S.O.
Abbey of Gethsemani
Trappist, Kentucky

Dear Tom:

I can't imagine a better epigraph for the book than the quote from St. Paul. We'll put it either on the title page or opposite.

As long as Mr. Ferry of the Center for Study of Democratic Institutions gets formal release, publishes after book is out, and runs credit line stating the peace essay is from SEEDS OF DESTRUCTION, there's no problem. But, of course, this won't happen unless he writes me and we arrange matters between us.

Fine about Ramparts, Motive and The Critic, but please tell them to say the pieces are part of your forthcoming book, SEEDS OF DESTRUCTION, to be published by us.

Vincent McGee phoned and said they were <u>not</u> going to use the Diaspora piece now. He thinks he may persuade Father Ford to compile a book of his own writings. I endorsed the idea, and told him if Columbia University Press doesn't take it, we would.

I haven't yet heard from Commentary and will let you know at once. I hope the General releases the peace essay promptly.

With kindest personal regards.

Yours ever,
[Robert Giroux]

JULY 1, 1964

Abbey of Gethsemani
[Letterhead]

Dear Bob:

First of all, I am very grateful for the new books. I have started immediately on [Michael] Serafian and find it really brilliant, more exciting than anything I have read on the Council because it not only informs but interprets in depth. And I think he is very sound and judicious; he strikes me as being always on target and usually on the bull's eye. It is every bit as good as [Hans] Küng's first book (I haven't read the others).

What it really brings out is the crisis of authority resulting from the crisis of judgment in the Church. And how like this is to the same kind of crisis in the South: ruthless and blind attachment to a mystique that has lost its root in reality, willingness to sacrifice any value, even order itself, in the name of "Order," which has ceased to have genuine justification in life. There is going to be a really fantastic crisis of authority in religious, clerical and lay life in these next years if the curial types don't wake up and let go. The fact that managers are beginning to get a bit scared and a bit less absolute is not really going to help very much.

This book is very important, because so much of the writing about the Council has been tinged with a superficial optimism (or a rather aimless combativity) and has not really come to grips with the basic issue. It is true that things of fundamental importance have come up in the Council and great statements have been made: but the accomplishment so far is trivial. This must be faced. People are going around under the impression that the whole Church has really moved into the new era just because a few exceptional men like [Cardinal Augustin] Bea [S.J.] have done so.

Turning to business: McGee is sending you his text of the Monk-Diaspora, which is the complete text and the one you should use, as I do not think you have this text already. I believe it was revised since I sent it to you first.

No news from the General yet.

One more point: I hesitate to bother you. It amounts to a request for a favor, if possible. Though the publication of pictures of monks is now tolerated, still there exists a statute which says pictures are not to be printed in connection with the promotion of books. As this involves at best a dozen members of the Order and chiefly me, I think it would be well for me to comply, especially as the publication of my picture is distasteful to me personally. I know you have had the plate made, but if it is killed I think I can get Fr. Abbot to cover the expense. Do you mind very much? I would be happier if the awful image were not there.

All best wishes in Christ, always, and thanks again for the books.

Tom /s/

JULY 2, 1964

Rev. M. Louis, O.C.S.O.
Abbey of Gethsemani
Trappist, Kentucky

Dear Tom:
Too bad about <u>Commentary</u>. I enclose the note from their editor.
I would now like to try the New York Review of Books. It's a long shot, but it has an influential circulation and is very much "in." I'll let you know what they do.

Yours ever,
[Robert Giroux]

JULY 5 [1964]

Our Lady of Gethsemani
[Letterhead]

Dear Bob:
Still no news from the General.
Meanwhile, the Civil Rights law calls for an addition to the <u>Black Revolution</u>—herewith enclosed. It will bring everything up to date. Should it be called "Prologue" or something formal like that? Maybe. You decide.
As usual, delays + obstacles are making this a better book—I hope!
All the best.

In Xt,
Tom /s/

JULY 7, 1964

Rev. M. Louis, O.C.S.O.
Abbey of Gethsemani
Trappist, Kentucky

Dear Tom:
I thank you for your good words about the Serafian book. I wish some of the reviews had your perception of its quality and importance. Even

Wilfrid Sheed sneered at it as "turgid" and "unreliable," though it seems to me so obviously well-informed.

I hope you have seen the latest issue of <u>Commonweal</u>. The whole issue is devoted to Los Angeles—that scandal of the Catholic world. If their Cardinal [James Francis McIntyre] considers integration not a moral issue but a political one, that is odd thinking for a prelate and one can say he is wrong-headed. But when he forbids his priests to speak on this subject, that is a scandal.

Vincent McGee sent me your revision for "The Monk and the Diaspora" and I will see that this version is used.

If you will be happier without the photo on the back of the book, we shall drop it. Actually, it has a great deal of character and, to judge from comments around the office, strikes readers as impressive. However, I should have asked your permission before going ahead, and if this is your final word, we shall drop it. This adds one more item to the Orwellian side-effects of the book!

With kindest personal regards.

Yours ever,
[Robert Giroux]

P.S. Your new introduction just came in, and I'm delighted. It "up-dates" everything. I hope we soon hear from the General and can finally publish.

JULY 14, 1964

WESTERN UNION
ROBERT GIROUX
FARRAR STRAUS CO
19 UNION SQUARE WEST NYK

PEACE ESSAY FULLY APPROVED[.] NO CHANGES[.] NO FURTHER DELAY.

TOM MERTON

JULY 27, 1964

Abbey of Gethsemani
[Letterhead]

Dear Bob:

This is just a note to say that the official date for the imprimi potest is July 21, 1964. I think you have the names. Or don't you? It seems to me that actually the only name that should be printed, from the Order, is Dom Ignace Gillet, O.C.S.O., Abbé Général (or Dom Ignatius Gillet, Abbas Generalis).

There have been too many other censors on all the other articles. Too many by far, and few deserve commemoration. Except Frs. Paul [Bourne, O.C.S.O.] and Charles [English, O.C.S.O.], but they are not the only ones; there were others I have forgotten and can't track down.

[Senator Barry] Goldwater got it, then. He presents no special problem to me, as there is no question whatever in my mind that it would be a gross infidelity to the Christian conscience to vote for him.[1] Unfortunately, this is perhaps not known to the majority of Catholics. I suspect that he will get more votes than people have anticipated. There are enough nuts in the country to put him in the white house, but some of them will perhaps be distracted by other issues and concerns. As for [President Lyndon Baines] Johnson, I can't say I am too keen on his policies either, at least foreign. I don't see how I can vote for him. Is there anybody else around, besides prohibitionists and American Nazis?

The other day I sent Naomi the Liturgy book, so you should have it soon. I have seen the galleys of her own book [*More Than Sentinels*], incidentally, and it is, of course, interesting if only because we are all in it, but I think it is a good book in its own right too.

Best wishes always, in Christ,
Tom /s/

P.S. Did anything come of the poem? If you let me have it back, I can always end up sending it somewhere like Commonweal.

1. In a short note dated July 15, 1964, RG, who likewise opposed the nomination of Senator Goldwater, thanked TM for informing him of the abbot general's permission to allow the essay on peace to be published.

JULY 30, 1964

Farrar, Straus & Company, Inc.
[Letterhead]
Robert Giroux
Editor-in-Chief

Rev. M. Louis, O.C.S.O.
Abbey of Gethsemani
Trappist, Kentucky

Dear Tom:
Many thanks for yours of the 27th with the official date for the imprimi potest. Corrected proofs had already gone back with the old date, and we'll change it to the new one on the page proofs. I suppose we will have to send a new copy to the censor here in New York. As you know, we received the imprimatur on the galley proofs; I shall explain the changes to them and ask for a new date from them.

Your poem is still at the New York Review of Books and I have not heard from them. If they don't take it, I would like to send it to the <u>Atlantic Monthly</u> or <u>Harper's</u>, or do you consider them too stuffy?

I'm delighted to hear about the Liturgy book and look forward to receiving it from Naomi. I'm writing her about her own book which is very interesting to me for the reason you state, though I somehow feel it might have been more interesting.*

I think you're absolutely right about a big Goldwater vote. I can't believe, however, that it will be big enough to make him President. The thought of becoming an expatriate had never entered my mind until the Republican Convention; now I can understand why it sometimes happens. (Imagine Cardinal McIntyre forbidding an archbishop his diocese!)

With kindest personal regards.

Yours ever,
Bob /s/

*This is easy to say, but quite another matter in <u>writing</u> a book!

AUGUST 14, 1964

Rev. M. Louis, O.C.S.O.
Abbey of Gethsemani
Trappist, Kentucky

Dear Tom:

I have a number of things to report. First of all, the New York Review of Books [October 1946] has taken your poem ["Picture of a Negro Child with a White Doll"]. Barbara Epstein phoned to say how much she liked it. She will send me a tearsheet just as soon as it appears, and I'll forward it. Second, I've just read your piece on "Honest to God" in <u>Commonweal</u> [August 21, 1964] and want to tell you how fine I think it is. In fact, I would very much like to see you develop this theme into a book. You are the only writer I know who really seems to understand the nature of the crisis Christianity is in, or who honestly admits there is one. (The bishops don't see it and I'm afraid the Third Session [of the Second Vatican Council] is going to march backwards very firmly; farewell [Pope] John [XXIII]'s aggiornamento.) I'll come back to the book. Third, the name of this firm is to become Farrar, Straus & Giroux and one of the first books I will have the honor of seeing this imprint on is SEEDS OF DESTRUCTION, which makes me very happy. Fourth, the page proofs of your book are due next week, while I'm away in Maine. I've asked Anne Brown, my secretary, to send off the Master Set to you at once, together with one duplicate set that you can keep. Will you mail your corrections back to her as speedily as you can? We'll have to resubmit for an imprimatur here, and so on, but I hope we can keep to our January publication date.

Naomi hasn't yet sent me the Liturgy Book, but I'm expecting it soon and looking forward to reading it. There are still problems to be faced on ART AND WORSHIP, the biggest being the effects of Council action, since liturgy is the one area in which progress seems to be happening, and I hope you will want to revise the text accordingly.

With the publication of SEEDS that leaves us one book to go, and the "crisis" book or "alienation" book or whatever expresses the theme of "a world where Christianity is no longer popular or even acceptable" will, I hope, be one you will consider. I know you want to give Naomi a book for Doubleday, and I understand and do not want to compete with her. I also know I have been at fault in the past and have annoyed you, for which I hope you have forgiven me. Anyway, I wanted you to be the first to know the imprint news, about which I am terribly happy. (I've not yet told Naomi.) It will be a thrill to see the new title page of SEEDS OF DESTRUCTION.

With affectionate regards.

Yours ever,
[Robert Giroux]

AUGUST 25, 1964

Abbey of Gethsemani
[Letterhead]

Dear Bob:

Thanks for your letter with the wonderful news. Congratulations! I too will be very happy and proud to be author of one of the first books over the new imprint of Farrar, Straus & Giroux. This is splendid. I am glad other books of mine will be along over the same imprint.[1] I hope Naomi has sent you the liturgy one by now.

You know that I respond warmly and positively to your suggestion for a book about the Church and the World of today. But honestly, it is terribly difficult to commit myself to the project, not because I wouldn't want to write it, and not because I could not say a thing or two. But, unfortunately, the Higher Superiors in Rome would be very negative. I would not want to write the book and then have it completely stopped. The General has been very tough about the French translation of "Monk in Diaspora." All kinds of objections to it. Thinks I am sitting in judgment on all the religious orders, putting myself above Rome, etc., etc. In effect, six pages of "who do you think you are?" It would be much worse if I tried the book you suggest and came anywhere near telling the truth. If I did, I would just have to join your team of anonymous authors. And even that would mean trouble, as they would certainly find out about it.

On the other hand, if I get stuff out essay by essay, there might be some hope of eventually building up a book. That would be the better way to approach it, and we can at least keep that in mind as a possibility. I will see what comes.

What strikes me most about the General's letter is the total incredulity with which he meets the kind of estimate of things that is in Monk and Diaspora. It is just not possible that things will not go on full steam ahead, with all the banners flying and the silver trumpets blowing all over the place, as they have done since Constantine. He was especially vexed by the camels of Périgueux, which he mentioned more than once.

The new encyclical [*Ecclesiam Suam*] confirms a great deal of what is said in [Michael Serafian's] The Pilgrim, doesn't it? The engines have been put in reverse, with a fair amount of whistle blowing toward the other boats in the harbor to show that we are all friends and that we expect them eventually to see the light and follow our lead in respectful submission. Backwards.

The more I hear about Goldwater, the less I like it. Great numbers of people in this part of the country are for him. Johnson's warlike exploits in Viet Nam have not brought him any votes, but have confirmed people in thinking Goldwater is right.

Best wishes always. And again, I am very happy about the news.

Cordially in Christ,
Tom /s/

1. TM's letter to NB, dated August 28, 1964, shows less enthusiasm for continuing his relationship with RG: "I think we [TM and RG] could finish out the contract and say I would send him another book later on, so as not to break connections brutally and completely. He wants me obviously to do something more for him. But I know how delicate this two-publisher business can be, and so I leave it to you to figure out what is best. I am perfectly willing to send a book his way later, after you have had a couple, for old times' sake and because he is now one of the partners and so on."

SEPTEMBER 18, 1964

Farrar, Straus & Company, Inc.
[Letterhead]
Robert Giroux
Editor-in-Chief

Rev. M. Louis, O.C.S.O.
Abbey of Gethsemani
Trappist, Kentucky

Dear Tom:

I am sending you under separate cover the first two books under the new imprint, one of which is a wild novel by James Purdy, CABOT WRIGHT BEGINS, and the other Robert Lowell's new poems, FOR THE UNION DEAD.

I realize how difficult it is for you to commit yourself to a project as "controversial" as the church and the world today. I was, of course, responding to that essay in <u>Commonweal</u> and perhaps if you proceed as you suggest, essay by essay, there might be some hope of eventually building up a book. It really is <u>the</u> burning subject of our time; the Council has made it so and it is going to be confronting us for a long time to come, even if the Council proves to be abortive.

We have had very good response from the Catholic Book Club in New York and the Catholic Literary Foundation in Milwaukee on SEEDS OF DESTRUCTION. The latter has definitely taken it as a selection; the former has two favorable votes and one negative, but Anne Fremantle is still to be heard from and I am sure she will be for the book. In any event, the book is now in the final stages of printing and we should have finished copies within a few weeks.

I am enclosing the latest "Letter from Vatican City" in this week's New Yorker. Rynne is a little more optimistic than Serafian and I hope he's right!

With affectionate regards.

Yours ever,

Bob /s/

SEPTEMBER 21, 1964

Abbey of Gethsemani
[Letterhead]

Dear Bob:

You might be interested in this "elegy" for Flannery O'Connor.[1] I have not submitted it to anyone. It was written with a magazine like Jubilee in mind, hence the paragraph at the beginning. But I will not send it to Ed Rice until I have your opinion on it. I think probably Jubilee or Commonweal would be the best place (with or without that introductory paragraph).[2]

Have you published anything of hers since "The Violent [Bear It Away]"? Is there anything more? She is a great loss. I just recently read her first book of short stories.

Pope Paul [VI]'s speech opening the III Council session is a bit of an improvement over the encyclical. Everyone seems to feel that this session will be really decisive one way or the other.

Best wishes always, in Christ,

Tom /s/

P.S. The magazine Fellowship, published by the Fellowship of Reconciliation, would be interested in publishing some bits of the peace section of the new book. Could you perhaps send them that? To James Best, F.O.R., Box 271, Nyack, N.Y.

1. In a short note dated September 24, 1964, RG encourages TM to publish his elegy in *Jubilee*.
2. TM, "Flannery O'Connor—A Prose Elegy," *Jubilee*, November 1964, 49–53.

OCTOBER 9, 1964

Farrar, Straus & Giroux, Inc.
19 Union Square West
New York 3, N.Y.

Rev. M. Louis, O.C.S.O.
Abbey of Gethsemani
Trappist, Kentucky

Dear Tom:

We have had very good reports on LES PIERRES SAUVAGES by Fernand Pouillon, a novel about the building of the Abbey of Thoronet in 1160. The French publisher is Éditions du Seuil. I would like to take it on here if I had some assurance that it was really "authentic" and worthwhile and I can think of no better judge than yourself. Would you take a look at it? I enclose a stamped envelope to return it in. It won't be easy to find the right translator, either, because of the technical terminology, but if it's good we'll just have to find the right one.

I also enclose an extraordinary letter that Pasternak wrote in 1937, that has just appeared in Encounter.

With all good wishes.

Yours ever,
Bob /s/

P.S. This session of the Council is positively marvelous, isn't it?

OCTOBER 19, 1964

Farrar, Straus & Giroux, Inc.
[Letterhead]

Rev. M. Louis, O.C.S.O.
Abbey of Gethsemani
Trappist, Kentucky

Dear Tom:

We have revised the jacket for SEEDS OF DESTRUCTION, as you requested, and I am happy to send it to you in final form herewith. We are expecting finished books in mid-November, so please tell Father Abbot it will be in time to send out during the Christmas season.

The book has been taken not only by the Catholic Book Club in New York but by the Catholic Literary Foundation in Milwaukee. The official publication date is January 4th.

With all good wishes.

Yours ever,
Bob /s/

P.S. [The publishing firm of] Jonathan Cape has taken Les Pierres Sauvages for England.

OCTOBER 26, 1964

Dear Bob:

Sorry to be a bit slow reporting on "Les Pierres Sauvages." I have been a bit tied up and have also had to go to town a few times to see the skin doctor about this "poison ivy," which after four months turns out to be something more mysterious. I think it is under control, but we still don't know the cause.

I think Pouillon's book is a good one and eminently publishable. The story of the construction of that marvelous place, Le Thoronet, is, of course, a great idea. I think in the main he does a good job of it. My only remark as a monk is that the book is crawling with anachronisms, as such books usually are. But they are so slight that most people will not pay any attention to them. I note, however, that in his mania for making every day a feast of some saint or other (including Holy Saturday) he has generously included saints who died three or four hundred years after Le Thoronet was built. On the whole, it is a good book and I think you ought to do well with it. The parts about the building are very interesting.

I look forward to "Seeds of Destruction" and note that in the advance copy of Schema 13 [*Pastoral Constitution on the Church in the Modern World*], which I have been able to get to, I find the same ideas on nuclear warfare as are in the book. They may be a bit modified in debate, though I see no reason for them to be so. This might be a telling point in connection with the publication of the book. We will see what they end up with.

This is just a hasty letter. More later. I hope you are well, and hope to see the new book soon. Congratulations especially on Lowell's new book. I may have mentioned it before, but there is no harm in praising it again. It is superbly done.

> Best wishes always in Christ,
> [Thomas Merton]

NOVEMBER 17, 1964

> Farrar, Straus & Giroux, Inc.
> [Letterhead]

Rev. M. Louis, O.C.S.O.
Abbey of Gethsemani
Trappist, Kentucky

Dear Tom:

The first copy of SEEDS OF DESTRUCTION came from the printer this afternoon and I have sent it to you by first-class mail. The official publication date is, of course, January 4th. Both the Catholic Book Club and the Catholic Literary Foundation are sending out their announcements and I enclose copies of both. That photograph by John Howard Griffin seems to be getting a great deal of circulation. It appeared as the cover of <u>The Sign</u> last month. It does not, of course, appear on the jacket.

I am most grateful to you for your report on LES PIERRES SAU-VAGES. In the end, we have decided not to go ahead with it. It is certainly publishable and somebody will do it, but I am really not enthusiastic about it for our list, and your comments were decisive in helping me to reach a decision.

Naomi has just sent me the script of SEASONS OF CELEBRATION, which I have just begun and about which I will be writing you shortly. I am delighted to have this and I hope we will be able to do it by Christmas 1965.

The last week of the Council seems to be particularly hectic, and I hope they settle the question of collegiality in some form or other. I hear such odd rumors about the success with which a handful of obstruction-ists frustrates the teaching authority of the Church and holds up the pas-sage of documents favored by the majority of the Fathers. Things should be clearer by early next week, and obviously a great deal of good work has been done.

With warmest regards.

Yours ever,

Bob /s/

NOVEMBER 21, 1964

Abbey of Gethsemani
[Letterhead]

Dear Bob:

Many thanks for the first copy of SEEDS OF DESTRUCTION and for other copies, which also arrived in time to be given out to members of the F.O.R. (peace movement and civil rights people) who were here on re-treat this week. We had rather an unusual retreat, with long, heated semi-nar sessions each day that were most rewarding and lively. However, one does not come out of it with any assurance that there is reasonable hope of permanently avoiding catastrophe, the way things are going. I wonder how rational and how human our world really is? Certainly, there are a lot of really heart-rending human aspirations. But our institutions do not seem geared to fulfill them.

I have been reserved about the third session, and still am not decided whether to feel elated about it or not. I think rather not. There have been some good moves and gestures, but definitely it seems that the established authority of the curia and the conservatives is set on blocking a real open-ing and aggiornamento. It is very difficult for me to feel a fully human op-timism about the immediate prospects of the Church in the world. One falls back on a theological hope (and, after all, this is not a bad place to fall!), which, however, may be fulfilled in ways that are not only quite outside the perspectives of the present human components of the Church, but may even completely contradict and reverse them. In other words, I think that few people are really looking into the religious depths of the present situation, and there is a general air of specious triumphalism even among liberals, which may turn out to be gravely deceptive.

I thank you again for not using the picture on the jacket. And I cannot help but feel that this is better for you and for the book as well as for me. I was very distressed at the picture on the cover of the Sign. It got there without anyone here knowing about it, and Naomi, of course, was not to blame. Maybe [John Howard] Griffin is handing it out on all sides. I will have to get after him.

You may be amused at the enclosed notes on the drawings now on exhibit in Louisville.

Best wishes always.

Cordially yours in Christ,
Tom /s/

P.S. If you have not already done so, could you perhaps send review copies of Seeds of D. to Bishop [John] Wright, Cardinal [Albert Gregory] Meyer and Cardinal [Joseph] Ritter (and anyone else like that you think of and also especially to Fr. Bernard Häring, C.Ss.R., Via Merulana 31, Rome. Also, of course, [Rabbi] Abraham Heschel.

NOVEMBER 24, 1964

Rev. M. Louis, O.C.S.O.
Abbey of Gethsemani
Trappist, Kentucky

Dear Tom:

Thank you for your good letter of the 21st. It is a pleasure to send review copies of SEEDS OF DESTRUCTION to Bishop Wright and Cardinals Meyer and Ritter, and particularly to send it to Father Häring. I am a great admirer of the latter's writing and I am hopeful of adding his work to our list. It seems clear to me that his work as a theologian has had a profound and salutary influence on the Council.

I relished your comments in the handsome little booklet put out in connection with the exhibition of drawings [at a college named after Mother Catherine Spalding] in Louisville. This is bound to be a "rare Merton item" and I am grateful to you for inscribing it. I only wish I could see the drawings!

With all good wishes.

Yours ever,
[Robert Giroux]

[DECEMBER 1964?]

Our Lady of Gethsemani
[Letterhead]

Dear Bob:

Could you please take care of this? It is perfectly all right with me, and I suppose with you also.

I have plenty of books and they are very handsome, thanks. Everyone seems to like them. I suppose I will begin getting the letters from Birchites when it is out on the market. (Got quite a few when I joined [Rabbi Abraham] Heschel et al. in signing a petition about the [Walter] Jenkins case.) Next year, I expect to be slightly less in circulation, more semi-eremitical, but this does not affect contacts with you. Best wishes for Christmas and the New Year, and all blessings.

In Christ,
Tom /s/

JANUARY 7, 1965

Farrar, Straus & Giroux, Inc.
[Letterhead]

Rev. M. Louis, O.C.S.O.
Abbey of Gethsemani
Trappist, Kentucky

Dear Tom:

In many ways I think Seasons of Celebration is your best book. Certainly it is one of your best books. I like it enormously and I am proud that we are publishing it. Even though Seeds of Destruction is just coming out (and you are getting a marvelous press, samples of which I enclose), we think we should publish the new book in the fall, around Advent, rather than hold it up until next January. Is that agreeable to you?

I do agree with Naomi that the opening chapter needs some rewriting, in view of the fact that other liturgical changes are taking place or will have taken place by the time the book comes out. This kind of correction is easy. I don't really see Naomi's other criticism however—namely, that some of the pieces don't fit into the liturgical structure of the book. (She says: "Maybe it's my dumbness, but I don't quite see the Good Samaritan unless Tom says it's one of the Sunday Gospels or something.") It seems to me that this criticism is clearly covered by the word "Homilies" in the subtitle of the book. It is possible that you may wish to reconsider the order of some of the homilies—for example, couldn't "The Community of Pardon" be transferred closer to "Ash Wednesday" and "Christian Self-Denial": and couldn't the essay of the Virgin Mary come just before or after the Christmas piece

["The Nativity Kerygma"]? Please let me know what you think of this and we'll get ready to put the book in galleys as soon as I hear from you.

I know I should not bother you with business matters but since the contract calls for the payment of five thousand dollars "on demand," rather than on publication, would you let us know whether it's all right with the monastery if we pay it during this month?

With warmest regards and all good wishes for the new year.

Yours ever,

Bob /s/

P.S. Since you may not see the magazine, I enclose the latest letter [by Xavier Rynne] from V[atican] C[ouncil].

JANUARY 11, 1965

Abbey of Gethsemani
[Letterhead]

Dear Bob:

Thanks for your letter, and I am delighted that you want to go ahead right away with SEASONS. I am willing to go over the first chapter, but you had better refresh my memory; I am not sure if I finally put the "Liturgical Renewal" chapter first in the text I sent in. That is the one concerning changes. If so, I will wait until after the beginning of Lent when the new changes go in. Is that the one? Will you also let me have anything you have under your hand on liturgical changes? We are fairly informed here but I am never quite clear what is what, as I get it from a welter of stuff that is read in the refectory. In any case, I am sure you don't want me to go into a great deal of detail on new changes, and I don't want to do that.

Why don't you just arrange the order of the chapters as suits you? Then if I have a strenuous objection I will let you know, but I don't think I shall. Of course, the Good Samaritan is for one of the Sundays after Pentecost. I don't think it matters terribly where that comes either, but I do think that all that is in the book should stay in it somewhere, because it is all relevant to the liturgical year.

As to the payment, I am sure the Abbey is delighted to get five thousand dollars any and every time it can, and if you want us to "demand it," I hereby do so. So if now is the time convenient to F, S & G, by all means send it along. Many thanks.

Thanks for the two reviews, and the Letter from VC (haven't read this yet). A rather fantastic-sounding declaration from Patriarch Maximos [IV] on the Jews was read in refectory yesterday. I guess in Antioch he has to take a decidedly Arab viewpoint.

Naomi told me that T. S. Eliot had died. That is a great blow, and I am sure you must feel it more than almost anyone. We are suddenly losing everyone. And that makes us realize how little we can afford to lose them, especially such as he. I reread Four Quartets this summer, and what a great thing it is. It is what I like best of his. I shall certainly pray for him, and will offer Mass for him when I get a chance. I have recently realized how close I myself am to being practically an Anglo-Catholic except on the point about the Papacy, naturally. I am much more Anglo than Irish American German Polish Catholic.

Best wishes for the New Year, and all blessings.

Cordially in Christ,
Tom /s/

JANUARY 15, 1965

Rev. M. Louis, O.C.S.O.
Abbey of Gethsemani
Trappist, Kentucky

Dear Tom:

I am happy to enclose a selection from the first batch of reviews. On the whole, the book is getting a fine press. I'm a bit disappointed that Thomas Greene of <u>America</u> [January 16, 1965] is so begrudging (he says it's depressing that so many are only now coming to the right conclusions, but I find this less depressing than that places like Los Angeles are not!) and that Dr. [Martin E.] Marty in the <u>Herald Tribune</u> uses the word "second-hand" so glibly (isn't his knowledge of the problem second-hand like most people's?).[1] Nevertheless, it's clear that the book is making an impact and the overall reviewing picture is certainly favorable.

With kindest regards.

Yours ever,
[Robert Giroux]

1. See TM's September 6, 1967, letter to Marty in *The Hidden Ground of Love: Letters on Religious Experience and Social Concerns*, 454–58.

MARCH 13, 1965

Abbey of Gethsemani
[Letterhead]

Dear Bob:

A friend of mine [probably James W. Douglass] who is very active in connection with Schema 13 has asked that we send some copies of <u>Seeds of Destruction</u> to the following bishops and cardinals. I was wondering if you would see fit to do this, as the boys in the gatehouse are sore at me for sending out books to translators for free. Here are the addresses:

Card[inal] Franz König, Rotenturmstrasse 2, Vienna I
Bischof Josef Schröffer, Eichstätt, Bayern, Germany
Bischof Otto Spülbeck, Meissen, East Germany and a review copy to
Der Christ in der Welt, Schottengasse, 3a, I, 58 Vienna.

They also suggested sending one to Karl Rahner [S.J.], Theologisches Fakultät, München.

Reading the reviews carefully, I see that those who don't know too much about the situation regard the book as important, and those who do know it, don't. In a way, the reactions have been largely slanted by a revulsion from the piece on Negroes, so that there has not been much attention paid to the one on war, which is less hortatory. I don't believe all hostile criticism, but my general impression is that the book is really a failure, from my point of view. I am just not in a position to write a book like that, and perhaps I was deluded in even trying to do so. But I thought I had to say something, and I did, come what may. It may do a little good in spite of everything. But I suppose, in the end, I had better chalk it up as another illusion that I have worked my way out of. I hope. But I do still think the section on war is fairly good, as also the diaspora piece.

Don't forget me when you have a copy of the new Flannery O'Connor! When comes the liturgy book? I am meditating on the new changes daily, as I say Mass. Actually, I see them as completely provisional, just a step to something else. But the Mass is a lot simpler and more clear. Saying Mass in the novitiate chapel, I have not been involved in English yet; there is no need for it there. We have some English readings in the conventual Mass, and there is still more in the Mass for the brothers. Personally, I think monks would be well advised to hold on to Latin in their choir, but, naturally, one must consider the needs of new people coming in. Yet the younger ones seem more satisfied with Latin than an intermediate group ordained in the last ten years.

Best wishes always. I keep you in my Lenten prayers.

Cordially in Christ,
Tom /s/

MARCH 15, 1965

Rev. M. Louis
Abbey of Gethsemani
Trappist, Kentucky

Dear Tom:
I take delight in assisting in any way I can with the work on Schema 13. I hope your book does have a good influence on the three bishops concerned. We have sent copies to them by airpost, as well as to Karl Rahner, and the review copy to Der Christ in der Welt in Vienna.

SEEDS OF DESTRUCTION seems more timely than ever in the present U.S. climate. It's true that reviewers so often write about the book they think the author should have written instead of the book they have just read. It's selling well, and from that point of view, it is a success. Did you see the latest piece in Commonweal? I enclose a copy just in case.

The Flannery O'Connor book will come from the printer in April, and I'll see that you get an advance copy. We quote you on the jacket. Robert Fitzgerald has written a long and marvelous introduction, which throws a good deal of light on this extraordinary writer.

We plan to do the liturgy book late this year, and I hope to have proofs by sometime in May. The vernacular Mass seems to be going over well in New York; I can't help noticing that at St. Vincent [Ferrer]'s [Church] the later and better-attended Masses are said by the younger Dominicans. There was one old-timer, an octogenarian, who still insisted on saying the prayers after Mass as late as last summer. On the whole, the people are taking it rather better than some of the clergy. Cardinal [Francis] Spellman's gesture to the Rev. Reeb has had a very good effect.[1] So have those marching nuns whose presence in demonstrations here would certainly have been unheard of only a few months ago.

With all good wishes.

Yours ever,
[Robert Giroux]

1. Cardinal Spellman donated $10,000 to the Good Samaritan Hospital in Selma, Alabama, in honor of Rev. James Reeb, a Unitarian minister murdered in Selma during the civil rights movement.

APRIL 29, 1965

Abbey of Gethsemani
[Letterhead]

Dear Bob:

Thanks for Flannery O'Connor's new book [*Everything That Rises Must Converge*], which, of course, I have read immediately. It has all of her usual power, sometimes more. Some of the stories have a really brutal impact, and with reason. I think that she has an almost prophetic insight into what ails everybody. It is instructive to read her and see her violent, misled, obsessed people in action, and to compare our national folly in Vietnam, for example. One wonders if we are really a nation of the damned. Sartre seems to think so, and though Sartre can make a big show of being friends with the publican Saint Genet [Sartre wrote a book on Jean Genet], he does not have the courage to be seen by the Third World speaking to an American.

The book has a significant pattern. The first and last stories say deeper and more detached things about the race situation than anyone else has had to say. And the title sums it all up neatly. I like the ironical echo of Teilhard [de Chardin, S.J.]. (Teilhard is good and admirable, but to see him right one must have the underside of the rug in view and Flannery surely shows that.)

I very much enjoyed the Enduring Chill, which perfectly settles the hash of us liberals [*sic*]. The Comforts of Home was great, the bull in Greenleaf (the coy, rural suitor death) is one of the great bulls of all mythology. All the stories are fine, though I did feel that the wonderful idea of Parker's Back did not rocket and explode the way a Flannery story should.

But the one story of all, the greatest and most perfect is Judgment Day. This is the best thing she ever wrote and one of the best stories anybody ever wrote. It is a terrific thing, and in a whole new dimension. If she was beginning to write something like that, just imagine what might have come if she had not died. It says everything, and the brutality is absent, and there are so many levels of meaning that one cannot begin to fathom them. I am still dazed by it, and by the skill with which she handled it, and by the meaning she packed into it. It is a great metaphysical poem of the South. And very humorous and compassionate. She was at last getting into the depths of compassion, which probably killed her.

Thanks for this wonderful book, Bob.

All the best always, in the Lord,

Tom /s/

APRIL 30, 1965

Rev. M. Louis, O.C.S.O.
Abbey of Our Lady of Gethsemani
Trappist, Kentucky

Dear Tom:

I thank you for the marvelous letter on Flannery O'Connor's new book, and I'm taking the liberty of quoting it to Bob Fitzgerald. Especially, I like what you say about "Judgment Day"—that and "The Enduring Chill" are my two favorites. Well, "Revelation" too—to make a third. It is quite a book.

We've been putting together the quotes on SEEDS OF DESTRUCTION, and I've just been handed the enclosed. It really makes an impressive grouping. Incidentally, the sales are keeping up exceedingly well. It's well over 10,000 already.

The design of SEASONS OF CELEBRATION is almost ready, and galley proofs should be starting by the end of May or early June.

With all the best.

As ever,

[Robert Giroux]

JULY 3, 1965

Abbey of Gethsemani
[Letterhead]

Dear Bob:

The Myna Lockwood book [*A Mouse Is Miracle Enough*] just came in, and I want to acknowledge it. I will let you know about my ideas when I have read it. Perhaps I could pass it on to one of the monks who has been catching birds, possums, snakes and God knows what for company.

What I do want to say is that I like Karl Stern's new book [*The Flight of Woman*] very much indeed. I am finishing it now, and have enjoyed it all the way through. The theme is most important and he treats it very well, with all his usual insight. I am very glad he has written it, and hope he will be understood, though I don't know what people are going to do about it. That reminds me: he mentions [Paul] Evdokimov, on the theology of woman: it is a marvelous book, and if it has not yet been translated into English, I recommend it. Perhaps it has, though, I seem to have heard that an English translation was around. I was especially moved by Karl's chapter on [Søren] Kierkegaard, which really makes plain the mystery of his relations with Regina.

Thanks also for the Third Xavier Rynne volume, which I will value as a source of reference on the Third Session.

With all my best wishes always.

Cordially in Christ,
Tom /s/

JULY 15, 1965

Abbey of Gethsemani
[Letterhead]

Dear Bob:

I told this man that I would pass his letter on to you, and that you could send him proofs if he wanted them. But I also warned him that almost everything in the book had previously appeared in a magazine. The only exception is, I think, Community of Pardon. I would not send him proofs until it is certain that he can use them.

Speaking of proofs, will they be coming along soon? I am quite tied up at the moment, but naturally I will make room for them in order to get them back without delay.

I really enjoyed Karl Stern's book and I hope you told him so. I have been intending to write him, but am so far behind with answering people that I have not been able to yet.

Naomi has a ms. of a book for you that I think you will like.[1]
With best wishes always.

Cordially yours in Christ,
Tom /s/

1. In a letter dated July 6, 1965, TM sent NB the manuscript of *Mystics and Zen Masters* to be published by FSG. "After this, then, I am publishing with Doubleday. What do you want to start with? You have never said anything about that partial manuscript of Journal material which I sent you a long time ago. Did you even get it? I think it would be a good starter." In a letter dated July 26, 1965, RG wrote to NB: "As I told Tom, the contract has now been more than fulfilled and there is no question about another option." In effect, RG ceased being TM's editor at this time. Doubleday hoped to publish TM's next book, entitled *Faith and Violence* (as noted in a letter from NB to TM dated August 4, 1965).

JULY 16, 1965

Rev. M. Louis, O.C.S.O.
Abbey of Gethsemani
Trappist, Kentucky

Dear Tom:

It isn't often that I can send you a book that I absolutely know you will enjoy. It's Tom Wolfe's THE KANDY-KOLORED, TANGERINE-FLAKE STREAMLINE BABY, which will soon reach you by separate cover.

I have just been advised by our production department that galley proofs of SEASONS OF CELEBRATION will be coming through on July 26th. I will get them to you as soon after that as possible. Meanwhile, I am writing to Father [Arthur] McNally [C.P.] at The Sign regarding "Community of Pardon," which I hope he will take.

I'm absolutely fascinated by your last paragraph, and I can hardly wait to see what the book is, and whether it's by you or by Naomi?

With warmest regards.

Yours ever,
[Robert Giroux]

JULY 26, 1965

Rev. M. Louis, O.C.S.O.
Abbey of Our Lady of Gethsemani
Trappist, Kentucky

Dear Tom:

Naomi has sent me the manuscript of MYSTICS AND ZEN MASTERS, and I think it is a very good book. It came as a surprise, and that made it all the nicer. I am most grateful to you for letting us have this, to complete our five-book contract.

In order to avoid drawing up a new contract, may we consider MYSTICS
AND ZEN MASTERS as being one of the five books, and consider ART
AND WORSHIP as the option book? This merely means that we would be
following the terms for advance and royalties as with the other four books,
and would hold ART AND WORSHIP as an option book for a future date
if we can succeed in working out the editorial problem. I have written
Naomi to tell her that with the delivery of this book, we acknowledge that
any contractual obligations have been more than fulfilled.

The proofs of SEASONS OF CELEBRATION came from the printer
this morning and I am sending them to you under separate cover. There
is a set of Master Proofs, to be returned to me, and a duplicate set for you
to keep. Now that I see the book in type, it seems to me that the essay on
"Liturgy and Spiritual Personalism" should come at the beginning rather
than at the end. (It is listed correctly in the Table of Contents.) If you
agree, will you mark proofs accordingly?

Did I tell you that I am off to Greece on August 20th? I can hardly wait.
With warmest regards.

Yours ever,
[Robert Giroux]

JULY 29, 1965

Abbey of Gethsemani
[Letterhead]

Dear Bob:

The proofs just arrived, and I want to let you know about them before
I take off with them to the hospital. Nothing serious; I just have to lie
around a few days and get the right diet and be observed, so I will read
them at leisure and get them off to you on my return "hopefully" as they
say cured.

Thanks too for your letter. One thing Naomi probably did not say, but
that I would like to say clearly: I do plan and hope ("hopefully") to let you
have another book here and there from time to time. The fact that we
wind up this particular five-book contract at this point does not mean no
books ever as far as I am concerned. But I do feel that since Naomi is
being so helpful as a nurse so to speak, she should get some of the books
for Doubleday.

New Directions is bringing out some selections of Gandhi I edited with
a preface, not really a whole book of mine.[1] This is way beyond proofs; [it]
is a paperback. I expect it (another adverb) "momentarily."

And now, finally, Tom Wolfe's KKTFSB. It is a magnificent book. What
good writing, what an eye, what a vocabulary (what is *infarcted*?). Some of
the pieces really jump out at you: the one on Cassius Clay, for instance,

and the one on the teen tycoon who got off the plane, name escapes me. Are these people real? They must be, hah? I am adjusting my perspectives, my Church and the world perspectives. I am in favor of these people, though not of Las Vegas (the old ladies with the work gloves at the machines). This is a marvelous book, the kind Lax and I and Rice were always dreaming of when we sat in the woods above Olean [New York]. We just never got around like this cat. Thanks for this tremendous book.

I certainly hope you enjoy Greece. Lax is on the island of Kalymnos. He says in Athens they shoot tourists but on Kalymnos it is always quiet and peaceful. Maybe you had better go see him if Athens gets rough. For my part, when I get back from the hospital, "hopefully" I will finally become a hermit—this is serious. I will live in a cottage I have in the woods, and come down to the monastery only once a day to say Mass and get a cooked meal. And doubtless pick up some mail.

All the best always, and best wishes for your trip and everything.

Cordially in Christ,
Tom /s/

P.S. What I really meant to say is that the way you propose handling things in your letter is fine with me; I think it makes sense, and let's do it that way.

1. Mahatma Gandhi, *Gandhi on Non-Violence: Selected Texts from Non-Violence in Peace and War*, ed. TM (New York: New Directions, 1965).

AUGUST 10, 1965

Farrar, Straus & Giroux, Inc.
[Letterhead]
Office of the Editor-in-Chief

Father M. Louis, O.C.S.O.
Abbey of Our Lady of Gethsemani
Trappist, Kentucky

Dear Tom:

Many thanks for returning the proofs so promptly. I am relieved to learn that you are out of the hospital, and I hope that all goes well with you.

I like the Author's Note and the other changes you have made in the text, and I am putting these through. I assume you will not want to see page proofs and that you'll trust us to see that all these changes have been made before we print.

Two problems remain before we can wind up production: (1) The amendment of the contract, a purely formal matter. I enclose the letter of emendation in duplicate herewith, which should be signed by Father

Abbot since he signed the original contract. Will you pass it on to him and ask him to return only one signed copy to me? (2) The copyright page of SEASONS OF CELEBRATION presents certain complications. We must note where all the pieces first appeared and the copyright line under which they appeared, in order to arrange for assignments. I am enclosing a list of the essays, and I will be grateful if you will simply put this information next to each of the fifteen pieces. I remember that "The Nativity Kerygma" was published in a handsome limited edition as a book. Would you put down the copyright line that appeared in the book? If the copyright name given is other than your own or the Abbey, we shall have to write for an assignment. In such cases, I am wholly dependent on you for the address to which we must apply. We will do all the paper work and clear it for you, provided you give us all the necessary details. I am sorry to dump this on you at the last minute, but I do not know where else to turn.

I was very happy to have your letter of July 29th, and I very much appreciate your saying that this does not necessarily mean no books from you ever in the future. It will mean a great deal to me if we can continue to publish some of your work in the years to come.

With affectionate regards and best wishes for your continued wellbeing.

Yours ever,
Bob /s/

P.S. I knew you would like the Tom Wolfe! If I get to Kalymnos, I'll call on Lax. (We may not be allowed in Athens!) N.B. We also need the wording for the "Ex Parte Ordinis"![1]

1. See the letter dated July 22, 1951.

AUGUST 10, 1965

Dear Bob:

The enclosed essay ["Zen Buddhist Monasticism"], which I think you will like, logically belongs in the MYSTICS AND ZEN MASTERS book, so I am sending it along. You will know where to place it.

Naomi and I will take up with New Directions the problem of the book they are bringing out this fall.[1] I did not realize that there was another one besides the Gandhi selections, really held over from spring because of printer's lethargy. I certainly don't want three of my books coming out in one season.

Best wishes, and hope you will have a great trip.

Cordially in Christ,
[Thomas Merton]

1. TM, *The Way of Chuang Tzu* (New York: New Directions, 1965).

AUGUST 17, 1965

Abbey of Gethsemani
[Letterhead]

Dear Bob:

This will arrive in your absence, but someone can take care of it: First, as regards the copyright lines for various articles in SEASONS OF CELEBRATION.

Nativity Kerygma, Copyright 1958 by the Abbey of Gethsemani
The Good Samaritan, Copyright 1962 by the Abbey of Gethsemani
The following appeared in Worship Magazine, Collegeville, Minn.
Liturgy and Spiritual Personalism
Church and Bishop in St. Ignatius
Time and the Liturgy
Advent, Hope or Delusion?
Ash Wednesday
Easter: the New Life
Homily on Light and the Virgin Mary
The Name of the Lord
From the Critic Magazine, Chicago: Liturgical Renewal, the open approach
From Commonweal: Christian Self-Denial
In Silentio was the prologue to a book Silence in Heaven, pub. by Thames & Hudson and by someone else in this country, but I understand you obtained rights to it at one time. Do I remember correctly?
The Sacrament of Advent in St. Bernard was published in French in Dieu Vivant, but that does not count. It has not, in fact, been printed before in English.
Community of Pardon: you will know if Sign magazine took this or not.
I think that covers the lot.

Father Abbot is signing and returning the letter about MYSTICS AND ZEN MASTERS.

Best regards always.

Cordially yours,
[Thomas Merton]

AUGUST 30, 1965

Abbey of Gethsemani
[Letterhead]

Dear Bob:

In addition to the article on "Zen Monasticism," which I sent you recently, I think this one on "Orthodoxy and the World" also belongs logically in the <u>Mystics and Zen Masters</u> book. I don't want to keep heaping new additions on you, but I do think they belong and should go in. You will judge. I hope your trip to Greece was a pleasant one. Things are very delightful down here, with nice fall-type weather beginning early, though it is still warm.

Hoping to hear that you have returned in good health, and that all goes well.

Cordially yours in Christ,
Tom /s/

OCTOBER 21, 1965

Farrar, Straus & Giroux, Inc.
[Letterhead]
Office of the Editor-in-Chief

Rev. M. Louis, O.C.S.O.
Abbey of Our Lady of Gethsemani
Trappist, Kentucky

Dear Tom:

I have just sent you by separate cover the first advance copy of SEASONS OF CELEBRATION to come from the press.

I liked the excerpts from your Notebooks very much. <u>Harper's</u> sent us a tearsheet [of "Few Questions and Fewer Answers"], and I presume they will be appearing in the November issue. I must tell you about a phone call that they apparently inspired from a reporter on the New York <u>Times</u>. He deduced from them that you were leaving the Trappist Order! I told him that this "rumor" was at least as old as THE SEVEN STOREY MOUNTAIN and to forget it!

Your essay ["Notes on Christian Existentialism"] in the new issue of <u>The Critic</u> is splendid. I must say they've done a first-rate job of presentation too—starting with the cover itself.

I hope that all goes well with you. My trip to Greece was terrific, and I wound up in Rome for the opening of the Council, in a ringside seat. I must say that the Pope's demeanor was most impressive: he carried the crozier that later turned up at the Yankee Stadium; and he kept waving aside the men who carried the <u>sedia gestatoria</u> and who kept shrugging their shoulders, as much as to say, "Are we going to be out of jobs too?" His announcement of the bishops' synod galvanized everyone and was the beginning of the new Pauline look (which I hope stays new). I thought his U.N. speech superb.

Yours ever,
Bob /s/

OCTOBER 26, 1965

Abbey of Gethsemani
[Letterhead]

Dear Bob:

Many thanks for the new book. It is very handsome, and I am happy to get it. I think that it ought to turn out all right.

I am glad you liked the existentialism essay. You will be interested to hear that someone who is bringing out a series of paperbacks with collections of essays about various authors, has asked me to do one on Flannery O'Connor.[1] I don't know who is doing this, I mean what publisher. The editor teaches at St. Louis U[niversity]. But, in any case, if you have some particularly good essays on her in mind, I would be glad to hear about them and, if possible, get copies. The idea is to collect ten or twelve first-class essays together into a book and then write an introduction.

I rather envy your Greek journey. I don't suppose you wound up on Mount Athos, but places like Delphi have always attracted me too. I imagine I probably could do without Athens, though perhaps the Acropolis is really something.

The censors have suggested some slight corrections in Mystics and Zen Masters. They are so slight that they could easily wait for the proofs. I have not, by the way, had two extra essays censored yet, the one on Zen Monasticism and the other on Orthodoxy and the World. Shall I go ahead with them?

All the best always, in the Lord,
Tom /s/

1. While TM never wrote another article on O'Connor, a section from "The Other Side of Despair" was included as "Excerpt on Flannery O'Connor" in *Women Writers of the Short Story: A Collection of Critical Essays*, ed. Heather McClave (Englewood Cliffs, NJ: Prentice-Hall, 1980), 145–49.

DECEMBER 9, 1965

Dear Bob:

Some time ago you mentioned the existentialism article in the Critic. I have rewritten it and it seems to me that this, too, would be a good addition to Mystics and Zen Masters. Naomi agrees, and hence I am sending it along to you for inclusion in the book. I never got an official statement one way or the other whether you intended to use the other two pieces I sent, "Zen Monasticism" and "Orthodoxy and the World." Let me know about this, so that I can get them censored. I will send all three and take care of them all at once. One of the censors on this book is a difficult one, however, and I hope he does not get nasty about existentialism. All three have been cleared with Naomi. Let me know then, please, and I will get busy with them.

Under separate cover, I am sending you my Chuang Tzu book, as something that might divert you over Christmas. It is a book I myself like; there is less of myself in it, and I certainly like Chuang Tzu. I hope you will too.

So I will let Chuang bring you my Christmas greetings, but, in the meanwhile, I will not forget you in my prayers. Everything is going nicely. The hermit life seems to agree with me. I still have various difficulties, mostly connected with social life: like getting unstuck from a peace movement in which people have a tendency to wave flaming draft cards about in the air stating: "This comes to you with the courtesy of Thomas Merton our sponsor." I find out about it three weeks after it happened.

Best wishes always. Take care of yourself and have a good Christmas.

With all cordial friendship in Christ,
[Thomas Merton]

DECEMBER 22, 1965

Rev. M. Louis, O.C.S.O.
Abbey of Gethsemani
Trappist, Kentucky

Dear Tom:

I couldn't agree more about adding "The Other Side of Despair" to MYSTICS AND ZEN MASTERS, and also "Zen Monasticism." I'm less sure about "Orthodoxy and the World," the review of the two books by Fr. [Alexander] Schmemann. Would you consider recasting the letter a bit, more in the form of an essay? I think it might work in that case.

The inscribed copy of the Chuang Tzu arrived, and I've read it with pleasure—read "in it" would be more accurate, because it has to be digested slowly with lots of double takes. I like your rendering of the poems very much. Jay should be congratulated on the production, a beautiful book. It gives me some ideas for MYSTICS AND ZEN MASTERS. (Years ago I worked on a book with Mai-mai Tzu whose illustrations Jay borrowed from Bollingen.)

A happy Christmas to you, Tom. The windup of the Council seems on the whole to have been pretty good (according to Xavier You-know-who, whose long piece I'll send you). I'm glad those anathemas from the 11th century have been wiped out, and it was ironic justice for Jacques Maritain to stay at the Pope's side on the last day, when the "message to the intellectuals" was read out. (Shades of the days when Maritain couldn't get a job in a Catholic university!) Even blind old [Cardinal Alfredo] Ottaviani pleaded for an end to war and advocated a "world government" which must have frightened some U.S. bishops. It's all very odd. With the bishops out of Rome (except for the Synod), it will be interesting to see how quickly the Curia reverts to the old ways.

With warmest regards.

Yours ever,
[Robert Giroux]

JANUARY 6, 1966

Abbey of Gethsemani
[Letterhead]

Dear Bob:

I have sent off the Existentialism piece for censorship and hope it will not be too long. If it has to go to the same censors who did the rest of the book, it might meet with a little opposition. Let us hope not. The other is cleared. As to the one on Orthodoxy, perhaps it would be best just to drop it. I don't really have enough material about other authors, which is what I would need to recast it.

I know the [Chinese painter] Mai Mai Sze book [perhaps *The Way of Chinese Painting: Its Ideas and Technique* (1959)] and am crazy about it. It is not the one that J. [Laughlin] used, though. He used another collection straight from China, which is in some ways less good. I did not always like the choices. The fighting cock on p. 109 probably could not last five rounds with an average horsefly. The illustrations in Mai Mai Sze that I would especially like to see used are the great classic bamboos and other such that are reproduced more elaborately in the first volume. Or some of the great Japanese and Chinese Zen painters.

Thanks for the good Xavier Rynne piece on the fourth session. On the whole, I was happy with the way it went. I have had to go through the Constitution on the Church in the World, to do a piece for Tom Burns who unaccountably does not want to use the Race section of Seeds of Destruction. I wrote a longish piece on the Constitution which is being typed. It rambles a bit perhaps. Actually, I thought the English version of the Constitution was appalling. What twentieth-century man would recognize himself as being addressed by that gibberish? But the material is basically good, I think. If I get my commentary eventually mimeographed, I will send a copy along. I was glad to hear about Maritain being there on the last day of the Council. Glad also that the hermit Charbel Makhlouf was beatified.[1] It is an auspicious beginning for my own hermit career here. Sister Luke [Tobin, S.L.], our observer, brought me back a relic, which I have here in the hermitage.

All best wishes for the New Year, and all blessings.

Cordially in the Lord,
Tom /s/

1. See the letter dated March 29, 1951.

MARCH 11, 1966

Rev. M. Louis, O.C.S.O.
Abbey of Gethsemani
Trappist, Kentucky

Dear Tom:

I hope you will understand our reasoning on the postponement of MYSTICS AND ZEN MASTERS. It is based solely on the fact that SEASONS OF CELEBRATION came out in December 1965. It's a marvelous book, and I think it will do just as well in the spring of 1967 as at any other time. I can see why there may be some pressure on Naomi to publish the other book in July, and I don't see why she should not go ahead with those plans if you are agreeable.

All the best.

As ever,
[Robert Giroux]

P.S. I am sending you Jean Stafford's scarey little book [*A Mother in History*] and the new Elizabeth Bishop [*Questions of Travel*] by separate cover.

MARCH 18, 1966

Dear Bob:

Actually, the idea of putting off MYSTICS AND ZEN MASTERS until 1967 is much better, as far as I am concerned. With the paperback of New Directions, we would be putting out three books in a year, otherwise, and I think that would be a bad idea all round. Hence, I much prefer to have one or other of the books come out later. Since this is what you prefer also, then I think we are all happy about it. I presume Naomi has no objections. I hope not.

However, I do think this one more Zen essay should go into the book. When you have read it, I think you will agree. So I am sending it along. It is appearing in a new rather flossy magazine called the Lugano Review ["The Zen Koan," 1966] edited in Europe by Jim Fitzsimmons, who you may or may not remember from Columbia.

We are having fine spring weather now, and I am glad to see it after a long rough winter in the woods, where I now live. Unfortunately, my zeal in chopping firewood has brought out an old back injury and I have to go in for an operation next week, which is tiresome.[1]

Best wishes always, and happy Easter. God bless you.

Cordially in Christ,
[Thomas Merton]

1. In a letter from NB to Father Abbot, dated January 27, 1966, she notes that she has recently talked to Ed Rice, who believes that TM is "in terribly poor health." While recovering from this surgery, TM met the nurse with whom he fell in love. For some of TM's poems about this relationship, see the limited edition: TM, *Eighteen Poems* (New York: New Directions, 1985).

JUNE 3, 1966

Farrar, Straus & Giroux, Inc.
[Letterhead]
Office of the Editor-in-Chief

Rev. M. Louis, O.C.S.O.
Abbey of Gethsemani
Trappist, Kentucky

Dear Tom:

I can't tell you how grateful I am for your marvelously perceptive comment on Walker Percy's THE LAST GENTLEMAN. I think it's one of the best novels I have ever read, and it will perhaps be the best that I have ever published. I also had a nice note from Percy, saying that he had heard from you directly.

We have an Anglican author on our list, who is very talented. She is Madeleine L'Engle, and she won the Newberry Medal, a kind of Pulitzer Prize for children's books, for A WRINKLE IN TIME, a copy of which I am sending you separately. I am enclosing herewith a play [published as *A Journey with Jonah*] she recently completed that I think Dick Walsh of the Catholic Hour should also see. I would be most interested to have your comments. There's no need to return this script. As you will see, Miss L'Engle wanted to present Jonah in a way that would appeal to children, but it seems to me that it is just as illuminating for adults.

With kindest regards.

Yours ever,
Bob /s/

SEPTEMBER 27, 1966

Farrar, Straus & Giroux, Inc.
[Letterhead]
Office of the Editor-in-Chief

Rev. M. Louis, O.C.S.O.
Abbey of Our Lady of Gethsemani
Trappist, Kentucky

Dear Tom:

We are now planning to go to press with MYSTICS AND ZEN MASTERS, and the copy-editor has raised a couple of queries which only you can answer. In the chapter entitled "From Pilgrimage to Crusade," there are two words missing in the quotation from St. Bernard. If you have a carbon of this chapter, the missing words are in lines 3 and 4 on page 15.

I would also like to know if you intend to write a preface. It seems to me that a short note would be appropriate — or indeed a long one if that is your inclination. Anyway, I am enclosing a copy of the contents as a reminder.

I was delighted to have a copy of CONJECTURES OF A GUILTY BYSTANDER, which I like very much. It brought back memories of The Sign of Jonas, but, of course, it's quite a different world we are living in now. Doubleday was very smart to make the arrangement with Life, and I think the serialization helped prepare the way for the book's success, about which I am happy for Naomi's sake as well as for yours.

Warmest regards.

Yours ever,
Bob /s/

SEPTEMBER 30, 1966

Dear Bob:

I was happy to get your letter and to learn that MYSTICS AND ZEN MASTERS is now in the works.[1] And I imagine that CONJECTURES ought to do something to stimulate interest in it and prepare the way. Certainly, I will be delighted to write a preface. I think from my own point of view the most effective way would be to write it after I have read the whole book in proof. I don't seem to have the entire ms. here, or I can't lay hands on all of it. I would plan a preface of about 1,500 words. Would you be willing to do it that way? I think it would make for a better preface.

A quote from St. Bernard: I can't locate a carbon of the typescript you have, but here is the printed article. On pages 12 – 13, there is a quote from St. Bernard, complete, and I imagine it is the one you refer to. Could this copy please be returned to me after the copy editor is through?

I am enclosing two other bits which you might be interested in. They logically fit into this book: one on Buddhism, the other on Orthodoxy in relation to the modern world. The Buddhism bit is to be in the next issue of Cross Currents [Fall 1966]. I leave you to decide if you want this material, but, in my opinion, it belongs in the book and will help the book. But, of course, there may be all sorts of other considerations and I am perfectly willing to let you decide as you know best. Meanwhile, I am pleased that the book is going ahead. It is one that I myself like — to some extent. When I look back at a lot of the books I have done in the past, I see they were perhaps not as worth doing as I thought at the time. But I suppose it is always that way, and they have fulfilled a function.

At the moment, I am writing mostly poetry and essays, and my concerns are all pretty "modern" at the moment, and on the literary side. Out of this, somewhere along the line, I am sure another book for you will come one of these days. Perhaps, something on modern French and Spanish poets. It is a possibility. Right now, I am deep in René Char [noted French poet]. If you have anything along those lines, I hope you will keep me in mind.

All the best always, and warm regards.

In Christ,

[Thomas Merton]

1. In a letter dated November 30, 1966, Mary Louise Vincent, RG's secretary, sent TM a list of queries concerning his book:

galley 2, line 1: Is this where footnote reference belongs?

galley 10, at end, 6 lines from bottom: Is this where footnote reference belongs?

galley 13, line 14: Is "untilate" right?

galley 15, after subhead—line 14: Ok "Lao Tzu," as on following passages?

galley 18, after subhead—line 27: Is Liu Wu-Chi right?

22, first paragraph after subhead: Ok to refer to him as Meng Tzu, as, earlier, author said he was going to call him thus, not Mencius?

22, after subhead—lines 14 & 16: Is Mo Tzu a different person from Mo Tsu on galley 13, 4th full paragraph? Or make spelling same?

22, verse ii: Should there be quote marks here too, as on i?

23, 2nd paragraph, lines 7 & 18: ok repeat "sapiential"? same paragraph, lines 14 & 15: ok sentence as altered?

4th paragraph, line 2: ok "most people"?—to avoid "they" to refer to "everyone."

25, line 6 after 2nd verse: ok close parenthesis where they now appear?

3rd paragraph after verse, line 5: ok sentence?

29, 3rd full paragraph, lines 2 ff: Is this sentence ok?

32, line 7 from end: Is this sentence ok now?

40, 4th paragraph, line 5: Does superior number refer to matter inside parenthesis only, or to whole sentence? If it refers to parenthesis only, put inside parenthesis.

44, 3rd paragraph, line 8: ok opening parenthesis where they are?

48 2nd paragraph after subhead, line 21: Where should opening quotes go?

52, 3rd paragraph, line 10: ok "Seraphi_n_," not Seraphi_m_? Throughout it's Seraphi_n_—please check throughout.

54, line 15: ok close quote where it is now?

galley 57, extract matter beginning with brackets: Is either expression in brackets or quotes part of the quotation? (If it's part of quote, it should be in parenthesis; if it's someone else's words, in brackets.)

58, first extract matter: Same question—brackets ok? Or is it part of the quotation?

3rd paragraph before the end: Is this right in text type and not as an extract?

60, lines 15 & 13 from end: Should this be in brackets, or is it part of quotation?

64, line 10: Is this word spelled correctly? Or should it be as on galley 65, last paragraph?

64, 3rd paragraph: Seraphi_n_ ok? and throughout

94, 2nd paragraph, lines 6 & 4 of paragraph: Ok words in parenthesis? Or should they be in brackets?

100, footnote 27: Where does reference go in text? Which of the two books of Suzuki do you mean?

101, note 15: Have I put the quotes in the right place? Are parenthesis correct? or brackets?

102, note 16: Please complete.

Note 27: What book does "op cit" here refer to? You've just mentioned two above?

Note 36: Please supply data

Note 45: Data missing.

103, note 16: Are brackets ok?

Please check Latin material with special care, as it was not checked in manuscript.

NOVEMBER 3, 1966

Rev. M. Louis, O.C.S.O.
Abbey of Gethsemani
Trappist, Kentucky

Dear Tom:

Our Copyright Department requires information about the original magazine publication of the essays in MYSTICS AND ZEN MASTERS. Could you note on the attached table of contents which essays were printed, where, and the date of publication, and return to me? We will then gather up assignments in the monastery's name, where possible.

I like BUDDHISM AND THE MODERN WORLD very much. Perhaps it should go into the book and even lead off the text. I'm awaiting the galleys (due mid-November) and we can decide then. Is that all right with you? Incidentally, did BUDDHISM AND THE MODERN WORLD appear in a magazine?

I enclose sample type pages herewith, and galleys should be following soon.

With best regards.

As ever,
[Robert Giroux]

NOVEMBER 8, 1966

Abbey of Gethsemani
[Letterhead]

Dear Bob:

I am returning the list of essays with more or less useable information about where those essays appeared in magazines. I am not at all sure of the dates, and in some cases they are very approximate indeed. But I came as close as I could.

More unfortunately, two of the magazines are so small that I can't accurately remember what they are or were called. But I have given the names of people to whom you could refer at the places where the magazines are published, who will know about the article and when they appeared. They will be glad to answer any query, I am sure. And Fr. [Illtud] Evans [O.P.] is the present editor of one of the magazines so he will be able to give you the proper clearance. Buddhism and the Modern World is supposed to come out in the Fall in Cross Currents, but I haven't see anything of this yet.

When the proofs are on hand, please let me know about how much room I will have for a preface: I don't plan to write much, as I said in my other letter.

I know Dom Gregorio Lemercier [O.S.B.] very well but have not read his book. I can imagine it would be very lively. He is under pretty heavy attack these days I believe. Hope he makes out.

With all my best wishes,
Tom /s/

P.S. I very much enjoyed your piece on T.S. Eliot in the special number of the Sewanee Review [Winter 1966].

NOVEMBER 29, 1966

Rev. M. Louis, O.C.S.O.
Abbey of Gethsemani
Trappist, Kentucky

Dear Tom:

I am sending proofs of MYSTICS AND ZEN MASTERS in duplicate. Please return one set to me with your corrections as soon as possible.[1]

I will have some additional queries for you later on about the original publications of some of the essays. One of them that you had listed for Jubilee, "Love and Tao" or "Two Chinese Classics," never appeared there. There are some other points also, which I'll forward to you later.

With warmest regards.

Yours ever,
[Robert Giroux]

1. According to a short note dated December 15, 1966, RG informed TM that the corrected proofs would arrive from the printer after Christmas.

DECEMBER 13, 1966

Dear Bob:

Here is the preface, short and sweet. Writing it has been my celebration of the twenty-fifth anniversary of my entrance into this community. The proofs are on their way back under separate cover and I hope the Christmas rush does not delay them too much.

You are right, "Love and Tao" was not in Jubilee. It was in the Catholic World, with some such title as Christian Contemplation needs Oriental Wisdom. Something like that. Perhaps at the end of 1962 or 1963. I should really keep records of these things. Moving up to the hermitage where I now am, I got rid of most of my files.

I am asking for the names of the censors and will let you have them—if possible, will slip them into this letter.

Anything else?

All my very best wishes for Christmas and the New Year.

With warm regards always,

[Thomas Merton]

P. S. By the way, did I ever tell you John Wu has written quite a good book [*The Golden Age of Zen* (1966)] on Zen (to which he asked me to do a preface)? I wonder if he has written to you about it? He is now in Taiwan writing a life of Sun Yat-sen.

DECEMBER 16, 1966

Abbey of Gethsemani
[Letterhead]

Dear Bob:

I am returning the queries of your proof reader. I think I have answered everything. What is not taken care of here is in the other set of proofs which I returned the other day. Hope by now you have them safely and that all is well.

Christmas is pretty close, already. Our cheese rush is over and for a long time it has looked like it would snow, on and off. We have already had quite a bit earlier in the winter. Once again I wish you all the best for Christmas and the New Year. Forgive me for not commenting yet on "Love Letters" by Madeleine L'Engle: I haven't got into it yet, whether the title put me off or what I don't know. But my novel reading is slow and infrequent, and I have been working on Faulkner anyhow; that is enough to keep me full for the time being. Later I will send you some reactions.

As ever, most sincerely,
Tom /s/

FEBRUARY 4, 1967

Abbey of Gethsemani
[Letterhead]

Dear Bob:

Since they are reading [Pie-Raymond] Régamey's book on art [*Religious Art in the Twentieth Century* (1963)] in the refectory, I am reminded daily of my own book on <u>Art and Worship</u>. I presume you have no further interest in it, and I for my part cannot see my way to publishing it in any case. So could you please return to me the manuscript which you probably still have there? I would like to file it here.

As I remember, there was a huge pile of pictorial material. Do you still have all that? Much of it was borrowed. Hold it, and if you let me know it is there to be sent, I could give you the address of the person. Or maybe it would be simplest just to get rid of it all. I certainly don't want it here. I don't think this man wants it back or expects it back after all this time. He has much the same stuff on slides, and better.

I am reading Flannery O'Connor's <u>Wise Blood</u> and am struck by the way she wrote all the essentials of the God is Dead and Secular City theologies ten and fifteen years in advance. Now the message of Haze Motes is the latest thing, and taken with utmost seriousness. I may write something on it. Have you seen any studies commenting of this aspect of her work that you can remember off-hand?

Would you please remember me when the new Tom Wolfe comes out? I like his style very much. The Neruda also, which I will probably review briefly. I am going to perhaps make a habit of doing notes on Latin American stuff for Continuum. Maybe.

All best wishes always, and as ever,

Most cordially in Christ,
Tom /s/

FEBRUARY 6, 1967

Farrar, Straus & Giroux, Inc.
[Letterhead]
Office of the Editor-in-Chief

Rev. M. Louis, O.C.S.O.
Abbey of Gethsemani
Trappist, Kentucky 40073

Dear Tom:

Many thanks for your letter of February 4th. I am enclosing the ms. of ART AND WORSHIP which, as you may recall, we had in the form of proofs (some of which are transparencies). I also enclose a copy of the dummy that Ed Rice designed for us and for which we paid him. The one enclosed is reduced from the master dummy (which is about the size of Jubilee).

We do have the pile of pictorial material—all the glossy prints of painting, sculpture and architecture—that we've kept here since 1958. If you will let me know to whom you wish it all to be sent (the large master dummy is with it), I'll ship it for you. If you want us to hold it, we can certainly continue to do so after nine years! Just let me know what you'd like us to do.

You're so right about Flannery and WISE BLOOD anticipating current theories years in advance. What an artist she was! I've seen nothing along these lines—not even in a recent Fordham Press book THE ACHIEVE-

MENT OF FLANNERY O'CONNOR, which is rather uneven. Do you know Robert Fitzgerald at Harvard, her literary executor? He'd be most interested in your view of Haze Motes being accepted as the last word fifteen years afterwards!

Thank you so much for sending me a copy of your mimeographed letter. It is full of wisdom and grace. These are hard times (intellectually) for many people who have been living in barricaded shelters much too long. It's not a "crisis of conscience" at all. It's just that the light of day has finally penetrated the shelters, and the light is of course blinding to eyes unaccustomed to it.

We expect bound copies of MYSTICS AND ZEN MASTERS on March 30th. I hope you like the jacket design.

With warmest regards.

Yours ever,
Bob /s/

P.S. Tom Wolfe's [book, *The Electric Kool-Aid Acid Test* (1968)] been postponed until May 24th, and I'll send it then.

APRIL 13, 1967

Dear Bob:

Many thanks for the first copy of <u>Mystics and Zen Masters</u> [that I] received last week. I hope it does fairly well—or indeed very well. I don't expect good reviews: perhaps I have published too much, but I don't seem to have much luck in that respect these days. But you have done a good job on the book, for which many thanks.

Will you please send copies for consideration to Tom Burns at Burns & Oates, and to my agent in Germany—Dagmar Henne, Agency Hoffman, Seestrasse 6, 8 München 23.

And could you please send review copies to:

Dr. Winston King, (complimentary rather than rev[iew]) Vanderbilt Divinity School, Nashville, Tenn.
Dr. Masao Abe, 362 Kamigorjo-Bamba-cho, Kamigyo-ku, Kyoto, Japan
Journal of Ecumenical Studies, Temple University, Philadelphia, Pa. 19122
Japanese Religions, Doshishe University, Kyoto, Japan
Fr. William Johnston, S.J., Monumenta Nipponica, Sophia University, 7 Kioi-cho, Chiyoda-ku, Tokyo, Japan
Dr. Graham Taylor, Editor, Newsletter Review, 1025 Pine Ave. Montreal, 2PQ Can[ada]
Cambridge Buddhist Assn, 3 Craigie St., Cambridge Mass 02138

I'd be very grateful, and I hope some good will come of it.

There is one other thing I'd like to ask: as my manuscripts are being brought together in a special collection at Bellarmine College, Louisville, I wonder if you would be willing to let me have those that you still have on file there for this collection—and any other material of mine that would be useful to them? Please let me know about this. It can be sent direct to Fr. John E. Loftus [O.F.M. Conv.], Bellarmine College, 2000 Norris Place, Louisville 5.[1]

My very best wishes to you, and thanks again,
[Thomas Merton]

1. In a letter to Father Loftus dated August 2, 1967, RG said he was sending Bellarmine College "manuscripts and other materials now in our office," concerning *The New Man*, *Seeds of Destruction*, *Seasons of Celebration*, *Disputed Questions*, and *The Secular Journal*.

JUNE 16, 1967

Dear Bob:

Many thanks for the reviews, and I have also been meaning to thank you all for the fine ad in the NY Review. I very much appreciate it. And I hope the book is going well.

The [Pablo] Neruda book [perhaps *The Heights of Macchu Picchu* (1966)] is beautifully done, and I hope really to do a note on it, at least, in some magazine. I may do a series of articles on Latin American poets. Right now however it is the hot weather and the afternoons are too steamy to write. One can read and pile up stuff for future work.

I hope you will do more of Neruda. Of course there is already some of the best of his stuff around. Do you know Rafael Alberti? I'll send a piece I did on him ["Rafael Alberti and His Angels," *Continuum* (Spring 1967)].

With my very best regards, always,
[Thomas Merton]

JUNE 23, 1967

Farrar, Straus & Giroux, Inc.
[Letterhead]
Office of the Editor-in-Chief

Rev. M. Louis, O.C.S.O.
Abbey of Gethsemani
Trappist, Kentucky

Dear Tom:

It was good to hear from you. I'm delighted to learn from Nancy Wilson Ross that she has done a long piece on your book for the New York Times Book Review. It is scheduled to appear sometime in July and we have had confirmation of this fact in our office because they phoned for a copy of the Ed Rice photograph.

I am glad you like the Neruda book. We may be doing more poems of his, but apparently he has his translation rights in such a snarl between England and America that it will take a bit of unraveling. I like the Ben Bellit versions of his poems in the Grove edition, but Nathaniel Tarn is more accurate, though a bit prosaic, and the Spanish text itself helps by being there in our edition.

Many thanks for your piece on Rafael Alberti, whose work I do not know and which I now think I should explore. Elizabeth Bishop is very keen about a Brazilian poet named [Carlos Drummond] de Andrade. Do you know his work?

With warmest regards.

Yours ever,

Bob /s/

AUGUST 2, 1967

Farrar, Straus & Giroux, Inc.

[Letterhead]

Office of the Editor-in-Chief

Rev. M. Louis, O.C.S.O.
Abbey of Gethsemani
Trappist, Kentucky

Dear Tom:

Just a note to tell you that I've sent a batch of your mss. and proofs to Father Loftus at Bellarmine [College].

I also found a batch of pictures for ART AND WORSHIP and I assume you would like these forwarded to you. Is that OK? I'll hold them until I hear from you.

As ever,

Bob /s/

AUGUST 11, 1967

Dear Bob:

Thanks very much indeed for sending the mss., proofs and so on to Bellarmine for their collection. That will cheer them immensely. They have a couple of girls working very devotedly on that collection and there is real interest.

Thanks, too, for all the new books, which I think I probably acknowledged a month or so ago. But my correspondence has gone haywire this summer and I am only just catching up. Anyway, I have been enjoying

THE CHINESE LOOKING GLASS which makes admirable light reading for supper time—not, of course, in the community but in the hermitage where I now live, eat, work, etc., alone. It is a grand life.

It was nice of Nancy Wilson Ross to turn out such [a] pleasant review in the Times, and I am grateful all round. Hope it is helping the book. I agree with you about Virginia Kirkus—no it was the Jesuit you meant— but all those critics who think a collection of essays is not a book. Personally, those are often the books I find best. Suzuki hardly wrote anything else. And, as you say, there is [Edmund] Wilson. And Virginia Woolf. And E. M. Forster, forsooth.

Ed Rice has had to sell Jubilee to a bunch of bloodthirsty people who gave him a nasty deal on it. It is good that he is out of there, as he was practically doing the whole thing single-handed and it was too much. But he certainly did a fine job for seventeen years. I suppose now the magazine will become at once successful and putrid.

Best always, and thanks again,

[Thomas Merton]

AUGUST 15, 1967

Farrar, Straus & Giroux, Inc.

[Letterhead]

Office of the Editor-in-Chief

Rev. M. Louis, O.C.S.O.
Abbey of Gethsemani
Trappist, Kentucky 40073

Dear Tom:

It's good to hear from you, as always. I had heard about the sale of Jubilee and I had hoped it would mean more freedom, financially and editorially, for Ed. What a lousy deal for him, after creating one of our best magazines and carrying it on single-handed for so long.

Your sentence, "It is a grand life," pleases me very much. I'm afraid I've not been very good at getting into my letters the very high regard I've had for you over thirty years. Did I tell you I went to the Virgin Islands last winter and literally stumbled onto Bob and Nancy Gibney?[1] What a shock, after all those years! It was all so strange that when a horse walked into their living-room, I hardly noticed it.

With warmest regards.

As ever,

Bob /s/

P.S. Did you know that some Washington magazine, *Voyages*, is devoting an issue to Bob Lax?

1. Robert Gibney was one of TM's closest friends at Columbia College. Once TM had entered the monastery, they did not keep in contact with one another.

NOVEMBER 18, 1967

Dear Bob:

Quite some time ago, nearly eight weeks I think, I sent you a manuscript for your book, in answer to your request. Not having heard anything since, I want to check and see if you got it. Anything is likely to happen to mail here: mine might not have got out and one from you might not have got in. But anyway, since I haven't heard I thought I ought to write you. Could you let me know if you got the piece and if it is ok? If you did not, I'll send another copy.

I hope all is going well with you and with the project.

Best wishes always,

[Thomas Merton]

JANUARY 25, 1968

Dear Bob:

Thanks for your wire about Sy Freedgood. I also got a call from the Methodist minister out there at Bridgehampton [on Long Island], who was asked by Sy's wife Anne to contact me. Funny: [John] Slate buried from the Synagogue and Sy from the Methodists![1] Very sad and tragic about Sy [who died in a house fire]. I am most sorry for Anne. When Sy was down here last year I found him living close to desperation, in a strange exalted way. He nearly destroyed himself in a car smash up on the way out from Louisville. Yet somehow there was some of his mad humor about it, a kind of intelligent distance and detachment. As I say, I worry more about Anne tormenting herself. Sy in some strange way probably turned up a winner in spite of everything.

Lax is back in the country and I am relieved to have him out of Greece and away from Middle Eastern wars . . . Jubilee without Rice is pitiable.

We have a new Abbot [Dom Flavian Burns, O.S.C.O.], young and solid and open. Things seem promising.

I have been happy about Mystics and Zen Masters. The Japanese are the first to be translating it (taking the Zen parts mostly). I hope it has been selling well: I think it is a fairly good book, considering.

Sometime, I want to give you another book, and have been thinking of a collection of literary essays which I have been putting out here and there: [William] Faulkner, Edwin Muir, [John] Milton and [Albert] Camus (in Sat[urday] Review last year), [Louis] Zukofsky, [Rafael] Alberti, [William] Styron, and other things like that. A little more time to let it grow. As a collection of literary essays and criticism, it would surely be homogeneous enough. Let me know what you think. Perhaps it could be for end of 1969? I'd have to work all that out with Naomi, but foresee no objections.

Finally: a friend of mine in Atlanta [June Yungblut] has done a thesis on Samuel Beckett, which I think is quite good. I told her I would mention it to you, in case you might be interested in seeing it as a possible book. It is a doctoral dissertation for Emory University Divinity School. She is a friend of Tom Altizer's, and her work was begun under Cleanth Brooks, at Yale I guess. Or is that possible? Anyway C. Brooks is in it somewhere.

My very best always.

Cordially,

[Thomas Merton]

1. John Slate, a friend of TM at Columbia College who later became a lawyer, visited TM in early April 1967 to help establish the Merton Legacy Trust.

JANUARY 30, 1968

Farrar, Straus & Giroux, Inc.
[Letterhead]
Office of the Editor-in-Chief

Rev. M. Louis, O.C.S.O.
Abbey of Gethsemani
Trappist, Kentucky 40073

Dear Tom:

It's good to hear from you. I had a phone call from John Brooks, a writer-neighbor of the Freedgoods, about Sy's death, and wired you at once. Jean Stafford told me they read your telegram at the service in Bridgehampton; she thought it a fine statement. I had not seen Sy for years but heard about him through Jean, who lived nearby.

I'm delighted to hear the Japanese are translating MYSTICS AND ZEN MASTERS. It's a great compliment to that part of the book. I'm even more pleased that you want me to do another book and I'd like nothing better in 1969, or whenever it might be ready. I'd like it if you could work in a few writers and poets nearer to the current upheaval or revulsion or whatever it is. Tom Wolfe is doing a book on Ken Kesey (see page 33 of catalogue), for example; do you know Kesey's writing? I'm sending you our Cesare Pavese [*The Selected Works of Cesare Pavese*] by separate cover; this may interest you too. Incidentally, I seem to have lost touch with Naomi and haven't heard from her for many months.

Thanks too for the tip on the Beckett thesis. I'll check this with the Noonday editors, but I'm afraid its chances are dim.

I heard Lax was back and I intend to ask Ed Rice where to reach him. With all good wishes.

As ever,

Bob /s/

FEBRUARY 7, 1968

Dear Bob:

Many thanks for your letter of the 30th ult[imate], as the old guys used to say. Thanks even more for Pavese. I thought his Moon and the Bonfires was superb and I am glad that none of the four in this collection have been read by me before. I agree that he is worth writing about and perhaps I shall include him. Ken Kesey, I don't know except by reputation. Is he good?

And now let me make a long overdue acknowledgement. It turns out that by an act of poetic justice, I have fully learned how foolish I was not to let publishers handle all foreign business for me. That woman, Marie Tadié, whom I had the imprudence to allow to act as my agent in France became a most grasping, arbitrary and unreasonable person to deal with. She tried to get all my Spanish and Italian business into her hands and would not allow me to let anyone in France translate anything of mine, even the smallest article, without it passing through her hands. Well, we finally decided to drop her as agent—as she was impossible. For this, she is suing the monastery for fifteen thousand dollars. Our case is fortunately in the hands of a good lawyer.

Meanwhile, having learned, I have resolved to let publishers handle all foreign rights in the future. Could Farrar, Straus & Giroux pay heed to my contrite state and take over, especially for Mystics and Zen Masters? Only Japan has bought this as yet. France, Spain and Italy have got most of the others (Tadié did really sell books!), but, as far as I know, that is about all. If inquiries come in, then, will you please work from there? And I'll send on any to you. About Mystics and ZM, the Spanish agent A.C.E.R. (who actually did the work for Tadié) has written that he has an offer of some sort and wants to handle it. I'll dig out his letter and send it, if it is ok. But, of course, I leave everything to you. I want to be "shot of it," as Kentuckians say. I've had enough!

Finally, speaking of new books and trends; there are a couple of things in the FSG catalog that interest me greatly (besides the two Tom Wolfes, [Hans Erich] Nossack's Impossible Proof, and [Donald] Barthelme's Unspeakable Practices). Both look particularly stimulating. I liked the other Fuentes book you sent some years ago. If there is anything else you think especially important . . .[1]

Thanks again, Bob. I can dig into the files and get a list of what has been sold where in the last few years, if you like.

> Best always,
> [Thomas Merton]

1. TM did not tell RG that he had sent to Doubleday the manuscripts of two new books, a novel entitled *My Argument with the Gestapo* (1969) and *Vow of Conversation*. The latter, a journal recording TM's life in 1964–65, was eventually published in 1988 by FSG.

JUNE 22, 1968

Dear Bob:

I can't seem to recall seeing a letter about <u>Raids [on the Unspeakable</u> (1966)] and [the Italian publishing firm of] Garzanti. Of course, that is perfectly all right. Go right ahead. While we are on that subject, since I am no longer dealing with Marie Tadié (have definitely dropped her), I wonder if Erich Linder [at Agenzia Letteraria Internazionale in Milan] would want to handle the sale of MYSTICS AND ZEN MASTERS. In future, I'll probably try to get all my publishers to handle foreign rights from their NY offices, but in this case there is still a problem as we have continued to handle Farrar, Straus & Giroux books ourselves. This is just one exception. I could send a copy to Milan if he doesn't mind. Probably Garzanti wants it.

As to the reversion of rights on NEW SEEDS from Burns & Oates: fine. I understand Tom Burns is no longer there. I don't particularly want to continue dealing with them. They are pretty square.

I still haven't caught up with work after getting back from California— but the trip was wonderful.[1] Surprisingly we have had nice weather most of June (when it is usually so tropically hot here).

> Best always, and many thanks,
> [Thomas Merton]

1. TM had gone to California to give some conferences to the Trappistine nuns at Our Lady of the Redwoods in Whitethorn.

Epilogue

When I presided at the Mass of the Resurrection on an early September morning in 2008 for my editor and dear friend of twenty-five years, Bob Giroux, I thought how the death of this incredible editor at one of the world's major publishing houses coincided with the passing of an era, when handheld printed books were being replaced by portable electronic tablets that contain thousands of books, any one of which can be called up in an instant without the realization of the beauty of the literary artifact itself. The thought, care, and good judgment that Giroux put into each of Merton's books that he edited helped to make Merton the most successful American spiritual writer of the twentieth century. Alas, today's emails between author and editor, often written in haste, have the tendency to reduce the variables of human communication about important matters to bullet points for immediate attention.

On those occasions when we visited Gethsemani together, Bob seemed to relax, putting aside the daily pressures of his life and touching the all-too-palpable spirituality of the abbey. He would join the monks for the recitation of the Canonical Hours, sometimes for Matins, Lauds, Prime, or Tierce, but usually for Vespers and Compline, not because anyone goaded him into doing it but because he felt it most appropriate as he touched the deepest wellsprings within himself. I don't remember him chanting, rising or bowing along with the monks in the sanctuary; rather he would just sit there absorbing the prayers and communing with whatever spiritual life he had developed over the years, most likely thinking about, I always believed, his good friend Tom, whose life and books had meant so much to him. Bob always felt peace in the uncluttered abbey church, originally built in 1866, especially when the chants and hymns allowed him to reflect on how he had changed since he and a small band of Columbia friends witnessed Merton's ordination.

With Merton's former secretary Brother Patrick Hart we would wander some of the back roads on the abbey grounds. I would just listen as the two of them reminisced about the ways that Merton had changed the attitudes of generations of monks. Comparisons between the past and the present were inevitable, though neither Bob nor Brother Patrick overly praised the past as they commented on the declining number of men entering the monastery. Once the three of us spent an hour or so poking around Merton's former hermitage, where Merton had spent many hours quietly praying, writing, and studying. Ironically Abbot James Fox, after his retirement, would also become a hermit at Gethsemani. It certainly did not escape Bob's attention that Merton and Fox are buried side by side in the abbey cemetery. I recall that Bob, having heard a number of rumors that had been circulating, speculated whether Merton would have left Gethsemani and put aside his life as a monk. He was glad to learn that Merton had written Brother Patrick while on his Asian journey saying that he considered himself a monk of Gethsemani, as he had been for twenty-seven years, and that he intended to remain so for the rest of his days.

During his trip to India, Sri Lanka, and Thailand, Merton had become, in Gabriel Marcel's words, a *homo viator*, a pilgrim trying to find a place to discover and explore new dimensions for an ecumenical conversation that seemed most appropriate after the Second Vatican Council. As Merton mentioned in a talk titled "Marxism and Monastic Perspectives," delivered in Bangkok just hours before he died, "The world refusal of the monk is something that also looks toward an acceptance of a world that is open to change." Gethsemani, like Henry David Thoreau's Walden Pond, contained in some important ways a microcosm of the world, but Merton felt the need for new vistas that would help him in the process of self-transformation and spiritual renewal. Above all he wanted a firsthand awareness of what other monastic traditions could offer not only for himself, but through his books for others. The Dalai Lama once praised Merton (they met three times near Dharamsala in the Himalayas) for having a more profound understanding of Buddhism than any other Christian he had known. In addition he mentions in his autobiography, *Freedom in Exile*, that Merton introduced him to the "real meaning of the word Christian."[1]

As a Trappist monk, Merton led a life one might consider fuller than the lives of some of the other monks at Gethsemani, in that he constantly explored what was both within and without himself. More than any other Trappist in the history of the order, I believe, he had an immense and loyal reading public, though Bob sometimes admitted that Merton had written and published too much. Merton's last letters to Bob during the year of Merton's death nevertheless reveal that he felt the pull and tug of his relationship with Farrar, Straus & Giroux, while his agent Naomi Burton was putting pressure on him to publish with Doubleday. Bob became a trustee of the Merton Legacy Trust when Naomi Burton retired, and remained a trustee until his death. He told me he never really did know whether his professional relationship with Merton had run its course. It was an unresolved question. Out of devotion to his friend, he kept a cache of Merton typescripts in his apartment in Tinton Falls, New Jersey, which he donated to the Bellarmine University Merton Center in Louisville. Yet to his credit and out of the deep commitment to his friend of thirty-five years Bob was instrumental in publishing (of the forty or so posthumous Merton books) *Love and Living* (1979), *The Nonviolent Alternative* (1980), and, from 1985 to 1994 (just before his retirement), five important volumes of Merton's letters, ensuring that Merton's legacy would continue through the ages.

NOTE

1. Dalai Lama, *Freedom in Exile: The Autobiography of the Dalai Lama* (New York: HarperCollins, 1990), 189.

Appendix

The Seven Storey Mountain. New York: Harcourt, Brace, 1948.
The Waters of Siloe. New York: Harcourt, Brace, 1949.
The Ascent to Truth. New York: Harcourt, Brace, 1951.
The Sign of Jonas. New York: Harcourt, Brace, 1953.
The Last of the Fathers: Saint Bernard of Clairvaux and the Encyclical Letter, Doctor Mellifluus. New York: Harcourt, Brace, 1954.
No Man Is an Island. New York: Harcourt, Brace, 1955.
The Living Bread. New York: Farrar, Straus & Cudahy, 1956.
The Silent Life. New York: Farrar, Straus & Cudahy, 1957.
Thoughts in Solitude. New York: Farrar, Straus & Cudahy, 1958.
The Secular Journal. New York: Farrar, Straus & Cudahy, 1959.
Disputed Questions. New York: Farrar, Straus & Cudahy, 1960.
The New Man. New York: Farrar, Straus & Cudahy, 1961.
Seeds of Destruction. New York: Farrar, Straus & Giroux, 1964.
Seasons of Celebration. New York: Farrar, Straus & Giroux, 1965.
Mystics and Zen Masters. New York: Farrar, Straus & Giroux, 1967.
Love and Living. Edited by Naomi Burton Stone and Patrick Hart, O.C.S.O. New York: Farrar, Straus & Giroux, 1979.
The Nonviolent Alternative. Edited by Gordon C. Zahn. New York: Farrar, Straus & Giroux, 1980.
The Hidden Ground of Love: Letters on Religious Experience and Social Concerns. Edited by William H. Shannon. New York: Farrar, Straus & Giroux, 1985.
A Vow of Conversation: Journals 1964–1965. Edited by Naomi Burton Stone. New York: Farrar, Straus & Giroux, 1988.
The Road to Joy: Letters to New and Old Friends. Edited by Robert E. Daggy. New York: Farrar, Straus & Giroux, 1989.
The School of Charity: Letters on Religious Renewal and Spiritual Direction. Edited by Patrick Hart, O.C.S.O. New York: Farrar, Straus & Giroux, 1990.
The Springs of Contemplation: A Retreat at the Abbey of Gethsemani. Edited by Jane Marie Richardson, S.L. New York: Farrar, Straus & Giroux, 1992.
The Courage for Truth: Letters to Writers. Edited by Christine M. Bochen. New York: Farrar, Straus & Giroux, 1993.

Witness to Freedom: Letters in Times of Crisis. Edited by William H. Shannon. New York: Farrar, Straus & Giroux, 1994.

Striving towards Being: The Letters of Thomas Merton and Czeslaw Milosz. Edited by Robert Faggen. New York: Farrar, Straus & Giroux, 1997.

Survival or Prophecy? The Letters of Thomas Merton and Jean Leclercq. Edited by Patrick Hart, O.C.S.O. New York: Farrar, Straus & Giroux, 2002.

Index

PATRICK SAMWAY, S.J.,

professor emeritus of English at St. Joseph's University
in Philadelphia, is the author or editor/co-editor of twelve books,
including *Walker Percy: A Life*, selected by the New York Times
Book Review as one of the notable books of 1997.